SECOND EDITION

THE BRISTOL PROJECT

People, places and themes

Alan Bilham-Boult
Heather Blades
John Hancock
Mike Ridout
Consultant:Keith Orrell

OCR
RECOGNISING ACHIEVEMENT

Heinemann

Heinemann Educational Publishers
Halley Court, Jordan Hill, Oxford, OX2 8EJ
a division of Reed Educational & Professional Publishing Ltd
Heinemann is a registered trademark of Reed Educational
& Professional Publishing Ltd

OXFORD MELBOURNE AUCKLAND
JOHANNESBURG BLANTYRE GABORONE
IBADAN PORTSMOUTH NH (USA) CHICAGO

First edition published 1999

Second edition published 2001

ISBN 0 435 35281 4

05 04 03 02 01
10 9 8 7 6 5 4 3 2

Designed and typeset by Hart McLeod

Picture research by Virginia Stroud-Lewis

Original illustrations © Heinemann Publishers 1999
Illustrated by Jeff Edwards, Sheila Betts and Tim Oliver
Cover design by Carla Turchini

Printed and bound in the UK by Bath Colour Books

Location of chapter photographs

Chapter 1: Malvern Hills, UK
Chapter 2: Satellite image of Mount St Helens, USA
Chapter 3: Old steelworks, Germany
Chapter 4: Favela in Rio de Janeiro, Brazil

Acknowledgements

The publishers would like to thank the following for permission to reproduce copyright material.

Maps, diagrams and extracts

7 C John Betjeman, Collected Poems/John Murray (Publishers) Ltd; 12 A Water Services Association; 20 A, 124 C, 207 B Maps reproduced from Ordnance Survey maps with the permission of The Controller of Her Majesty's Stationery Office © Crown copyright; Licence No; 398020; 30 A, 55 D, 94 B, 100 A, B, 176, 192 A, B, C, D, E, G Guardian Newspapers Limited; 33 K, 97 D The Daily Telegraph; 54 A, 58 E Met Office; 71 A Courtesy of Worcester Evening News; 81 G GCSE Bitesize Revision Geography/BBC Education; 83 F, 98 A, 120 B, C, 136 D, 146 B, 147 C David Waugh, The New Wider World/Thomas Nelson & Sons Limited, 1998; 84 A, 96 B Simon Ross, Hazard Geography/Longman Group UK Limited; 88 C British Overseas Development/Department for International Development; 93 C Geography/The Geographical Association; 99 C Investigating Geography: Environments, M Stacey and J Lucas, Addison Wesley Longman Australia Pty Ltd; 119 D MAFF, Tokyo; 122 A, 125 D British Steel plc; 126 A, 135 C Mel Rockett, Themes in Human Geography/Thomas Nelson & Sons Limited, 1987; 130 A, B Geography Review/Philip Allan; 131 C, 150 B, C Examination Papers for GCSE Syllabus C, Bristol Project 1998/OCR; 137 F Peterborough City Council; 139 C © Third Way 1988 Reprinted by permission from the Christian current-affairs magazine Third Way; 139 D R Prosser, Tourism/Thomas Nelson & Sons Limited, 1982; 139 F, 182 B © Times Newspapers Limited, 1909/15; 143, 144 Rainforest Action Network, San Francisco; 148 B from HUMAN DEVELOPMENT REPORT 1994 by United Nations Development Programme. Copyright © 1994 by United Nations Development Programme. Used by permission of Oxford University Press Inc; 149 D © Times Newspapers Limited, 1998 151 E, 156 A, B © George Philip Ltd. Cartography by Philip's; 151 F Friends of the Earth; 151 G, 153 D Oxfam; 152 C Tearfund; 155 F Daewoo (UK) Limited; 159 C, D Fair Trade Federation, Gettysburg; 187 D Harlow Council; 193 J © GMPTE, 1999, Manchester; 213 E, 217 A Aimée Hagger; 216 C Brian Greasley, Project Fieldwork/Bell & Hyman.

Photographs

Cover photo by Corbis UK Ltd. ACE Photo Agency (19H, 25A, 85C, 107/1, 107/3, 107/4, 107/7, 107/8, 109 top and centre, 134 right and left, 144A, 148Bi,ii,iii, 165A, 166B, 175D, 182E, 197D); Actionaid (152B); Aerofilms (26C, 29D, 114B, 200A, 200C); Associated Press (70 bottom, 101C, 149D, 185E); BBC Photograph Library (40A); British Steel (124A); Bruce Coleman Collection (143D, 166A, 169G, 202A 203B, 211C,); Cambridge Newspapers (194M); Cardiff Bay Development Corporation (127F); Corbis UK (83E, 85D,E, 99E, 109 bottom, 118B, 129E, 132 left and right, 140 left, 144C); Daewoo Cars (154D, 155F); Emscher Park, Germany (105); Environmental Images (30A, 30D inset, 58A, 61E, 102C, 110C, 111F,G,H, 116C, 117E,F, 119F, 214C); Farmers Weekly Picture Library (113D, 117D); Hutchison Library (64C, 89D, 108A,); John T Blakeston (30E, 31G, 32A,C,D,F); La Redoute (133E); Lincoln Cathedral (61F); London Aerial Photo Library (29C, 187C, 196A,B,C); Monica Almeida/NYT Pictures (185C); NASA (83D); Network Photographers/ Paul Lowe (108B)/ Martin Mayer (107/6)/Gerard Sioen/Rapho (140 right, 148Biv); News Team International Ltd./Steve Hill (72A)/Mike Sharp (71A, 102B); Oxfam (110D)/ Shafiqul Alam (91D)/Shafiqul Alam/DRIK (149C)/ Jeremy Hartley (99D)/James Hawkins (152A); PA News/Adam Butler (70 top)/Toby Melville (70 centre); Panos Pictures/Guiseppe Bizzarri (158B)/ Trygve Bolstad (113C)/Sean Sprague (146A)/Zed Nelson (148Bv); Photoair (21C, 22A); Popperfoto (96A)/AFP (133C)/AFP/Eddy Nedeljkoic (103D)/Reuters (80E, 80F, 92B)/Reuters/Mario Laporta (73B); Press Association (8A); Rex Features/SIPA Press (123E); Robert Bosch Limited (128B); Roger Bamber (33K); Roger Scruton (7a); Science Photo Library/Tony Craddock (110A)/Earth Satellite Corporation (69, 141B)/ESA/PLI (51B)/Michael Marten (118C)/Russ Munn (110B)/NASA (86A)/W.T.Sullivan III (208A); Skyscan Photolibrary/Colour Library Books (7d); Skyscan Photolibrary/John Farmar (23F)/London Aerial Photo Library (5)/NPA (22D); South American Pictures/Tony Morrison (180C); The Leprosy Mission (153E); Tony Stone Images (76B); Vine House Farm (115F inset); Warren Collection/Museum of Fine Arts, Boston (7G); White Scar Cave, Ingleton, North Yorkshire (11C,D,E). All other photographs supplied by the authors and Steve Cutting.

The publishers have made every effort to trace the copyright holders. However if any material has been overlooked or incorrectly acknowledged, we would be pleased to correct this at the earliest opportunity.

Tel: 01865 888058 email: info.he@heinemann.co.uk

Contents

How to use this book

This textbook has been written specifically to match OCR Specification C, the Bristol Project, but it will provide the content for any GCSE Geography course. A number of design features have been incorporated to ensure comprehensive coverage of the course in an easy-to-use and interesting format.

Specification coverage

The framework taken is that of the first four *themes* (those that appear in the terminal examination), with special attention being paid to the *minimum place and scale requirements*. Each of the first four chapters covers one theme from the specification, and the specification key ideas are outlined briefly on the opening page of each chapter. Within the chapter, the specification content is broken down into double-page spreads, numbered at the beginning of each new topic.

Theme 5, 'Sustainable Development', has been woven through the other four themes in the manner in which most schools teach it. The opening page of each chapter briefly indicates what has been included from Theme 5.

Enquiry approach

An enquiry approach has been promoted throughout the text, both through using the specification's 'Questions for Enquiry', and through the nature of the content and the tasks set. Where appropriate the specification 'Questions for Enquiry' appear as headings within the text. Other questions have also been used as headings, and together with the range of resources and stimulus material used, it is hoped that this will develop an enquiry approach and encourage further investigation into the topics covered.

Qs, Questions and the Decision Making Exercise

There are three levels of questions included within *People, Places and Themes* that aim to reinforce knowledge and understanding, whilst also providing effective practice at exam-style questions.

Qs

These are usually relatively short questions that may require lengthy and detailed answers from students. They directly test knowledge and understanding of the topic or resource being studied. They may also require some extended individual or group research to supply the necessary answers. Some of the Qs are role plays and many encourage students to think beyond the immediate topic.

Questions

These are available at the end of most sub-sections, and also use the Questions for Enquiry where appropriate, as well as trying to set extended tasks that reflect the vocabulary, content and skills of the syllabus. These questions have marks allocated out of a total of 25, as are the terminal examination questions. However, it must be stressed that these are **not** sample examination questions and they have not been subjected to OCR's vetting procedures. They are intended to help students become used to exam-style vocabulary and command words, and to get them used to the discipline of answering questions with marks. Because of this they deliberately do **not** usually follow the 2, 2, 6, 6, 9 structure of exam questions.

Decision Making Exercise (DME)

In preparation for the Decision Making Exercise, each of the first four chapters has included at least one task following a DME-type format. In the case of chapters three and four, this involves a full set of DME tasks using the **Background**, **Options** and **Decision framework**. Clearly these are not actually DMEs since they do not provide a full set of resources. They are intended to familiarise the pupils with the style and format of this sort of task in a variety of contexts. These questions are out of 20 or 60 marks depending upon the number of tasks set.

Using practical skills

An additional chapter on skills has been included to help deliver the internal assessment, enquiry-approach and skills components of the course. It is envisaged that teachers will use this chapter as and when appropriate in delivery of the themes and internal assessment.

Physical systems and environments

Theme 1

Geomorphic processes and landforms

Atmospheric processes and climate

Physical environments and systems

Theme 5

Exploitation and management of natural resources

Resolving issues

Introduction

Why study physical systems and environments?

Our activities are frequently affected by the weather. At school break, at weekends, during holidays, weather conditions may alter our plans. Economic activities such as farming can be seriously affected. Extremes of weather in Britain are not very common, but the weather is very changeable and a lot of money is spent trying to understand and predict the weather to help us in our decision making.

Many countries around the Mediterranean have popular tourist resorts. Tourists are attracted by the hot, sunny days throughout the summer. Why is the weather around the Mediterranean so different from that in Britain?

It is not only the weather that attracts people to different tourist destinations, scenery and landscape also attract people. Sheer Cornish cliffs, haunting Norfolk marshes or the contrasting uplands of the Peak District and Snowdonia appeal to large numbers of people, but why are the landscapes in Britain so varied?

Too many visitors can damage an environment. Too many cars produce exhaust gases which may be altering world climates and changing our weather. How will this affect us? If we care about our future we need to understand how landscapes form, and why the weather changes. It will help us manage activities better and improve the quality of the environment for everyone.

Questions for enquiry

To gain a better understanding of physical systems and environments the following key questions will be investigated in this chapter:

- What are the landforms that make up a selected landscape like?
- What physical processes are operating on the selected landscape?
- What evidence is there of how landforms are influenced by geology and past and present processes?
- How are landforms being influenced by human activity?
- How do weather conditions reflect processes in the atmosphere at the local scale?
- What influences the patterns of climate in the British Isles?
- How does the global atmospheric system affect the climate in particular places?
- Is the climate changing?
- How can systems' ideas help the study of
  - river basins
  - water in the atmosphere
  - habitats including their soil and vegetation?
- What are the consequences of people's use of resources?

Themes

The answers to these questions will be sought by examining a number of themes:
- The hydrological cycle and the river basin system
- The landscapes and processes associated with rivers, ice and sea
- Atmospheric processes and climate
- Environmental systems – the links between climate, soils, vegetation and human activity.

People and places

This chapter looks at how physical systems function at different scales. Are there areas around the school that are warmer or windier than others? Why is the landscape and the weather of the Lake District so different from that around London and yet they are only six hours apart by car? Comparing the climate of the British Isles to that of Japan or a country close to the Equator helps us to understand how global patterns and natural systems are closely linked. Human activity which interferes with systems in one part of the world can easily affect areas that are quite distant. This has implications for us all.

A

Littondale, North Yorkshire

Where are they?

Landscapes and the weather are often described in the media and in photographs. Many writers and artists have tried to take things further by portraying a sense of place in their prose, poetry or pictures. Here are some examples.

N

Q

1 Try to link the examples labelled **A – G** with the places on the map labelled **1-7**.

2 Select a photograph of a natural landscape or the weather and try portraying your sense of place in writing.

C

'Where deep cliffs loom enormous, where cascade
Mesembryanthemum and stone-crop down,
Where the gull looks no larger than a lark
Hung midway twixt the cliff-top and the sand,
Sun-shadowed valleys roll along the sea.
Forced by the backwash, see the nearest wave
Rise to a wall of huge translucent green
And crumble into spray along the top
Blown seaward by the land-breeze.'
John Betjeman, *Sunday afternoon service in St Enodoc Church*

5

B

Seven Sisters, East Sussex

6

D

Crag Lough, Northumberland

0   100   200 km

2

G

Stour Valley, Suffolk

E

'Flat, with an unrelieved and monotonous flatness…. From the raised banks of the Leem, it stretched away to the horizon, its uniform colour, peat black, varied only by the crops that grew upon it – grey-green potato leaves, blue-green beet leaves, yellow-green wheat; its uniform levelness broken only by the furrowed and dead-straight lines of ditches and drains, which… ran like silver, copper or golden wires across the fields…'
Graham Swift, *Waterland*

1

7

F

'Do you see yon mountain? … Its name is Ben Alder; it is a wild desert mountain full of hills and hollows…. For the best part of three nights we travelled on eerie mountains and among the well-head of rivers, often buried in mist, almost continually blown and rained upon, and not once cheered by any glimpse of sunshine.'
Robert Louis Stevenson, *Kidnapped*

4

3

7

Weathering

Geomorphic processes

- How has the surface of the Earth achieved its present form?
- What are the forces that shape landscapes?
- How fast does change take place?

Weathering is just one of the five main processes that shape the landscape: weathering, mass movement, erosion, transportation and deposition.

DEFINITIONS

Weathering: the break-up of rocks in the place that they are found, by the action of the weather, chemicals, plants and animals, e.g. rain water enters cracks in rocks. If the water freezes and thaws it will slowly break the rock into fragments.

Mass-movement: when rocks, loosened by weathering, move downhill under the influence of gravity and without a transporting agent such as water, e.g. rock falls.

Erosion – transportation – deposition: rivers, waves, ice and wind erode rocks, transport the fragments away and, when they can no longer carry them, deposit them in another place, e.g. waves erode cliffs and carry the broken rock away and deposit it as beaches further along the coast.

These processes act continually upon the landscape, slowly changing its shape and appearance. Sudden events such as avalanches, earthquakes and river floods can alter a landscape very quickly, sometimes in seconds. Events such as these do not happen very often, but they can change a landscape dramatically.

Q

What parts did the five processes in the Definitions box play in causing this sudden rockfall (**A**)? How will weathering and the sea change this landscape in the future?

A

Beachy Head, East Sussex

Over time rain water enters the rock between the sand grains — the rock is permeable.

Surface flaking allows water to fill small crevices behind.

Water expands on freezing, pushing the sand grains apart. With continued freezing and thawing the rock is weakened and fragments fall to the ground.

Weathering of a sandstone headstone

B

Q

1 If a headstone is highly polished, will physical weathering still be a problem?
2 How will the amount of weathering differ:
   a) at different parts of the same headstone
   b) depending where the headstone is located in the cemetery
   c) depending where the cemetery is located?

Weathering processes

Weathering is often the initial process operating on any landscape or landform. Your bicycle, outside paint-work on a house and rocks will be changed if exposed to the weather over a period of time. Weathering involves the decomposition of the Earth's surface at one place. It does not involve the removal of the loosened material. That is erosion.

Weathering processes can be divided into three types: physical, chemical and biological.

Physical weathering

Freeze-thaw   This is the most common method. It involves the alternate freezing and thawing of water found in joints or surface crevices. **B** demonstrates the effects on a headstone made of sandstone. The thickness of beds and the patterns of joints will significantly affect the rate at which weathering takes place.

Pressure release   Deep in the core of the Earth, rocks are kept under pressure by the weight of overlying rocks. Over millions of years rocks at the surface are eroded and weathered. With less pressure the rocks expand, crack and form **joints**.

Exfoliation Rock surfaces are weakened and crack as they expand and contract when heated by the sun during the day but cool rapidly at night.

Wetting and drying of rocks. On sea cliffs salt water enters cracks in the rocks. If the water dries out salt crystals will grow, breaking the rock up. If clays dry out they shrink and deep cracks appear. In times of drought, this can cause serious damage to buildings.

Chemical weathering

This breaks down the rock by chemical reactions, most involving rain water (**C**).

Biological weathering

This is the effect plants and animals have on rocks. Both physical and chemical weathering are involved.

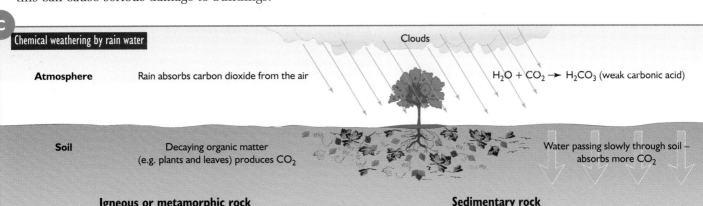

C

Chemical weathering by rain water

Clouds

Atmosphere   Rain absorbs carbon dioxide from the air $H_2O + CO_2 \rightarrow H_2CO_3$ (weak carbonic acid)

Soil   Decaying organic matter (e.g. plants and leaves) produces CO_2 Water passing slowly through soil – absorbs more CO_2

Igneous or metamorphic rock   **Sedimentary rock**

Rock

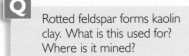
Granite

Sandstone

Limestone

Common minerals form granite: quartz, feldspar, mica. Weak acid 'rots' feldspar and rock disintegrates. Unweathered 'core-stones' are found surrounded by layers of weathered rock, like the layers of an onion.

Sand grains are often quartz which are cemented together by weaker compounds such as iron. The weak acid attacks the cement and carries it away in solution. The rock easily disintegrates into individual sand grains.

Limestone is composed mainly of calcium carbonate. Calcium carbonate + weak carbonic acid → Calcium bicarbonate. $CaCO_3 + H_2CO_3 \rightarrow Ca(HCO_3)_2$. Calcium bicarbonate is soluble – the rock is dissolved and carried away by underground water. Joints and bedding planes are gradually widened.

Q Rotted feldspar forms kaolin clay. What is this used for? Where is it mined?

Q What colours in the rock and water will indicate a content of iron compounds?

Q Water containing a lot of calcium bicarbonate in solution is known as 'hard' water. What is the effect of hard water on water pipes and kettles?

Is weathering different from erosion?

As weathering proceeds the fragments of weathered rock are available to be carried or transported away by the sea, running water, ice, wind or gravity (e.g. rock falls). Other fragments will dissolve and be carried away in solution. The process of removing weathered material is known as *erosion*. Erosion would be difficult and very slow if the rocks were not being broken up beforehand by the weathering processes. **A** shows the steep slopes above the lake of Wastwater in the Lake District. The mountain top is 500m above sea level. Large quantities of loose rock have accumulated on the steep valley sides known as **screes**. They rise 200m above the lake and extend below the surface into the deepest lake in the Lake District (76m). They are a spectacular feature. Rocks near the top, loosened by weathering, fall down the slope under gravity, forming a fan-like shape. This process is known as *mass movement*.

Screes at Wastwater, the Lake District

A

Q

1 Many people visit Wastwater for its scenery. Create a diagram for a display board to explain how the screes at Wastwater have formed. Your labels should draw the visitors' attention to the ridge (500m), lake, rock faces of freeze-thaw weathering, rock falls, large angular rock fragments, vegetation growing on screes.

2 In **A** vegetation is growing on some parts of the screes. What does this tell you about the supply and movement of scree today?

Have weathering processes been more active in the past?

The type and rate of weathering vary in different climates. Chemical weathering is most active in hot, moist tropical areas close to the Equator. Freeze-thaw will be active in places with plenty of rainfall and temperatures which keep rising and falling above and below freezing point. If temperatures are too low then the water will not melt and release the fragments of rock. Weathering will be much slower.

During the last 600,000 years, a series of warmer and colder periods than present have affected the British Isles. The screes at Wastwater consist of huge amounts of fallen rock but only small amounts of rock are breaking away from the rock faces today.

Experts think the screes were mainly formed about

10,000 years ago, when the climate was much colder. In mountain areas freezing and thawing was much more active particularly on outcrops of well-jointed rocks.

Evidence of past climates can be found in most landscapes in the British Isles. In Norfolk aerial photographs show large areas of *patterned ground*, formed of stones in the soil. Today, weathering is only producing these features where temperatures frequently fall to −5°C, not too common an event in Norfolk today! Experts cannot agree how Hay Tor (**B**), a granite outcrop on Dartmoor was formed, but chemical weathering was far more active during periods when the climate was warmer than it is today.

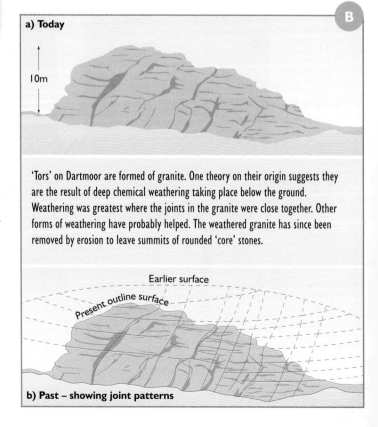

B

a) Today

10m

'Tors' on Dartmoor are formed of granite. One theory on their origin suggests they are the result of deep chemical weathering taking place below the ground. Weathering was greatest where the joints in the granite were close together. Other forms of weathering have probably helped. The weathered granite has since been removed by erosion to leave summits of rounded 'core' stones.

Earlier surface

Present outline surface

b) Past – showing joint patterns

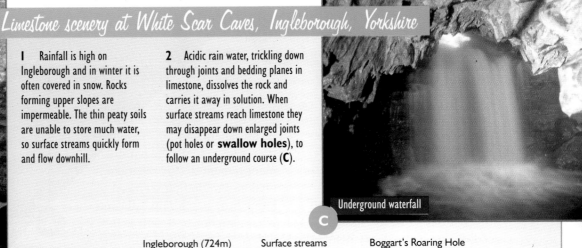
Underground waterfall

C

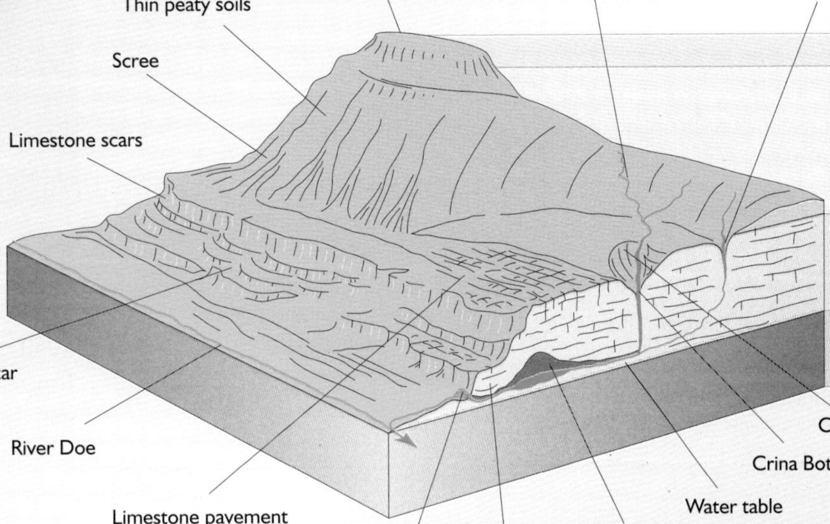

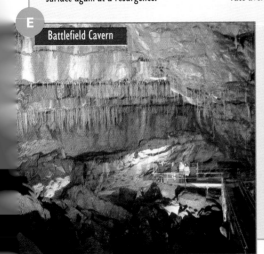
Limestone pavement

F

1 Rainfall is high on Ingleborough and in winter it is often covered in snow. Rocks forming upper slopes are impermeable. The thin peaty soils are unable to store much water, so surface streams quickly form and flow downhill.

2 Acidic rain water, trickling down through joints and bedding planes in limestone, dissolves the rock and carries it away in solution. When surface streams reach limestone they may disappear down enlarged joints (pot holes or **swallow holes**), to follow an underground course (**C**).

7 Valleys in limestone areas are often steep-sided gorges. Bare cliffs of limestone or 'scars' outcrop on the valley side. The valley may have been eroded by a surface stream in the past, which has now disappeared underground, giving a dry valley. Some dry valleys are formed when a cave roof collapses.

6 Solution under soil widens joints. If soil is removed by erosion, such as glacial action in the past, the weathered limestone is exposed as limestone pavement. Deep joints known as **grikes** and upstanding blocks as **clints** (**F**).

Diagram labels:
- Ingleborough (724m)
- Thin peaty soils
- Scree
- Limestone scars
- Surface streams
- Boggart's Roaring Hole (potholes and swallow holes)
- Millstone Grit (impermeable)
- Yoredale Beds (slate and sandstone – impermeable)
- Carboniferous limestone (many joints and beds – permeable)
- Slate (impermeable)
- Raven Scar
- River Doe
- Limestone pavement
- Resurgence
- White Scar Cave System
- Crina Scars
- Crina Bottom
- Water table
- Large cave/cavern

5 A saturated layer or **water table** forms in limestone above impermeable rocks. Level of 'table' rises and falls depending on rainfall. Sudden rises can fill cave systems, creating dangerous situations for cavers. In valley, river bubbles out at surface again at a resurgence.

4 Calcium (released by chemical reaction between rain water, limestone rock and carbon dioxide) is either deposited on cave walls as flowstone or grows slowly as **stalactites** (from ceiling) (**E**) and **stalagmites** (from floor) (**D**). Growth rate average is 1cm/200years.

3 Joints and bedding planes are slowly enlarged by solution, stream erosion and rock falls to form caves. *Solution:* Greater in warmer periods that separated cold glacial times in past. Many large cave systems were formed more than 70,000 years ago during the warmer periods that separated cold glacial times. *Stream erosion:* After heavy rain or rapid snowmelt, fast-flowing streams erode rock channels. *Rock falls:* If joints are close together, solution eventually weakens the rock and causes rock falls from cave roof.

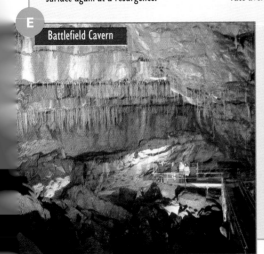
Battlefield Cavern

E

Deposition of calcite

D

Questions

1 Give two reasons why water in streams is naturally acidic. *(2)*

2 Describe the chemical weathering process that can take place when rain water seeps through the joints and fissures in limestone. *(3)*

3 Using examples from limestone areas, show how landforms are the result of both the processes of weathering and erosion. *(10)*

4 Describe how some landforms are the result of both past and present processes. *(10)*

Total: 25 marks

The hydrological cycle

How important is water to us?

Water is essential to all life; the human body is 90 per cent water. A large tree requires many hundreds of litres daily. Each person in the UK uses about 150 litres per day. **A** shows how this is used. **B** shows the heavy demands made by industry, such as the Llanwern Steel Works in South Wales (page 124). The cost of water has been rising – the average unmetered bill per household is now about £250 per year.

Most people take water for granted unless there is a problem when there is either too much (floods) or too little (droughts). Demand is also increasing. We are buying more domestic machines, such as

dishwashers and power showers, than ever before. The careful management of this resource is vital and to do that we need to know how much rain falls and what happens to it as it makes its way to the sea. We need to know how the natural system works.

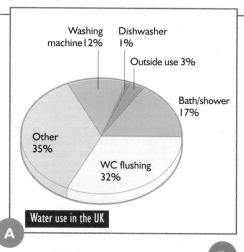

A Water use in the UK

Industrial use of water	B
Litres of water used to make:	
Average car	30,000
One tonne of steel	4,500
One tonne of ready mixed concrete	450
A pint of beer	4.5

Q

1 **A** shows 35 per cent of water use as 'Other'. What might this include?

2 We are urged to 'Save Water! Use the graph and table to help identify where savings could be made?

The hydrological cycle

The total amount of water available on the planet is limited. It exists in three states: gas, liquid and solid. The circulation of water between the oceans, atmosphere and land is known as the *hydrological cycle*. This can be studied at the global and the river basin scale.

The global system

Since there are no net gains or losses, this cycle is known as a closed system (**C**). The rate at which water moves through the system will vary; some will be stored for thousands of years in the deep oceans and ice caps. In contrast water remains only a short time in the atmosphere before returning to Earth as precipitation.

Q

1 Which are the two largest 'stores' of water?

2 How might they be affected if global temperatures increased or decreased?

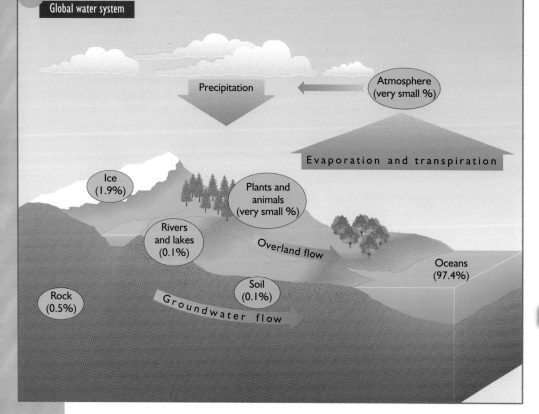

C Global water system

Precipitation

Atmosphere (very small %)

Evaporation and transpiration

Ice (1.9%)

Plants and animals (very small %)

Rivers and lakes (0.1%)

Overland flow

Oceans (97.4%)

Rock (0.5%)

Soil (0.1%)

Groundwater flow

The river basin system

The river basin is part of the hydrological cycle and can be studied as a system. Water moves by a variety of routes through the drainage basin, e.g. infiltrating the soil.

INPUTS		STORES		OUTPUTS
(water enters the drainage basin, e.g. precipitation)	**flows** ➡	(water is stored for different lengths of time, then released, e.g. as **groundwater** and **base flow**)	**flows** ➡	(water leaves the basin, e.g. as streamflow)

Since inputs vary and outputs of water are lost for good from the basin this is an 'open' type of system.

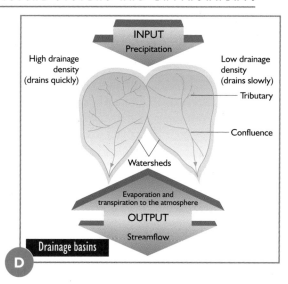

D Drainage basins

The drainage density for a drainage basin $= \dfrac{\text{total length of streams (m)}}{\text{area of the basin (m}^2)}$

The higher the density, the quicker water drains through the basin and the risk of sudden or flash floods is greater.

E The water system

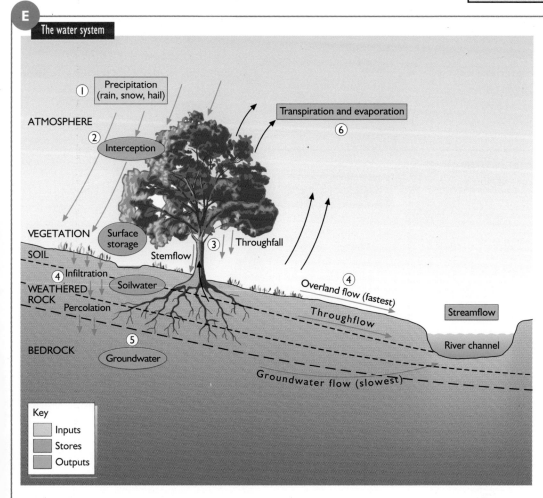

Precipitation falls to the ground. Rainfall varies in intensity and seasonally. 'Heavy' showers fall at over 10mm/hour (**1**). Most of it is intercepted by vegetation.

Interception is greatest in summer when trees are in leaf (**2**). Water reaches the soil through the trees, throughfall, or along the stem/trunk of trees and plants, stemflow (**3**). At the soil surface water can either flow as **overland flow** following the steepest slope to the stream (soil erosion may result if vegetation is thin) or it can infiltrate into the soil (**4**).

Infiltration rates vary depending on the permeability of the soil. Dry, sandy soil is more permeable than clay. Saturated (waterlogged) soil is the least permeable and infiltration is at its slowest. On entering the soil, water moves either downhill as **throughflow** or by percolation moving down vertically to form groundwater stores (**5**). Permeable rocks such as chalk and sandstone have large storage capacities. Large amounts of water in the soil enter the roots of plants and trees and evaporate through their leaves – **transpiration** (**6**). The water is then lost to the system.

Key
- Inputs
- Stores
- Outputs

RIVER HYDROGRAPHS

River discharge is the amount of water in the river passing a given point at a given time, measured in cumecs (cubic metres per second).

Changes in discharge are measured at a gauging station and recorded on a **hydrograph** (**C**).

The shape of the discharge curve in a hydrograph is related to:
- the quantity and intensity of the rainfall
- the different routes taken by the water to reach the river.

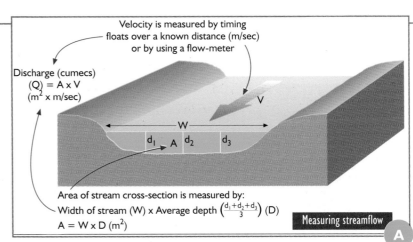

Velocity is measured by timing floats over a known distance (m/sec) or by using a flow-meter

Discharge (cumecs)
(Q) = A x V
(m^2 x m/sec)

W

d_1 A d_2 d_3

Area of stream cross-section is measured by:
Width of stream (W) x Average depth $\left(\frac{d_1 + d_2 + d_3}{3}\right)$ (D)
A = W x D (m^2)

Measuring streamflow

A

The period between the time of maximum rainfall and the time of peak discharge is called the **lag time**. Lag times are very important: a river with a short lag time and high discharge can cause sudden floods. In **B** the river in basin 1 is more likely to cause flooding than in 2.

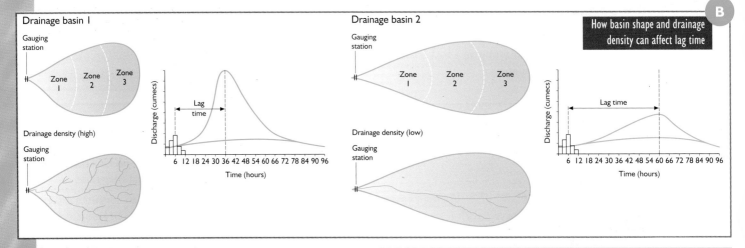

B

How basin shape and drainage density can affect lag time

Drainage basin 1

Gauging station

Zone 1 | Zone 2 | Zone 3

Drainage density (high)

Gauging station

Lag time

Discharge (cumecs)

6 12 18 24 30 36 42 48 54 60 66 72 78 84 90 96
Time (hours)

Drainage basin 2

Gauging station

Zone 1 | Zone 2 | Zone 3

Drainage density (low)

Gauging station

Lag time

Discharge (cumecs)

6 12 18 24 30 36 42 48 54 60 66 72 78 84 90 96
Time (hours)

CASE STUDY *EU: River Lymn, Lincolnshire*

FACT FILE

Basin area: 61.6 sq km
Gauging station: Partney Weir
Annual mean flow (1962-98): 0.49 cumecs (m^3/sec)

Highest recorded flow (26 April 1981): 13.34 cumecs (m^3/sec)

Mean annual precipitation (1988-97): 610mms

Max height in basin: 141m OD (Tetford Hill)
Height at Partney Weir: 15m OD
Water abstraction: Some abstraction for irrigation and for stock
Geology: Sandstone ridges and clay valleys
Soils: Light, dry permeable soils on sandstone
Heavy, wet impermeable soils on clay
Land use: Mostly arable (grain, rape, sugar beet) on sandy soils
Mixed farming on clay soils with more grass
Isolated woodlands on steeper slopes
Small rural villages, no housing estates or urban developments

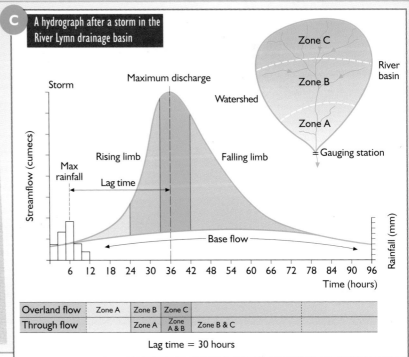

C A hydrograph after a storm in the River Lymn drainage basin

Storm

Maximum discharge

Zone C

River basin

Watershed

Zone B

Max rainfall

Rising limb

Falling limb

Zone A

= Gauging station

Lag time

Streamflow (cumecs)

Base flow

Rainfall (mm)

6 12 18 24 30 36 42 48 54 60 66 72 78 84 90 96
Time (hours)

Overland flow	Zone A	Zone B	Zone C	
Through flow		Zone A	Zone A & B	Zone B & C

Lag time = 30 hours

Basins 1 and 2 are similar in size and receive similar amounts of precipitation, but their hydrographs are very different because of factors such as:

Rock type	Impermeable rocks, low infiltration, high **surface run-off** and high drainage density	Permeable rocks, high infiltration, greater throughflow and groundwater flows
Soil	Thin soils: soils are quickly saturated — decreased infiltration, increased surface run-off	Deeper soil: increased infiltration and soil water storage
Relief	Steep slopes: surface run-off faster	Gentle slopes: increased infiltration, slower surface run-off
Vegetation	Moorland grass and heather: little interception, greater run-off	Woodland and forest: high interception and evaporation, root systems absorb large amounts of water, increased loss through transpiration
Land-use	Urban areas: concrete and tarmac impermeable, little storage, rapid run-off through drains	Rural areas: more interception and storage, reduced run-off
Management	Land drainage pipes in arable areas increase throughflow	Dams built to store water and control river discharge
Water demands	Low demand	High demand: water extracted from bore-holes (less groundwater) and rivers (lower discharge) for domestic water supply, industry and irrigation

D

The Environment Agency is responsible for managing river basins in the UK. It tries to predict what might happen if, for example, there is a heavy rainstorm or if more water is taken for domestic supplies. It produces hydrographs to show variations in discharge and rainfall over the 'water year' (Oct–Sept). **F** shows how three similar storms do not produce the same increases in discharge in the River Lymn. Seasonal changes in the main 'stores' and other outputs will affect how discharge responds to storms at different times of the year.

E

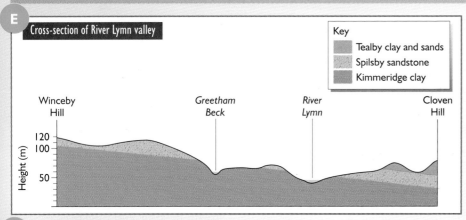

Cross-section of River Lymn valley

Key
- Tealby clay and sands
- Spilsby sandstone
- Kimmeridge clay

F

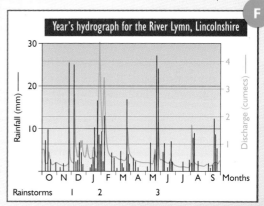

Year's hydrograph for the River Lymn, Lincolnshire

G

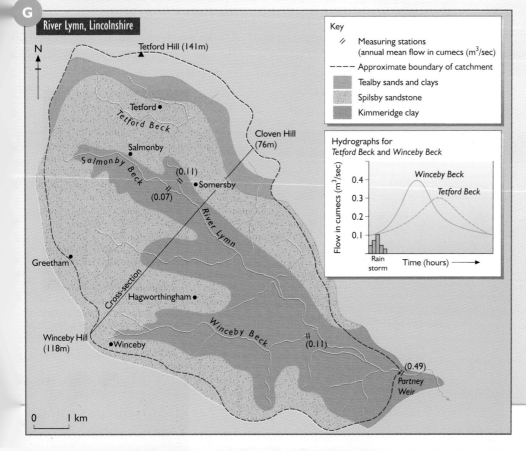

River Lymn, Lincolnshire

Key
- // Measuring stations (annual mean flow in cumecs (m³/sec)
- --- Approximate boundary of catchment
- Tealby sands and clays
- Spilsby sandstone
- Kimmeridge clay

Hydrographs for *Tetford Beck* and *Winceby Beck*

Questions

1 Suggest reasons why the sources of many of the tributaries of the River Lymn are close to the junction of the Spilsby Sandstone and the Kimmeridge Clay. (2)

2 Use the resources to explain why the average flow of Tetford Beck is much higher than Salmonby Beck. (6)

3 The storm hydrographs are shown for Tetford and Winceby Becks (**G**).

a) Describe two differences between the two hydrographs and,

b) Use the map (**G**) and geological cross-section (**E**) to suggest reasons for them. (7)

4 Compare the discharge pattern of the River Lymn from November to March with that of April to October. (5)

5 How might the River Lymn hydrograph change if a large, new housing estate was built at Tetford? (5)

Total: 25 marks

River landscapes

The two river valleys in **C** are very different landscapes. Which landscape has been most affected by human activities? Why do rivers and their valleys change so much between upland and lowland areas? What physical processes, acting upon the rocks, have produced these two contrasting landscapes?

River energy

A river begins at its source and flows towards the sea. The slope the river follows is called the long profile (**A**). The steepest parts are normally those close to the source, with gradients becoming gentler towards the sea. As more tributaries join the river, the amount of water, or the discharge (see page 14) of the river will increase. So, discharge will normally increase towards the sea. Also, as a river flows downhill it gains energy. The amount of energy available will increase with discharge.

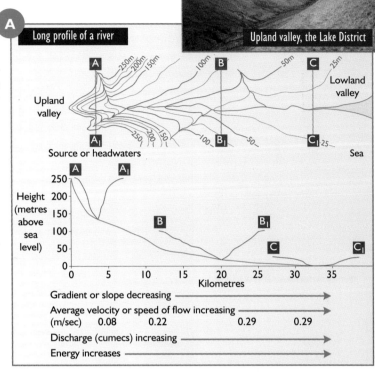

A Long profile of a river

Upland valley, the Lake District

Upland valley

Source or headwaters

Lowland valley

Sea

| | A | A₁ | B | B₁ | C | C₁ |

Gradient or slope decreasing →

Average velocity or speed of flow increasing (m/sec)

| 0.08 | 0.22 | 0.29 | 0.29 |

Discharge (cumecs) increasing →

Energy increases →

How is this energy used?

Most energy, about 95 per cent, is used or lost in friction and turbulence as the river flows along its channel (**B**). Friction and turbulence will be greatest in upland channels (**C**). If more energy is available in the lowland sections and less energy lost, then the speed at which a river flows, called velocity, will increase.

All rivers have the most energy and flow fastest when they are full. This is called **bank-full** stage (**C**).

Surplus energy is used by the stream to erode and transport, or carry away, materials.

The more energy that a river has and the faster it flows, the more it is able to erode and transport.

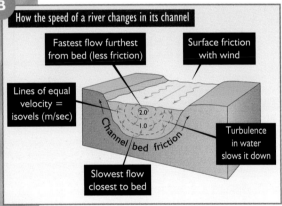

B How the speed of a river changes in its channel

Fastest flow furthest from bed (less friction)

Surface friction with wind

Lines of equal velocity = isovels (m/sec)

2.0
1.0

Channel bed friction

Turbulence in water slows it down

Slowest flow closest to bed

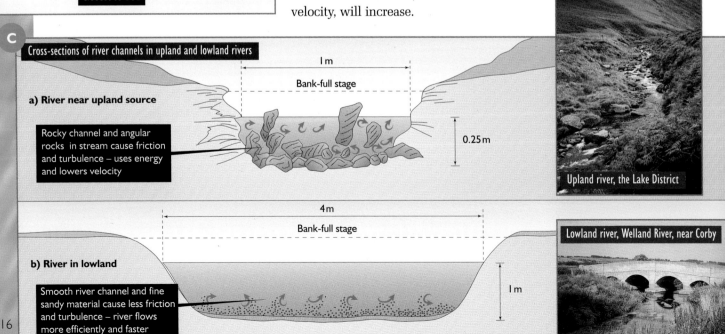

C Cross-sections of river channels in upland and lowland rivers

1 m
Bank-full stage

a) River near upland source

Rocky channel and angular rocks in stream cause friction and turbulence – uses energy and lowers velocity

0.25 m

Upland river, the Lake District

4 m
Bank-full stage

b) River in lowland

Smooth river channel and fine sandy material cause less friction and turbulence – river flows more efficiently and faster

1 m

Lowland river, Welland River, near Corby

What are the processes associated with rivers?

Erosion and transportation in streams are closely linked, since the material transported is used by the river to further erode its channel (**D**). Most erosion and transportation therefore takes place at bank-full stage.

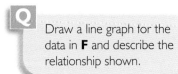

A river is most efficient at bank-full stage

Transportation

Load can be carried in three ways (**E**):

- bedload (along the streambed)
- saltation (by a series of hopping movements along the bed)
- **suspended load** (above the bed)
- solution (dissolved in the water).

Discharge (Cumecs)	Suspended load (grammes per second)
0	0
1	10
2	60
3	170
4	400
5	700

F

Q Draw a line graph for the data in **F** and describe the relationship shown.

Discharge will determine the ability of a river to transport load. **F** shows how the amount of suspended load changes as the discharge increases. The more water the more sediment.

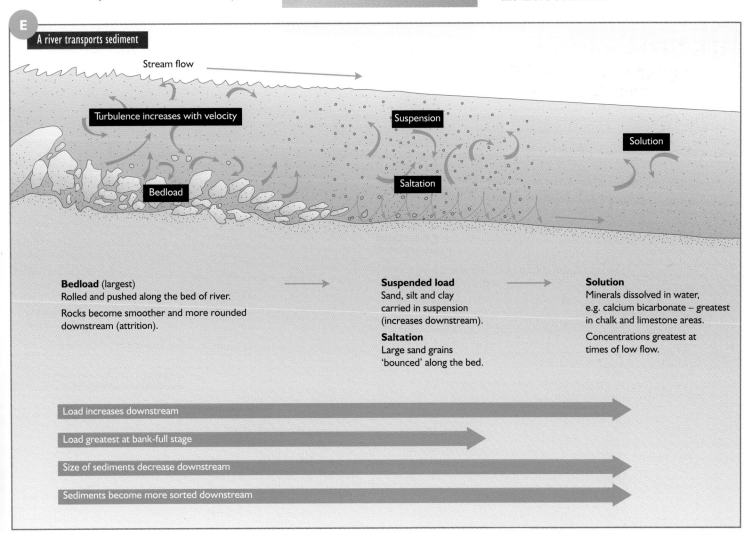

A river transports sediment

Bedload (largest)
Rolled and pushed along the bed of river.
Rocks become smoother and more rounded downstream (attrition).

Suspended load
Sand, silt and clay carried in suspension (increases downstream).

Saltation
Large sand grains 'bounced' along the bed.

Solution
Minerals dissolved in water, e.g. calcium bicarbonate – greatest in chalk and limestone areas.
Concentrations greatest at times of low flow.

Load increases downstream

Load greatest at bank-full stage

Size of sediments decrease downstream

Sediments become more sorted downstream

Erosional processes

There are four processes:

1 **Abrasion or corrasion** When material carried by the river rubs against its banks and bed, it smooths and shapes the rocks in the channel (**A**). The suspended load causes most abrasion. The swirling action of pebbles caught in rock cavities can create potholes (**B**).

2 **Attrition** Rocks transported by the river collide, break up into smaller pieces and become smoother and more rounded as they progress downstream.

3 **Hydraulic action** The immense force of the water removes material from the river banks and bed. At very high velocities (e.g. waterfalls) this can break rocks apart and is known as cavitation.

4 **Corrosion** The result of chemical processes when water dissolves chemicals in the rock. This is important where rivers pass over areas of limestone or chalk rock, such as in the Yorkshire Dales or South Downs.

Abrasion smooths rocks in channel bed — A

Potholes in streambed — B

Depositional processes

Deposition will occur when a river no longer has enough energy to transport the load it is carrying. For example, when a river enters a lake, velocity and turbulence lessen as energy is reduced (**C**).

Given time, the processes of erosion, transportation and deposition balance out. The slope of the long profile of the river and the size and shape of the river channel is a result of this balance. Human interference with the river – straightening the channel or building a dam – upsets the balance (**D**).

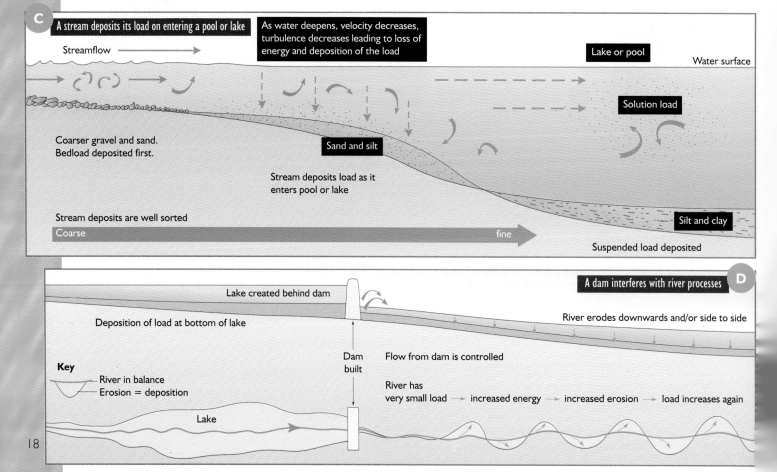

C — A stream deposits its load on entering a pool or lake

As water deepens, velocity decreases, turbulence decreases leading to loss of energy and deposition of the load

Streamflow

Lake or pool

Water surface

Solution load

Coarser gravel and sand. Bedload deposited first.

Sand and silt

Stream deposits load as it enters pool or lake

Stream deposits are well sorted

Coarse — fine

Silt and clay

Suspended load deposited

D — A dam interferes with river processes

Lake created behind dam

River erodes downwards and/or side to side

Deposition of load at bottom of lake

Dam built

Flow from dam is controlled

Key

River in balance
Erosion = deposition

River has very small load → increased energy → increased erosion → load increases again

Lake

What river landforms are there in upland areas?

Many rivers have their headwaters or sources in upland areas where precipitation is high and evapotranspiration low. Soils are thin with little vegetation and rocks are often impermeable. Most water moves down the slopes as overland or throughflow, making lag times short. When rain falls, river discharge can increase very quickly. Since the course of the river is steep and rocky, the flow, at bank-full stage, will be very turbulent with sufficient surplus energy to move large loads. The rocks are rolled along as bedload and become more rounded.

The river uses its load to cut downwards (vertical erosion). In arid areas and areas of limestone this can create a gorge (**E**). In mountain areas in the British Isles, however, the steep valley sides become unstable. Weathered rock tumbles downhill into the river and the slopes become less steep to form a V-shaped valley (**F**). At the same time the river also erodes from side-to-side (lateral erosion) creating **interlocking spurs**.

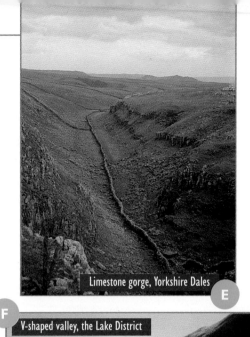
Limestone gorge, Yorkshire Dales **E**

F
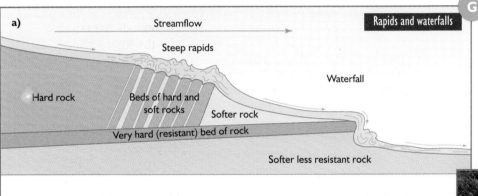
V-shaped valley, the Lake District

G

a) **Rapids and waterfalls**

Streamflow

Steep rapids

Waterfall

Hard rock

Beds of hard and soft rocks

Softer rock

Very hard (resistant) bed of rock

Softer less resistant rock

b)

Overhanging rock eventually collapses. Waterfall moves upstream

Steep-sided gorge left as waterfall retreats upstream

Hard rock

Softer rock undercut

Great turbulence causes corrasion and cavitation and creates deep plunge pool

Very turbulent water

Rocks in plunge pool (abrasion)

Waterfall, Skye, Scotland **H**

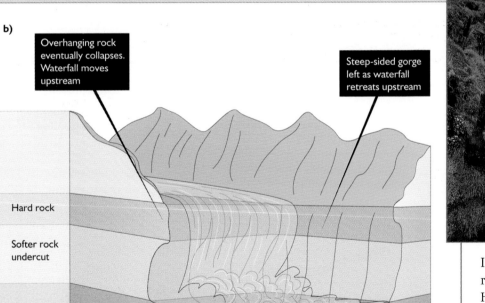

In upland areas the long profile of the river is generally steeper and uneven. Harder, more resistant rocks can cause rapids – sections of very fast and turbulent flow – and waterfalls (**G**). Waterfalls are often also found where tributary streams enter larger valleys that have been deepened by glaciers in the past, known as hanging valleys (see page 37).

CASE STUDY EU: Long Mynd valley profiles – Ashes Hollow and Quinny Brook

FACT FILE

Long Mynd, Shropshire

Height: 500m OD

Slopes: Gentle slopes at the top; very steep-sided valleys on south-east side

Geology: Ancient (Pre-Cambrian), hard, impermeable rocks with very hard beds of different rocks causing waterfalls

Precipitation: High all year: 800–1000mm per year (snow cover on the top in winter)

Soils: Thick peaty soils on the gentle slopes of the highest ground; thin acid soils on the steeper slopes

Vegetation: Grass and heather moorland used for hill sheep farming

Q Describe the river channel and landforms that you might expect to find in Ashes Hollow valley.

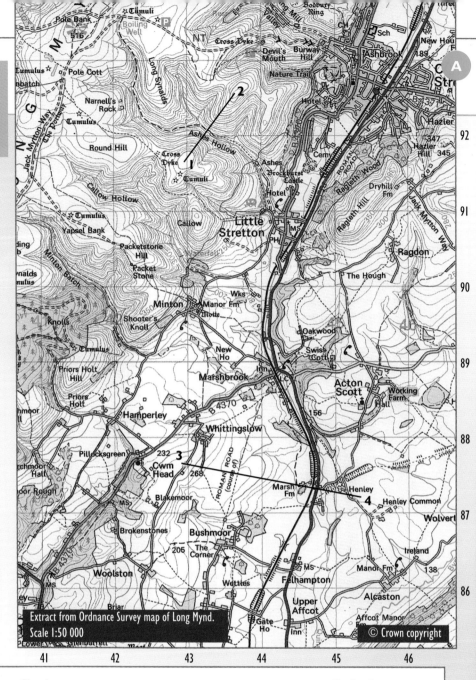

Extract from Ordnance Survey map of Long Mynd.
Scale 1:50 000
© Crown copyright

A

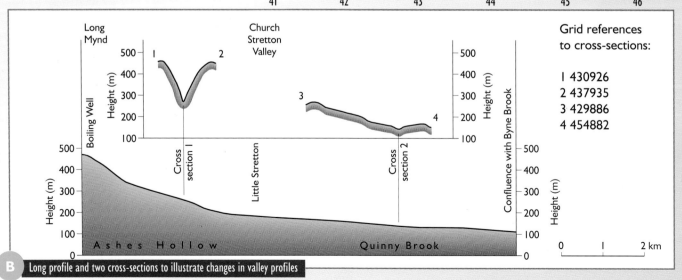

Grid references to cross-sections:

1 430926
2 437935
3 429886
4 454882

B Long profile and two cross-sections to illustrate changes in valley profiles

What are river landforms in lowland areas like?

In lowland areas as rivers approach the sea, vertical erosion is slower. River velocity and discharge, however, is higher than in uplands, and rivers are able to transport large amounts of fine sediment, particularly when full (**C**).

As the river moves from side to side in its channel, it causes lateral erosion, the load helping to erode the banks by corrasion. **F** shows that erosion is greatest on the outer part of the bend, where the river has most energy. In time, larger bends or *meanders* develop with river cliffs marking zones of undercutting. Deposition takes place in areas of least energy and point bars develop (**E**). At the same time the valley is being widened and the V-shape opens out with a flat valley floor. Most of these changes take place when the river is at bank-full stage. Eventually, if the meanders become extreme, the river cuts through the 'neck' of the meander and follows a straighter course once again (**E**). The abandoned meander is left as an **ox-bow lake**.

The River Trent at its confluence with the River Idle. Its colour suggests it is carrying a large suspended load.

C

River meanders in the UK

D

E

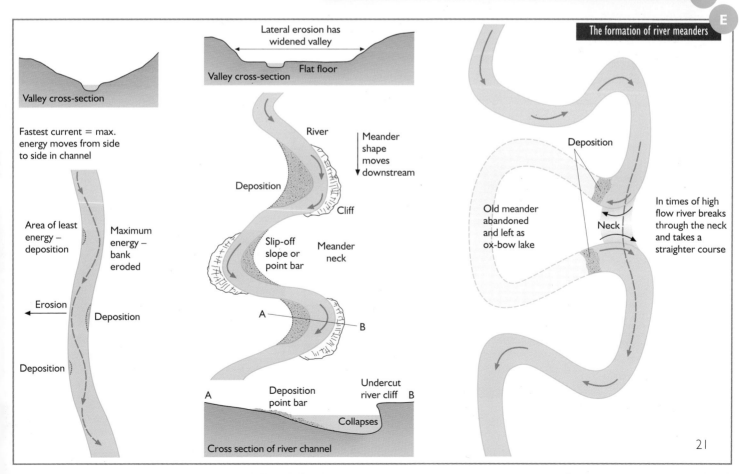

The formation of river meanders

Valley cross-section

Fastest current = max. energy moves from side to side in channel

Area of least energy – deposition

Maximum energy – bank eroded

Erosion

Deposition

Deposition

Lateral erosion has widened valley

Valley cross-section   Flat floor

River

Meander shape moves downstream

Deposition

Cliff

Slip-off slope or point bar

Meander neck

A

B

A   Deposition point bar   Undercut river cliff   B

Collapses

Cross section of river channel

Deposition

Old meander abandoned and left as ox-bow lake

Neck

In times of high flow river breaks through the neck and takes a straighter course

21

Meanders on River Welland, near Corby

A

Floodplains

In times of very high discharge the river may overflow its channel and flood the flat valley floor, which is known as the floodplain (**B**). The river will be carrying a large suspended load. As the water floods out of the channel, there is a sudden loss of energy, and large amounts of sediment will be deposited on the bank, forming **levées** (**C**). Further deposits will be left across the floodplain every flood adding another layer. These deposits are known as **alluvium**.

Along the Mississippi River, deposition over a long period has raised the levées and the river flow is now higher than the floodplain. When the river burst through the levée in 1993, flooding was very extensive.

Deltas

Large amounts of the suspended load carried by rivers ends up in the sea, where it is transported along the coast by waves and tidal currents. The River Nile in Egypt carries a large amount of sediment into the Mediterranean Sea, but the waves and tides are not strong enough to take it away, so the sediment is deposited at the mouth of the river, forming a *delta* (**D**).

The deposits split the river into several channels, called **distributaries**. These spread the sediments over a wide area, giving the delta distinctive shapes.

The River Nene floods near Peterborough

B

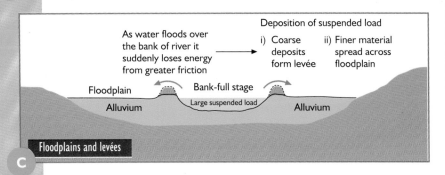

As water floods over the bank of river it suddenly loses energy from greater friction

Deposition of suspended load
i) Coarse deposits form levée
ii) Finer material spread across floodplain

Floodplain   Bank-full stage
Alluvium   Large suspended load   Alluvium

Floodplains and levées

C

Aerial view of The Nile delta

D

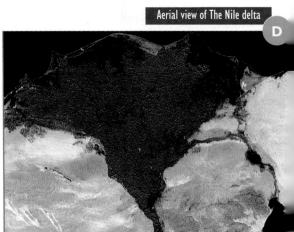

The Nile and Mississippi deltas **E**

Changes in sea level

If sea level falls, rivers will need to adjust. They will erode vertically for a time before forming a new floodplain. Parts of the former floodplain will be left as **river terraces** (**G**). Since they are made of fertile alluvium and are well drained, terraces were often chosen by the Anglo-Saxons for village sites as for example, along the Trent valley.

If sea level rises, it will flood the floodplains nearest to the sea and form estuaries such as at the mouth of the Thames, or that forming Southampton Water. Rivers deposit sediment in the estuary, which at low tide, is exposed as mudflats and salt-marshes (**F**). A rise in sea level would also flood and destroy low-lying deltas threatening the lives and livelihoods of the people living there. Fourteen million people live and farm on the Nile delta alone.

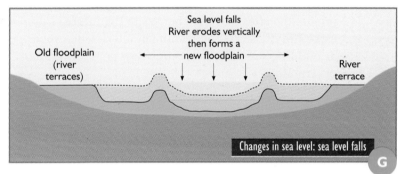

Changes in sea level: sea level falls **G**

Sea level rises: Exe estuary, Devon, at low tide **F**

Questions

1 Use the aerial photograph (**A**) to make a sketch map of the course of the river. Annotate with evidence of erosion, deposition and abandoned channels. *(12)*

2 River engineers have straightened the channel. Explain what effects this might have on river processes. *(6)*

3 Choose one landform from **A** and explain its formation. *(5)*

4 How might a drop in sea level affect the River Nene in **B**? *(2)*

Total: 25 marks

Coastal landscapes

What are coasts?

The coast is the narrow zone where the land, sea and atmosphere meet. Waves and tidal currents interact with the different rocks and sediments forming the land, to shape and produce erosional and depositional landforms such as cliffs and beaches. Weathering processes such as freeze-thaw will affect the rocks on cliff faces, while rivers often supply large amounts of **suspended load** for the sea to transport and deposit. The coastal zone is a very active place and changes occur on a daily basis as the weather alters and the tides rise and fall. Most change takes place during storms when beaches and weak cliffs can be eroded very rapidly. The longer term effects of changing sea levels will threaten low-lying coasts, but all coastlines will have to adjust to the new conditions. It is important that we understand how coastal processes work in order to predict the effects of any changes in the future, especially those caused by human interference such as building sea-walls or creating new land for farming or airports.

Shaping the coasts

Waves do most of the work in shaping coastal landforms. When wind blows over water, surface waves are formed which move in the direction of the wind. The stronger the wind and the longer it blows over the water the larger the wave is likely to become. The distance a wind can blow over the sea is known as the *fetch*. On the Cornish coast waves approaching from the south west may have a fetch of thousands of kilometres, as their origin is in the stormy South Atlantic Ocean. Since these waves approach from the same direction as the **prevailing wind**, they are known as the *dominant* waves. They are responsible for most of the work of erosion, transportation and deposition. They will be long, low waves or 'swell', providing excellent conditions for surfing. Along the Yorkshire and Lincolnshire coasts, the dominant waves come from the north east.

How do waves erode?

In open, deep sea a wave moves forward but a float on the surface will move only up and down since the water itself moves in a circular motion (**1**). A float will not move forward. As a wave approaches the shore the water depth decreases and friction against the sea bed causes the bottom of the wave to move slower than the crest. The circle is increasingly distorted (**2**); the wave increases in height until it finally plunges forward as a breaker (**3**). The energy of the wave is released and the work of erosion, transportation and deposition takes place. On open coasts, these are the dominant processes in the area between low and high tides (**4**). They will be most active in stormy conditions, when high winds create large high-energy waves.

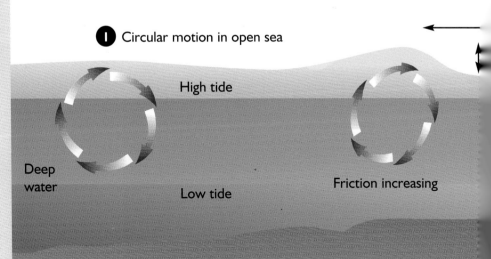

At high tide the deeper water allows bigger waves with greater energy to reach the cliffs increasing erosion

1 Circular motion in open sea

High tide

Deep water

Low tide

Friction increasing

Erosional processes

There are four main processes of erosion:
- **hydraulic action** – as a wave breaks against a cliff it traps air that is compressed into cracks in the rock, causing blocks to be loosened and broken away over time.
- **corrasion** or **abrasion** – the moving water bombards the cliff with rock fragments and drags others backwards and forwards over rock surfaces, wearing them away.

- **attrition** – the rock fragments themselves rub against each other, reducing their size and making them more rounded.
- **corrosion (solution)** – salt water is able to corrode the minerals in some rocks, causing the rock to dissolve.

Waves crashing against cliffs

A

Coasts with cliffs

Where there are cliffs wave action will be concentrated at the base; a *wave-cut notch* (**5**) will be eroded which eventually will lead to the cliff above collapsing (**6**). The cliff face will retreat leaving a sloping rock surface called a *wave-cut platform*, which is covered at high tide (**7**). At low tide this platform is exposed often trapping many rock-pools. The speed of erosion will of course depend on the strength of the rock forming the cliff. Weathering action, such as freeze-thaw, may loosen rock fragments on the upper cliffs, which will then fall away (**8**). The eroded rock will fall onto the wave-cut platform where it will be used in the process of *corrasion* (**9**). Gradually *attrition* will reduce it in size and it will be transported away. This will happen very quickly when the cliffs are formed of weaker rock such as clay.

6 Cliff collapses and retreats

Weathering of rock

8

Vertical joints

Horizontal beds or layers of rock

Cliff collapses along weak joints

3 Breaker

5 Wave-cut notch

Undercutting – erosion along bedding planes and joints

Wave length ⟶

Wave height

2 Increasing distortion

7 Wave-cut platform extending as cliff retreats

9

Q With the help of diagrams, describe how high, steep storm waves will cause most erosion to a cliff when they break (use the correct terms for the processes of erosion).

4 Inter-tidal zone

Headlands and bays

A coast is formed of strong and weak rocks (**A**). The weaker rocks are eroded more quickly and form bays while the stronger form headlands. As this coast develops over time, erosion increases on the headlands which often creates steep cliffs. The eroded material is reduced by attrition and transported into the bays. Here the waves have less energy and the material is deposited to form beaches.

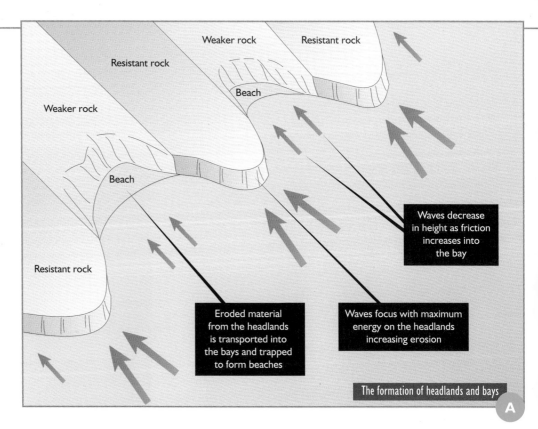

Weaker rock

Resistant rock

Resistant rock

Weaker rock

Beach

Beach

Resistant rock

Waves decrease in height as friction increases into the bay

Eroded material from the headlands is transported into the bays and trapped to form beaches

Waves focus with maximum energy on the headlands increasing erosion

The formation of headlands and bays

A

As a headland is eroded, the cliff retreats leaving a *wave-cut platform* (**B1**). Erosion will be greatest where there are weaknesses in the rock such as joints and faults. Chalk and limestone, for example, have many joints; the largest of which may be widened to form *caves* (**B2**). Wave pressure inside the cave may cause the roof to partially collapse, which creates a

blowhole (**B3**). As the headland is exposed caves may be enlarged to form *arches* (**B4**). If the roof of the arch collapses isolated *stacks* are left rising from the wave-cut platform (**B5**). Stacks are very exposed – weathering and erosion will gradually reduce them to *stumps* (**B6**).

B

The formation of headland features

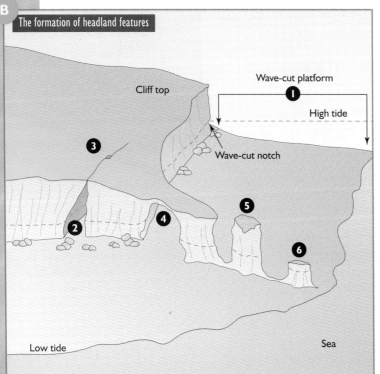

Cliff top

Wave-cut platform

1

High tide

Wave-cut notch

3

2

4

5

6

Low tide

Sea

C

Chalk cliffs of Flamborough Head

How do waves transport material?

Rock eroded from cliffs, and material carried down to the sea by rivers, is moved or transported by the waves. When a wave breaks, some of the water will flow up the beach, a movement known as **swash**. Its return back down the beach is the **backwash**. Beach material, eroded or disturbed by the wave breaking, is transported up and down the beach by these movements of water.

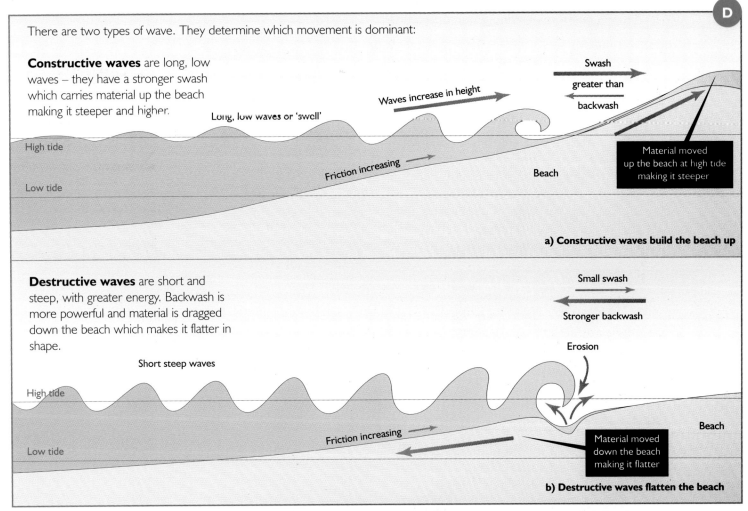

There are two types of wave. They determine which movement is dominant:

Constructive waves are long, low waves – they have a stronger swash which carries material up the beach making it steeper and higher.

Long, low waves or 'swell'

Waves increase in height

Swash greater than backwash

Friction increasing

High tide

Low tide

Beach

Material moved up the beach at high tide making it steeper

a) Constructive waves build the beach up

Destructive waves are short and steep, with greater energy. Backwash is more powerful and material is dragged down the beach which makes it flatter in shape.

Short steep waves

Small swash

Stronger backwash

Erosion

High tide

Friction increasing

Low tide

Beach

Material moved down the beach making it flatter

b) Destructive waves flatten the beach

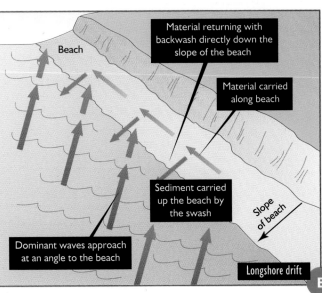

Longshore drift occurs where waves can also transport material along the beach (**E**). If the dominant wave approaches the beach at an angle, the swash will carry material up and across the beach. However, the backwash carries it back down the beach by the steepest slope. Another wave will then move it up and across the beach once more.

Beach

Material returning with backwash directly down the slope of the beach

Material carried along beach

Sediment carried up the beach by the swash

Slope of beach

Dominant waves approach at an angle to the beach

Longshore drift

Questions

1 Describe the landscape found at Flamborough Head (**C**). Take care to use the correct geographical terms.   (5)

2 Make an A4 poster informing the public how the different landforms found at Flamborough Head have been formed. Draw a sketch of the headland in the centre and surround it with labels and diagrams explaining the processes and stages of formation of the different landforms.   (20)

Total: 25 marks

What coastal landforms of deposition are there?

In shallow or sheltered areas, such as a bay, wave energy decreases – the material or load can no longer be transported and deposition takes place. Beaches are the most common landform resulting from deposition.

The shape and size and height of a beach depends on:

- the type of wave (**D**, page 27)
- the tidal range (the difference in height between low tide and high tide)
- the nature of the beach material (**A**).

Beaches are constantly changing however. In winter, high winds and storms cause more destructive waves. Sand is removed, sandy beaches become lower, and often more pebbles are visible. In summer, storms are less frequent and constructive waves are dominant. Sand is returned to the beach, which then becomes higher and more sandy.

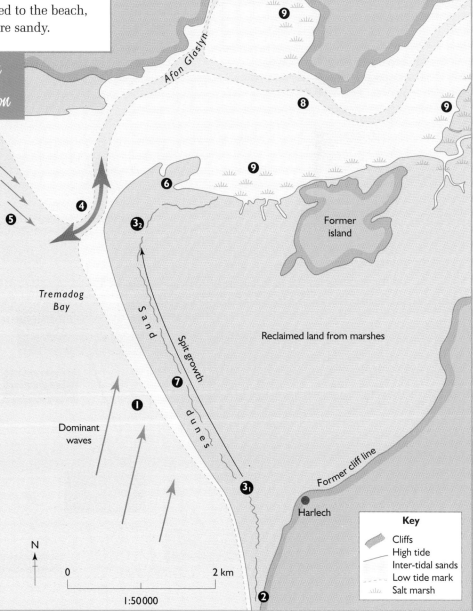

Sand beaches have low slopes

Pebble beaches are steeper

Storm beach has largest pebbles thrown up by the largest high-energy waves

Cliff

High tide

Tidal range

Low tide

Ridge

Runnel

Beaches differ in shape and size

A

B

CASE STUDY *EU: The Afon Glaslyn estuary – coastal deposition*

In **B**, a beach has formed along the coast and longshore drift is transporting material to the north (1). The former coastline changes direction at the mouth (**C**) of a river **estuary** (2), but material, transported by longshore drift, has slowly been deposited across the estuary mouth to form a *spit* of sand and pebbles (3₁ – 3₂). The spit will continue to grow until erosion by tidal and river currents moving in and out of the estuary (4) equals the amount of new material supplied by longshore drift. If secondary waves (5), from the north west are strong enough, the spit may develop a curved end (6). If the tidal and river currents are very weak, deposition may continue right across the estuary mouth creating a *bar*.

When the tide is low the sand on the beach dries out. Finer sand can be moved by the dominant winds which transport it up to the top of the beach, where it is trapped by vegetation to form *sand dunes* (7). In the shelter of the spit (8), the tidal waters in the estuary will no longer have the energy to transport even fine material. Sand, silt and clay will be deposited and trapped by plants forming *salt marshes* (9).

Afon Glaslyn

Former island

Tremadog Bay

Reclaimed land from marshes

Sand dunes

Spit growth

Dominant waves

Former cliff line

Harlech

N

0   2 km

1:50000

Key

Cliffs
High tide
Inter-tidal sands
Low tide mark
Salt marsh

How have past processes influenced our coasts?

Sea level changes

During the last ice age, large quantities of water froze to form the great advancing ice sheets (page 34). With less water in the oceans, sea level dropped. It is estimated that it fell by over 100 metres. As sea level fell, rivers rapidly eroded downwards, which deepened their valleys. After the ice age, when the ice sheet melted, sea level rapidly rose and drowned the lower part of these over-deepened valleys. These long, deep inlets of the sea are known as *rias* (e.g. Dartmouth, **D**). Estuaries in eastern England, such as the Thames, Wash and Humber have similar origins. In Norway, glaciers eroded and deepened former river valleys. As the climate became warmer and the ice sheets melted, they flooded to form *fjords* (**E**).

The Afon Glaslyn estuary

C

D Ria: Dartmouth

Raised beaches

In Scotland, with the weight of the ice sheets removed, the land has risen slightly faster than the rise in sea level. Former coastal landforms such as cliffs and beaches are now several metres above present sea level. These are known as *raised beaches* (**F**).

E Sogne Fjord, Norway

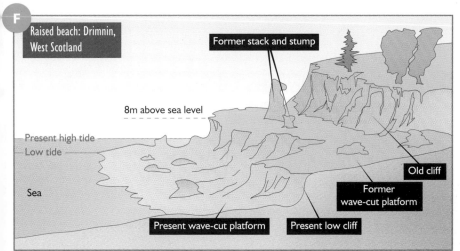

F Raised beach: Drimnin, West Scotland

Former stack and stump

8m above sea level

Present high tide

Low tide

Sea

Old cliff

Former wave-cut platform

Present wave-cut platform

Present low cliff

Q

1 Use **A**, or a named beach that is familiar to you, to describe the changes you might find if, at low tide, you walked from the top of a beach down to the water level.

2 What changes to the present processes might result in a bar forming right across the mouth of the Afon Glaslyn estuary in **B**?

3 Use **D** and **E** to describe the differences in the landscapes of a ria and a fjord.

COASTAL MANAGEMENT

How are coasts being influenced by human activity?

The Environment Agency is responsible for ensuring that coastal erosion does not endanger people's lives and livelihoods in the UK. This has become much more difficult as:

- severe gales have become more frequent in the last ten years, and are likely to increase as a result of global warming (**A**).
- global warming may increase sea level by half a metre by the year 2050; the low-lying coastal areas of south-east England are particularly at risk.
- The British Isles are tilting, with the south-east coast sinking into the North Sea at 150mm per 100 years.
- many more people live in coastal settlements; older people often retire to the coast and buy bungalows.

Five options can be considered:

Do nothing! Let the natural processes of erosion continue until a new balance is achieved. This is unlikely to be an option where coastal settlements exist or extensive flooding may result.

Prevent and discourage Planning controls can prevent further housing being built in vulnerable areas. Insurance companies can make the cost of insuring some coastal properties too high to be affordable.

Managed retreat Do not protect the present coast but defend it further inland. This may be possible in low-lying areas of farmland such as around the Wash estuary, and in Essex.

Build 'hard' defences Construct concrete sea walls (**B**), rock armour (**C**), sea bees (**D**) and **groynes** (**E**). These are very expensive.

Use 'soft' solutions Build up beaches with sand dredged from many kilometres offshore – called **beach nourishment** (**F**). This is expensive but the solution is efficient, economic, sustainable and attractive and likely to be the most favoured method of sea defence in the future. The tourist industry favour this option.

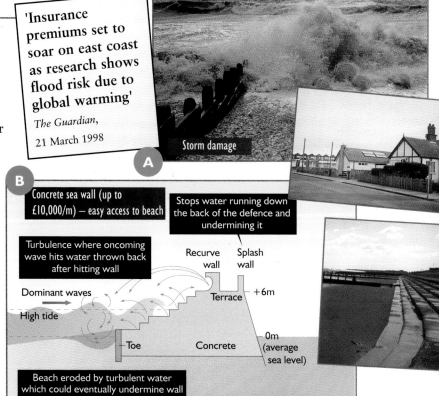

'Insurance premiums set to soar on east coast as research shows flood risk due to global warming'

The Guardian, 21 March 1998

A Storm damage

B Concrete sea wall (up to £10,000/m) – easy access to beach

Stops water running down the back of the defence and undermining it

Turbulence where oncoming wave hits water thrown back after hitting wall

Recurve wall | Splash wall

Dominant waves

Terrace +6m

High tide

Toe | Concrete | 0m (average sea level)

Beach eroded by turbulent water which could eventually undermine wall

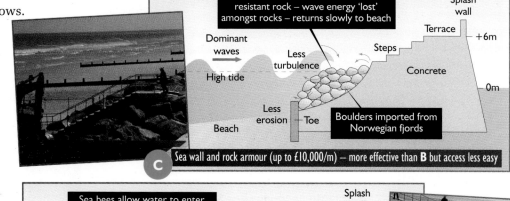

Rock armour: 3-tonne boulders of resistant rock – wave energy 'lost' amongst rocks – returns slowly to beach

Splash wall

Dominant waves

Terrace +6m

Less turbulence

Steps

High tide

Concrete

Less erosion | Toe

0m

Beach

Boulders imported from Norwegian fjords

C Sea wall and rock armour (up to £10,000/m) – more effective than **B** but access less easy

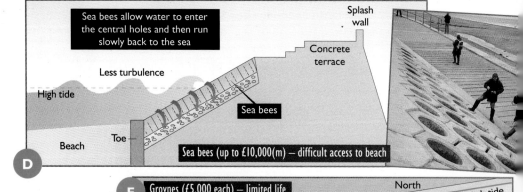

Sea bees allow water to enter the central holes and then run slowly back to the sea

Splash wall

Concrete terrace

Less turbulence

High tide

Sea bees

Beach | Toe

D Sea bees (up to £10,000(m) – difficult access to beach

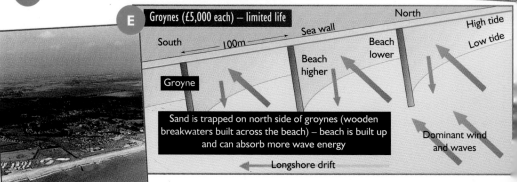

E Groynes (£5,000 each) – limited life

North

Sea wall

High tide

South

100m

Beach lower

Low tide

Beach higher

Groyne

Sand is trapped on north side of groynes (wooden breakwaters built across the beach) – beach is built up and can absorb more wave energy

Dominant wind and waves

Longshore drift

Q

1 Using **D**, draw a labelled cross-section to show why sea bees are an effective sea defence.

2 Use **F** to help explain the four advantages given in favour of beach nourishment.

Sand dredged from banks several kilometres offshore pumped onto beach and then 'shaped' by bulldozers – beach is higher, absorbs more wave energy and better for leisure

'Hard' defence still gives extra protection in times of exceptional storms

New beach absorbs the wave energy

High tide

+6m

0m

Old beach level

Concrete

Beach nourishment

F

In the past problems of coastal erosion have been dealt with in an isolated way providing solutions for specific locations. The effects on other parts of the coast were often ignored.

In **G**, the village of Mappleton in Yorkshire was threatened by erosion of the weak rock of the low cliffs. Sea defences were built to protect the cliff base and control the wave processes. The strategy was successful – a higher sandy beach was deposited and waves were prevented from undercutting the cliff any further. North of the point, however, the beach was starved of sand. It became narrower and lower, which allowed more waves to reach the cliffs and undercut them. It caused faster cliff retreat and loss of farmland.

Today, engineers consider the whole coastline, and try to choose solutions that take account of much larger patterns of erosion, transportation and deposition (**H**).

"To rebuild the beaches along the long and vulnerable coastline of the east coast is a massive programme which will never be completed."
Environment Agency

G

Mappleton, Yorkshire

H

Protecting the east coast

N

Skegness

Kings Lynn

Norwich

Peterborough

Great Yarmouth

Ipswich

Harwich

Key

Dredging site

Beach nourishment sites

Flood risk areas

0   50 km

"Tackling the issue demanded a new approach. Previously the tendency had been to look at isolated problems in specific locations and to design solutions to solve them. Now for the first time it was necessary to look at the whole of the coastline. In this way the full extent of the loss of beaches, the offshore movement of beach materials and other factors could be identified to produce a comprehensive assessment of the effect of defence schemes on adjoining areas and the remainder of the coast."
National Rivers Authority

Questions

Photograph **G** of Mappleton is looking south.

1 Make a labelled sketch or map to:
   a) show the nature of the coastal landforms (cliffs and beach) and the wave processes
   b) identify the different coastal defences
   c) show the effects of the defence works on the cliffs and beach.   *(10)*

2 How far do you think these defence works have been successful ?   *(8)*

3 What physical, economic and social factors make it unlikely that the east coast programme of sea defences will ever be completed?   *(7)*

Total: 25 marks

31

CASE STUDY
EU: The Holderness coast

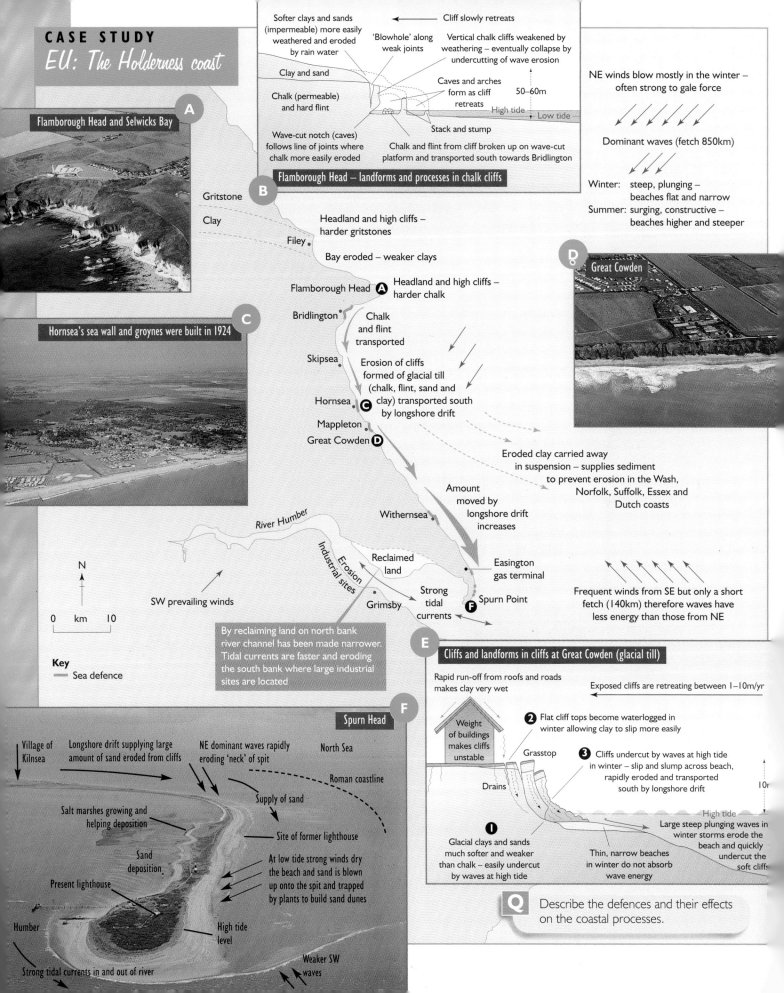

A
Flamborough Head and Selwicks Bay

C
Hornsea's sea wall and groynes were built in 1924

Flamborough Head – landforms and processes in chalk cliffs

Softer clays and sands (impermeable) more easily weathered and eroded by rain water

Cliff slowly retreats

'Blowhole' along weak joints

Vertical chalk cliffs weakened by weathering – eventually collapse by undercutting of wave erosion

Clay and sand

Chalk (permeable) and hard flint

Caves and arches form as cliff retreats

50–60m

High tide   Low tide

Wave-cut notch (caves) follows line of joints where chalk more easily eroded

Chalk and flint from cliff broken up on wave-cut platform and transported south towards Bridlington

Stack and stump

NE winds blow mostly in the winter – often strong to gale force

Dominant waves (fetch 850km)

Winter: steep, plunging – beaches flat and narrow
Summer: surging, constructive – beaches higher and steeper

D
Great Cowden

Gritstone
Clay
Filey
Headland and high cliffs – harder gritstones
Bay eroded – weaker clays

Flamborough Head **A** Headland and high cliffs – harder chalk

Bridlington   Chalk and flint transported

Skipsea   Erosion of cliffs formed of glacial till (chalk, flint, sand and clay) transported south by longshore drift

Hornsea **C**

Mappleton

Great Cowden **D**

Eroded clay carried away in suspension – supplies sediment to prevent erosion in the Wash, Norfolk, Suffolk, Essex and Dutch coasts

Withernsea   Amount moved by longshore drift increases

River Humber

Industrial sites

Erosion

Reclaimed land

Grimsby   Strong tidal currents

Easington gas terminal

F Spurn Point

Frequent winds from SE but only a short fetch (140km) therefore waves have less energy than those from NE

N

SW prevailing winds

0   km   10

Key
— Sea defence

By reclaiming land on north bank river channel has been made narrower. Tidal currents are faster and eroding the south bank where large industrial sites are located

E
Cliffs and landforms in cliffs at Great Cowden (glacial till)

Rapid run-off from roofs and roads makes clay very wet

Exposed cliffs are retreating between 1–10m/yr

Weight of buildings makes cliffs unstable

2 Flat cliff tops become waterlogged in winter allowing clay to slip more easily

Grasstop

3 Cliffs undercut by waves at high tide in winter – slip and slump across beach, rapidly eroded and transported south by longshore drift

Drains

10r

High tide

1 Glacial clays and sands much softer and weaker than chalk – easily undercut by waves at high tide

Thin, narrow beaches in winter do not absorb wave energy

Large steep plunging waves in winter storms erode the beach and quickly undercut the soft cliffs

F
Spurn Head

Village of Kilnsea

Longshore drift supplying large amount of sand eroded from cliffs

NE dominant waves rapidly eroding 'neck' of spit

North Sea

Roman coastline

Supply of sand

Salt marshes growing and helping deposition

Site of former lighthouse

Sand deposition

At low tide strong winds dry the beach and sand is blown up onto the spit and trapped by plants to build sand dunes

Present lighthouse

Humber

High tide level

Strong tidal currents in and out of river

Weaker SW waves

Q
Describe the defences and their effects on the coastal processes.

THE HOLDERNESS COASTAL SYSTEM

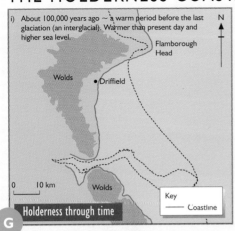

G Holderness through time

i) About 100,000 years ago ~ a warm period before the last glaciation (an interglacial). Warmer than present day and higher sea level.

Key — Coastline

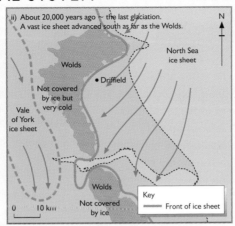

ii) About 20,000 years ago ~ the last glaciation. A vast ice sheet advanced south as far as the Wolds.

Key — Front of ice sheet

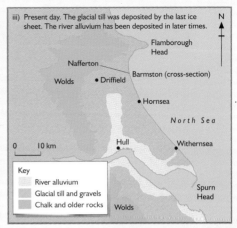

iii) Present day. The glacial till was deposited by the last ice sheet. The river alluvium has been deposited in later times.

Key
- River alluvium
- Glacial till and gravels
- Chalk and older rocks

I Coastal towns 'lost' by erosion since Roman times

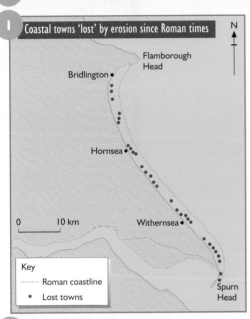

Key
- - - Roman coastline
- • Lost towns

Two sisters have lived for over 70 years in their farmhouse on the Holderness coast. They recall their childhood walks to the sea, past barns, the stackyard, a pond, a field full of bullocks and the coastguards' lookout point. Now all are gone.

'When the waves crash against the cliffs, the servants' bells tinkle eerily in the kitchen of this, once handsome, farmhouse. The floor tremors and the cracks in the ceilings widen…. In the summer it's usually lovely and peaceful here. But in the winter the gales are frightening. You think "Oo, stop" when you hear the waves. If the wind is on the sea you can hear the rollers and the house shudders. The trouble is nobody's going to buy the house. We just hope we can sell the bricks and things inside like the tiles and fireplaces.'

The Daily Telegraph, April 1995

H Barmston: geological cross-section

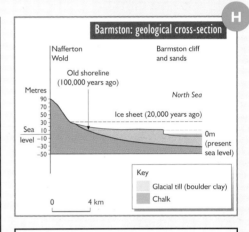

Key
- Glacial till (boulder clay)
- Chalk

'We may have to sacrifice the Holderness coastline if we are to protect cities and industry along the Humber, and other coastlines in Lincolnshire, Norfolk, Suffolk, Essex and even the Netherlands.'
A university geographer, an expert on coastal processes

J A proposal to defend the coast at five points only

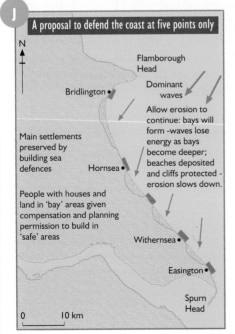

Main settlements preserved by building sea defences

People with houses and land in 'bay' areas given compensation and planning permission to build in 'safe' areas

Dominant waves

Allow erosion to continue: bays will form - waves lose energy as bays become deeper; beaches deposited and cliffs protected - erosion slows down.

K

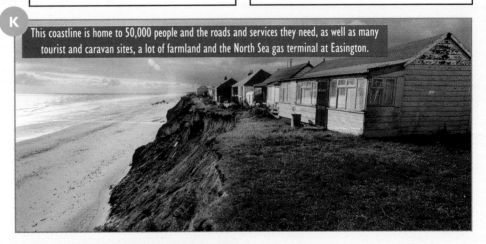

This coastline is home to 50,000 people and the roads and services they need, as well as many tourist and caravan sites, a lot of farmland and the North Sea gas terminal at Easington.

Decision making exercise

For the Holderness coast or for a lowland coast threatened by erosion, which you are familiar with, suggest how you think the coastal area chosen should be managed in the future. Refer to the five options for coastal management on page 30.

You could suggest one approach or a combination of several. Give reasons for your decisions and why you rejected alternative strategies. (20)   *Total: 20 marks*

Glacial landscapes

The valley in **A** is large and deep. Its sides are steep, rocky and straight, as though they have been scraped clean. Its bottom is flat, with large amounts of loose rock, now mostly concealed by vegetation. It has an open U-shape rather than a V-shape found in valleys cut by rivers in upland areas. A river flows through the valley today, but it is small compared to the valley. This valley has been carved by a powerful process. What process can this be?

A Upper Wasdale in the Lake District

Is the climate changing?

The past two million years have been a period of global climatic change. It is known as the Quaternary Period. In the British Isles the climate has fluctuated many times between very cold 'glacial' and warm 'interglacial' conditions. A detailed sequence of changes has been obtained by investigating the sediments from deep drill holes in the ocean bed. On land, sorting out the effects of these changes is much more difficult since upland areas will not be the same as lowland and the effects of earlier periods will have been eroded and destroyed by later events.

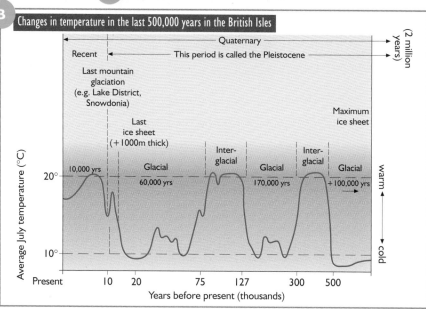

B Changes in temperature in the last 500,000 years in the British Isles

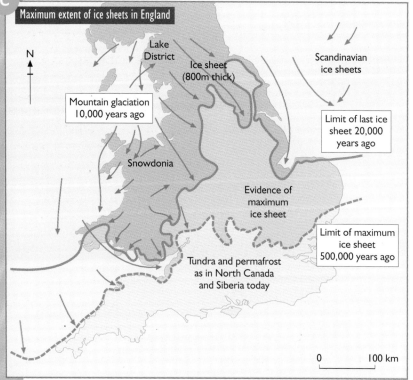

C Maximum extent of ice sheets in England

The graph (**B**) shows that the British Isles has had several 'glacial' periods in the last 500,000 years. The effects of two of them are shown on the map in **C**. Huge ice sheets extended across the British Isles and only the very south has remained unglaciated.

Temperatures today are like those of an interglacial period. A very cold period has not occurred for 10,000 years! Is Britain still in the ice age? Will the ice sheets return?

Q

1 Using **C** and a map of England describe how far the ice reached at its maximum. State the names of places.

2 Name an area where it may be possible to still investigate the effects of the older ice sheet.

3 How long have present-day rivers had to change the landscape left by the last ice sheet?

34

Glaciers or ice sheets?

Glaciers are moving masses of ice, which are mostly confined to mountain valleys. *Ice sheets* are more extensive. They flow out from the polar regions covering most of the landscape completely. In the past *ice caps* have covered upland centres such as Snowdonia and the Lake District.

How does glacier ice form?

Glacier ice is dense blue ice (**D**) that can only form in areas receiving heavy snowfall, most of which remains throughout the year. The weight of the accumulating snow gradually squeezes the air out from the layers below forming **névé**, and eventually glacier ice (**E**).

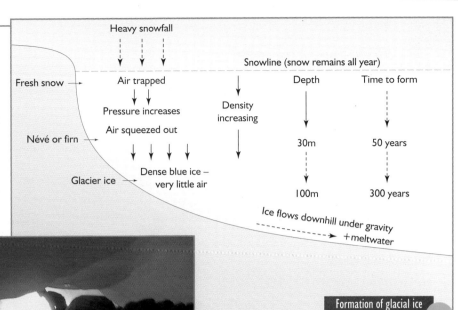

Heavy snowfall

Fresh snow → Air trapped

Pressure increases

Néve or firn → Air squeezed out

Glacier ice → Dense blue ice – very little air

Snowline (snow remains all year)

Density increasing

Depth	Time to form
30m	50 years
100m	300 years

Ice flows downhill under gravity + meltwater

Formation of glacial ice **E**

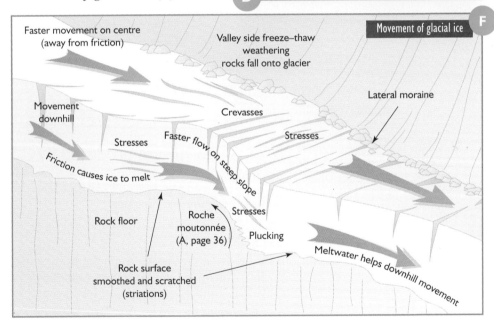

Ice cave **D**

Faster movement on centre (away from friction)

Valley side freeze–thaw weathering rocks fall onto glacier

Movement of glacial ice **F**

Movement downhill

Crevasses

Lateral moraine

Stresses

Faster flow on steep slope

Stresses

Friction causes ice to melt

Rock floor

Roche moutonnée (A, page 36)

Stresses

Plucking

Rock surface smoothed and scratched (striations)

Meltwater helps downhill movement

How do glaciers move?

As the ice thickens and becomes heavier, it moves downhill on a layer of meltwater. Pressure with the rock melts the base of the ice and this produces meltwater (**F**). The ice moves at different rates causing stresses and large cracks or *crevasses* to develop. Thicker ice sheets are colder and are often frozen to the rock. They move very slowly, particularly in lowland areas.

Is there a glacier system?

G shows the glacier as a system with inputs, stores, flows and outputs. As the ice reaches lower altitudes or latitudes temperatures rise and melting or **ablation** increases. If **accumulation** (amount of ice gained) exceeds ablation then the amount of ice in store increases, and the ice front advances. In the past, glacial periods of thousands of years of intense cold allowed the ice sheets to advance from the polar regions across large areas of Northern Europe and North America. During the last century, most glaciers have been shrinking and retreating – ablation exceeds accumulation.

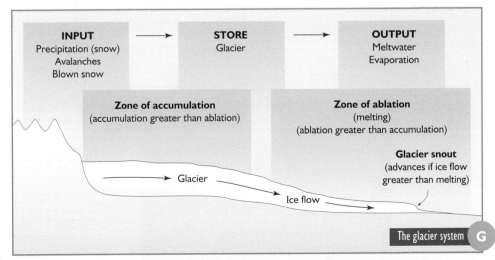

INPUT	STORE	OUTPUT
Precipitation (snow) Avalanches Blown snow	Glacier	Meltwater Evaporation

Zone of accumulation (accumulation greater than ablation)

Zone of ablation (melting) (ablation greater than accumulation)

Glacier snout (advances if ice flow greater than melting)

Glacier

Ice flow

The glacier system **G**

How does ice erode?

Ice alone cannot erode solid rock very easily. As the climate becomes colder however, vegetation decreases and freeze-thaw weathering increases. The surface rocks are shattered into loose angular fragments. As the ice moves forward the loose rock is frozen into the glacier and increases its ability to erode.

A Roche Moutonnée – a rock formed under the ice through abrasion and plucking

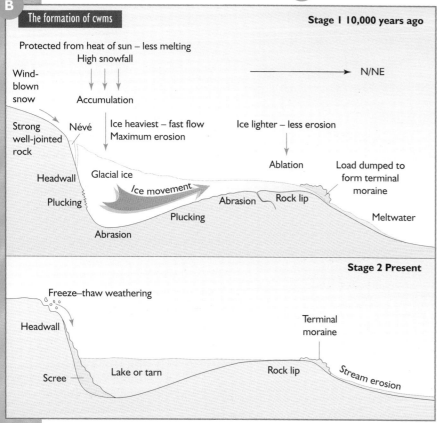

Erosion under the ice takes place in four ways:

- shovelling or scooping-up of the loose surface rock into the lower layers of ice
- **abrasion** – the moving rock fragments act like coarse sandpaper, scratching and eroding rock surfaces
- **plucking** – ice freezes to the rock and pulls it apart along joints and weaknesses in the rock (**A**)
- **meltwater erosion** – powerful streams of meltwater in ice tunnels carry stones and pebbles which smooth the surface of the rock.

What landforms are produced by erosion?

Cwms, corries or cirques

The deep basin in **D** probably started as a rock hollow high up on the mountainside, but it has been gradually deepened by erosion, during several glacial periods (**B**). These deep hollows are known as cwms (in Wales), **corries** or cirques, and are dramatic features in high upland areas such as those of North Wales and the Lake District.

The block diagram (**C**) shows that several deep cwms have formed near the summit of Cadair Idris, creating a *pyramidal peak*. Between the cwms narrow, knife-edge ridges have formed called *arêtes*.

D Cwm Cadair Idris

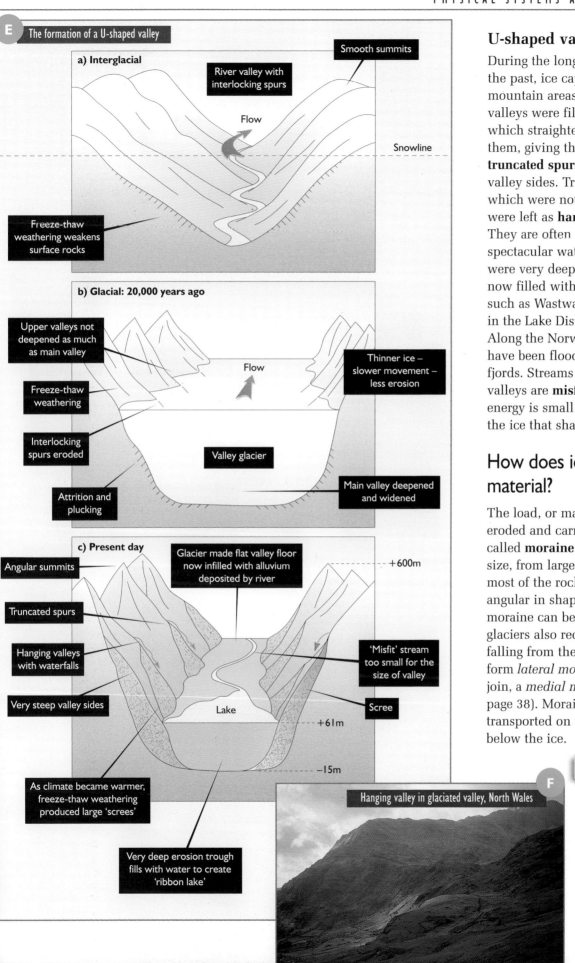

E The formation of a U-shaped valley

a) Interglacial

Smooth summits

River valley with interlocking spurs

Flow

Snowline

Freeze-thaw weathering weakens surface rocks

b) Glacial: 20,000 years ago

Upper valleys not deepened as much as main valley

Flow

Thinner ice – slower movement – less erosion

Freeze-thaw weathering

Interlocking spurs eroded

Valley glacier

Attrition and plucking

Main valley deepened and widened

c) Present day

Angular summits

Glacier made flat valley floor now infilled with alluvium deposited by river

+600m

Truncated spurs

Hanging valleys with waterfalls

'Misfit' stream too small for the size of valley

Very steep valley sides

Lake

Scree

+61m

As climate became warmer, freeze-thaw weathering produced large 'screes'

−15m

Very deep erosion trough fills with water to create 'ribbon lake'

F Hanging valley in glaciated valley, North Wales

U-shaped valleys (E)

During the long glacial periods in the past, ice caps covered the mountain areas of Britain and river valleys were filled with moving ice which straightened and deepened them, giving them a U-shape. Steep **truncated spurs** were left along the valley sides. Tributary valleys, which were not deepened as much, were left as **hanging valleys** (**F**). They are often marked today by spectacular waterfalls. Some valleys were very deeply eroded and are now filled with deep narrow lakes such as Wastwater or Derwent Water in the Lake District (**A**, page 34). Along the Norwegian coast they have been flooded by the sea to form fjords. Streams occupying the broad valleys are **misfit streams**; their energy is small compared to that of the ice that shaped these landscapes.

How does ice transport material?

The load, or material, which is eroded and carried by the ice is called **moraine**. Moraine varies in size, from large boulders to fine clay; most of the rock fragments are angular in shape. Large amounts of moraine can be transported. Valley glaciers also receive rock fragments falling from the valley sides, which form *lateral moraine*. If two glaciers join, a *medial moraine* is formed (**A**, page 38). Moraine is therefore transported on top, within and below the ice.

Q Make a sketch of the landscape in **F**, carefully labelling: steep valley sides, flat valley floor, hanging valley, waterfall, truncated spur, arête, scree, misfit stream.

What landforms are associated with glacial deposition?

When ablation or melting occurs the ice will deposit the load it is carrying. This is known as moraine or **glacial till**. These deposits form various features (**A**):

- **Terminal moraines** mark the furthest position reached by the ice. If the *ice front* remains stationary for a period of time, the melting ice provides a continual supply of moraine, which forms a ridge along the ice margin.
- **Recessional moraines** As the ice front retreats any stationary periods will be marked by ridges (**A**).

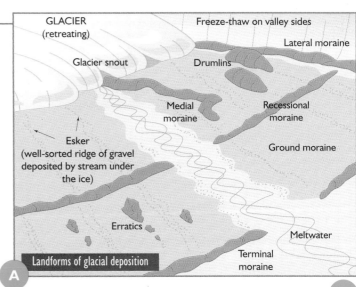

GLACIER (retreating)

Freeze-thaw on valley sides

Lateral moraine

Glacier snout

Drumlins

Medial moraine

Recessional moraine

Ground moraine

Esker (well-sorted ridge of gravel deposited by stream under the ice)

Erratics

Meltwater

Terminal moraine

A Landforms of glacial deposition

Terminal moraines can be found on the rock lip of cwms (**B,** page 36) and at the limits of vast ice sheets. A low ridge in the Lincolnshire Fenlands, called the Stickney Moraine (**B**) marks the furthest extent of the last ice sheet. A photograph taken 20,000 years ago looking south from West Keal church, would have shown an ice sheet to the east ending in a wall of ice, perhaps 50m high.

The Stickney terminal moraine is composed mostly of clay which contains many rock fragments that have their origin in northern Britain and Scandinavia.

Erratics (**A**) are rocks transported and deposited in an area of different rock type. Along with moraines they provide evidence of past ice movements.

Ground moraine (glacial till or **boulder clay**) is a layer of unsorted stones, sand and clay that is left covering the former land surface when it melts and retreats. Most lowland areas in the British Isles are extensively covered with these deposits (**C**).

Drumlins (**D**) are formed moraine, but they have a streamlined shape. Moraine may have been deposited by stationary ice, but then the ice moved forward again, moulding the moraine into drumlin shapes. Drumlins are usually found in large groups (**D**).

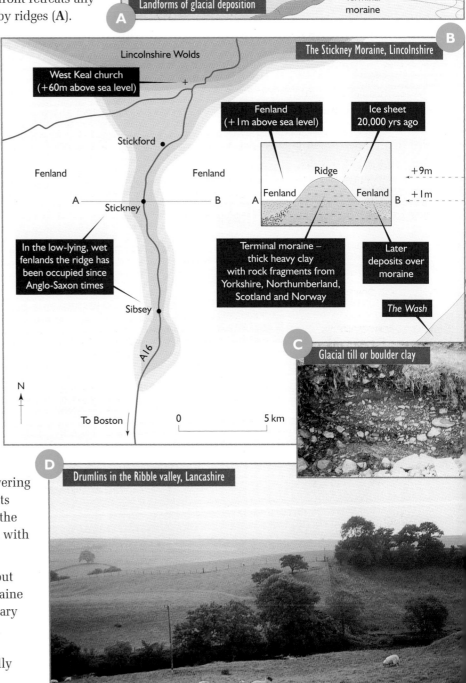

B The Stickney Moraine, Lincolnshire

Lincolnshire Wolds

West Keal church (+60m above sea level)

Stickford

Fenland

Fenland

A ——— Stickney ——— B

In the low-lying, wet fenlands the ridge has been occupied since Anglo-Saxon times

Sibsey

A16

N

To Boston

0   5 km

Fenland (+1m above sea level)

Ice sheet 20,000 yrs ago

Ridge

+9m

Fenland   Fenland   +1m

A   B

Terminal moraine – thick heavy clay with rock fragments from Yorkshire, Northumberland, Scotland and Norway

Later deposits over moraine

The Wash

C Glacial till or boulder clay

D Drumlins in the Ribble valley, Lancashire

North Downs landscape

Q

Look back at map **C**, page 34.

1 Which areas of England are unlikely to have a cover of ground moraine?

2 Much of East Anglia is covered with ground moraine called 'chalky boulder clay'. How might East Anglia's farming benefit from this?

Eskers (**A**) are long winding ridges that have formed beneath the ice. They are composed, however, of well-sorted material, which is usually gravel. They have probably been sorted and deposited by meltwater streams flowing in ice tunnels at the base of the ice, and then left as ridges when the ice melts.

What is a periglacial environment?

Periglacial environments have:

* short, cool summers and long, very cold winters
* permanently frozen ground (**permafrost**) often to great depths
* little vegetation
* freeze-thaw weathering in summer which shatters rocks into angular fragments

DEFINITION

Periglaciation: the processes and landforms found in areas subject to long periods of sub-zero temperatures.

* waterlogged soils in summer, when the sun melts the top of the frozen ground
* mass movement as the waterlogged soils slide downhill over the top of the impermeable frozen ground below (**solifluction**). The smooth scarp slope of the North Downs (**E**) is formed of chalk, but it has been strongly affected by solifluction in the past (**F**).

Today, vast areas of the world, such as the tundra of Canada and Siberia, are affected by periglacial conditions. In the past, when ice sheets extended over much of Britain, southern Britain was also a periglacial zone. As the ice sheets advanced and retreated, the rest of Britain would also have been under periglacial conditions.

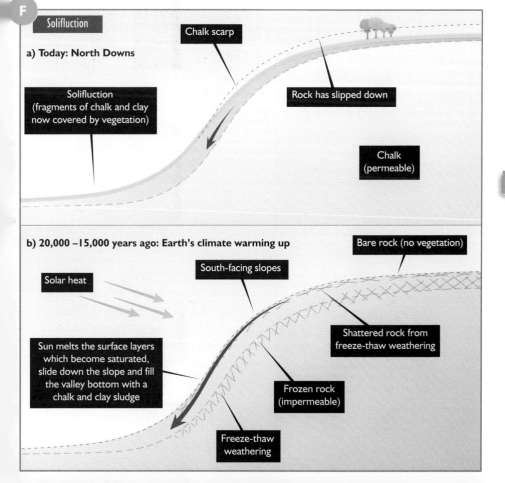

F

Solifluction

a) Today: North Downs

Chalk scarp

Solifluction (fragments of chalk and clay now covered by vegetation)

Rock has slipped down

Chalk (permeable)

b) 20,000–15,000 years ago: Earth's climate warming up

Bare rock (no vegetation)

South-facing slopes

Solar heat

Sun melts the surface layers which become saturated, slide down the slope and fill the valley bottom with a chalk and clay sludge

Shattered rock from freeze-thaw weathering

Frozen rock (impermeable)

Freeze-thaw weathering

Questions

1 When was your local area under, or nearest to, glacial conditions during the last ice age? (2)

2 Use the diagram of Cadair Idris (**C**, page 36) to describe the landscape. (7)

3 Choose **two** landforms from the Cadair Idris diagram. For each, what evidence is there of how they were formed? (10)

4 How might human activity make use of this environment? (6)

Total: 25 marks

Weather and climate

How has the *weather* affected you today? How has it changed since yesterday? The weather forecast describes the changes expected over the short term – generally the next 24 hours. The weather in the British Isles can be described as very variable, and the news services try to keep us informed by broadcasting forecasts many times during the day. Forecasts are mostly concerned with changes in temperature, sunshine, cloud cover, precipitation and wind speed (**A**).

Interest in the weather is hardly surprising since it affects not only our day-to-day activities, but also important decisions taken in industries such as farming, building, transport and leisure. Special forecasts are made for farmers and shipping. Major airports have their own weather stations.

TOMORROW Blizzards Win GALES

A TV weather forecaster

A

> ### DEFINITIONS
> **Weather** is the short term, hour-by-hour or day-by-day, changes in the state of the atmosphere
>
> **Climate** is described by the averages of weather readings taken over a long period of time – generally 30 years.
>
> **Microclimate** describes the climate and weather that is found in relatively small, very local areas (e.g. a wood, a town, or a mountain valley).

Q Discuss how the weather forecast in **A** is likely to affect decision-making the next day.

What affects weather conditions locally?

Consider how the following affect microclimates:

- altitude
- exposure and shelter
- water
- buildings and concrete.
- aspect
- coasts
- vegetation

Each can affect temperatures, wind and precipitation and lead to a relatively unique microclimate in a locality.

Mountain and valley microclimates

In mountain areas (**B**) temperatures, wind and precipitation are affected by differences in altitude (height), aspect (direction a slope faces) and slope. The tops of mountains are very exposed. Compared to valleys it is colder, more windy and wetter. In the winter there will be more snow which will take longer to melt than in the valleys. The valleys are more sheltered from the high winds and freezing temperatures. Trees and hedges give greater protection compared to the bleak, open moorland found high up on the fells.

Within valleys there are also differences, such as in Great Langdale in the Lake District where farming, settlement and the tourist sites for camping and caravans mostly cluster on the south-facing slopes. In alpine valleys in Austria and France, the best ski-slopes are found above the tree line on the north-facing slopes.

Q How does **B** help to explain why these locations are preferred? Why are the microclimates on the south and north sides of the valley more different in winter?

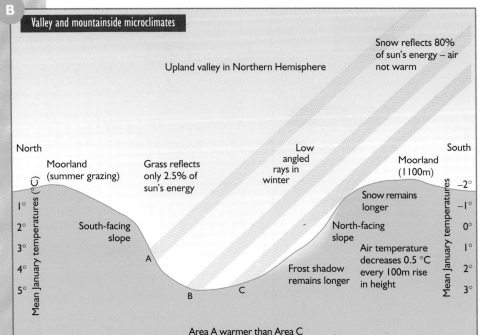

B Valley and mountainside microclimates

Upland valley in Northern Hemisphere

Snow reflects 80% of sun's energy – air not warm

North
South

Moorland (summer grazing)

Grass reflects only 2.5% of sun's energy

Low angled rays in winter

Moorland (1100m)

South-facing slope

Snow remains longer

North-facing slope

Frost shadow remains longer

Air temperature decreases 0.5 °C every 100m rise in height

A

B

C

Area A warmer than Area C

Mean January temperatures (°C): 1° 2° 3° 4° 5°

Mean January temperatures: −2° −1° 0° 1° 2° 3°

Coastal microclimates

Along coasts, in the afternoon on hot summer days, a cool onshore breeze often springs up to bring some relief from the high temperatures (**C**). These breezes are the result of local differences in temperature between the land and the sea. Water heats up more slowly than the land. It takes more solar energy to raise the temperature of water by 1°C, than it does to heat the same mass of rock or soil. By mid-afternoon temperature differences are greatest and the cooler air over the sea moves onshore, forcing the warmer air to rise.

Once heated, water retains its heat for a longer time than the land. At night the sea will be warmer than the land. If warm, moist air from over the sea extends over the land it will be cooled. Condensation may take place and, during the night, mist and fog forms. Fog is similar to cloud but it occurs at ground level. Fog is more common in areas near the coast.

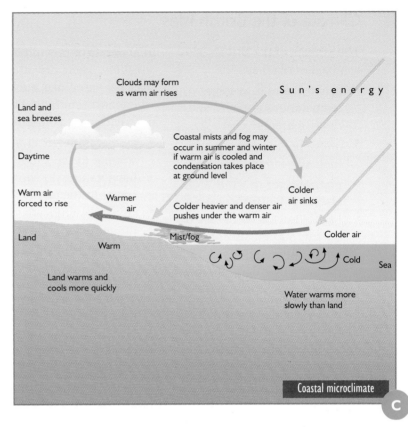

Coastal microclimate

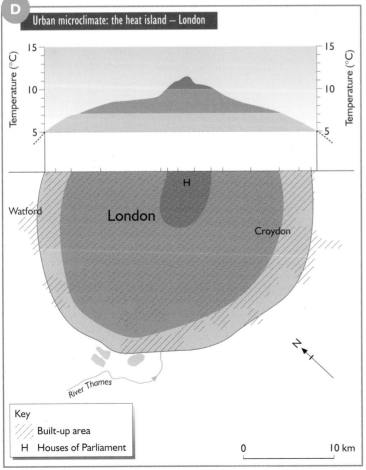

Urban microclimate: the heat island — London

Urban microclimates

Urban areas are generally warmer than the surrounding countryside. Measurements in London show the centre around Oxford Street and Westminster can be 6°C warmer than suburban areas such as Croydon. This is known as the *urban heat island effect* (**D**).

In summer the concrete and tarmac areas around your school are hotter than the playing field. Concrete, bricks and tarmac absorb more heat energy than grass and release it more slowly. The centres of cities are therefore warmer, particularly at night and during the winter, than their surrounding areas. Tall buildings also funnel the wind, increasing its strength, and can shade some areas from the sun.

Questions

1 Describe what other heat sources in the city will increase the heat island effect? (4)

2 Describe the differences in microclimates as you cross the valley in **B** in winter. (6)

3 Explain, with examples, how microclimate is likely to affect human activities (such as family, settlement and tourism) in this valley. (9)

4 What features might a forest microclimate have? (6)

Total: 25 marks

Climate of the British Isles

The climate of the British Isles can be described as:

- *cool temperate*: average temperatures are mild and rarely extreme
- *moist*: precipitation is fairly high all year and reliable
- *maritime*: air or wind reaching the British Isles has to travel over the sea or ocean: this can affect the temperature and moisture in the air, particularly if the winds come from the west.

This is a general description. If the country is divided into four areas (**B**) each has a distinctive character based on differences in amounts of precipitation or sunshine. There are often seasonal variations, such as when most rain falls. The main differences are as follows:

- temperatures in summer are warmer in the south
- temperatures in winter are cooler in the east
- sunshine hours are greatest in the south
- total rainfall is highest in western areas
- the number of wet days is greatest in the west
- in eastern areas more rain falls in summer months
- in western areas more rain falls in winter months.

1 Produce diagrams to compare the four weather stations for the following:

   - yearly temperature range
   - max./min. temperatures
   - total precipitation
   - seasonal differences in precipitation
   - wet days per year
   - sunshine hours.   (12)

2 Find data from the graphs in **B** to support each of the seven differences about the British Isles climate listed in the text opposite.   (9)

3 What additional differences can you think of? Support your answers with data.   (4)

Total: 25 marks

A

Climate data for four stations

		J	F	M	A	M	J	Jly	A	S	O	N	D	Temp. Range/ year	Precip. total/ year	Wet days*/ year	Sunshine hours/ year	Max/min temperatures
Onich	Temperature (°C)	2.9	2.9	5.5	7.3	10.7	13.5	14.4	13.7	11.2	8.4	5.6	3.9	11.5			1058	25.9/–7.1 °C
	Precipitation (mm)	203	162	127	133	94	125	160	154	190	214	181	236		1979	239		
Dundee		2.5	3.4	5.5	8.4	10.9	14.3	15.9	14.7	11.9	8.2	5.3	3.8	13.4			1348	26.3/–6.7 °C
		65	47	49	43	62	55	89	72	61	76	71	71		761	182		
Cambridge		2.7	3.5	6.4	9.1	12.3	16.0	17.4	17.2	14.1	9.2	6.1	3.5	14.7			1490	30.6/–8.6 °C
		49	35	36	37	45	45	58	55	51	51	54	42		558	12		
Falmouth		3.9	5.5	7.1	9.1	12.0	15.2	16.5	16.9	14.8	11.0	8.8	6.4	13.0			1683	25.0/–3.4 °C
		128	91	84	61	70	58	72	77	86	102	129	132		1090	193		

* Wet day = precipitation > 0.25mm

B **Climate of the British Isles: a summary**

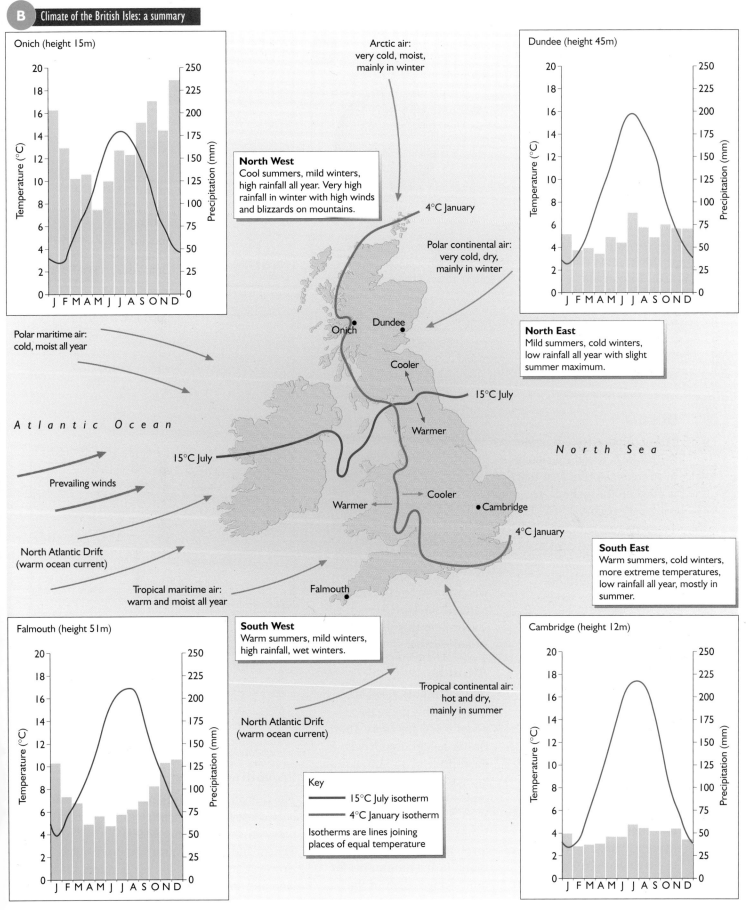

Onich (height 15m)

Dundee (height 45m)

Arctic air:
very cold, moist,
mainly in winter

North West
Cool summers, mild winters,
high rainfall all year. Very high
rainfall in winter with high winds
and blizzards on mountains.

4°C January

Polar continental air:
very cold, dry,
mainly in winter

Polar maritime air:
cold, moist all year

Onich   Dundee

Cooler

North East
Mild summers, cold winters,
low rainfall all year with slight
summer maximum.

15°C July

Atlantic Ocean

Warmer

15°C July

North Sea

Prevailing winds

Cooler

North Atlantic Drift
(warm ocean current)

Warmer

Cambridge

Tropical maritime air:
warm and moist all year

Falmouth

4°C January

South East
Warm summers, cold winters,
more extreme temperatures,
low rainfall all year, mostly in
summer.

Falmouth (height 51m)

South West
Warm summers, mild winters,
high rainfall, wet winters.

Cambridge (height 12m)

Tropical continental air:
hot and dry,
mainly in summer

North Atlantic Drift
(warm ocean current)

Key

——— 15°C July isotherm

——— 4°C January isotherm

Isotherms are lines joining
places of equal temperature

TEMPERATURE

Latitude

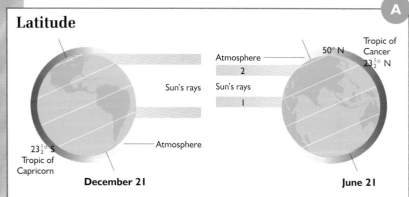

December 21

June 21

The Earth moves around the sun on its orbit with its axis inclined. Summer in the northern hemisphere occurs when the North Pole is tilted towards the sun. The sun is overhead at the Tropic of Cancer (23½ °N) where its energy will be most concentrated (1). Further north, due to the curvature of the Earth, the sun is lower in the sky, and the same amount of energy is spread across a larger surface area (2). The incoming radiation will also pass through a greater thickness of the Earth's atmosphere and more energy is absorbed and scattered by gases and dust.

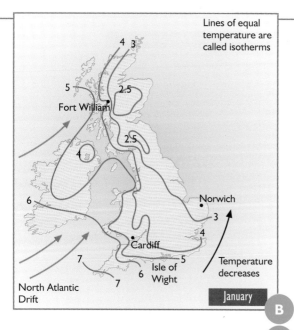

Oceans

The oceans surrounding the British Isles warm up slowly in summer, storing heat that is released throughout the winter (**C**, page 41). Temperatures over the land are therefore kept cool in summer (**C**), but warm in winter (**B**) – a *maritime climate*. They are rarely extreme. The range between average January and July temperatures is about 10°C. In Berlin, at a similar latitude to London, the temperature range is 20°C. Berlin is far from the moderating effects of the sea. It has a more extreme *continental climate*.

In addition a warm ocean current, the North Atlantic Drift or Gulf Stream, crosses the Atlantic from the Gulf of Mexico, bringing warm water to western European coasts. On the exposed Mull of Galloway in south-west Scotland, temperatures are mild enough for sub-tropical plants to survive and flourish. Without the Gulf Stream, it is estimated that winter temperatures would be up to 15°C lower in the British Isles! In winter temperatures decline from west to east (**B**) since the water in the North Sea without the Gulf Stream is cooler than that along the Atlantic coasts.

Altitude

As shown in **B**, page 40, temperatures decrease at about 0.5°C for every 100m rise in height. Ben Nevis, at an altitude of 1344m, has an annual mean temperature of only –0.3°C compared to +7°C in Fort William, which is nearby and close to sea level. In winter snow is found in the mountains for much longer than in the valleys.

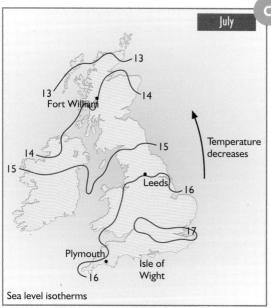

Q

1 Use **A** to explain why winter temperatures are so much lower in the north of the British Isles.

2 Explain why the largest ski resort in the British Isles is located on the north-facing slopes of the Cairngorm mountains in Scotland.

Prevailing winds

The prevailing winds blowing across the British Isles come from the south west. In winter they pass across the warmer waters of the Gulf Stream and so will warm western Britain. However, in summer the sea is colder than the land and so the winds have a cooling effect.

PRECIPITATION

Precipitation is the name given to rain and its different forms such as drizzle, sleet, hail and snow. **D** describes the processes resulting in precipitation. There are three important conditions. There must be:

- air, which is forced to rise and cool
- sufficient uplift and cooling for the air temperature to drop to condensation level or *dewpoint*, when the air becomes saturated and water vapour condenses to form visible droplets (clouds)
- sufficient minute particles of dust, salt and soot in the air (nucleii) to attract water vapour. Condensation takes place on the particle and droplets form.

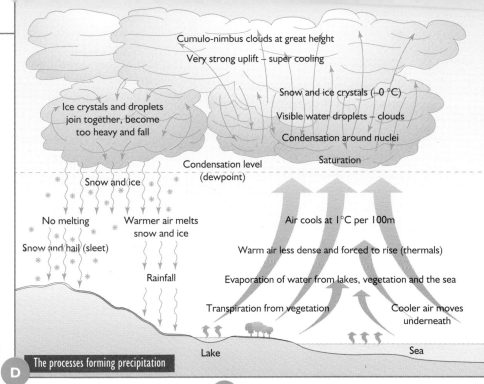

Cumulo-nimbus clouds at great height

Very strong uplift – super cooling

Snow and ice crystals (–0 °C)

Ice crystals and droplets join together, become too heavy and fall

Visible water droplets – clouds

Condensation around nuclei

Saturation

Condensation level (dewpoint)

Snow and ice

No melting

Warmer air melts snow and ice

Snow and hail (sleet)

Rainfall

Air cools at 1°C per 100m

Warm air less dense and forced to rise (thermals)

Evaporation of water from lakes, vegetation and the sea

Transpiration from vegetation

Cooler air moves underneath

Lake

Sea

D The processes forming precipitation

Types of rainfall

Most rain that falls in the British Isles is relief or frontal rain. Convectional rain occurs usually in summer.

Relief rain

Air moving towards any range of hills has to rise. **E** shows how this may result in precipitation. In **F** the highest rainfall totals of over 1600mm per year coincide with the high mountain areas found in western Britain. They force the warm, moist prevailing winds to rise and cool. Note how most of eastern Britain is in what is called a **rain shadow**.

Convectional rain

On hot summer days, in the afternoon, large clouds can quickly develop which may result in heavy rainstorms with thunder and lightning. The ground has been heated throughout the day and the upward movement of warm air becomes very strong and fast evaporating any moisture available (**D**). Thermals rising at over 20m/second, take air rapidly above condensation level producing large raindrops and heavy downpours of rain. In equatorial areas such storms occur regularly each afternoon.

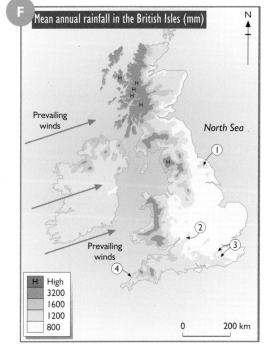

F Mean annual rainfall in the British Isles (mm)

N

Prevailing winds

North Sea

Prevailing winds

H	High
	3200
	1600
	1200
	800

0   200 km

Q

1 Use an atlas to help explain the higher precipitation at places 1, 2 and 3 on **F**.

2 Why does 4 only receive moderate precipitation, yet it is very exposed to the prevailing winds?

In the British Isles they are local and infrequent. They occur more in south-east England where summer temperatures are higher. This helps to explain why rainfall is highest in the summer months in places such as Cambridge (**B**, page 43).

E Relief rainfall in the Lake District

West

Saturated air
Rain falls

East

Windward slope (clouds form)

Lee slope (rain shadow)

Drier air

Condensation level

Condensation level

Sinking air warming at 1°C/100m

Warm moist westerly airflow

Rising air cools at 1°C/100m

Drier air – less rain

Sea

	Coastal Plain	Lake District	East England
Altitude	50m	1000m	100m
Rainfall	1000mm	3000mm	700mm

Frontal rain

The changeable weather in the British Isles is well known. One of the main causes is the frequent passage of **depressions**, or low pressure systems, across the country from west to east. They produce a rapidly changing pattern of weather making it very difficult to make accurate forecasts.

Depressions develop over the North Atlantic Ocean where northward-moving warm, moist tropical air meets cold polar air pushing south (**Aa**). **Fronts** occur where the two different air masses meet and are unable to mix (**Ab**).

The depression deepens and becomes more extensive as the whole system is driven eastwards under the influence of fast-moving jet streams in the upper atmosphere. Winds, in the northern hemisphere, spiral inwards in an anti-clockwise direction, increasing in strength as they approach the centre of the depression (**Ac**).

The cold front travels faster, gradually catching up with the warm front. The warm, moist air between the fronts is squeezed upwards producing the sequence of weather patterns shown in **B**. Where the cold front finally catches up with the warm front it is known as an **occluded front** (**Ad**).

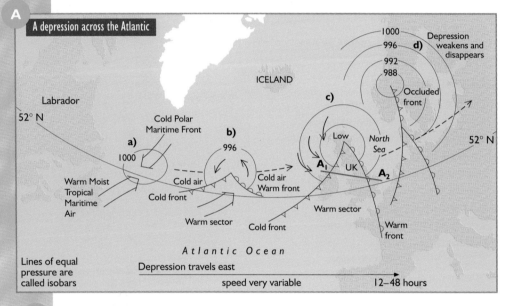

A A depression across the Atlantic

Labrador
52° N
Cold Polar Maritime Front
b)
a)
1000
996
Warm Moist Tropical Maritime Air
Cold air
Cold front
Cold air
Warm front
Warm sector
Cold front
c)
Low
North Sea
Warm sector
Cold front
1000
996
992
988
d)
Depression weakens and disappears
Occluded front
ICELAND
A1   UK   A2
52° N
Warm front

Lines of equal pressure are called isobars

Depression travels east

Atlantic Ocean

speed very variable
12–48 hours

Anticyclones

Anticyclones are areas of high pressure (**D**). They are slower moving than depressions and can remain over the country for several days. They 'block' the progress of depressions, which are forced to take more northerly or southerly routes. The weather is more stable and less variable. Air is descending so skies are clear and winds are light. The Earth warms by day but cools rapidly at night. In summer and autumn hot, fine weather is common with temperatures above average.

Convectional rain storms may develop during afternoons. In extreme cases summer heatwaves can occur, as in August 1990. Prolonged high pressure and lack of rainfall may also produce drought conditions. In winter the clear calm conditions can give bright, crisp weather, but frosts are likely, due to night-time cooling.

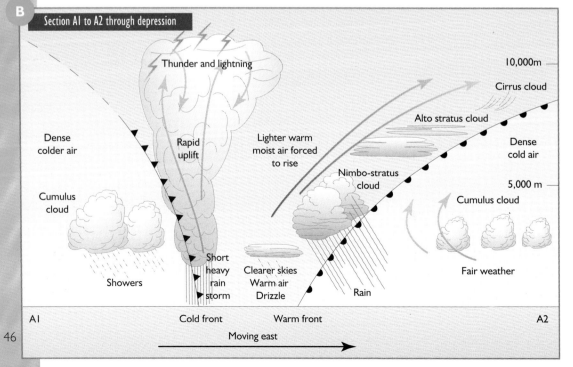

B Section A1 to A2 through depression

Thunder and lightning
Dense colder air
Rapid uplift
Lighter warm moist air forced to rise
Cirrus cloud
Alto stratus cloud
Dense cold air
Nimbo-stratus cloud
Cumulus cloud
Cumulus cloud
10,000m
5,000 m
Showers
Short heavy rain storm
Clearer skies
Warm air
Drizzle
Rain
Fair weather
A1
Cold front
Warm front
A2
Moving east

Forecasting

To provide an accurate forecast of the weather, meteorologists need to be able to plot the path, speed and development of each depression. Using data from weather stations, maps are produced called **synoptic charts**. They show the state of the weather at any one time. The data for each station is plotted using a set of symbols (**E**). **Isobars**, or lines joining places with equal

pressure, are drawn and the fronts marked on. The skill of the weather forecaster is to use these charts together with computer models and radar and satellite images to predict the short-term changes in the weather for different parts of the country. **C** shows the satellite image for a depression passing over the British Isles during the winter. **D** shows one for a September anticyclone.

C

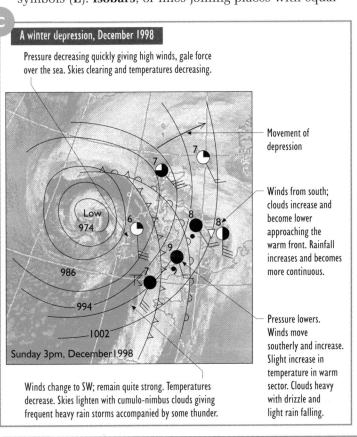

A winter depression, December 1998

Pressure decreasing quickly giving high winds, gale force over the sea. Skies clearing and temperatures decreasing.

Movement of depression

Winds from south; clouds increase and become lower approaching the warm front. Rainfall increases and becomes more continuous.

Pressure lowers. Winds move southerly and increase. Slight increase in temperature in warm sector. Clouds heavy with drizzle and light rain falling.

Sunday 3pm, December 1998

Winds change to SW; remain quite strong. Temperatures decrease. Skies lighten with cumulo-nimbus clouds giving frequent heavy rain storms accompanied by some thunder.

D

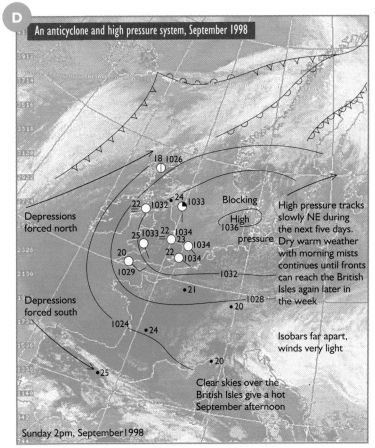

An anticyclone and high pressure system, September 1998

Depressions forced north

Depressions forced south

Blocking High pressure 1036

High pressure tracks slowly NE during the next five days. Dry warm weather with morning mists continues until fronts can reach the British Isles again later in the week

Isobars far apart, winds very light

Clear skies over the British Isles give a hot September afternoon

Sunday 2pm, September 1998

E Summary key to weather maps

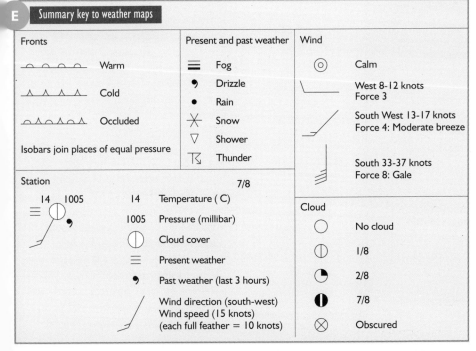

Fronts	Present and past weather	Wind
Warm	Fog	Calm
Cold	Drizzle	West 8-12 knots Force 3
Occluded	Rain	South West 13-17 knots Force 4: Moderate breeze
Isobars join places of equal pressure	Snow / Shower / Thunder	South 33-37 knots Force 8: Gale

Station 7/8
14 — Temperature (C)
1005 — Pressure (millibar)
Cloud cover
Present weather
Past weather (last 3 hours)
Wind direction (south-west)
Wind speed (15 knots) (each full feather = 10 knots)

Cloud: No cloud, 1/8, 2/8, 7/8, Obscured

Questions

Refer to the satellite image of a depression over the British Isles (**C**).

1 Describe the differences you would expect to find in the weather between the Isle of Wight and the Lake District. (6)

2 Describe the weather over northern Scotland. (4)

3 How might the weather in London change during the following 24 hours? (6)

4 Describe **five** differences between the weather associated with a depression and an anticyclone in summer. (5)

4 What conditions lead to anticyclones over the British Isles? (4)

Total: 25 marks

How do other climates differ from that of the British Isles?

CASE STUDY *Contrasting climates*

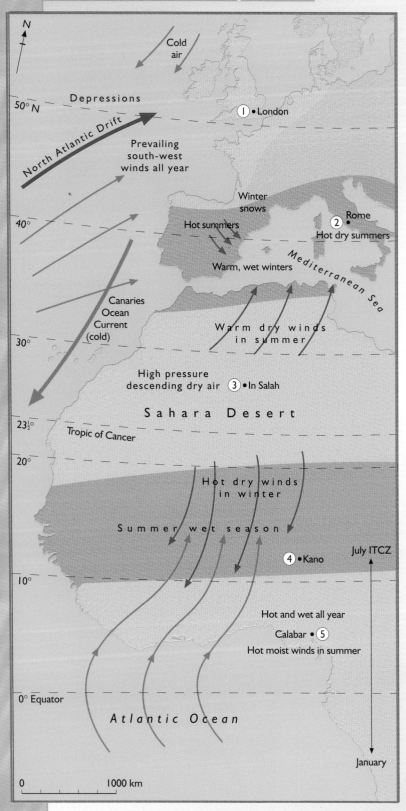

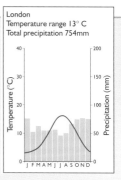

London
Temperature range 13° C
Total precipitation 754mm

1 London

Cool, maritime climate — warm, moist south-west prevailing winds all year and the warm North Atlantic Drift keep temperatures moderate. Eastward travelling depressions give reliable rainfall all year and very changeable weather.

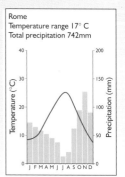

Rome
Temperature range 17° C
Total precipitation 742mm

2 Rome

Mediterranean climate — summers are hot and dry. From June to August solar heating is much stronger than in London. Winds are light and the air stable so skies remain cloudless and the land and sea receive maximum heat. Occasional afternoon convectional thunderstorms can give brief heavy falls of rain. In winter months warm, moist winds from the south west bring depressions and frontal rainfall, similar to the UK. However temperatures remain much warmer because of the more southerly latitude and the warming influence of the Mediterranean Sea.

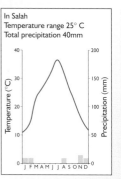

In Salah
Temperature range 25° C
Total precipitation 40mm

3 In Salah

Hot desert climate — sub-tropical high pressure dominant all year. Warm, dry descending air gives clear skies with extreme daytime temperatures and cold nights. Large annual range in temperature (25⁰C) due to continental position and considerable winter cooling of the land surface. Low (40mm), unreliable rainfall, generally occurs in sudden heavy convectional storms. Coastal areas have less extreme temperatures due to cold ocean current (Canaries Current).

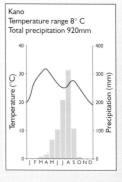

Kano
Temperature range 8° C
Total precipitation 920mm

4 Kano

Tropical continental climate (savanna) — low latitude gives high temperatures all year (no month below 20⁰C). Overhead sun in summer (June) shifts ITCZ north; south-west, on-shore winds bring warm, moist air into low-pressure area. Summer heating gives strong convectional currents and heavy rainfall from June to September (wet season: 741mm). The amount of rain can be unreliable. During winter months, continental position allows some cooling. ITCZ moves south, north-east Trade Winds develop bringing dry air from desert areas (Harmattan Wind). Winter dry season (November — February).

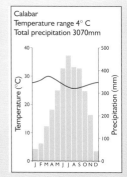

Calabar
Temperature range 4° C
Total precipitation 3070mm

5 Calabar

Tropical equatorial climate (tropical rainforest) — located close to the Equator, sun high in the sky all year therefore constant high temperatures (lowest temperature 26⁰C). There is only a small seasonal change (annual temperature range 4⁰C). Daily temperatures are more variable with night-time cooling after very hot days (daily temperature range 10⁰C). Air is very moist and humid, particularly in summer with on-shore winds. Heavy thunderstorms most late afternoons. Rainfall very high all year (3070mm).

Global climate

The climate graphs in **A** show how climates change from London going south towards the Equator. Differences can be seen in:

• average temperatures
• seasonal changes in temperatures (temperature range)
• total rainfall
• seasonal variations in rainfall (wet and dry season).

The map of world climates (**B**) shows that the climate stations in the case study are representative of broad bands of climate that spread across the African continents north of the Equator and around the Mediterranean Sea. Latitude is obviously an important influence on the pattern of global climates.

The cool maritime climate of the British Isles and Western Europe does not spread so extensively across the continent. If, however, the other areas in the world that have the same climate, are located, another pattern emerges. This climate is found at similar latitudes to the British Isles both north and south of the Equator and on western coasts of continents. It would seem that the influences of sea, ocean currents and prevailing winds, that are so important in understanding the climate of the British Isles, are part of a global pattern. High mountain areas have their own climate but the types of climate found either side of large mountain ranges are often very different. Look at the different climates found north and south of the Alps or west and east of the Rocky Mountains in the USA. High mountains or relief often act as barriers to the world wind patterns and help to influence the global patterns of climate.

Q Summarize the differences between the **five** climates on page 48 under two columns headed Winter and Summer.

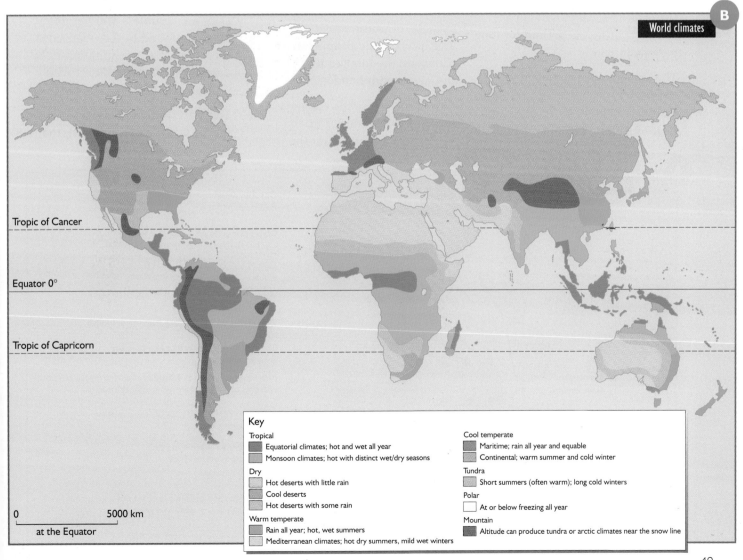

World climates | B

Tropic of Cancer

Equator 0°

Tropic of Capricorn

0 — 5000 km
at the Equator

Key

Tropical
- Equatorial climates; hot and wet all year
- Monsoon climates; hot with distinct wet/dry seasons

Dry
- Hot deserts with little rain
- Cool deserts
- Hot deserts with some rain

Warm temperate
- Rain all year; hot, wet summers
- Mediterranean climates; hot dry summers, mild wet winters

Cool temperate
- Maritime; rain all year and equable
- Continental; warm summer and cold winter

Tundra
- Short summers (often warm); long cold winters

Polar
- At or below freezing all year

Mountain
- Altitude can produce tundra or arctic climates near the snow line

How does the global system affect climates?

The global pattern of climate is affected by:

- latitude
- land and sea
- relief
- ocean currents.

Latitude

The Equator receives greater amounts of solar heating than latitudes further north or south. Places therefore nearer the Equator are much warmer than those closer to the Poles. (Compare mean annual temperature for Calibar with London on page 48.) Nearer the Poles precipitation will be more variable with lower temperatures. More will fall as snow, covering the ground for long periods in winter.

The amount of solar energy received by each hemisphere varies because of the tilt of the Earth and its orbit around the sun. This gives summer and winter seasons. Places nearer the Poles have greater differences between summer and winter in temperature and precipitation. (Compare the annual temperature range in Calibar with that in Rome.)

A shows how the large amounts of energy received by areas close to the Equator lead to vast cells of moving air (e.g. the Hadley Cell), which transfer heat from the Equator towards the polar regions.

At the Equator air, warmed from below, becomes less dense and is forced to rise as strong convection currents, creating low pressure at the surface (ITCZ). Convectional currents of warm, moist air cool to give heavy, daily thunderstorms. (Compare the total annual rainfall in Calibar with London.)

Strong, steady winds converge to fill the low pressure from the north and the south, but the spinning of the Earth diverts the winds slightly to the right in the northern hemisphere and they become the north-east Trade Winds. In the southern hemisphere winds are diverted to the left, producing the south-west Trade Winds.

Air in the upper atmosphere flows away from the Equator and cools. Cooling air becomes denser, heavier and descends back to the surface on the polar sides of the 'Cell', causing zones of high pressure at about 30⁰ north and south of the Equator (sub-tropical high pressure zone). Descending air warms and becomes drier, skies are cloudless and hot desert areas are found in these latitudes. (Compare total precipitation in In Salah in the Sahara Desert with Calabar.)

The ITCZ or low pressure zone moves north and south with the

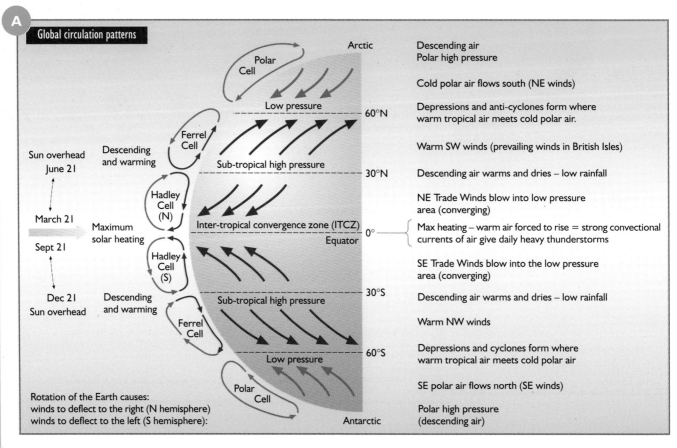

A

Global circulation patterns

Arctic	Descending air Polar high pressure
Polar Cell	
Low pressure — 60°N	Cold polar air flows south (NE winds)
	Depressions and anti-cyclones form where warm tropical air meets cold polar air.
Ferrel Cell	
Sun overhead June 21 — Descending and warming	Warm SW winds (prevailing winds in British Isles)
Sub-tropical high pressure — 30°N	Descending air warms and dries – low rainfall
Hadley Cell (N)	NE Trade Winds blow into low pressure area (converging)
March 21 — Maximum solar heating	Inter-tropical convergence zone (ITCZ) — 0° Equator	Max heating – warm air forced to rise = strong convectional currents of air give daily heavy thunderstorms
Sept 21	
Hadley Cell (S)	SE Trade Winds blow into the low pressure area (converging)
Dec 21 Sun overhead — Descending and warming	Sub-tropical high pressure — 30°S	Descending air warms and dries – low rainfall
Ferrel Cell	Warm NW winds
Low pressure — 60°S	Depressions and cyclones form where warm tropical air meets cold polar air
Polar Cell	SE polar air flows north (SE winds)
Rotation of the Earth causes: winds to deflect to the right (N hemisphere) winds to deflect to the left (S hemisphere):	Polar high pressure (descending air)
Antarctic	

overhead sun. In June there will be low pressure (ITCZ) over the Tropic of Cancer (23.5°N). Warm, moist Trade Winds from over the Atlantic Ocean bring heavy summer rains. In December when the overhead sun is south of the Equator the sub-tropical high pressure zone moves south over the Tropic of Cancer. The hot descending air gives a winter dry season. (Compare the summer and winter rainfall at Kano.)

Around 60° north and south of the Equator the global circulation of air produces another zone of low pressure, where warm tropical air from the south west converges with cold polar air. Depressions form and at the fronts warm air is forced to rise over the cold denser air causing frontal rainfall. In the British Isles depressions can occur throughout the year providing a steady, reliable rainfall. Further south, in Rome, depressions are rare in summer, which is therefore drier and hotter than in the British Isles. (Compare the climate graphs for London and Rome.)

High pressure over the Poles, creates cold polar deserts.

Explain why there is very little cloud cover over North Africa in **B**.

Land and sea

Land masses become much hotter than the water in the oceans in summer, but lose heat much faster during the winter. Continental areas therefore have more extreme climates than coastal areas. (London and Berlin are at similar latitudes but the annual temperature range in Berlin is 20° (+20°C – 0°C). Compare this to London.)

Hot land masses in summer warm the air above, which expands and rises creating low pressure areas and convectional currents. Summer thunderstorms are therefore more common in Berlin than in London and precipitation is more variable and unreliable through the year.

Relief

Temperature decreases with altitude. Warm, moist winds are forced to rise over the mountains, cool and cause relief rain. Mountains in the Scottish Highlands, the Alps, Japan and the Cameroon Mountains near Calibar all have more extreme temperatures and far wetter climates than the surrounding lowlands.

High, extensive mountain ranges, such as the Alps, Himalayas and the Andes, interrupt or block the global patterns of airflow (**A**) and act as boundaries between very different climates either side. (Compare the climate graphs for Niigata and Tokyo on either side of the central mountains of Japan, page 53.)

Ocean currents

In the northern hemisphere ocean currents flowing northwards carry warm water from the tropics towards the polar areas. The North Atlantic Drift or Gulf Stream keeps winters in the British Isles warmer and the summers cooler than those in Central Europe (**A**, page 48).

Prevailing winds from the south west, passing over the ocean current are warmed and pick up large amounts of moisture. The precipitation, caused when the air is forced to rise over mountains or at fronts, provides the British Isles with a reliable precipitation all year. (Look at the distribution of precipitation for London.)

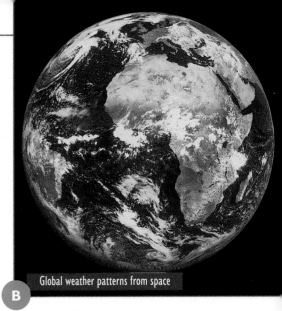

B Global weather patterns from space

Cold ocean currents from colder polar waters have a contrasting effect. Those flowing south along coasts in the northern hemisphere keep summer temperatures cooler and the air drier than normal for that latitude. Coastal fogs occur when warmer air from over the land is cooled by the cold water, e.g. the cold Californian current keeps the coastline around San Francisco much cooler than inland and causes many days of coastal fogs.

In tropical areas warm ocean currents, such as the Kuro Siwo (**A**, page 52) which flows north towards Japan, are the source of the large amounts of energy and moisture that can result in the development of intense depressions or typhoons (page 86).

Questions

Choose and name a contrasting climate to that of the British Isles.

1 Describe the main features of its climate. (6)
2 Name **two** other areas of the world that experience the same climate. (2)
3 Contrast this climate with that of the British Isles. (8)
4 Explain how factors such as latitude, relief and oceans lead to the contrasts given in question 3. (9)

Total: 25 marks

What influences Japan's climate?

The climate of Japan is influenced by large-scale and more local factors:

Large-scale factors:

- seasonal changes in wind patterns (**A** and **B**), as a result of:
  - seasonal changes in global pressure systems
  - differences in heating and cooling of large landmasses and the oceans.
- the effects of latitude – the main islands spread over nearly 16° of latitude from north to south, the same as from Glasgow to Southern Italy.
- warm and cold ocean currents (Japan experiences both).

Local factors:

- the effects of relief – high mountains through the centre of Japan force both winter and summer winds to rise affecting precipitation.
- typhoons – tropical depressions develop over the South Pacific Ocean. As they travel north, they become more intense, sucking up large amounts of moisture and increasing in wind strength (**B**).

Questions

1 Which climate station
   a) receives most precipitation
   b) has the coldest monthly temperature? (2)

2 Compare the climates of Nemuro and Tokyo (6)

3 Suggest reasons why the winter rainfall in Niigata is much greater than in Tokyo. (8)

4 With the aid of a diagram, explain why the climate of Kagoshima is different from that in Nemuro. (9)

Total: 25 marks

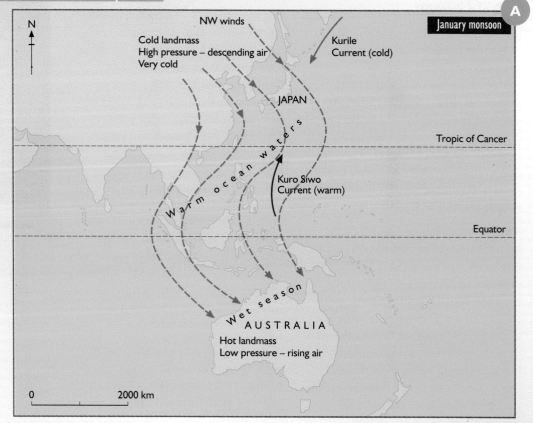

A January monsoon

NW winds

Cold landmass
High pressure – descending air
Very cold

Kurile Current (cold)

JAPAN

Warm ocean waters

Tropic of Cancer

Kuro Siwo Current (warm)

Equator

Wet season

AUSTRALIA
Hot landmass
Low pressure – rising air

0   2000 km

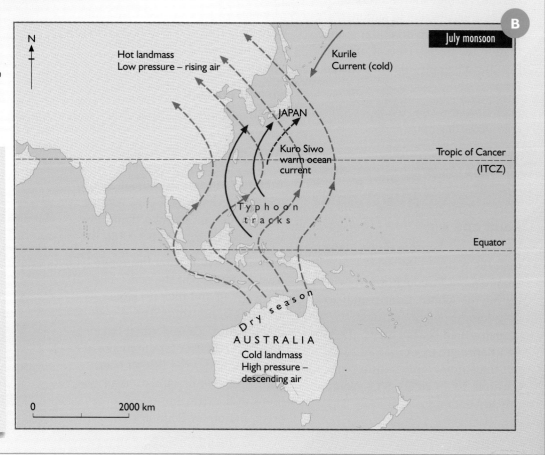

B July monsoon

Hot landmass
Low pressure – rising air

Kurile Current (cold)

JAPAN

Kuro Siwo warm ocean current

Tropic of Cancer
(ITCZ)

Typhoon tracks

Equator

Dry season

AUSTRALIA
Cold landmass
High pressure – descending air

0   2000 km

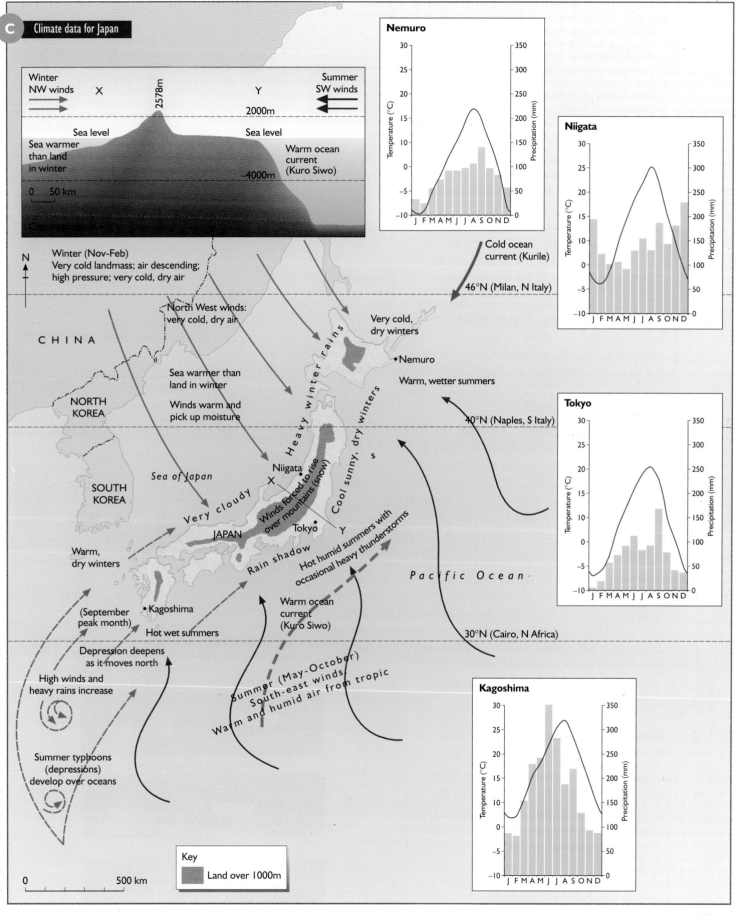

C Climate data for Japan

Climate change

Is the climate changing?

Changes in global climates are not new. Section 1.5 (Glaciation) shows that there have been several large fluctuations in the last 200,000 years, let alone the many years of the Earth's history before that. Fossil evidence from South Wales, shows that 120,000 years ago elephant, hyena and hippopotamus roamed the area. Yet by 18,000 years ago, a vast ice sheet covered much of the British Isles, and reindeer occupied the same area.

Such events occurred naturally, but changes today *appear* to be largely the result of human activities. Are these changes permanent or short-term fluctuations? Scientists are not yet in agreement.

What is the evidence?

Rising global temperatures   Extreme temperatures appear to be occurring more frequently. **A** shows records for a single day in August 1998. (Note the drought in the USA referred to on page 97.) Long-term records, kept since 1860, show an upward trend in recent years (**B**). It is now accepted by many that **global warming** is happening and will continue for some years. A rise of 2 to 4°C is expected by the year 2100.

Increasing storms   The global frequency of high winds and tropical storms appears to be increasing. A warmer atmosphere provides more energy and warmer ocean temperatures can trigger more intense hurricanes. Over the last ten years a series of hurricanes have been the worst of the century (page 86). Higher winds mean larger and more powerful waves, threatening sea defences and engulfing low-lying coastal communities. Are these long-term changes or are more people living in vulnerable low-lying coastal areas, so that losses are greater?

Changing ocean currents   Many scientists believe that changes in ocean currents El Niño and La Niña in the South Pacific Ocean (**C**) disturb climate patterns world-wide and explain many unusual events, such as very wet weather in California and the droughts in the Sahel of Africa. Evidence suggests that El Niño is happening more often.

Glowing, glowing…gone?

Britons flee killer heat in Europe

Hottest year for planet Earth

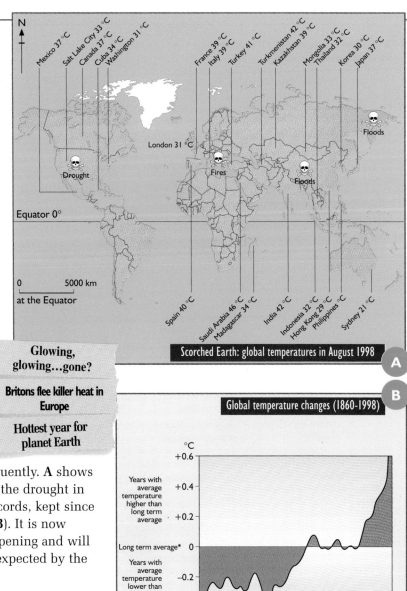

Scorched Earth: global temperatures in August 1998

A

B

Global temperature changes (1860-1998)

°C
+0.6

Years with average temperature higher than long term average   +0.4

+0.2

Long term average*   0

Years with average temperature lower than long term average   −0.2

−0.4

1860 1880 1900 1920 1940 1960 1980 2000
Year

*Long term average based on 1961-90

C

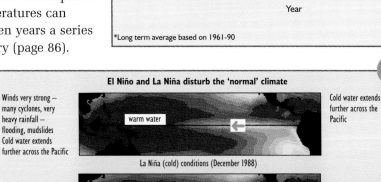

El Niño and La Niña disturb the 'normal' climate

Winds very strong — many cyclones, very heavy rainfall — flooding, mudslides
Cold water extends further across the Pacific

warm water

Cold water extends further across the Pacific

La Niña (cold) conditions (December 1988)

Hot with heavy rainfall

warm water

Cold water welling up from ocean deeps rich in microscopic food for fish

Normal conditions (December 1990)

Winds do not develop, very little rain — crops fail, forest fires more likely

warm water

No cold water coming from deeps — warm temperatures bring storms and hurricanes with flooding; no food supply — no fish

El Niño (warm) conditions (December 1997)

Shrinking Antarctic ice sheets
Satellite images have shown large cracks in the ice sheets around Antarctica (**D**). Many glaciers are shrinking. If this is a result of global warming then continued melting will add large amounts of water to the oceans increasing sea levels. Satellites recording this information are fairly recent; longer records will confirm the trends.

What causes global warming?

Greenhouse gases (GHGs), such as carbon dioxide (CO_2), occur naturally in the atmosphere. About a hundred years ago a Swedish scientist, Svante Arrhenius, suggested that certain gases in the atmosphere acted like glass in a greenhouse. They allow the sun's rays through but trap the heat radiated from the Earth, that would otherwise disappear into space. This is known as the **greenhouse effect** (**F**). Without them we would freeze or boil, and the Earth would resemble the planet Mars, and be

uninhabitable. The gases circulate between the atmosphere, oceans, vegetation and animals, which maintains a temperature balance within the atmosphere. Natural changes in the balance help to explain the warmer periods and colder 'ice ages' in the past.

Since the Industrial Revolution, human activities have been increasing the amount of GHGs in the atmosphere and adding new ones (**E**). Many countries are to blame, some more than others.

The natural systems can no longer maintain the balance: as more gases accumulate and as more heat is trapped in the atmosphere, global warming takes place. Even if emissions are reduced, the amounts of extra gases already in the atmosphere will ensure that temperatures will continue to increase well into this century.

Q Suggest explanations for the different CO_2 emissions shown in **E**.

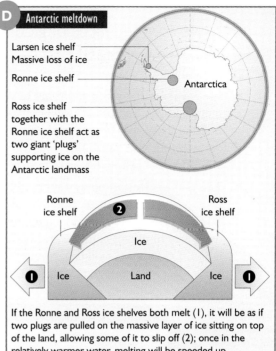

D Antarctic meltdown

Larsen ice shelf
Massive loss of ice

Ronne ice shelf

Ross ice shelf together with the Ronne ice shelf act as two giant 'plugs' supporting ice on the Antarctic landmass

Antarctica

If the Ronne and Ross ice shelves both melt (1), it will be as if two plugs are pulled on the massive layer of ice sitting on top of the land, allowing some of it to slip off (2); once in the relatively warmer water, melting will be speeded up.

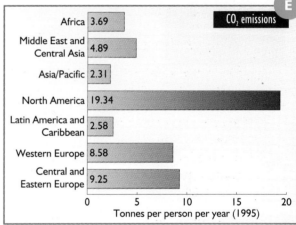

E CO_2 emissions

Region	Tonnes per person per year (1995)
Africa	3.69
Middle East and Central Asia	4.89
Asia/Pacific	2.31
North America	19.34
Latin America and Caribbean	2.58
Western Europe	8.58
Central and Eastern Europe	9.25

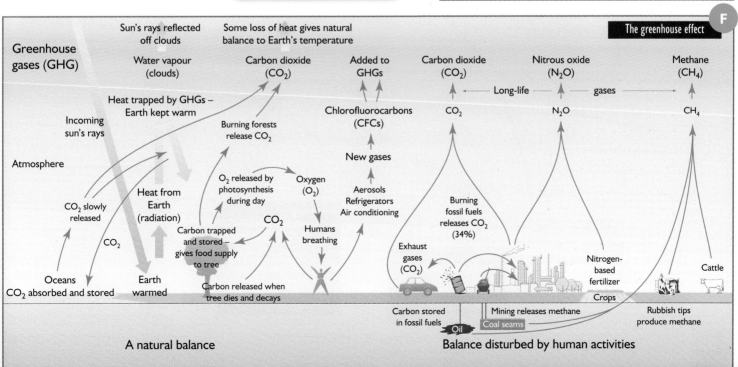

F The greenhouse effect

Greenhouse gases (GHG)

Sun's rays reflected off clouds

Some loss of heat gives natural balance to Earth's temperature

Water vapour (clouds)

Carbon dioxide (CO_2)

Added to GHGs

Carbon dioxide (CO_2)

Nitrous oxide (N_2O)

Methane (CH_4)

Heat trapped by GHGs – Earth kept warm

Incoming sun's rays

Atmosphere

Burning forests release CO_2

Chlorofluorocarbons (CFCs)

Long-life gases

CO_2

N_2O

CH_4

CO_2 slowly released

Heat from Earth (radiation)

O_2 released by photosynthesis during day

Oxygen (O_2)

New gases

Aerosols
Refrigerators
Air conditioning

Burning fossil fuels releases CO_2 (34%)

Nitrogen-based fertilizer

Cattle

CO_2

Carbon trapped and stored – gives food supply to tree

CO_2

Humans breathing

Exhaust gases (CO_2)

Crops

Oceans CO_2 absorbed and stored

Earth warmed

Carbon released when tree dies and decays

Carbon stored in fossil fuels

Oil

Mining releases methane
Coal seams

Rubbish tips produce methane

A natural balance

Balance disturbed by human activities

Possible consequences of global warming

The expected effects of global warming are considerable.

- **Sea levels will rise**, **threatening low-lying coasts**. Even without additional water in the oceans from melting ice sheets, an increase in water temperature will cause the water to expand, as in a boiling kettle, and sea level to rise.

- **The global circulation system might alter**. Changes in temperature may cause winds and rainfall patterns to alter. In some areas it will get drier and in others wetter. Farming will need to adapt if existing populations are to be sustained. Large areas of sparsely populated land in northern Europe, Asia and North America, will become warmer and agricultural opportunities will improve.

- **Extreme weather events may increase**, such as hurricanes, heavy rains, heat-waves and droughts. Agriculture and industry will need to adapt; large vulnerable populations will need protection from water shortages and coastal and river flooding. As so often LEDCs will probably be most at risk.

Q

Look at the map of the British Isles in **A**.
1. How will your area be affected?
2. What could you do locally to cut down on global warming?

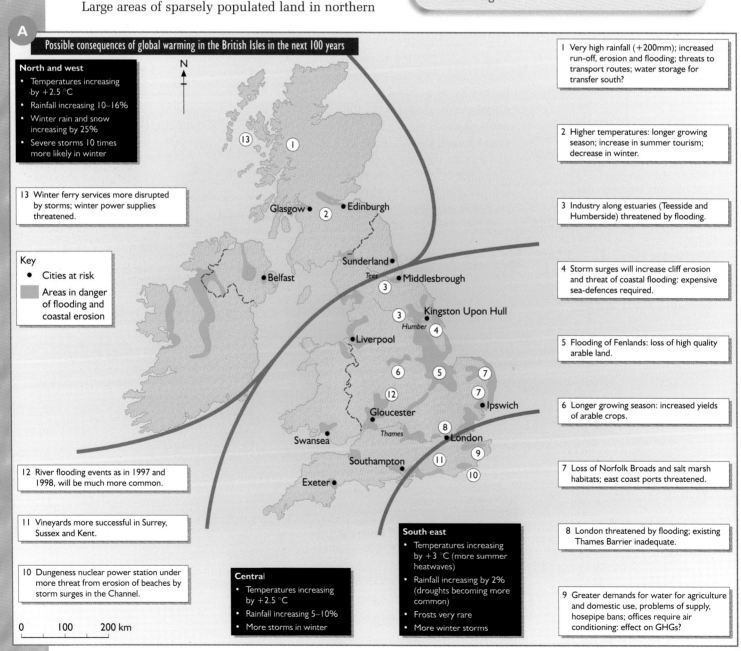

A

Possible consequences of global warming in the British Isles in the next 100 years

North and west
- Temperatures increasing by +2.5 °C
- Rainfall increasing 10–16%
- Winter rain and snow increasing by 25%
- Severe storms 10 times more likely in winter

13 Winter ferry services more disrupted by storms; winter power supplies threatened.

Key
- • Cities at risk
- ▨ Areas in danger of flooding and coastal erosion

12 River flooding events as in 1997 and 1998, will be much more common.

11 Vineyards more successful in Surrey, Sussex and Kent.

10 Dungeness nuclear power station under more threat from erosion of beaches by storm surges in the Channel.

0   100   200 km

Central
- Temperatures increasing by +2.5 °C
- Rainfall increasing 5–10%
- More storms in winter

South east
- Temperatures increasing by +3 °C (more summer heatwaves)
- Rainfall increasing by 2% (droughts becoming more common)
- Frosts very rare
- More winter storms

1 Very high rainfall (+200mm); increased run-off, erosion and flooding; threats to transport routes; water storage for transfer south?

2 Higher temperatures: longer growing season; increase in summer tourism; decrease in winter.

3 Industry along estuaries (Teesside and Humberside) threatened by flooding.

4 Storm surges will increase cliff erosion and threat of coastal flooding: expensive sea-defences required.

5 Flooding of Fenlands: loss of high quality arable land.

6 Longer growing season: increased yields of arable crops.

7 Loss of Norfolk Broads and salt marsh habitats; east coast ports threatened.

8 London threatened by flooding; existing Thames Barrier inadequate.

9 Greater demands for water for agriculture and domestic use, problems of supply, hosepipe bans; offices require air conditioning: effect on GHGs?

Cities on map: Glasgow, Edinburgh, Belfast, Sunderland, Middlesbrough, Kingston Upon Hull, Liverpool, Gloucester, Ipswich, London, Swansea, Southampton, Exeter
Rivers: Tees, Humber, Thames

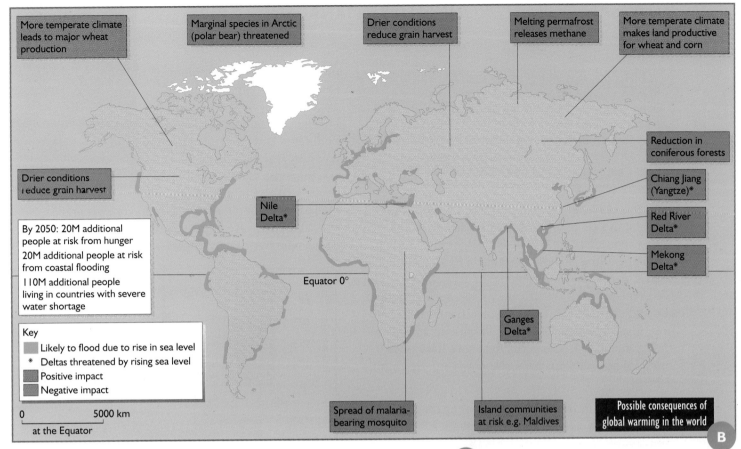

More temperate climate leads to major wheat production

Marginal species in Arctic (polar bear) threatened

Drier conditions reduce grain harvest

Melting permafrost releases methane

More temperate climate makes land productive for wheat and corn

Reduction in coniferous forests

Chiang Jiang (Yangtze)*

Drier conditions reduce grain harvest

Red River Delta*

Nile Delta*

Mekong Delta*

By 2050: 20M additional people at risk from hunger
20M additional people at risk from coastal flooding
110M additional people living in countries with severe water shortage

Equator 0°

Ganges Delta*

Key
Likely to flood due to rise in sea level
* Deltas threatened by rising sea level
Positive impact
Negative impact

0   5000 km
at the Equator

Spread of malaria-bearing mosquito

Island communities at risk e.g. Maldives

Possible consequences of global warming in the world

B

How can we adapt to the change?

Global agreements

The threats, resulting from climate change, to communities across the world, have been recognized by the United Nations. International meetings have resulted in agreements to reduce greenhouse gas emissions (**C**).

However, there are problems. Most future growth in emissions is expected from developing regions in Asia and South America who have not signed the agreement. Many scientists believe that levels of greenhouse gases are already too high; reductions of 5.2 per cent will have little effect on global warming during the next 100 years.

Reducing the impact

It is almost certain that climates are changing. We will have to adapt. It will be important to do the following at the very least:

- Develop plans for sustainable settlement in low-lying areas (especially where population densities are high and crop production is important, such as in Bangladesh).
- Improve water supplies and encourage more efficient ways of using water.
- Be better prepared for extreme weather events such as tropical storms.
- Encourage research to improve farm production in semi-arid areas, which are likely to grow in size.

C

1992	Rio Earth Summit	Agreement to a 5.2 per cent reduction in emissions by about 2010. Signed by 38 industrialized countries.
1997	Kyoto Conference	
1998	Buenos Aires Conference	

Questions

Global climatic change is predicted to continue for at least the next 100 years.

1 State **two** effects it may have in west Scotland. (2)

2 Give a reason for **each** of the effects you have described in question 1. (4)

3 Describe **two** different areas that are at risk from an increase in sea level. Explain why they are at risk. (7)

4 For an area that you have studied:

a) describe the possible effects of global warming, and

b) discuss the steps that might be taken to adapt to the effects you have described.

(12)

Total: 25 marks

HOW CAN OUR ENVIRONMENT BE MANAGED?
Summer-time smog

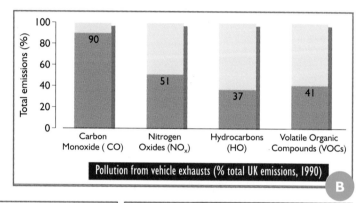

An increasing problem: summer-time smog – a health hazard

A

> **DEFINITION**
>
> **Ozone** is a naturally occurring gas found throughout the atmosphere. At ground level it is a pollutant, which has doubled since the Industrial Revolution. In the upper atmosphere the ozone layer protects the Earth from harmful ultraviolet radiation.

Until the 1950s, thick, yellow, unhealthy smogs were common in British towns and cities during winter. They were caused by smoke and sulphurous gases in the air, resulting from the burning of fossil fuels, such as coal, for heating and cooking. In many MEDCs this is a problem of the past. Cleaner fuels, such as natural gas, and central heating have replaced coal and open fires. Many houses today are built without a fireplace and open chimney. Clean Air Acts have been passed and most governments have successful smoke control policies.

Today the major threat to clean, healthy air is the exhaust of cars, lorries and other vehicles, which emit a wide variety of pollutants (**B**). It is their effect on ozone that is the problem. Only small amounts of ozone are found naturally in our air, but the combination of pollutants and sunlight sets off a complex series of chemical reactions (**C**). Concentrations of ozone will rise in areas with many cars and on days when temperatures and sunshine hours are high. The result is summer-time smog, which seriously affects air quality (**E**).

Pollution from vehicle exhausts (% total UK emissions, 1990)

y-axis: Total emissions (%) 0–100

- Carbon Monoxide (CO): 90
- Nitrogen Oxides (NO$_x$): 51
- Hydrocarbons (HO): 37
- Volatile Organic Compounds (VOCs): 41

B

Ozone formation at ground level

Sunlight (ultra-violet radiation)

Cars and lorries → Carbon monoxide (CO), Nitric Oxide / Nitric Dioxide (N$_x$), Hydrocarbons

Power stations → Volatile organic compounds (VOCs)

→ Complex chemical reactions (increases with higher temperatures) → OZONE → Summer-time smog

Daytime (hot sunny days)

Urban areas – many vehicles – slow moving

C

Health impacts

Summer-time smog → Breathing problems → Increase in hospital admissions and premature deaths ← Increased sensitivity to pollen

D

E

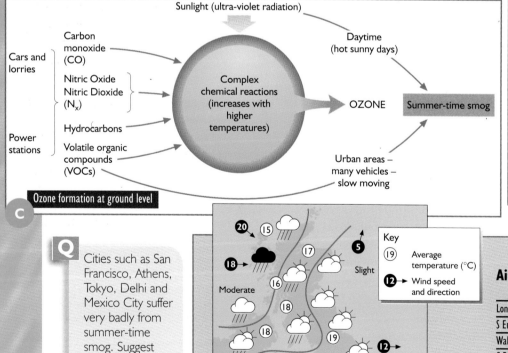

Key
- ⑲ Average temperature (°C)
- ⓬→ Wind speed and direction

Moderate / Slight

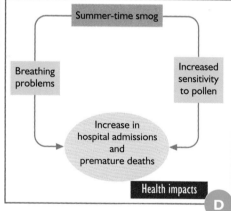

Weather and air quality

Air quality	11.8.98 NO$_2$	O$_3$	12.8.98 NO$_2$	O$_3$
London	Poor	Md	Md	Md
S England	Md	Md	Md	Md
Wales	Md	Md	Gd	Md
C England	Md	Md	Md	Md
N England	Md	Md	Md	Gd
Scotland	Md	Gd	Gd	Gd
N Ireland	Gd	Gd	Gd	Gd

Met Office, Bracknell August '98

Q Cities such as San Francisco, Athens, Tokyo, Delhi and Mexico City suffer very badly from summer-time smog. Suggest reasons why such different cities have this problem.

Pollution control

In the British Isles a network of air pollution monitoring sites has been established so that the public can be kept informed of pollution levels (**F**). The UK government health standard is set at 50 parts per billion. **F** shows sites where, in 1997, pollution levels rose above the health standards on more than 30 days. Recent research shows that pollution may be worse, but there are not yet enough monitoring sites to record it. **H** is an example of a government campaign.

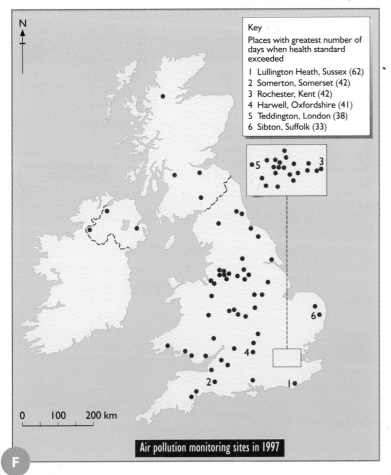

Key
Places with greatest number of days when health standard exceeded
1 Lullington Heath, Sussex (62)
2 Somerton, Somerset (42)
3 Rochester, Kent (42)
4 Harwell, Oxfordshire (41)
5 Teddington, London (38)
6 Sibton, Suffolk (33)

0   100   200 km

Air pollution monitoring sites in 1997

F

H

Don't choke Britain
✓ Cycle for a day
✓ Limit cars in city centres
✓ '2 persons + only' car lanes
✓ Improve/cheaper public transport
✓ City cars use different fuels
✓ Car engine checks (emissions)
✓ Improve driving habits – less acceleration

A government campaign 1998

The ozone layer

Ground level ozone should not be confused with the ozone layer high in the Earth's atmosphere (**G**). This upper layer is formed as the sun's rays react with oxygen. It forms a protective shield, which absorbs ultraviolet rays from the sun. Ultraviolet rays can cause skin cancer. They can also destroy micro-organisms in the sea that are important food supplies for fish.

In 1986 scientists in Antarctica discovered a hole in the shield of ozone. This meant greater amounts of the dangerous rays were reaching Earth. The hole is being eroded by gases called chloroflourocarbons (CFCs). They were used in refrigerators, polystyrene and aerosols (e.g. hair sprays). CFCs have been rising, accumulating in the stratosphere, and gradually destroying the ozone layer.

CFCs were banned in 1990 but there is already so much in the atmosphere that the ozone hole is likely to grow until 2020. Measurements in 1998 show that the hole had increased considerably in the previous twelve months. A further hole is also growing over the Arctic (**G**). Precautions are being taken in Australia and Argentina: people are being advised to keep their skin covered if out in the sun. Much larger populations could be affected if the Arctic hole spreads.

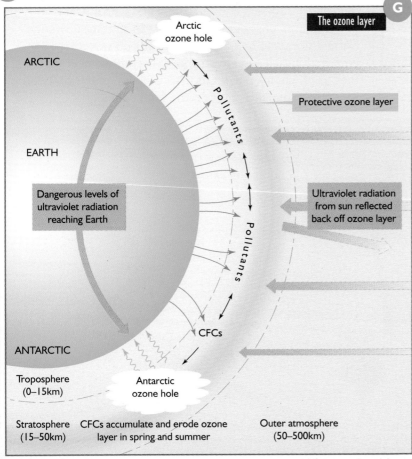

The ozone layer

G

Arctic ozone hole

ARCTIC

EARTH

Protective ozone layer

Pollutants

Dangerous levels of ultraviolet radiation reaching Earth

Ultraviolet radiation from sun reflected back off ozone layer

Pollutants

CFCs

ANTARCTIC

Antarctic ozone hole

Troposphere (0–15km)

Stratosphere (15–50km)   CFCs accumulate and erode ozone layer in spring and summer

Outer atmosphere (50–500km)

Acid rain

Rain is slightly acidic because carbon dioxide is dissolved as the droplets form and fall through the atmosphere. It is sufficiently acid to dissolve limestone and create the distinctive scenery and landforms shown on page 11. This rain has a pH of about 5.6. In Europe and North America, much of the rain that falls has a pH reading of between 5 and 3. Note where these values are on the pH scale of acidity (**A**). Rain with a pH of 3.5 is a hundred times more acid than normal and is very polluted.

The main ingredients of this pollution are sulphur dioxide (SO_2) and nitrogen oxides (NO_x) which are given off from sources such as coal-fired power stations and car exhausts. **B** shows the sources of these in the UK. The pollution can reach the ground locally as gas or dry deposition (**C**), or it can dissolve in water droplets and be carried by winds far from the source to eventually fall as rain or snow (wet deposition). High chimney stacks and

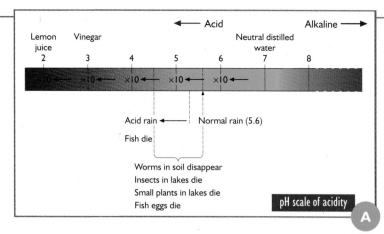

pH scale of acidity **A**

south-west prevailing winds mean much of the pollution produced in the British Isles is blown to Norway and Sweden – countries that produce little themselves. The maps in **D** show how pollution patterns have changed since 1960. Higher temperatures usually accelerate chemical reactions so acid rain may increase in the future with global warming.

> **Q** Describe and suggest reasons for the changing patterns of 'risk' shown in **D**. What changes might occur over the next fifty years?

What are the effects of acid rain...
on ecosystems?

During the last 30 years, trees have been dying in increasing numbers across Europe and North America (**E**). More than 25 per cent of the forests in southern Sweden, Germany, Poland and Slovakia have been severely damaged. Lakes and streams have become so acid that they are lifeless – devoid of insects, frogs, plants and fish. The pollutants have got into the food chain.

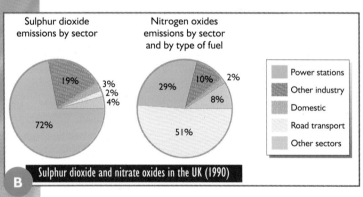

Sulphur dioxide and nitrate oxides in the UK (1990) **B**

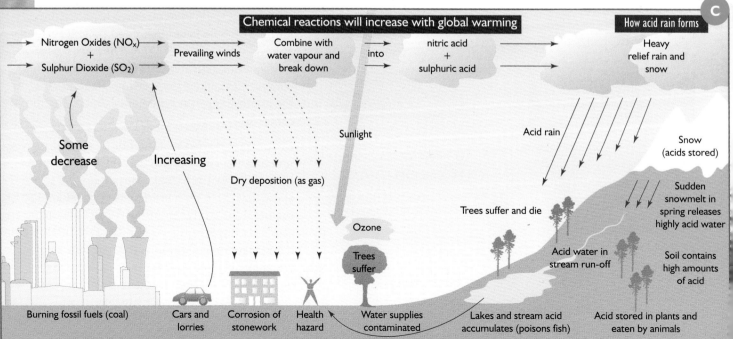

How acid rain forms **C**

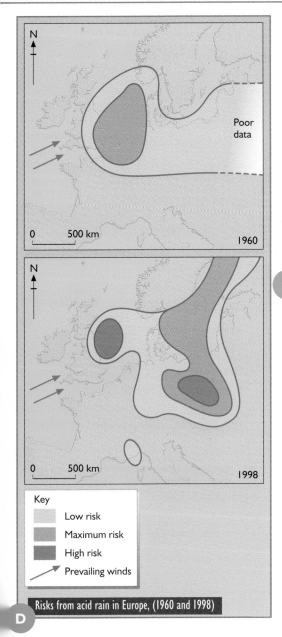

Key

Low risk

Maximum risk

High risk

Prevailing winds

Risks from acid rain in Europe, (1960 and 1998)

D

Questions

1 Examine **F** on page 59 and suggest reasons for the distribution of sites with readings above the health standard in 1997? (6)

2 Why do you think ozone pollution at ground level might be more dangerous during anticyclonic (high pressure) conditions during the summer? (6)

3 Explain how ozone in the atmosphere can be both an advantage and disadvantage. (6)

4 Why is acid rain pollution difficult to control? (7)

Total: 25 marks

Effects of acid rain on vegetation

E

Effects of acid rain on Lincoln Cathedral

F

... on buildings?

Acid particles deposited on buildings, statues such as on Lincoln Cathedral (**F**), and bridges cause corrosion. Buildings of natural stone such as limestone and marble are particularly at risk. Conservation is very costly, but safety considerations (railway viaducts) and heritage value (castles, cathedrals, major houses) must be taken into account.

... on people?

Dry deposition can have direct effects on people's health, causing respiratory problems, coughs and headaches. Indirectly, water supplies can be contaminated and toxic chemicals can be stored in fruit, vegetables and animals.

HOW CAN ACID RAIN BE REDUCED?	
SOLUTION	**PROBLEM**
1 **Reduce SO$_2$ emissions from power stations**	
• burn low sulphur coal	Expensive to import: affects UK coal mines
• burn alternative fuels with low sulphur content (e.g. North Sea gas or oil)	UK coal mines would close: unemployment
• remove sulphur from coal	Expensive
• burn limestone with coal to absorb SO$_2$	Requires new, expensive boilers: higher fuel prices
• 'end of pipe' technologies, removing SO$_2$ in the chimney by spraying gases with a mixture of limestone and water.	Very expensive, but mixture produces gypsum, a mineral used in plasterboards.
2 **Reduce NO$_x$ emissions from cars**	
• fit catalytic converters	Expensive to buy
• use 'cleaner' fuels	
• improve car engines.	
3 **Use alternative energy sources:** HEP, wind, solar, tidal.	Time, expense, political will?
4 **International agreement** (e.g. Kyoto protocol 1997)	All countries need to agree and abide by agreement
5 **Laws and taxes**	Difficult and expensive to enforce
6 **Public awareness**	
• turn off lights	
• insulate houses	
• use the car less	

Ecosystems

The environment includes the rocks and soils, vegetation, animals, humans, water, the atmosphere and climate. An **ecosystem** describes how all these factors interact with each other. An ecosystem is composed of living organisms and their dead remains; and the non-living rocks, atmosphere, rain and sunshine. The interactions between these can be shown on a systems diagram (**A**). The principal input is sunlight, or solar energy. This is absorbed by green plants, used in photosynthesis, and passed through the system as food. Plants are eaten by insects and animals; animals consume each other. The plants, insects and animals all act as temporary stores of energy. Each

time energy is transferred, as when a fox consumes a rabbit, some energy is lost from the system. Eventually, plants and animals die. They decompose and provide nutrients such as nitrogen and calcium, which can be absorbed by

roots and used to feed plants. Then the **nutrient cycle** starts again.

Ecosystems exist at all scales, from a rock pool on the seashore to large-scale global systems, such as the tropical rainforest (**B**).

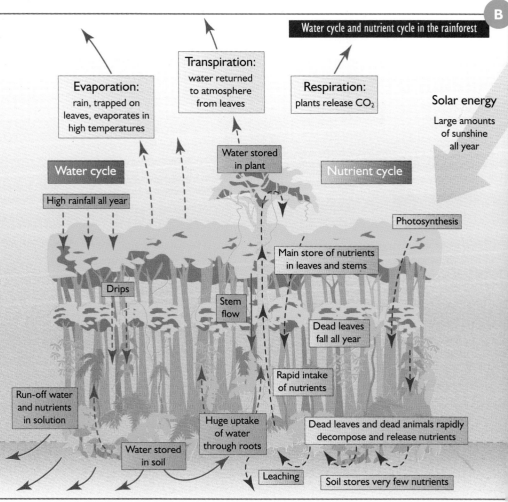

A An ecosystem

Sun's energy

Gases lost to atmosphere (H_2O, CO_2, etc.)

Precipitation

Total amount of living material = BIOMASS

Respiration and transpiration

Photosynthesis

Primary producers (plants)

Consumers (animals)
primary (herbivores) → secondary (carnivores)

Decomposers (insects, worms and micro-organisms)

Nutrient store
minerals, gases, water

Rock weathering
physical, chemical, biological

Run-off

Key
Inputs
Outputs
Flows or transfers
Stores

B

The tropical rainforest ecosystem

This system is characterized by:

- **High productivity** — rainforests receive high amounts of solar energy and rainfall and the amount of biomass produced is much greater than any other ecosystem. Trees grow very close together and compete for light and energy by growing very tall.
- **Biodiversity** — this ecosystem contains the greatest variety of plant and animal life. Up to 100 different trees can be found in an area the size of a football pitch, compared to ten or less in woodlands in the UK. Brazil has over 55,000 different species of plants.
- **Fragility** — rainforests have matured over very long periods of time. Relationships between the plants, animals and the soil are often complex; any interference can be very damaging.

Water from the high rainfall circulates through the system:

- It provides sufficient moisture to prevent plants and animals from wilting in the high temperatures.
- It aids rapid decomposition and the release of nutrients in the soil.

Water cycle and nutrient cycle in the rainforest

Evaporation: rain, trapped on leaves, evaporates in high temperatures

Transpiration: water returned to atmosphere from leaves

Respiration: plants release CO_2

Solar energy
Large amounts of sunshine all year

Water stored in plant

Water cycle

Nutrient cycle

High rainfall all year

Photosynthesis

Main store of nutrients in leaves and stems

Drips

Stem flow

Dead leaves fall all year

Rapid intake of nutrients

Run-off water and nutrients in solution

Huge uptake of water through roots

Water stored in soil

Dead leaves and dead animals rapidly decompose and release nutrients

Leaching

Soil stores very few nutrients

What are the links between climate, vegetation and soils?

Forest structure

C

Climate

- Limited seasonal change (no winter or dry season)
  - constant high temperatures (24 – 28 °C)
  - daily temperature range greater than monthly
  - high rainfall all year (+1500mm)
  - daily convectional storms during late afternoon.
- In mountain areas relief rain and convectional storms increase rainfall to +2500mm.
- Climate provides a continual growing season; large supply of solar energy and rapid rates of growth and decay.

Trees

- Evergreen, shedding leaves and growing new continuously, maintaining photosynthesis and preventing competition.
- Leaves dark green and waxy, limiting moisture loss in the high temperatures but allowing water to run off easily in heavy storms.
- No single specie of tree dominates; individual trees such as mahogany, are widely spaced.
- Different species flower and fruit at different times, providing continual food supply (no seasons).
- Shallow rooted, competing for space and nutrients from the soil — many develop buttress supports.
- Many species probably yet to be discovered?

Insects and animals

- Vast number of different species: Brazil has over 1500 different birds and over 450 species of reptile.
- Many have adapted to living in trees and occupy the canopy layers, feeding on the abundant food supplies of flowers, fruit and seeds. Many are yet to be discovered?

Soils

- Rapid chemical weathering of the rocks creates very deep soils (10–100m)
- Water percolating through the soil from the high rainfall carries away valuable salts — leaching.
- Soils are rich in iron oxide and red in colour — latosols.
- They are very acid with a pH of less than 6.5.
- Soils are generally infertile, because decomposition of leaves and other organic matter and the uptake of the nutrients produced are so rapid.

Forest structure diagram

Epiphytes – plants living in the tree crowns for light (not parasitic)

Woody climbers (lianas)

Dense unbroken cover

Trees adapted to shade

Dense undergrowth along river banks

River floods bring nutrients

Fish, reptiles, amphibians

Dense tree trunks, little undergrowth; mosses and ferns

Shallow root systems

Leaching of minerals (e.g. calcium)

+50m — Emergent layer – birds and insects — Maximum sunlight, rain and wind; temperatures lower at night

+45m

+40m

+35m — Canopy layer – animals living here rarely visit floor — Trees compete for light; nearly all rain intercepted

+30m

+25m — 15% sunlight; rain drips through canopy; hot and humid

+20m

+15m — Lower canopy layer – animals living in trees here visit floor — 10% sunlight; dark and gloomy, very little change in temperature

+10m

Buttress roots for tall trees

+5m — Shrubs/herbs

Ground level — Very few dead leaves on surface — Warm, moist soil

Seeds from trees germinate quickly

Iron-rich layers (latosol)

Weathered soil

Weathered rock

−100m — Parent rock

Climate graph for Uaupés

D

Temperature (°C) / Rainfall (mm)

J F M A M J J A S O N D

Mean temperature 25°C   Total rainfall
Temperature range 2°C   2845mm

What are the links between human activities and the rainforest?

The rainforest has long been used by forest-living tribes of people, who have adapted their lifestyle and agriculture to benefit from and sustain the local environment. Increasingly, however, countries, such as Brazil, have looked to the resources of the forest, its rivers and the rocks beneath, to provide them with energy and raw materials for new industrial development and for exports. All these activities have used and exploited the opportunities provided by the climate, vegetation and soils, with very different outcomes.

The main human activities linked with the rainforest are:

- farming and settlement
- deforestation for timber, mining, hydro-electric power schemes (high rainfall supplies large rivers with a continuous supply of water) and transport
- tourism.

1 Farming and settlement

Traditional farming – shifting cultivation (B)
Local or indigenous people, such as the Yanomami in north-west Brazil, live within the forest and use it to provide all their needs. From hunting, gathering and cultivating they obtain their food, drink, clothing, fuel, building materials, medicines and much more. A number of small plots are quickly cleared by 'slashing and burning' (C). They are cultivated for a few years before being abandoned and the forest and soils left to recover.

A Secondary forest

Several plots chosen to be cleared: undergrowth cut and most trees felled by hand but not uprooted; some trees left spaced out across the plot, to give protection to the soil, and provide food, e.g. bananas

Plots burned, destroying weeds and seeds and producing large amount of ash

Planting commences as soon as possible. Ash dug into soil during planting to provide fertilizer and reduce acidity. A mixture of crops grown, e.g. manioc, sweet potato, cassava and vegetables

Regrowth of secondary forest. Nutrient cycle re-established and system recovers in 15-20 years

Plots abandoned

Farmers move or select different plots to clear

Crop yields decrease after 2–3 years

Loss of trees exposes soil to fierce sun and heavy rain. Leaching and run-off increase making soils very infertile

B Traditional farming cycle practised by indigenous people

The traditional farmers use the climate, vegetation and soils to their advantage:

- heavy rainfall all year ensures a reliable fresh water supply
- shelter trees such as bananas (D) are kept to protect the soil and crops from the fierce sun and heavy rain

C Shifting cultivation in Brazil

D Banana trees

- the continual growing season allows several crops to be cultivated in succession throughout the year
- the continual fruiting of different trees throughout the year provides a continuous supply of foods to be gathered
- large numbers of animals and reptiles provide a food supply from hunting
- rich variety of plants such as trees, lianas, epiphytes and fungi provide building materials, ropes, baskets, hunting weapons and medicines
- burning the forest helps destroy weeds, plant diseases and harmful insects, while providing ash to help soil fertility
- by cultivating a plot for only two or three years farmers recognize the limited fertility of the soil and the dangers of soil erosion if exposed too long to the hot sun and heavy rain
- regrowth of secondary vegetation and the rapid decomposition cycle returns nutrients to the soil and allows farmers to return after about ten years.

However better health care is causing an increase in population of indigenous farmers which threatens the system by extending the period that plots are cultivated and reducing the time they are left to recover . Nutrients are lost from the soil by leaching, the soil hardens in the hot sun and run-off increases in the heavy rains leading to soil erosion.

Agroforestry This is a combination of arable farming, tree crops and forestry.

It takes advantage of the climate providing a continuous growing season which allows a wide variety of crops and vegetables to be grown throughout the year. The vegetation also helps agroforestry by providing:

- a large variety of trees. These valuable crops (e.g. cocoa, rubber, brazil nuts, mangosteen) can be grown in small commercial plots
- trees that are used to protect the soil from the sun and heavy rains
- small forest areas that are slowly cleared and provide income from timber
- the decaying matter to sustain biodiversity, food chains and soil nutrients.

Large-scale ranching and cultivation Large areas of the forest have been burnt and cleared for extensive cattle ranches, such as on the Mato Grosso Plateau (**A**, page 66). This too is linked to the climate, vegetation and soils. The continuous growing season and high rainfall provides pastureland for large numbers of cattle throughout the year.

However, the heavy rainfall causes leaching of nutrients and soil erosion where the forest has been converted to grasslands. Because of this wealthy ranchers tend to clear further forest for new land rather than trying to manage existing pastures.

Small-scale crop farming Farmers have been resettled on 100ha plots close to new roads, such as the 6,000km Trans-Amazonian Highway, built through the forest.

Here the forest ecosystem is affected by:

- over exposure of soils to the sun and heavy rains as farmers are often not familiar with the rainforest environment
- the production of good crop yields in the short-term when soil nutrients are high
- farmers not rotating crops or allowing secondary forest to regrow because of the small plots
- rapidly declining soil nutrient levels leading to reduced yields as the land is used more intensively to provide an income. This in turn leads to increased soil erosion until the farmer is unable to make a living
- the plot being abandoned or sold to ranchers and a new clearing being made in the forest

How is the system being threatened?

Population increase

Medical aid, health care and other services are reaching these people, so populations are increasing quickly.
- More plots are needed to maintain food supplies.
- Deforestation by commercial and other users reduces the area available for the cultivators to 'shift' their plots.
- Plots are cultivated for longer periods.
- Abandoned plots are not given sufficient time to recover.

Exploitation

Industrial and agri-businesses exploit the rainforest, deforesting huge areas for:
- logging
- mining
- ranching
- hydro-electricity
- transport.

Government resettlement

Schemes for landless rural people and urban poor cause deforestation along roads.

Climate change

Deforestation may increase the effects of El Niño. El Niño has caused changes in the normal wind patterns and brought drought to the rainforests of Indonesia and Roraima in NW Brazil. Large areas have been devastated by fires, some out of control for three months.

2 Deforestation

Deforestation of the world's rainforests continues at an alarming rate. In Brazil it continues despite:

- bans on new licences for new mahogany logging concessions
- appointment of government inspectors
- intense international pressure.

Analysis of satellite images of the Amazon shows that between 1995 and 1996 an area of more than 60,000 sq km – twice the size of Belgium – was cut down, burned and cleared (**A**). It is estimated however that 80 per cent of the forest remains intact.

Problems

Deforestation has led to a number of problems at a range of scales from local to global (**B**).

- Hardwoods such as rosewood and mahogany are in demand for furniture by MEDCs.
- Individual, valuable trees, such as mahogany, are widely spaced. A lot of other trees have to be destroyed to reach them.
- Large-scale soil erosion causes river flow and sediment loads to increase. Downstream this can cause flooding, kill aquatic life, ruin fishing, silt up dams and make navigation difficult (**B**).
- Loss of soil and exposure of hard laterite surfaces slows forest recovery. It is likely to take at least 100 years for the secondary forest to regrow.
- The variety of life or bio-diversity is reduced; food webs are destroyed:
  - research into plants with medicinal value curtailed
  - the gene pool is reduced and research into breeding drought-resistant plants combating the effects of climate change could be affected.
- Global oxygen levels may be reduced, since oxygen is produced during photosynthesis.

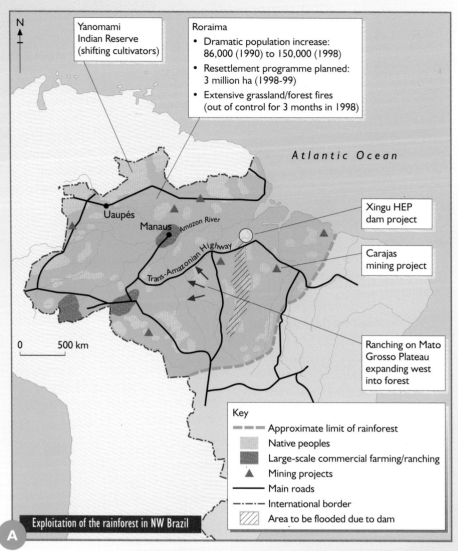

A Exploitation of the rainforest in NW Brazil

- Yanomami Indian Reserve (shifting cultivators)

Roraima
- Dramatic population increase: 86,000 (1990) to 150,000 (1998)
- Resettlement programme planned: 3 million ha (1998-99)
- Extensive grassland/forest fires (out of control for 3 months in 1998)

Atlantic Ocean

Uaupés
Manaus
Amazon River
Trans-Amazonian Highway

Xingu HEP dam project

Carajas mining project

Ranching on Mato Grosso Plateau expanding west into forest

Key
- – – – Approximate limit of rainforest
- Native peoples
- Large-scale commercial farming/ranching
- ▲ Mining projects
- —— Main roads
- —·—·— International border
- ▨ Area to be flooded due to dam

- Reduced transpiration and evaporation of moisture into the atmosphere and increased run-off is likely to:
  - reduce local rainfall. Drier conditions increase fire risk.
  - affect the global water cycle, increasing aridity.
- Burning forests contribute up to 35 per cent of global carbon dioxide emissions, adding to the greenhouse effect and increasing global warming.

3 Tourism

Tourism has developed in the rainforest as it has become more accessible to people from MEDCs. There is an increasing demand for more adventurous holidays. Tourists are attracted by the tropical rainforest in itself and the exciting variety of plant and animal life that exist there. There are no seasonal changes in the climate which allows tourism throughout the year.

However, large-scale tourism involving the construction of new airports, hotels and road and river access results in forest clearance, erosion of river banks and forest paths and disturbance of the fragile system. Local people are unlikely to benefit. Tourism on a large scale is likely to be destructive and harmful to the fragile ecosystem. However, most of the tourism in the Brazilian rainforest is small scale and aims to sustain the environment and provide income to local communities which will help maintain the total forest system. This is known as *ecotourism* (see page 144).

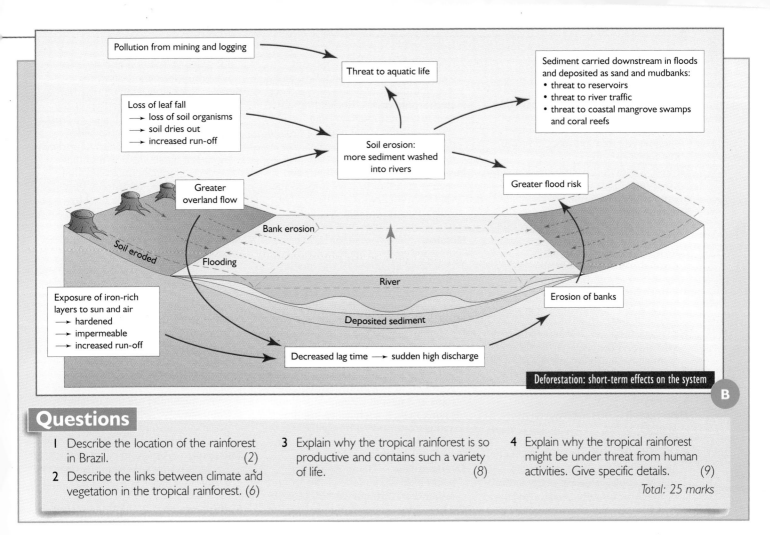

Deforestation: short-term effects on the system

- Pollution from mining and logging → Threat to aquatic life
- Loss of leaf fall
  - → loss of soil organisms
  - → soil dries out
  - → increased run-off
- Soil erosion: more sediment washed into rivers
- Sediment carried downstream in floods and deposited as sand and mudbanks:
  - threat to reservoirs
  - threat to river traffic
  - threat to coastal mangrove swamps and coral reefs
- Greater overland flow
- Greater flood risk
- Soil eroded
- Bank erosion
- Flooding
- River
- Deposited sediment
- Erosion of banks
- Exposure of iron-rich layers to sun and air
  - → hardened
  - → impermeable
  - → increased run-off
- Decreased lag time → sudden high discharge

B

Questions

1 Describe the location of the rainforest in Brazil. (2)

2 Describe the links between climate and vegetation in the tropical rainforest. (6)

3 Explain why the tropical rainforest is so productive and contains such a variety of life. (8)

4 Explain why the tropical rainforest might be under threat from human activities. Give specific details. (9)

Total: 25 marks

GLOSSARY

Ablation   The melting of ice forming a glacier or ice sheet.

Acid rain   Rain that has been polluted by chemicals, mainly sulphur dioxide from factories and power stations, and is responsible for the acidification of rivers and lakes and widespread destruction of fish and forests in Europe and North America.

Accumulation   Addition of snow or ice to glacier or ice sheet.

Alluvium   Deposits of fine sediments left across a floodplain after a river has been in flood.

Anticyclone   An area of high atmospheric pressure, where light winds spiral outwards in a clockwise direction (northern hemisphere).

Backwash   The return flow of water down a beach after a breaking wave.

Bank-full discharge   The volume or amount of water flowing in a river when water fills the channel to the top of the banks.

Beach nourishment   Replacing beach material, lost through erosion by the sea, with sand and shingle dredged from sources offshore and then pumped onto the beach to make it higher.

Base flow   The normal flow or discharge of a river that comes from springs and groundwater flow.

Boulder clay   Deposits left covering the ground after the retreat of an ice sheet or glacier, e.g. the chalky boulder clay covering large areas of East Anglia.

Clint   The remaining upstanding blocks of a limestone pavement after the joints in the rock have been widened by solution.

Corrie   An armchair-shaped hollow eroded into a mountainside by moving ice at a glacier's source. Also known as cwms and cirques.

Depression   An area of low atmospheric pressure, where winds spiral inwards in an anti-clockwise direction (northern hemisphere).

Distributary   The branching of the main channel of a river into several separate channels, which spread out across a delta.

Drainage basin   The area of a river's watershed that is drained by the river and its tributaries.

Ecosystem   A system that shows how a community of plants and animals are related to their physical (non-living) environment.

Estuary   The lowest part of a former river valley that has been drowned by the sea and is now tidal.

Exfoliation   The weathering of rocks by heating and cooling that causes a rock to shed layers, similar to an onion.

Front   Boundaries between different types of air-masses found in depressions (e.g. cold front).

Glacial till   Deposits left covering the ground after the retreat of an ice sheet or glacier (also known as boulder clay).

Global warming   The theory that the Earth's temperatures are rising due to human activities (including the deforestation of the rainforests) leading to the excessive build up of carbon dioxide in the atmosphere which increases the natural **greenhouse effect**.

Greenhouse effect   The natural effect of gases that act like a greenhouse, trapping heat in the lower atmosphere and maintaining a stable temperature. These gases (e.g. carbon dioxide) allow short-wave incoming radiation from the sun to pass through, but prevent some of the long-wave radiation reflected from the Earth escaping.

Grike   Joints in limestone widened by solution, which with the **clints** produce a 'pavement' effect.

Groundwater   Water moving or stored well below the ground surface, often in the underlying rocks.

Groyne   A barrier of wood or concrete, built from the high tide mark, out across the beach to help reduce **longshore drift** and encourage the deposition of sand to make the beach higher.

Hanging valley   A tributary valley which joins the main river valley from above and may 'hang' hundreds of metres above the main valley. It is often marked by a waterfall.

Hydrograph   A graph showing the changes in the discharge of a stream over a period of time.

Igneous rock   Crystalline rocks that are mostly formed when molten magma cools within or at the surface of the crust (granite, basalt, volcanic rocks).

Infiltration   The movement of water from the surface into the soil, rock or beach.

Interception   Precipitation trapped by vegetation instead of falling directly onto the soil.

Interlocking spurs   Series of projections in river valley which appear to overlap or 'interlock' when seen from the top or bottom of the valley.

Isobar   A line linking equal values of atomospheric pressure. Also isotherms (temperature), isohyets (precipitation), isovels (river velocity).

Joints   Vertical fractures or cracks in rock layers caused by rocks cooling, expanding or drying out over long periods of time.

Lag time   The time delay, measured on a **hydrograph**, between maximum rainfall during a storm and the peak discharge or flow in the river.

Levée   A natural or artificial raised bank alongside a river.

Longshore drift   The movement of beach sediments along the shore. Waves approaching the beach at an angle will carry material up and across the beach. However, the **backwash** carries it back down the beach by the steepest slope and sediment is moved along the beach in a dominant direction.

Metamorphic rock   Rocks, formally igneous or sedimentary, that have been altered by heat and/or pressure deep in the Earth's crust (e.g. slate, marble).

Misfit stream   A stream that now seems too small to have formed the valley through which it flows. The valley may have been originally eroded by a larger river or glacier.

Moraine   Sediments that have been transported by glaciers or ice sheets. Described as lateral (side), medial (middle), terminal (end) and recessional (temporary halt in the retreat of a glacier or ice sheet).

Névé   Snow crystals, about one year old, and compacted by the weight of the fresh snow above.

Nutrient cycle   The movement of nutrients required by plants for food. Nutrients are taken up through the roots and passed through the plant. Living matter, such as leaves, dies and is decomposed by bacteria in the soil to release fresh nutrients for the root systems to absorb.

Overland flow   The movement of water over the surface of the ground rather than through the soil or rocks.

Ox-bow lake   The abandoned part of a meander after a river has straightened its course by eroding through the neck of the meander.

Percolation   The movement of rain water vertically down through the soil.

Permafrost   Ground that is permanently frozen through most of the year, often to many metres deep.

Permeable rocks   Rocks which allow water to pass through (e.g. sandstone, chalk). Also, pervious rock, which is a type of permeable rock where water moves through the rock along joints and bedding planes (e.g. Carboniferous Limestone).

Prevailing winds   The direction from which winds in an area most commonly blow (e.g. The British Isles have prevailing winds from the south west).

Rain shadow   An area of low rainfall found in the lee of mountains that cause air to rise and heavy relief rain to fall.

River long profile   Cross-section of river's course from source to mouth.

River terrace   The remains of a former floodplain that have been left when the river eroded downwards and formed a new floodplain at a lower level. Terraces are often used for gravel extraction and have fertile, well-drained soils for farming.

Scree   Rock, loosened by weathering, falls and rolls to the bottom of the slope and piles up in heaps of broken angular rock on the valley side.

Sedimentary rocks   Rocks, deposited by water, ice or wind, which have hardened and cemented together over time. They are usually formed in layers or strata, separated by bedding planes (e.g. sandstone, limestone, chalk, clay).

Solifluction   The flow of soil and rock down a slope which has become soaked or saturated with water. A major process of transportation on slopes in periglacial regions (those regions with permafrost), where the water from summer thaws cannot soak away due to lower levels of frozen ground.

Stalactite   A mass of calcite suspended from the roof of a limestone cave. Calcium carbonate crystals (calcite) are precipitated from water, which has slowly percolated through joints and fissures, dripping from the cave roof.

Stalagmite   A mass of calcite which has grown upwards from the floor of a limestone cave as water drips onto the floor.

Surface run-off   Rainfall that, when it hits the ground, runs down the slope over the surface, rather than sinking into the soil or rocks.

Suspended load   Sediment carried along in the water of a river or in the sea.

Swallow hole   Joints in Carboniferous Limestone, which have been enlarged by solution and erosion, where streams often disappear underground.

Swash   The movement of water up the beach after a wave has broken.

Synoptic chart   A map showing conditions in the atmosphere, such as temperature, air pressure and precipitation, at a stated time

Throughflow   The movement of water through the soil or rock close to the surface of the ground.

Transpiration   The loss of moisture from a plant into the atmosphere generally through its leaves.

Truncated spur   An **interlocking spur** that has been eroded by a valley glacier to now form part of the steep side of a U-shaped valley.

Water table   The surface of the saturated layer or **groundwater** store in a **permeable rock**.

Natural hazards and people

Introduction

Tornado damage, Selsey, West Sussex, 1998

Why study natural hazards?

Few weeks pass by without news of a natural disaster somewhere in the world. Modern technology means that their aftermath appears on our television screens or in our newspapers almost immediately. While most are sudden and unexpected, some, such as floods, are confidently predicted before they actually happen. Some knowledge of natural hazards can help us deal with them and minimize their impact.

All of us are affected by natural hazards whether it is fog on the way to school, the risk of a hurricane in Florida, floods in Bangladesh, or a major drought in Africa. They affect us all either directly or indirectly. Some cause death and severe damage, others are inconvenient and disruptive. While this may not affect us personally, it will affect large numbers of people somewhere in the world. Most of us, however, will contribute in some way to the financial cost of coping with natural hazards. Through charity donations, taxes or by extra charges for services, we will contribute towards helping to clear up afterwards or in attempting to reduce their impact in the future. An understanding of why, how and where different types of natural hazard occur should help us to predict them more accurately and take steps to reduce their impact.

Questions for enquiry

To gain a better understanding of natural hazards the following key questions will be investigated in this chapter:

🌍 What different kinds of natural hazards are there?

🌍 Where do different kinds of hazard occur?

🌍 What physical processes are responsible for natural hazards?

🌍 How do people's activities affect natural hazards?

🌍 How do natural hazards affect people in parts of the world that are at different levels of development?

🌍 How can people be protected from natural hazards?

🌍 Can natural hazards be predicted and controlled?

Themes

The answers to these questions will be sought by examining six natural hazards:

- earthquakes
- volcanic eruptions
- tropical storms
- flooding
- drought
- fire.

In addition, this chapter will investigate:

- how hazards are classified
- plate tectonic theory
- why people continue to live in hazardous areas despite the risks.

Flooding, River Severn, 1998

People and places

Some natural hazards operate at a local scale while others work globally. This chapter will look at how different parts of the world can be affected in varying ways and by different sorts of hazards. LEDCs, such as Bangladesh and Sudan, are seen to suffer extreme hardships. In contrast, MEDCs, such as Japan and the USA, are seen to be far better equipped to cope with the consequences of natural hazards. In the UK and elsewhere in the European Union, natural hazards are also seen to affect people.

Highway 166 collapses in rain storms, California, 1998

WHAT ARE NATURAL HAZARDS?

DEFINITION

A **natural hazard** is a natural event which is perceived by people as a threat to life and property. It may be generated from within the Earth (earthquakes, volcanoes), occur upon the surface (landslides, avalanches, floods), or happen within the atmosphere (high winds, drought, snow, fog).

What different kinds of hazard are there?

Q What recent natural hazards have hit the headlines? Make a list of events, locations and dates.

A and **B** show some of the natural hazard events at the start of 1998. It was a most unusual period when a whole series of natural events occurred that threatened life and property.

B 1998

2 JANUARY
Strong winds from the south west hit the UK.

5 JANUARY
Widespread flooding occurred along the River Severn. At Worcester river levels were 4m above normal, causing homes to be evacuated, roads to be closed and the county cricket ground to be submerged.

8 JANUARY
A **tornado** hit Selsey in West Sussex, reaching speeds of up to 150km/hr. It left a narrow path of destruction as roofs were ripped off, chimneys blown down, trees felled and hundreds forced to leave their homes.

13 JANUARY
The **volcano**, Mt Etna, erupted again in Sicily, southern Italy.

15 JANUARY
Quebec, Canada experienced a freak 'ice storm'. Freezing temperatures at ground level turned rain into ice as it fell, bringing down pylons and leaving most of the province without electricity.

23 JANUARY
An **avalanche** swept down a mountainside in the French Alps above the ski resort of Les Orres. Ten children were killed and twenty two injured.

10 FEBRUARY
North-east Afghanistan suffered an **earthquake** killing an estimated 4,000 people. Rescue attempts were hindered by the remoteness of the area.

23 FEBRUARY
A tornado in Florida reached speeds of 330km/hr and killed 38 people.

24 FEBRUARY
Heavy rain due to 'El Nino' occurred all along the eastern Pacific coast causing **floods** in Ica, in the Peruvian desert, and **mudslides** in California.

27 FEBRUARY
Gales cause havoc in Northern England. An aeroplane was blown 200m across the runway at Leeds Airport and a lorry was blown over and blocked the A1(M) motorway.

It's bad, but it has been worse

Worcester cricket ground under water, January 1998

WORCESTER'S watery problems this week pale in significance compared to the two "great floods" which have hit the city this century.

The floods of 1947 and 1924 caused havoc and devastation in the Faithful City.

But even they are no match for the worst flood on record, which happened in Worcester in 1886 when the river rose 20 feet higher than normal.

In the harsh winter of 1947 the flood came after months of exceptional rainfall and a snow thaw in the Welsh mountains.

The situation was so bad that St John's was completely cut off from the rest of Worcester.

A Dunkirk-style operation took place to ferry people over the bridge on coaches, open-back lorries and horse-drawn carts, while a 15-minute train service was set up between Foregate Street and Henwick.

Newport Street bus station was completely under water and Upton and surrounding villages were cut off by road.

River levels set to stay for 24 hours

Twister!

'There was a tremendous clap of thunder ...I thought the whole place was falling'

Ten children are killed as avalanche hits school party

Courtesy of *Worcester Evening News*, January 1998

A Newspaper extracts of natural hazards, January 1998

Natural or man-made?

Natural hazards are not always just due to natural events. Many of them are also made far worse by human causes. An avalanche is a good example of this. The rapid downhill descent of a mass of snow may be triggered off by man-made explosions, skiing or even the action of people clearing slopes for more ski-runs. Even so the hazard is still essentially a 'natural' event with gravity and weather conditions (snow and temperature) at work.

Fog – the M42 crash

Fog is another example of a natural hazard. On the morning of Monday 10 March 1997, fog caused Britain's biggest (at that time) road vehicle pile-up on the M42 motorway. **A** shows an aerial view and a fact file of the devastation that resulted from this multiple crash.

FACT FILE

- Dense fog, 40m visibility.
- Driver error a contributory factor, 27 charged with offences following the crashes.
- Six separate crashes, involving both carriageways and all six lanes.
- 160 vehicles in total involved in the crash.
- Emergency services impeded by the blocked motorway.
- Three died and 90 injured, 15 of them seriously.
- M42 closed for a day.
- Heat so intense that vehicles and the road surface melted.

An aerial view of the M42 crash

A

How severe?

Fog is not normally seen as a severe hazard, whereas something that can kill thousands of people, such as an earthquake, is. The severity of natural hazards can be assessed by the numbers injured, the cost of the damage caused and the size of area affected. The assessment of the severity will, in turn, be affected by:

- the type of location affected (large city or remote countryside)
- the likelihood of it occurring
- the degree of preparation that is possible and has been undertaken for the hazard.

So, an unexpected hazard that kills a lot of people and causes much damage in a large city is very severe. On the other hand, a hazard in a remote area that happens frequently and affects few people is much less severe.

Q
In your opinion, was the M42 road accident primarily a natural or man-made hazard?

How frequent?

Some natural hazards occur frequently. For example, over 400 earthquakes were detected in just a two-day period before the Mount Pinatubo volcanic eruption in the Philippines in 1991. Others are isolated occurrences, such as the Italian mudslide disaster of May 1990 shown in **B**.

The frequency will vary with location. Parts of the USA is used to tornadoes and **hurricanes**, but the UK is not. Some hazards recur over a regular period in a precise location, such as the annual flooding of a river.

How long?

The duration of different natural hazards varies considerably. At one extreme earthquakes last for a matter of seconds, whereas at the other extreme global warming is thought to last for decades.

For the sake of simplicity, a three-fold classification is suggested.

- Short term: lasting for less than a day – earthquakes.
- Medium term: lasting for more than a day, less than a month – river floods.
- Long term: lasting for more than a month – many volcanic eruptions.

Where in the world?

Some natural hazards are very localized, such as tornadoes in the Midwest of the USA. Others are global in their distribution; river flooding, for example, occurs in areas all over the world. In-between, other phenomena are concentrated in certain areas, for example avalanches in mountain areas with snow, or hurricanes in the Tropics.

B Clearing up after the mudslide in Sarno, southern Italy, 6 May 1998

1 Either as a group or individually, make a list of as many natural hazards as you can.

2 Arrange the list in order of frequency and put them in a table as illustrated below. Rank the most frequent first and the least frequent last.

3 Fill in the second column, deciding whether the duration of the natural hazard is short (S), medium (M) or long term (L).

4 Use the severity index to grade each natural hazard as to how dangerous it is to people.

5 In the final column, make brief notes on the type of location where you normally find each natural hazard. Add specific examples wherever possible.

Type of natural hazard	Duration (short/medium/ long term)	Severity (1-5)	Distribution and examples

SEVERITY INDEX

1 None dead; few injured. Damage slight. Small area affected.

2 None dead; some injured. Damage fair. Local area affected.

3 Few dead; several injured. Damage considerable. Regional effects.

4 Few dead; many injured. Extensive damage. Regional or national effects.

5 Many dead; many injured. Few, if any, structures remaining standing. Multinational effects.

Plate tectonics

In order to understand the distribution of natural hazards, such as earthquakes and volcanoes, we need to study **plate tectonics**. According to the theory of plate tectonics, the Earth's **crust** is divided into seven large and twelve smaller **plates** (**C**). This crust is up to 90km thick and consists of cooler solid rock 'floating' on the hotter molten rock of the **mantle** (**A**). The plates are like postage stamps stuck on a football in terms of scale.

Plates consist of two types of crust – continental and oceanic. The older continental crust is mainly granite. It is between 25 and 90km thick, less dense than oceanic and it does not sink. Oceanic crust is mainly basalt, between 5 and 10km thick, dense and it is frequently being destroyed and replaced. It is therefore younger.

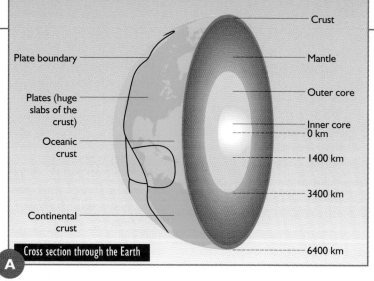

A | Cross section through the Earth

The plates 'float' like rafts on the mantle, generally moving just a few centimetres a year. Over millions of years this has caused continents to split apart and collide, so changing the relative position of the continents and oceans. This is known as **continental drift**. The cause of plate movement is thought to be convection currents generated by the hot temperatures from within the Earth (**B**). This is the same principle as boiling a saucepan of water, with the hot water rising and cooling then sinking to the bottom again.

Plates move in different ways:
* some plates move towards each other
* others move apart
* some slide past each other.

The places where they meet are known as **plate margins**. These are areas of great crustal stress and activity due to the movement of the plates. The different types of plate margin (**C**) give rise to many of the world's earthquakes and volcanoes, plus structural features such as fold mountains.

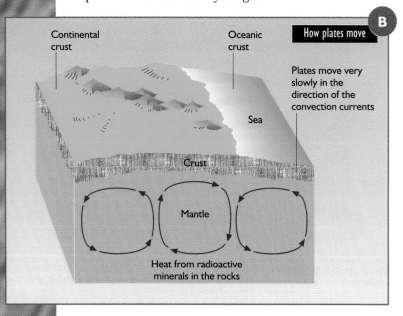

B | How plates move

Plates move very slowly in the direction of the convection currents

Q
1 What are plates?
2 State three differences between continental and oceanic crusts.

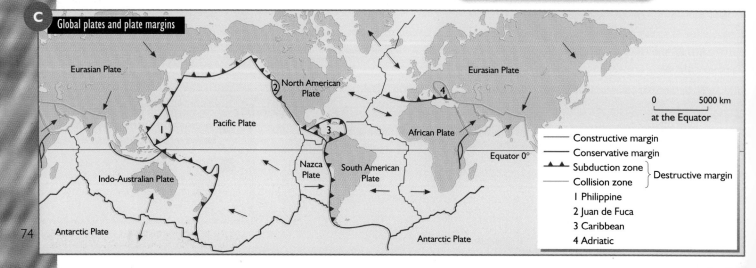

C | Global plates and plate margins

Eurasian Plate
North American Plate
Pacific Plate
African Plate
Nazca Plate
South American Plate
Indo-Australian Plate
Antarctic Plate
Eurasian Plate
Equator 0°
Antarctic Plate

0 — 5000 km at the Equator

—— Constructive margin
—— Conservative margin
▲▲▲ Subduction zone ⎫
—— Collision zone ⎭ Destructive margin

1 Philippine
2 Juan de Fuca
3 Caribbean
4 Adriatic

Types of plate margin

1 Destructive margins

Destructive margins are where plate is destroyed as two plates move together and collide. This will happen at either a **subduction** or **collision zone**.

a) Subduction zones These occur where an oceanic plate is moving towards a continental plate. The heavier oceanic plate consisting of denser material sinks below the lighter continental plate to form a subduction zone, and associated **ocean trench**. Diagram **D** shows this happening to the west of South America where the oceanic Nazca Plate meets the continental South American Plate. The heat from the mantle and friction from contact between the two plates causes oceanic plate to be destroyed. At the same time, quite violent earthquakes can be triggered by the increase in friction and pressure. The melting plate creates liquid **magma** that rises towards the surface to form volcanoes (e.g. Cotopaxi). This, together with the collision of the plates, pushes up fold mountains, such as the Andes.

Sometimes when oceanic and continental plates meet, the magma rises offshore from a continent. Then islands will form, following the line of the ocean trench. The shape of these gives them the name **island arcs**. Diagram **E** shows how this has happened to form Japan.

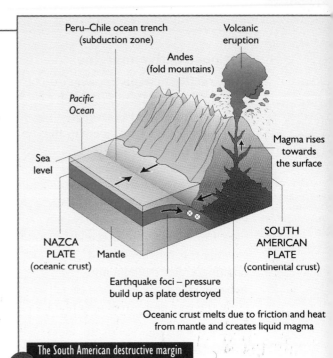

D The South American destructive margin

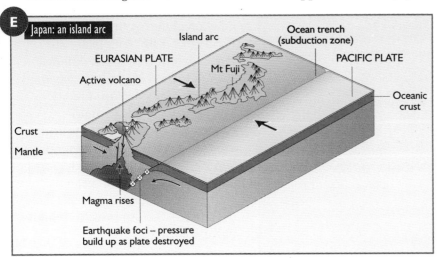

E Japan: an island arc

b) Collision zones These occur where two continental crust plates collide. Diagram **F** shows how this has happened as the plate carrying India has collided with the larger Eurasian Plate. Once, there was an ancient sea called Tethys between the two land masses. As the plates moved together at a rate of 5cm a year, the sea disappeared and the sea bed was pushed up and buckled to form the world's highest mountain chain, the Himalayas. This process is still continuing. Earthquakes are also associated with this collision, such as that at Latur, central India, in 1993, which killed 25,000 people.

Q How can sediments, which have been formed under the sea, be found high up in the Himalayas?

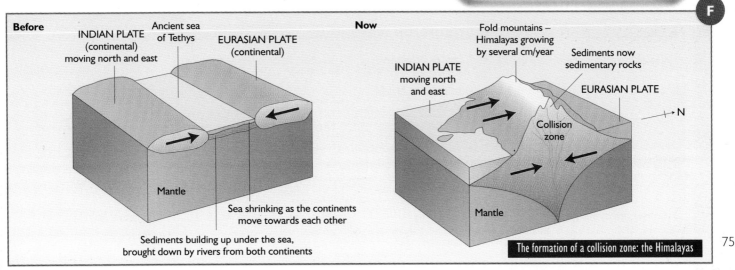

F The formation of a collision zone: the Himalayas

2 Constructive margins

Constructive margins are where two plates move away from each other and new crust is created. This most commonly occurs in the middle of oceans. Diagram **A** shows how the North American Plate is moving apart from the Eurasian Plate, so that the Atlantic Ocean is widening by about 3cm a year. Convection currents are causing this movement and creating a 'gap' called a **mid-oceanic ridge**. Magma rises to 'plug the gap' and forms new plate.

Where the magma builds up above the surface of the ocean, volcanic islands form. Iceland and the Azores are examples in the North Atlantic. Iceland did not exist two million years ago when Britain entered its last Ice Age. Iceland's location on the Mid-Atlantic Ridge means that it is a major site of volcanic and earthquake activity, but these tend to be of the more gentle variety. Surtsey was a volcano under the sea that erupted in 1963 to the south west of Iceland. Within four years an island of 2.8 sq km had been created.

Constructive margins can also be found on land. The East African Rift Valley is opening up and new land is being formed in the bottom of the valley.

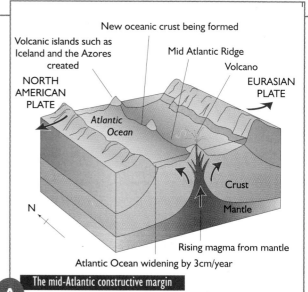

The mid-Atlantic constructive margin

3 Conservative margins

Conservative margins are where plates move alongside each other. Crust is neither created nor destroyed and no new landforms appear. However, these can be sites for violent earthquakes. In California, the San Andreas Fault marks the junction of the North American and Pacific Plates (**B**). Both plates are moving north west but at different speeds. Instead of slipping smoothly past each other, they tend to 'stick'. The pressure builds up until suddenly the plates jerk forward sending shock waves to the surface and triggering a sudden earthquake. Map **C** shows five such major earthquakes that have occurred along the 1040km San Andreas Fault in the twentieth century.

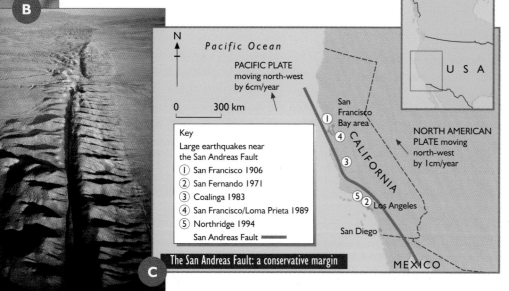

The San Andreas Fault: a conservative margin

Key

Large earthquakes near the San Andreas Fault

1. San Francisco 1906
2. San Fernando 1971
3. Coalinga 1983
4. San Francisco/Loma Prieta 1989
5. Northridge 1994

San Andreas Fault

Summary table of plate margin activity

Type of plate margin	Description of changes	Earthquake/ volcanic activity	Examples
1 Destructive margins a) Subduction zones	Oceanic moves towards continental crust, but being heavier oceanic sinks and is destroyed in a deep-sea trench. Island arcs and fold mountains both with volcanoes are formed.	Violent earthquake and volcanic activity	Andes, Nazca and South American Plates. Japan Island arc, Pacific and Eurasian Plates.
b) Collision zones	Two continental crusts collide and are forced up into fold mountains.	Earthquake activity/no volcanic activity	Himalayas, Indo-Australian and Eurasian Plates.
2 Constructive margins	Two plates move away from each other. New oceanic crust created, forming mid-oceanic ridges with volcanoes.	Earthquake and gentle volcanic activity	Iceland, Eurasian and North American Plates
3 Conservative margins	Two plates move sideways past each other – land neither formed nor destroyed.	Earthquakes can be violent/no volcanic activity	San Andreas Fault (California), Pacific and North American Plates.

Where are earthquakes and volcanoes found?

Plate tectonic theory explains why earthquakes and volcanoes occur. They are the result of movements within the Earth and, in particular, of the world's plates.

The distribution of the world's main earthquakes and volcanoes is shown in maps **D** and **E**. Match each of these with the map of the world's plate margins (**C**) on page 74. What do you notice?

Earthquakes

Map **D** shows that there is a well-defined pattern to the world's earthquakes. They

- occur in narrow belts
- follow all types of plate margin
- are near volcanoes
- occur on land and at sea
- are particularly concentrated around the Pacific Ocean.

Volcanoes

Some of the world's most famous and recent volcanic eruptions, together with their distribution, are shown on map **E**. The distribution again shows a distinct pattern. They

- occur in long, narrow belts
- are found most often at destructive plate margins, especially around the Pacific Ocean – 'The Pacific Ring of Fire'
- coincide with constructive margins
- are sometimes found away from plate margins
- are found on both land and at sea
- are less frequent than earthquakes.

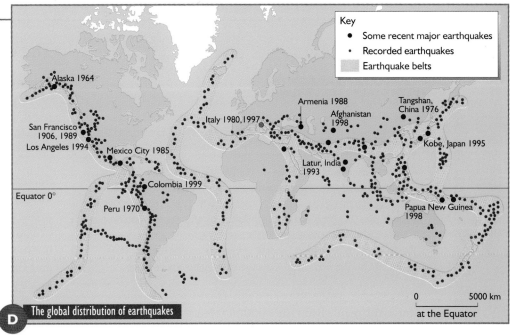

D The global distribution of earthquakes

Key
- ● Some recent major earthquakes
- • Recorded earthquakes
- Earthquake belts

0   5000 km
at the Equator

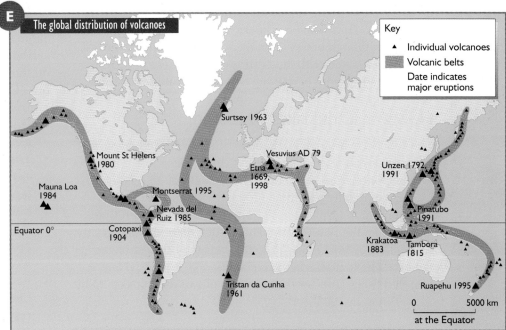

E The global distribution of volcanoes

Key
- ▲ Individual volcanoes
- Volcanic belts
- Date indicates major eruptions

0   5000 km
at the Equator

Questions

1 Copy and complete the table by :
   a) naming the two types of plate involved (oceanic or continental)
   b) giving the direction of plate movement (towards, away from or sideways past)
   c) naming an example
   d) adding any other features likely to be present. (20)
2 With the aid of a labelled diagram, explain how volcanoes are formed at constructive plate margins. (5)

Total: 25 marks

Tectonic landform	Two types of plate involved	Direction of plate movement	Example	Other features present
Island arc				
Violent earthquake				
Fold mountains				
Violent volcano				

Earthquakes

> **DEFINITIONS**
>
> An **earthquake** is a shaking or trembling of the Earth's crust. It consists of shock waves generated by a sudden movement deep within the crust. These move outwards like the ripples in a pond after a stone has been thrown in, and are responsible for the shaking of the Earth's surface.
> The source of the shock waves is known as the **focus**. The point on the Earth's surface above this is the **epicentre**.

Earthquakes result from the sudden release of pressures. In most cases this is caused by plate movements. As the plates try to move, pressure builds up until it is finally released as a sudden jerk. However, earthquakes do occur away from plate margins, although not as often or as destructively. These are usually associated with faults (lines of weakness in rocks), and can be triggered by mining activity or water extraction.

How are earthquakes measured?

The shock waves of an earthquake can be recorded on an instrument called a **seismograph**. Even the smallest tremor produces a trace on the graph. The strength of an earthquake is most commonly measured on the **Richter scale** (**A**). It is important to realize that each point on the scale is ten times greater than the point below. This means that the Mexico City earthquake of 1985 (measuring 8.1) was ten times stronger than the one that affected San Francisco in 1989 (7.1) and a hundred times stronger than the first of two earthquakes to hit Afghanistan in 1998 (6.1).

The effects of earthquakes

Primary effects These are the immediate effects caused directly by the earthquake itself. People are injured or killed and buildings and infrastructure are damaged or collapse.

Secondary effects These are the indirect effects resulting from the earthquake's primary damage. They include fires from broken gas pipes, people made homeless, businesses closing, communications failing and the psychological effects. Often these are greater than the primary effects.

Why do earthquakes affect different areas in different ways?

Table **B** shows some of the effects of selected earthquakes. The strength of the earthquake on the Richter scale is obviously important, but other factors can also be crucial:

- **Distance from the epicentre** The San Francisco earthquake was 80km away and so its effects were reduced.
- **The state of preparation for an earthquake** Areas such as California and Japan both expect tremors and have buildings and schemes to cope with them.
- **Population density** A densely peopled area such as Kobe/Osaka in Japan will be worse hit than a rural area. However, in north-east Afghanistan the remoteness of the area meant that it was difficult for the rescue services to get through and more people died as a result.
- **Type of land the area is built on** The Mexico City earthquake was made much worse by the silt, on which much of the city is built, turning to mud as the earthquake brought water to the surface – 'It wobbled like a jelly'.
- **Time of day** The Kobe earthquake was at 5.46am, so fewer people were about.
- **Time of year** It is harder to survive a winter earthquake if you are trapped or made homeless. After the Armenian earthquake of 1988 half a million homeless people suffered night-time temperatures of −20°C. Rescue services also find it more difficult to operate.

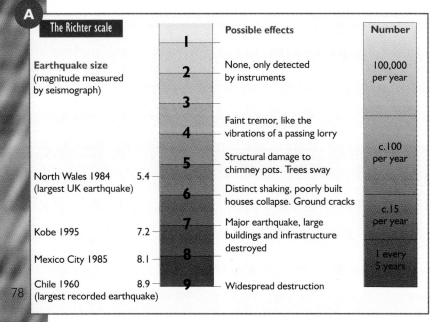

A

The Richter scale		Possible effects	Number
Earthquake size (magnitude measured by seismograph)	1 2 3	None, only detected by instruments	100,000 per year
	4	Faint tremor, like the vibrations of a passing lorry	c.100 per year
North Wales 1984 (largest UK earthquake) 5.4	5	Structural damage to chimney pots. Trees sway	
	6	Distinct shaking, poorly built houses collapse. Ground cracks	c.15 per year
Kobe 1995 7.2	7	Major earthquake, large buildings and infrastructure destroyed	
Mexico City 1985 8.1	8		1 every 5 years
Chile 1960 8.9 (largest recorded earthquake)	9	Widespread destruction	

The effects of selected earthquakes

Year	Place	Size (Richter scale)	Effects
1976	Tangshan, China	7.8	250,000 dead; 650,000 homeless
1985	Mexico City	8.1	10,000 dead; over 1,000 large buildings collapse
1989	San Francisco	7.1	62 dead; further 81 die when freeway collapses
1993	Latur, India	6.4	25,000 dead;150,000 homeless
1994	Los Angeles	6.7	57 dead; 20,000 homeless; over 100 fires
1995	Kobe, Japan	7.2	5,500 dead; 310,000 homeless
1998	NE Afghanistan (2 tremors)	6.1 / 6.9	February: 4,000 dead / June: 3,000 dead; 28 remote villages destroyed
1998	Papua New Guinea	7.0	Earthquake at sea triggers a tidal wave; 3,000 dead

C Location of Kobe

EURASIAN PLATE (continental crust)

JAPAN

Kobe

Tokyo

PACIFIC PLATE (oceanic crust moving 6.8 cm per year)

PHILIPPINE PLATE (oceanic crust)

N

0   1000 km

CASE STUDY *MEDC: The Kobe earthquake*

When did it happen? On Tuesday 17 January 1995 at 5.46am.

What happened? An earthquake measuring 7.2 on the Richter scale occurred 20km south west of Kobe. It lasted for a mere 20 seconds, but that was sufficient to result in Japan's deadliest earthquake since the Kanto earthquake killed 140,000 in 1923. The ground was moved 18cm horizontally and 12cm vertically. Hundreds of aftershocks were experienced – 616 by 8.00pm.

Where did it happen? The focus was 14km beneath the northern part of Awaji Island in Osaka Bay (**D**). Because it was so near to the surface and its epicentre so close to not only Kobe, but also the major urban areas of Kyoto and Osaka, it caused major devastation.

The area affected is in southern Japan next to the Pacific Ocean (**C**). Kobe is located on a narrow strip of land between Osaka Bay to the south east and the Rokko Mountains to the north west. The narrowness of the coastal plain at this point means that it serves a crucial role as a transport corridor, which includes the bullet train, linking south-east and north-east Japan. Kobe itself is a city of 1.4 million people and a major port responsible for 30 per cent of Japan's commercial shipping.

Why did it happen? Kobe lies on the Nojima Fault, above a destructive plate margin. Here the heavier, oceanic Philippine Plate is forced under the lighter, continental Eurasian Plate (**C**). Sudden movement of the fault caused this major earthquake.

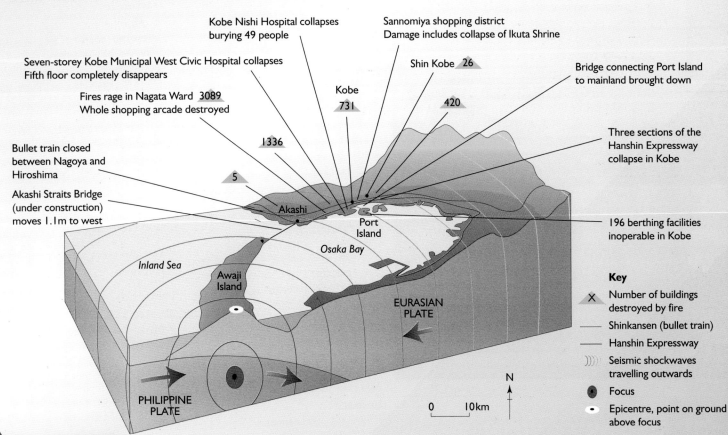

Kobe Nishi Hospital collapses burying 49 people

Sannomiya shopping district
Damage includes collapse of Ikuta Shrine

Seven-storey Kobe Municipal West Civic Hospital collapses
Fifth floor completely disappears

Shin Kobe   26

Bridge connecting Port Island to mainland brought down

Fires rage in Nagata Ward   3089
Whole shopping arcade destroyed

Kobe
731

420

Three sections of the Hanshin Expressway collapse in Kobe

Bullet train closed between Nagoya and Hiroshima

1336

5

Akashi Straits Bridge (under construction) moves 1.1m to west

Akashi

Port Island

196 berthing facilities inoperable in Kobe

Osaka Bay

Inland Sea

Awaji Island

EURASIA PLATE

PHILIPPINE PLATE

N

0   10km

Key

X Number of buildings destroyed by fire

— Shinkansen (bullet train)

— Hanshin Expressway

)))) Seismic shockwaves travelling outwards

● Focus

- Epicentre, point on ground above focus

What were the effects of Kobe?

Short-term effects

- A total of 5,477 deaths were officially attributed to the earthquake, together with 35,000 injuries.
- Nearly 172,000 houses collapsed, while numerous other buildings were also affected; 35 schools and 3 hospitals were completely destroyed.
- A further 7,500 homes were destroyed by fire which started when gas pipes fractured. Particularly affected were the closely packed wooden houses in the old city. A lack of water made fire-fighting difficult.
- At the peak of the earthquake 316,000 people were evacuated from their houses. They had to live in temporary accommodation, such as schools, parks and community centres, often with night-time temperatures as low as –2°C, and initially with a shortage of blankets, food and clean water.
- The transport network was devastated: twelve trains were derailed while a 130km section of the bullet train route had to be closed when five bridges collapsed. A 1km section of the elevated Hanshin Expressway also collapsed. On the day of the earthquake the city's traffic was grid-locked, delaying the emergency services.
- 196 berths at the ports of Kobe and Ashiya were destroyed. Exports from Kobe in January 1995 fell 46.9 per cent compared to the previous January.
- Water, gas and electricity supplies were disrupted. About one million homes were affected, while 285,000 telephone lines were also down.

F Western Kobe devastated by fires from the earthquake

Longer-term effects

- Inevitably, thousands of businesses were forced to close both in the short and long term.
- Extra jobs, however, were created in the construction and related industries.
- Overall, the estimated total cost of the damage was 10 billion yen.
- Kobe's population fell by 33,000 between January and June 1995, largely due to people moving away.

E Rescue teams search for victims

```
DIARY OF THE AFTERMATH

17 JANUARY 1995
Earthquake hits.

19 JANUARY
National government set up
emergency headquarters.

23 JANUARY
Number of homeless peaks at
316,000. More than half the
schools reopen. Electricity
supply resumes in all damaged
areas.

28 JANUARY
Final massive search for
survivors.

31 JANUARY
Eight residential districts
subjected to restrictions on
new buildings.

2 FEBRUARY
Earthquake refugees start
moving into temporary housing.

24 FEBRUARY
Kobe Steel reopens its damaged
factory.

28 FEBRUARY
Water supply fully restored.

1 MARCH
Underground shopping malls in
Kobe's popular Sannomiya
district reopen.

20 MARCH
Danger of aftershocks
subsides.

8 APRIL
Bullet train route fully
restored.

1 JULY
Bay-area part of the Hanshin
Expressway reopens.

1 AUGUST
Eastern terminal of Kobe port
reopens.

20 AUGUST
All remaining shelters for
earthquake homeless close.

23 AUGUST
Railway network is back to
normal.

1 SEPTEMBER
Japan observes Disaster
Prevention Day and rescue
drills are carried out in all
earthquake-hit areas.

14 OCTOBER
Kobe hit by a small
earthquake.

OCTOBER 1996
Hanshin Expressway fully
restored.

2005
Target year to complete the
Kobe City Recovery Plan
...earthquakes take a lot of
recovering from!
```

Can earthquakes be predicted and controlled?

Can earthquakes be predicted? So far no, or at least not with any accuracy. We know approximately where they should occur, but not when they will happen.

By studying past records of earthquakes, scientists believe it is possible to identify events that usually occur just before earthquakes. These can be used as warnings of imminent earthquakes. Such events include strange animal behaviour, changes in electrical conductivity and gas emissions from the ground, and a large number of small tremors.

Some scientists in California have suggested the 'Seismic Gap Theory'. This involves studying past seismograph records and working out the pattern of the shock waves. In this way they hope to work out the length of the gap until the pattern repeats itself, and so predict the next large earthquake.

What can be done?

Research to reduce the effects of earthquakes continues in Japan and the USA. It has included injecting liquid into faults to lubricate them and prevent the sudden jerks that cause an earthquake. However, there is little evidence so far that this works and it is generally agreed that for the moment the best thing is to learn to live with and prepare for earthquakes.

It is important to inform people living in earthquake-prone areas what to do in the event of an earthquake. This is why Japan has an annual Disaster Day on 1 September (anniversary of 1923 Kanto earthquake) and why rescue drills are practised in earthquake areas. Signs, leaflets and lessons in schools all help educate people too. In Kobe they are creating an Earthquake Memorial Park as a reminder of the danger.

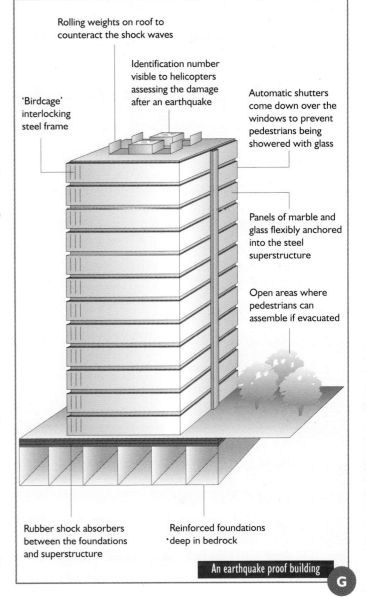

Rolling weights on roof to counteract the shock waves

Identification number visible to helicopters assessing the damage after an earthquake

'Birdcage' interlocking steel frame

Automatic shutters come down over the windows to prevent pedestrians being showered with glass

Panels of marble and glass flexibly anchored into the steel superstructure

Open areas where pedestrians can assemble if evacuated

Rubber shock absorbers between the foundations and superstructure

Reinforced foundations deep in bedrock

An earthquake proof building   **G**

Questions

1 Use a map of Japan to describe the location of Kobe.   (2)

2 The Kobe earthquake measured 7.2 on the Richter scale. What exactly does this mean?   (2)

3 Explain why an earthquake occurred at Kobe in 1995. You may use diagrams to assist your answer.   (6)

4 Why might an earthquake of similar size be far more destructive in an LEDC than in Kobe?   (6)

5 Summarize the effects of the Kobe earthquake in a table. List these, with specific detail, under two headings: 'primary effects' and 'secondary effects'.   (9)

Total: 25 marks

In San Francisco all inhabitants must have accessible emergency supplies, first aid kits and torches. Heavy items of furniture and equipment must be anchored securely to the wall or floor.

Greater action can be taken with more substantial and important buildings (**G**). Even individual homeowners will sometimes reinforce their houses with steel rods, while in San Francisco foundations must be strengthened if converting an attic to living space. More flexible gas and electricity cables can also be laid to help minimize damage in the event of an earthquake. However, this all costs money and the poorer parts of the world find it difficult to prepare for future disasters, not least because they often have more urgent priorities.

Volcanic eruptions

CASE STUDY
MEDC: Mount St Helens, 18 May 1980

Located in the sparsely populated Cascade Mountains, north-west USA (**B**), Mount St Helens, 2,950m high, was for 123 years an inactive volcano. Then, on 18 May 1980, the most powerful volcanic eruption in 60 years world-wide occurred. Volcanic activity had been building up for two months, which meant that scientists were on hand to monitor events. However, all were amazed at the scale of the eruption.

What caused the Mount St Helens eruption?

Like so many volcanic eruptions, it was caused by the rising of magma where an oceanic plate, the Juan de Fuca, descends under the continental North American Plate (diagram **A**). The resulting friction causes heat which turns the destroyed oceanic crust into magma. Over time the build up becomes so great that it forces its way to the Earth's surface.

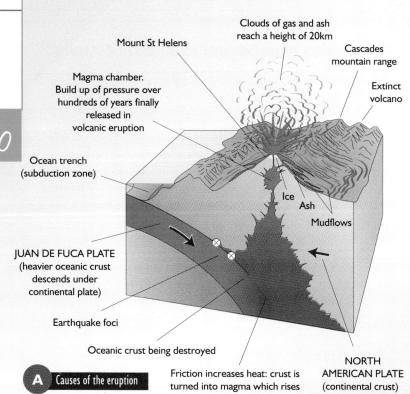

A Causes of the eruption

Build up to the eruption

20 March 1980	The volcano 'awakes' at 3.47pm with an earthquake of 4.0 on the Richter scale.
25 March	47 small earthquakes in 12 hours.
27 March	Small explosion forms a new crater 70m across.
30 March	Steam ejected.
1 April	Ground shakes – possible movement of magma and gas. Roads around volcano closed as tourists attracted by the hazard!
12 April	100m high, 2km in diameter, bulge appears on north side of volcano.
13 April– 17 May	Small-scale activity continues. Bulge grows 1.5m a day, indicating a build up of magma. Snow and ice melt on the mountain and local farm animals behave strangely.
18 May	Earthquake at 8.32am, 5.1 on the Richter scale, causes the bulge to slide forwards. A landslide of rock, ice and soil moves north at 250km/h, suddenly releasing pressure over magma. A vast explosion results sending a cloud of gas and volcanic ash (called a *nuée ardente*) into the air, devastating the area north of the volcano.
20 May	Volcanic gas cloud covers the whole continent.
By early June	Ash has blown completely around the world.

Diagram **C** shows how dramatically Mount St Helens was changed, much reduced in height and with a huge crater on one side.

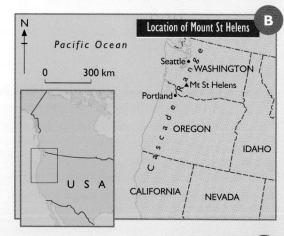

B Location of Mount St Helens

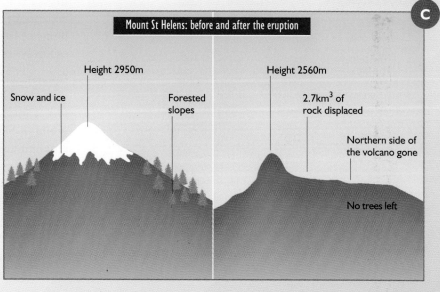

C Mount St Helens: before and after the eruption

Q Examine the satellite image of Mount St Helens at the start of this chapter (page 69).

1 Which part of map **F** is shown on the satellite image?

2 Identify the volcano, lava flows, mountain ridges, valleys and water.

D Mount St Helens

E Destruction following the eruption of Mount St Helens, 1980

Effects of the eruption on human activity

Landscape All vegetation 21km to the north of the volcano was levelled. Volcanic deposits (up to 150m deep) were left from the landslide and (up to 5m deep) from the **lava** flows.

Farming The volcanic deposits eventually increased soil fertility, but, in the short term, flooding led to losses of crops and livestock in the valleys. The ash also ruined an estimated 12 per cent of crops, especially fruit and alfalfa.

Forestry With such a large area of the forest to the north flattened, together with logging camps, the livelihood of loggers was devastated, although some ten million trees were replanted.

Communications Much sediment was deposited in the rivers and navigation on the Columbia River was disrupted. Flooding washed away road and railway bridges. Falling ash also got into the engines of cars in three US states.

Fishing Lava flows and ash clogged channels and raised water temperatures. As a result fish died and 250km of prime salmon and trout rivers were lost.

People Because of the warnings and monitoring of the volcano most people had evacuated to a safe distance. However, 63 still died, most from the poisonous gases that accompanied the eruption. Fortunately it was an area of low-density population, with only a few logging camps and tourist lodges.

Tourism Media interest both during and after the eruption attracted tourists to the area. In 1993 a tourist centre was opened at Mount St Helens attracting over one million visitors a year.

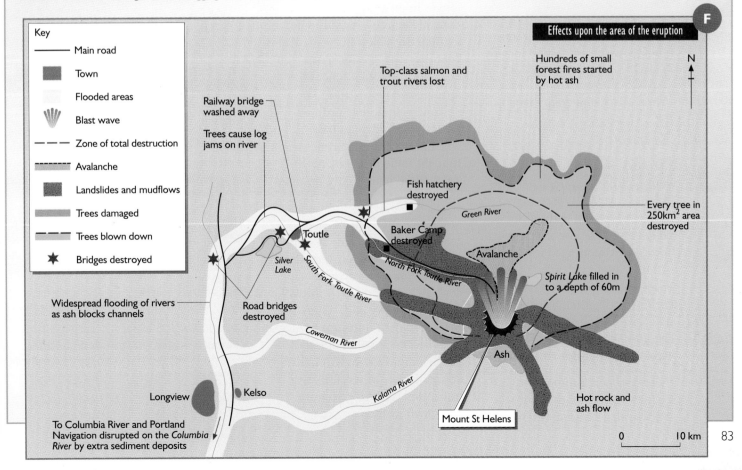

F Effects upon the area of the eruption

Key
— Main road
■ Town
▨ Flooded areas
▧ Blast wave
--- Zone of total destruction
······ Avalanche
▨ Landslides and mudflows
▨ Trees damaged
--- Trees blown down
★ Bridges destroyed

N

Top-class salmon and trout rivers lost

Hundreds of small forest fires started by hot ash

Railway bridge washed away

Trees cause log jams on river

Fish hatchery destroyed

Green River

Every tree in 250km² area destroyed

Toutle

Baker Camp destroyed

North Fork Toutle River

Avalanche

Silver Lake

South Fork Toutle River

Spirit Lake filled in to a depth of 60m

Widespread flooding of rivers as ash blocks channels

Road bridges destroyed

Coweman River

Ash

Longview

Kelso

Kalama River

Mount St Helens

Hot rock and ash flow

To Columbia River and Portland Navigation disrupted on the *Columbia River* by extra sediment deposits

0   10 km

	1	2	3	4
Margin type	Destructive	'Hot spot'	Constructive	Destructive
Volcano type	Composite	Shield	Usually shield	Composite
Eruption	Explosive	Gentle oozing	Usually gentle	Explosive
Products	Nuées, ash, lava	Lava	Lava, ash	Nuées, ash, lava
Example				
Margin/plate	Caribbean/S. American	Pacific	N. American/Eurasian	Juan de Fuca/N. American
Volcano	Soufrière, Montserrat	Mauna Loa, Hawaii	Surtsey, Iceland	Mount St Helens, USA

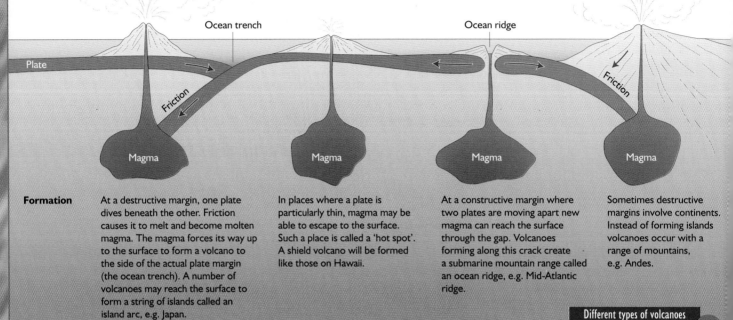

| Formation | At a destructive margin, one plate dives beneath the other. Friction causes it to melt and become molten magma. The magma forces its way up to the surface to form a volcano to the side of the actual plate margin (the ocean trench). A number of volcanoes may reach the surface to form a string of islands called an island arc, e.g. Japan. | In places where a plate is particularly thin, magma may be able to escape to the surface. Such a place is called a 'hot spot'. A shield volcano will be formed like those on Hawaii. | At a constructive margin where two plates are moving apart new magma can reach the surface through the gap. Volcanoes forming along this crack create a submarine mountain range called an ocean ridge, e.g. Mid-Atlantic ridge. | Sometimes destructive margins involve continents. Instead of forming islands volcanoes occur with a range of mountains, e.g. Andes. |

Different types of volcanoes

A

Types of volcanoes

Most volcanoes form at plate margins, because that is where there is a ready supply of magma. However, some are found well away from plate margins. These are known as **hot spots**. This is where the Earth's crust is particularly thin (**A**).

The shapes of the volcanoes and nature of the eruptions fall into two basic types. Where the magma emerging is fluid the volcano will be low and wide, with gently sloping sides. This is called a shield volcano. The eruption will be gentle. Where the magma is thick the volcano will have steeper sides and the eruption will be more violent. This is a composite volcano.

Volcanoes can also be classified by their history of eruptions. A volcano that has not erupted since records began and is no longer in an area of existing volcanic activity is said to be **extinct**. Snowdon in North Wales is an example. A **dormant** volcano is one that has not erupted for a long time. Those volcanoes that have erupted recently are called **active** volcanoes. Mount St Helens was thought to be dormant until 1980 when it suddenly became active after 123 years!

Volcanoes produce a variety of material. All produce lava flows, which, depending on how liquid they are, move away from the central cone. Most will throw ash into the sky and, where the blast is violent, produce a *nuée ardente*, the glowing cloud of gas, dust and steam (**C**). Lahars are mudflows of volcanic ash lubricated by water from snowmelt or heavy rain.

Q Using **A**, at what sort of plate margin are all the volcanic eruptions in **B** found? Why? (Map **E**, page 77 will help you.)

B

Details of major volcanic eruptions

Volcanic eruption	Year of eruption	Consequences
Vesuvius, Italy	AD 79	City of Pompeii destroyed
Mount Etna, Italy	1669	20,000 killed
Tambora, Indonesia	1815	Crops failed, causing famine and killing 80,000
Krakatoa, Indonesia	1883	Volcano caused tidal waves killing 36,000; global summer temperatures down 0.5°C following year
Mount St Helens, USA	1980	63 killed: every tree in a 250 sq km area destroyed
Nevada del Ruiz, Columbia	1985	25,000 killed; Volcano Disaster Assistance Programme created
Mount Pinatubo, Philippines	1991	350 killed; 500,000 evacuated after 2 months' monitoring
Mount Unzen, Japan	1991	38 killed

Can the volcanic hazard be predicted?

Volcanic eruptions are not rare. There are on average 60 a year. Careful monitoring enables scientists to predict likely eruptions and to arrange for people to be evacuated. The main warning signs are:

- **Earthquakes** Before an eruption there is usually a marked increase in the number and strength of tremors as the magma rises through the Earth's crust. The foci of these tremors also rise towards the surface.
- **Ground changes** The movement of magma underground also deforms the volcano surface. Before an eruption, bulging of a volcano is common, as is the opening up of cracks. Lasers are used to measure changes, while fixed tiltmeters measure any change in tilt of the slope. Radar images from satellites can also penetrate vegetation and measure surface changes accurately.
- **Ground temperatures** These too can be measured by satellite and may change as the magma rises in the volcano and lava flows appear. As a result snow and ice melt on some volcanoes.
- **Environmental changes** Magma movement underground can trigger changing gas emissions, with the amount of sulphur, chlorine and water vapour varying in the weeks prior to an eruption. Animals also often behave strangely.
- **Past volcanic history** Geological studies of previous volcanic deposits, together with historical records, can provide many clues to future eruptions.

C — Mauna Loa, Hawaii

D — Volcanologist takes samples at Mount Pinatubo, 1991

Q Using page 82, what warning signs were there of the Mount St Helens eruption?

E — Farming on the fertile slopes of Mount Etna, Sicily

Are there any benefits?

- Some countries such as Iceland have used the hot water and steam for **geothermal energy**. Hot springs can also lead to resort towns being created.
- Volcanic soils weather to become very fertile soils, which are excellent for intensive farming, as on the slopes of Mount Etna in **E**.
- The more adventurous traveller is keen to see volcanic sites, bringing in valuable revenue. When Mount Ruapehu in New Zealand erupted in 1995, 'volcano tours' were arranged within weeks of the eruption, including a 70-minute flight within 3km of the active crater.
- Volcanic rocks make good building stone, On a larger scale whole islands, such as Japan and Iceland, and much extra land is created from volcanic eruptions.

Questions

1 Use the world map **E** of volcanoes (page 77) and **B** (page 84) to describe the global distribution of volcanoes. (5)

2 Why are Italy and Iceland prone to volcanic activity? (2)

3 Briefly explain how volcanoes are formed at:
   a) destructive plate margins
   b) constructive plate margins
   c) 'hot spots'. (3 x 3)

4 What was the effect of the Mount St Helens volcanic eruption on:
   a) human activity
   b) the surrounding area? (9)

Total: 25 marks

Tropical storms

Tropical storms are intensive, low pressure weather systems known in different parts of the world as **hurricanes**, **cyclones**, **typhoons** or **willy-willies** (**B**). They are summer storms and found in low latitudes.

Hurricane Bonnie photographed from a space shuttle, 1998

A

What is the tropical storm hazard?

Tropical storms have three major effects: very strong winds; torrential rain; **storm surges**. Together, these can cause loss of life, considerable damage and severe economic impacts. They represent a major hazard.

Strong winds can in extreme cases exceed 250km/hr and often reach 160km/hr. These can flatten whole neighbourhoods, especially where housing is not very substantial. Trees are uprooted and man-made poles whisked away with their electricity lines. Anything not securely attached to the ground is at risk. The shanty towns of Santa Domingo in the Dominican Republic were destroyed by Hurricane Georges in 1998. It also destroyed 90 per cent of the country's agricultural crops, while in the USA 80,000 people were evacuated from affluent Florida Keys.

Torrential rain (up to 250mm a day) often follows. This can cause flooding as rivers overflow. The floods may also leave contaminated water increasing the risk of disease. A further risk is landslides from the heavy rain. In Honduras in1998, 10,000 died as **flash floods** swept away people and their makeshift housing as a result of Hurricane Mitch.

Storm surges are thought to cause 90 per cent of deaths resulting from tropical storms. They are a

rapid rise of sea level caused by the hurricane winds 'pushing' sea water on to the coast. If this coincides with a period of high tide, catastrophic coastal flooding can result. In Bangladesh's 1970 cyclone, 225,000 people and 280,000 cattle were drowned after a storm surge, 7m above normal high tide, swept across 26,000 sq km of the country.

How are tropical storms formed?

Tropical storms possess vast amounts of energy, derived from heat and moisture. They form:

- over warm tropical seas with a temperature of over 27°C
- in late summer/early autumn when sea temperatures are highest
- over vast areas of deep water
- in the Trade Winds belt, north and south of the Equator.

Their formation is not fully understood, but it involves the transfer of energy on a huge scale. Very moist, warm air rises rapidly from the surface of the sea (**C**). On meeting colder air high in the atmosphere it condenses to form clouds. If the surface of the sea

B

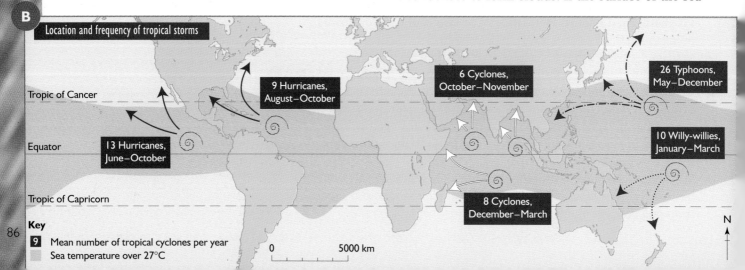

Location and frequency of tropical storms

Tropic of Cancer

9 Hurricanes, August–October

6 Cyclones, October–November

26 Typhoons, May–December

Equator

13 Hurricanes, June–October

10 Willy-willies, January–March

Tropic of Capricorn

8 Cyclones, December–March

Key

9 Mean number of tropical cyclones per year
Sea temperature over 27°C

0   5000 km

N

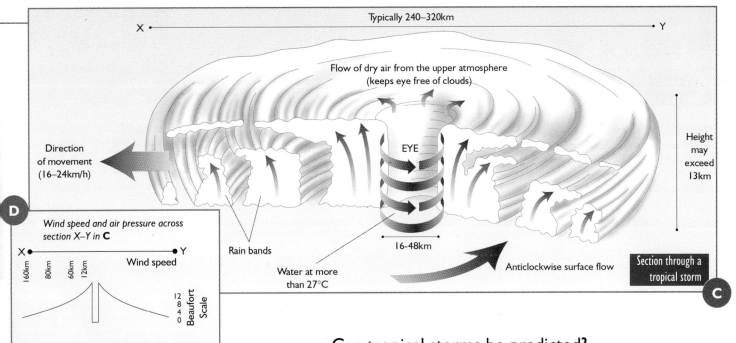

Typically 240–320km

X • ← → • Y

Flow of dry air from the upper atmosphere
(keeps eye free of clouds)

Direction
of movement
(16–24km/h)

EYE

Height
may
exceed
13km

Rain bands

16–48km

Water at more
than 27°C

Anticlockwise surface flow

Section through a tropical storm

C

D

Wind speed and air pressure across section X–Y in C

X • ← → • Y

160km 80km 60km 12km

Wind speed

12
8
4
0
Beaufort Scale

Air pressure

Pressure decreasing

is warm enough, the upward movement sucks in more warm air that evaporates more water and the storm builds. The more this happens the larger the source of energy and the longer the life of the storm. Strong winds are released by the process. These spiral violently upwards, driven by the rotation of the Earth. They are thrown outwards from the centre of the storm. In the centre develops an area of calm – higher temperatures and no cloud – known as the **eye** (**A**). **D** shows the contrast between the eye and the rest of the storm. The strong Trade Winds drive the storm across the globe from east to west. They lose their energy when they reach land or move into higher, cooler latitudes and the heat and moisture supply disappears.

Can tropical storms be predicted?

As technology improves, greater knowledge of tropical storms is gained. A specially adapted aeroplane is in use in the USA to fly through tropical storms as they form. This collects information to help predict the path of the storm. Satellite images (**A**), and advances in weather forecasting and interpretation also mean better prediction of the speed and path of storms. Yet it is still impossible to forecast them accurately. What is more, many of the areas that are affected by tropical storms are poorer LEDCs, which are often without the technology or money to have such forecasting systems.

Rather than improving forecasting, most progress has been made in improving precautions for tropical storms. Early warning systems, evacuation schemes, improved coastal defences, better trained emergency services and reinforced buildings all help reduce the storm effects. Yet once again there is a huge gap between the provision made by rich and poor countries. Hurricane Georges in 1998 hit both south-east USA and the Dominican Republic. For the USA the hurricane was regarded as a temporary inconvenience, which insurance and compensation payments would soon put right, but for the Dominican Republic it was a devastating disaster which will take years for the economy and individuals to recover from.

Q

1 On a copy of **C**, use diagram **D** to help you label:
   a) places of relatively high and low wind speeds
   b) a place of calm
   c) the point of most rapid drop of pressure.

2 Use the text to improve the annotation of your copy of diagram **C**.

E

Categories of tropical storm					
Storm type	**Central pressure** (millibars)	**Wind speed** (km/hr)	**Storm surge** (metres)	**Typical damage**	**Example/location/ damage**
Tropical depression		<55			
Tropical storm		55-119	<1.2		
Hurricane Category 1	>980	120–149	1.2–1.6	Minimal	Allison (1995), Florida/ minimal
Category 2	965–979	150–179	1.7–2.5	Moderate	Bob (1991), New England/ US $1.5 billion
Category 3	945–964	180–209	2.6–3.8	Extensive	Alicia (1983), Texas/ US $2.4 billion
Category 4	920–944	210–249	3.9–5.5	Extreme	Andrew (1992), Florida/ US $25 billion
Category 5	<920	>250	>5.5	Catastrophic	Camille (1969), Gulf Coast/ US $5.2 billion

Source: *Geographical Magazine*, October 1995

How do tropical storms affect people?

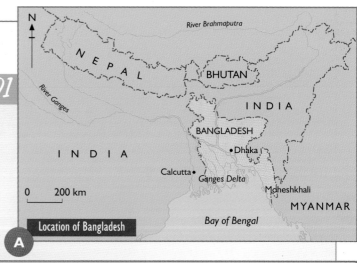

A Location of Bangladesh

In late April 1991 a tropical cyclone hit the east coast of Bangladesh (**A**). The worst hit areas included the exposed, flat offshore islands, such as Moheshkhali, and the delta of the Ganges and Brahmaputra rivers. 140,000 people died. Yet this was not a new experience for Bangladesh. 1970 had seen the most devastating cyclone in their history – 'Gorkie'. It killed over 225,000. Another in 1985 saw 40,000 die. Tropical storms are experienced each year, but why does Bangladesh suffer in particular?

- Bangladesh lies to the north of the Bay of Bengal (**A**) where cyclones are funnelled between the land masses of India and Myanmar.
- Bangladesh is adjacent to tropical seas with temperatures often above 27°C providing the heat and moisture to drive the cyclone.
- Most of Bangladesh is low-lying with 70 per cent of the total land area less than one metre above sea level. Not only does this mean that storm surges easily flood the land, there are also few higher areas to which escape can be made.
- Storm surges, as shown in diagram **B**, easily breach the earth embankments acting as coastal defences. There is little money available for protection of what will often be flimsy housing, yet densely populated land.
- Local people, many without telephones and televisions, may receive little or no advance warning of cyclones.

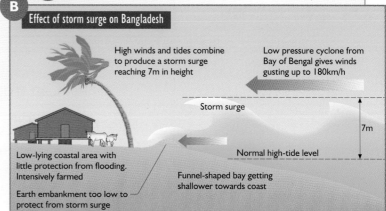

B Effect of storm surge on Bangladesh

High winds and tides combine to produce a storm surge reaching 7m in height

Low pressure cyclone from Bay of Bengal gives winds gusting up to 180km/h

Storm surge

Normal high-tide level

7m

Low-lying coastal area with little protection from flooding. Intensively farmed

Earth embankment too low to protect from storm surge

Funnel-shaped bay getting shallower towards coast

Effects of the cyclone

The newspaper article **C** shows how the 1991 cyclone affected one family. On the island of Moheshkhali winds reached 225km/hr and produced a 7m storm surge. The embankment was swept away, as were whole villages and many personal possessions.

- 12,000 died and 28,000 people were injured just on this island. One boy, called Amin, lost his mother and six brothers and sisters in the storm.
- Food shortages followed, as crops and food supplies were washed away and 48,000 cattle died.
- Farms were ruined.
- Many fishing boats were damaged too, badly affecting another source of food and employment. (The storm surge however did bring a vast quantity of fish – one person caught £500 worth of prawns the next day!)
- Clean water supplies were contaminated and diseases such as dysentery and cholera followed.

The cyclone hit the island at high tide. It was 11.00 pm, when it was dark, making the effects worse. In addition, no special significance was given to the warnings. The third red flag was raised, a sign to go to the special cyclone shelters, but many ignored this – they are used to cyclones and had not experienced a bad one here since 1970. The six shelters were not enough for all the people anyway. In total the economic damage was estimated at £60 million.

C

Cyclone devastation

ACHIYA AND AYUB ALI and their five daughters live in Nilkamal, Bangladesh. Like thousands of poor families living on the coast they are always threatened by floods and cyclones.

Achiya arrived in Nilkamal as Ayub's bride in 1968 – just two years before a major cyclone. Then in April 1991 came another, which was even more devastating. Thousands of people were killed. Countless others lost their homes and jobs. Children were separated from their parents.

The cyclone brought devastation to a region where it is hard to make a living at the best of times. Increasing land erosion means more and more farmers are losing their farmland. As fields disappear farm workers lose their jobs and are forced to find other ways of feeding their families. That is what happened to Ayub. For ten years he has struggled to earn enough by casual labouring jobs, and driving a rickshaw. However, Ayub and Achiya were among the lucky ones in that they and their daughters survived the terrible cyclone.

How? Ayub had heard that the cyclone was coming, and he remembered what 1970 had been like. So at 10pm that night, as the wind grew, he took his wife and daughters to the village school. Unlike their own house, which he knew could never stand up to high winds and waves, the school has strong concrete pillars. Then Ayub tied all six of them by the wrists and bound them to the sturdy pillars so that the wind would not carry them off. Ayub then went off to watch the tide. At last, at five in the morning, it started to go down. The danger was past, and Ayub hurried to untie his family and return home. A dreadful sight awaited them. The family's home was crushed and their possessions lay in thick mud. The straw and bamboo walls had collapsed and the roof lay on the ground. Worse still, Ayub's rickshaw, the only source of income they had, was lying on its side in the mud totally wrecked. Not that any of their neighbours would be able to afford rickshaw rides now. Not for a long time!

Can people be protected from cyclones?

Since 1991 there has been a massive programme of cyclone protection measures to protect Moheshkhali and its population.

Earth embankments These have been strengthened and new ones constructed (similar to the one constructed at Dhaka in **D**), so that they now surround the whole island.

Cyclone shelters 70 new ones have been built, paid for by overseas aid at a cost of £80,000 each. These huge structures are on stilts, so they will be above floodwaters, and are built to withstand strong winds.

Tree-planting programmes Mangrove trees have been planted along the shoreline (**E**). These are able to survive in shallow, salty sea water. They absorb part of the power of the storm surge waves. They also stabilize shifting silt and so protect the embankments. On land, trees have also been planted around buildings and roads to protect them and break up the power of the wind.

Community activities People are encouraged to take part in community activities (e.g. literacy

classes) in the cyclone shelters. This is to get people, especially women, used to the shelters (in the past some strict religious groups have been reluctant to let their women mix with men). The activities include education about the cyclone risk and what can be done to reduce their impact.

Will this be enough to protect this LEDC from future devastation? Or will it merely delay the inevitable?

The Dhaka embankment

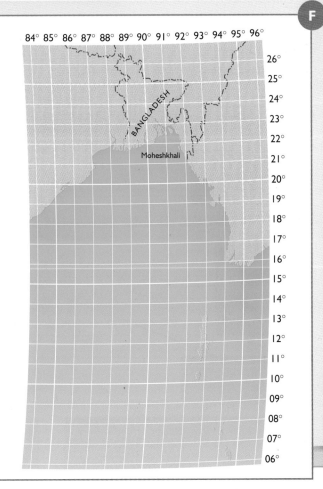
Mangroves planted along the shoreline

Questions

The cyclone began to form over the Bay of Bengal on 25 April 1991. The path of the storm was monitored by satellite over the next four days until the cyclone hit land on the night of 29 April. Details for the position of the eye of the storm are given in the table.

Date	Time	Position
25.4.91	09.00	89 00°E, 08 00°N
26.4.91	18.00	87 30°E, 09 50°N
27.4.91	24.00	87 30°E, 12 40°N
28.4.91	12.00	87 40°E, 13 50°N
28.4.91	24.00	88 20°E, 15 40°N
29.4.91	09.00	89 00°E, 17 00°N
29.4.91	16.00	90 00°E, 18 50°N
29.4.91	24.00	91 40°E, 20 40°N

1 On a copy of map **F**:
  a) plot the path of the cyclone, using the longitude and latitude coordinates given in the table
  b) add labels to show:
    • the time and date for each position
    • the start and end of the cyclone
    • any other information. (6)
2 Explain why the 1991 cyclone occurred and why it was so destructive. (9)
3 Draw up a table to show the 'short-term' and 'long-term' effects' of the 1991 cyclone. Include specific detail in your answers where possible. (10)

Total: 25 marks

River floods

A **flood** occurs when water overflows onto land not normally covered by water following a rise in water levels.

Floods are one of the most common and costly of natural hazards, causing death and widespread damage. 1998 was a particularly bad year with record flood levels in Bangladesh and China. In the UK flooding was much worse than usual along the Rivers Wye, Severn, Avon and Nene.

What causes flooding?

Some floods are caused by sea water (e.g. storm surges), but here our focus is on river floods, for which there are many different causes (**A**). Many are natural causes resulting from relatively 'extreme' climatic conditions (e.g. heavy rainfall), but increasingly people's activities are contributing to floods, often through mismanagement of their surroundings.

A Causes of river floods

- **Heavy rainfall** In 1952, in Lynmouth, Devon, 228mm fell in 24 hours. The entire main street was washed away and 34 people died.
- **Saturated ground** means that there is more surface run-off. This also contributed to the Lynmouth flood where it had rained heavily for two weeks.
- **Rapid snowmelt** In many mountain areas of the world a spring thaw causes flooding, e.g. the Alps and the River Rhône.
- **Deposition of silt** causes a rise in river-bed level and a reduction in channel capacity. This is happening in the Ganges Delta, Bangladesh (**B**).
- **Dam failure** In 1928 the St Francis Dam, California, collapsed killing 500 people.
- **Deforestation** in Nepal contributes to the flooding of the River Ganges by increasing surface run-off and soil erosion (**B**).
- **People build impermeable concrete and tarmac surfaces** in the river basin, increasing surface run-off and decreasing lag time.

CASE STUDY Bangladesh

Floods are commonplace in Bangladesh. However, the flood in July to September 1998 was regarded as the 'worst in living memory' (**D**). Bangladesh suffers particularly because 70 per cent of the country is less than one metre above sea level, and 80 per cent is floodplain. It is part of the largest delta in the world formed by the merging of three rivers – the Ganges, Brahmaputra and the smaller Meghna. During the annual **monsoons**, which bring torrential rain, these rivers burst their banks and flood the land. As diagram **B** illustrates the flooding is made much worse by humans.

However, these floods are also vital to Bangladesh's economic well being. Floodwater:
- provides nutrients that help renew fish stocks and improve soil fertility
- provides water for irrigation
- deposits silt that creates new land upon which many of them precariously live.

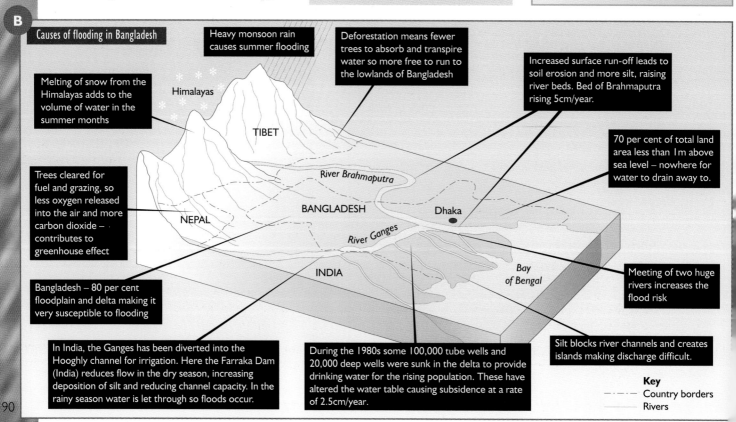

B

Causes of flooding in Bangladesh

Heavy monsoon rain causes summer flooding

Deforestation means fewer trees to absorb and transpire water so more free to run to the lowlands of Bangladesh

Increased surface run-off leads to soil erosion and more silt, raising river beds. Bed of Brahmaputra rising 5cm/year.

Melting of snow from the Himalayas adds to the volume of water in the summer months

Himalayas

TIBET

70 per cent of total land area less than 1m above sea level – nowhere for water to drain away to.

Trees cleared for fuel and grazing, so less oxygen released into the air and more carbon dioxide – contributes to greenhouse effect

River Brahmaputra

BANGLADESH   Dhaka

NEPAL

River Ganges

Bangladesh – 80 per cent floodplain and delta making it very susceptible to flooding

INDIA

Bay of Bengal

Meeting of two huge rivers increases the flood risk

In India, the Ganges has been diverted into the Hooghly channel for irrigation. Here the Farraka Dam (India) reduces flow in the dry season, increasing deposition of silt and reducing channel capacity. In the rainy season water is let through so floods occur.

During the 1980s some 100,000 tube wells and 20,000 deep wells were sunk in the delta to provide drinking water for the rising population. These have altered the water table causing subsidence at a rate of 2.5cm/year.

Silt blocks river channels and creates islands making discharge difficult.

Key
- – - – - Country borders
- ———— Rivers

Bangladesh climate

	J	F	M	A	M	J	J	A	S	O	N	D
Temperature (°C)	22	24	28	32	32	30	29	30	30	29	25	24
Rainfall (mm)	10	25	40	50	140	290	320	330	250	120	40	5

D Dhaka in flood, 1998

Q

1 Use the figures in **C** to draw a climate graph for Bangladesh.

2 Annotate the graph to show how both the rainfall and temperature figures contribute to flooding.

3 Explain how the monsoon, deforestation and dam building contribute to flooding in Bangladesh.

FACT FILE
The 1998 flood disaster

- The flooding lasted from July to September with the Ganges reaching its highest levels ever.
- 66% of the land area was underwater.
- 30 million were made homeless.
- 1,070 died, from drowning, snake bites and diarrhoea.
- Dhaka, the capital, was 2m underwater and almost completely cut off.
- Water and electricity in Dhaka was cut off and the sewerage system collapsed.
- Flood water contaminated fresh water supplies, leading to cholera, diarrhoea and dysentery.
- The entire annual stock of rice was destroyed.
- 668,529ha of crops were badly damaged (rice, jute, sugar cane and vegetables).
- 130,000 cattle were killed.
- 400 factories had to close and more than a thousand schools were destroyed.
- Communications were hit. Over 11,000km of road were damaged. Many road and rail bridges were swept away, all making the distribution of emergency food and drugs difficult.
- The disaster would have been much worse but for the flood embankments already there.

Flood prevention

Can the people of Bangladesh be protected from floods, as in many parts of the developed world? Or must they continue to 'live with floods'? Several measures have been introduced.

Levées Since 1947, 7,500km of flood embankments or levées have been built so that the rivers can hold more water before flooding.

Improved flood services The flood warning system, rescue services and flood shelters have been improved.

Re-afforestation has been undertaken in the Himalayas. In Nepal there is a project to plant fruit trees so that the land is more productive, while the trees prevent run-off into the rivers.

FAP In 1990 a long-term solution, the Flood Action Plan (FAP), was started. This is a joint venture between the government and international aid agencies, funded by the World Bank, to tackle the flooding problem in 26 regional planning areas.

International organizations ActionAid has concentrated upon providing schools, loans and employment, so that people living in the delta are in a stronger position to withstand the effects of the floods.

Difficulties with flood protection in Bangladesh

Poor international cooperation 92 per cent of the catchment area of Bangladesh's rivers is outside the country, so that Bangladesh depends upon other countries upstream. In the past there has been poor co-operation with India and Nepal because of political differences.

Cost The FAP construction costs were estimated at £1 billion over 30 years and the annual maintenance costs at about £100 million! Bangladesh is one of the poorest countries in the world and the interest payments alone would be a major problem.

Corruption Many Bangladeshis believe that officials have helped themselves to government money that should have been used for flood prevention. It is alleged that an embankment to protect Dhaka was not built due to this.

Different priorities The government has given a higher priority to investment in improving exports and services. This means that there is less money for repairing and building new flood protection schemes.

Size of problem With a rapidly growing population (forecast to double by 2030) and so much of the country to protect is it really possible to solve it?

Generally, developed countries benefit from a much greater level of flood protection than LEDCs such as Bangladesh. Nevertheless, large-scale floods, such as along the Mississippi (1993) and the Rhine (1995), do still occur. Losses of human life are relatively few, but the level of economic disruption can be great.

The Rhine is Europe's busiest river. It is 1320km long. Map **A** shows its course rising in the Swiss Alps from melting snow and passing through Switzerland, Germany, France and the Netherlands (where it is called the Waal) before entering the North Sea. The Rhine Basin includes a population of 40 million from 9 countries and some of the world's most important industrial and agricultural areas. Because of its importance, considerable flood protection has taken place – it is a 'controlled river' passing through a highly urbanized area with a high density of population.

In late January/early February 1995, the Rhine suffered catastrophic flooding. **A** shows the worst-affected areas. Disruption was greatest in the Netherlands where 75 per cent of the land is below sea level. 250,000 had to be evacuated as there were signs that the dykes were crumbling. The floods caused 27 deaths, disrupted drinking water and power supplies, telephones and roads. The estimated cost of flood damage in Germany alone was £640 million, without including indirect costs to the economy.

Causes

A natural phenomenon?

It is normal for rivers to flood and natural processes play a prominent role. The Rhine was no exception. Heavy rainfall (Switzerland had three-and-a-half times its average rain in January) meant that soils were saturated. This, combined with unusually mild temperatures that melted snow in the Alps, produced far too much water with which the basin could cope. Groundwater stores were also high as winter rain in the Rhine basin had increased by 40 per cent since 1900, following average temperature rises of 1° to 1.5°C.

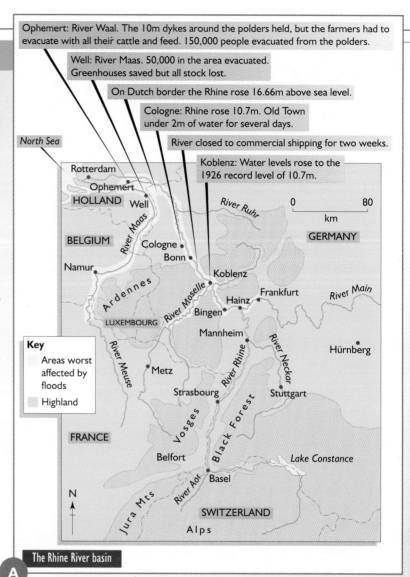

Ophemert: River Waal. The 10m dykes around the polders held, but the farmers had to evacuate with all their cattle and feed. 150,000 people evacuated from the polders.

Well: River Maas. 50,000 in the area evacuated. Greenhouses saved but all stock lost.

On Dutch border the Rhine rose 16.66m above sea level.

Cologne: Rhine rose 10.7m. Old Town under 2m of water for several days.

River closed to commercial shipping for two weeks.

Koblenz: Water levels rose to the 1926 record level of 10.7m.

The Rhine River basin **A**

Flooded Dutch motorway due to the Rhine floods of 1995 **B**

Or caused by humans?

Human actions made the problem of flooding much worse.

- **Building** Three times more land in Germany is built up than in 1900. This means the spread of impermeable man-made surfaces has increased the speed with which run-off enters the river channels.

- **Farming techniques** are more intensive, compacting soils and leading to more open land. Soils therefore store less water and surface run-off increases.

- **Clearing of vegetation** The damage by acid rain in the Black Forest, trees cleared for development and farmers cutting out hedges mean less vegetation to soak up water.

- **Channel changes** To reduce journey times for barges, the Rhine has been straightened and is now 50km shorter. Deepening and canalizing has also taken place. Together they speed up flow so that a flood surge takes two to three days, as opposed to five, to move downstream.

- **Embankments** (dykes) have been built closing off former floodplains. This creates a faster and deeper river flow. It has also led to more building on former floodplains as people think they are free of flood-risk.

How can people be protected from floods?

C shows a variety of approaches to flood protection. Note how some of them actually contributed to the 1995 floods by moving water more rapidly downstream to the Netherlands. Along the Rhine four main methods have followed the 1995 floods.

1 **Behavioural** At Well, in the Netherlands (**A**), the impact of the floods was reduced by heeding the flood warnings. Furniture was moved upstairs and carpets taken up, and, when the time came, 50,000 people were evacuated to reduce risk.

2 **Embankments (dykes)** These enable the river to hold more water. The Dutch have improved or built 600km of dykes since 1995. Most are simple earth dykes of sand and soil; some are protected by stone; others are reinforced with steel so that they can be taller and thinner. Construction work has involved demolishing houses and scarring the landscape, but they have been designed to withstand the worst floods for the next 1200 years! The total cost of the Dutch flood protection scheme was over £1,000 million.

3 **Retention basins** At Strasbourg (**A**), they have built an overflow basin for diverting some of the Rhine's water when the river is dangerously high. This reduces flow in the Rhine for ten to twelve hours and gives time for the water levels to drop naturally. There is an international plan to build sufficient retention basins to reduce river levels by 60cm. However, progress is slow because of opposition to building them from private landowners and national objections, such as 'why should the French build basins designed to help north German cities hundreds of miles away?'

4 **Artificial floodplains** In the Netherlands there is little room for retention basins. It is the most densely populated country in Europe. Instead they have built dykes back from the rivers and created forelands – areas that can flood giving the river more space (**D**). Such areas can be used for grazing animals or for recreational pursuits when not flooded, but they have meant arable farmers have lost land.

Methods of flood protection

Behavioural

Accepting the loss Nothing is done. This is especially common in the Third World.

Public relief funds After a flood a disaster fund is often set up. Following the Lynmouth flood for example, money was sent from all over the world. At the end of the first week £151,000 had been donated and when the fund closed in the summer of 1953 over £1,300,000 had been collected.

Flood insurance It is now possible in certain areas to insure property against flood damage.

Flood forecasting and warnings In areas with a history of flooding river gauges are used to forecast floods and warnings are given to the public via the media, sirens or police loudhailers.

Structural

Reservoirs These can be built in the upper courses of rivers to store water, so preventing sudden floods. The Clywedog reservoir in Wales has reduced flooding along much of the River Severn.

Channel enlargement Rivers can be deepened and widened, so that they are able to hold more water before they overflow.

Embankments Many towns are protected by concrete or brick embankments, which may be 2 or 3m high on either side of the river. They are common as they are relatively cheap to build.

Flood relief channels Artificial channels can be built around a town to take away excess water and prevent flooding.

Barrages Dams or barrages can be built across rivers (for example, the Thames barrier) but they are expensive.

Floodplain zoning Planning authorities can prohibit certain land uses in flood-prone areas.

Improving channel efficiency By dredging U-shaped channels, removing vegetation and straightening corners and bends.

Source: *Geographical Magazine Analysis*, January 1990

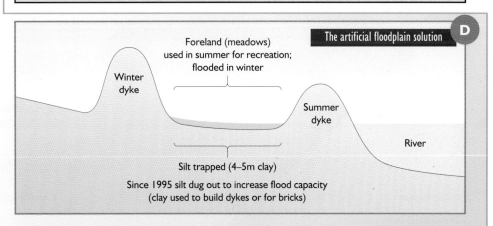

D The artificial floodplain solution

Foreland (meadows) used in summer for recreation; flooded in winter

Winter dyke

Summer dyke

River

Silt trapped (4–5m clay)

Since 1995 silt dug out to increase flood capacity (clay used to build dykes or for bricks)

The real difficulty in the Rhine Basin is co-ordinating a policy across national borders and finding solutions that balance the needs of different groups of people. Whatever is done, however, it must not be forgotten that flooding is mostly controlled by nature, and that people can only reduce the hazard to a limited degree.

Q

1 Why did the Netherlands suffer the worst effects of the Rhine floods?

2 Describe and explain the steps which are being taken to reduce flooding along the River Rhine.

How can environments best be managed?

River Yangtze in flood, August 1991

Flooding on the Yangtze

Flooding is nothing new to China. The world's worst ever flood occurred there in 1887 when the Huang He (Yellow River) burst its banks drowning 900,000 people and washing away 2 million homes. However, it is the flooding of the Yangtze River that has caused most problems to China. This is the world's third longest river at 5,600km. Its valley is home to 400 million people. It floods annually, but in 1931, 1934 and 1954 they were particularly catastrophic. Altogether over 300,000 have died from its floods in the twentieth century. However, the magnitude of the annual flooding seems to expand each year. The floods of the 1990s set new records (**A**). 1998 saw water levels surpass those of the 1954 flood.

Most of the flooding takes place in the lower Yangtze, downstream of a 190km picturesque, narrow, steep-sided section known as the Three Gorges (**D**). Here the world's largest dam is being built in a mainly rural area.

The 1998 flood

The Yangtze floods of 1998 lasted for two months (July and August). The monsoon rains, lasting a month longer than usual, and 'El Niño' (see chapter 1, page 54) were blamed for the floods. A staggering 240 million people (20 per cent of China's population) were affected and over 2,000 lives lost. At one point the river was 45m high. New dykes enabled the river to hold more water. These were deliberately destroyed, diverting water to the countryside, to save Wuhan, the capital of Hubei province (**B**). It is the region's largest industrial and trading centre. In places flood defences were 'swept away like sand castles' indicating the need for much greater flood protection against future flooding. It is to stop floods like this that the Three Gorges Dam project was proposed as long ago as 1919. The dam was started in 1994 (**B**).

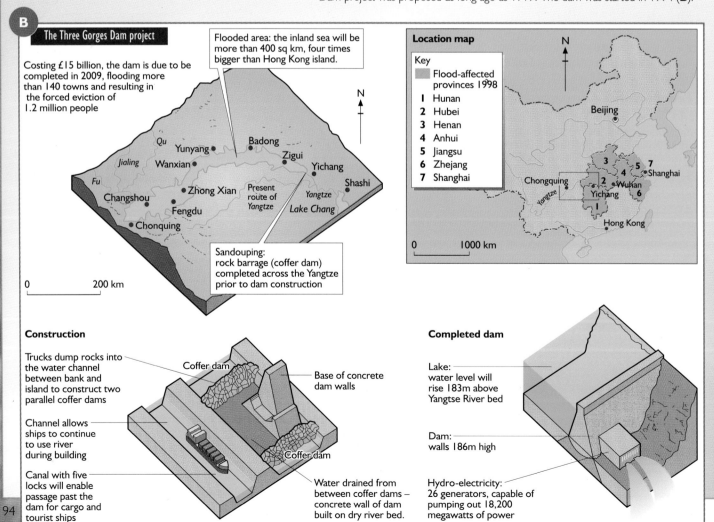

B

The Three Gorges Dam project

Costing £15 billion, the dam is due to be completed in 2009, flooding more than 140 towns and resulting in the forced eviction of 1.2 million people

Flooded area: the inland sea will be more than 400 sq km, four times bigger than Hong Kong island.

Qu Yunyang • Badong
Jialing Wanxian • Zigui
Fu • Zhong Xian Yichang
Changshou • Present Shashi
• Fengdu route of *Yangtze*
• Chonquing *Yangtze* Lake Chang

0   200 km

Sandouping: rock barrage (coffer dam) completed across the Yangtze prior to dam construction

Location map

Key
- Flood-affected provinces 1998
1 Hunan
2 Hubei
3 Henan
4 Anhui
5 Jiangsu
6 Zhejiang
7 Shanghai

Beijing
3 5 7
4 • Shanghai
Chongquing 2 • Wuhan
Yangtze Yichang 6
1

Hong Kong

0   1000 km

Construction

Trucks dump rocks into the water channel between bank and island to construct two parallel coffer dams

Coffer dam

Base of concrete dam walls

Channel allows ships to continue to use river during building

Coffer dam

Canal with five locks will enable passage past the dam for cargo and tourist ships

Water drained from between coffer dams – concrete wall of dam built on dry river bed.

Completed dam

Lake: water level will rise 183m above Yangtse River bed

Dam: walls 186m high

Hydro-electricity: 26 generators, capable of pumping out 18,200 megawatts of power

Why is there conflict over the Three Gorges Dam?

C

The Three Gorges Dam solution

For the scheme

- It will protect 50 million people and millions of hectares of farmland from flooding, thus raising grain and oil seed production.
- It will generate over 10 per cent of China's power with 'clean' HEP, replacing some polluting coal-fired power stations.
- It will store water for irrigation.
- The Yangtze will be navigable by 10,000 tonne ships as far as the inland port of Chongquing (**B**), quintupling the volume of shipping.
- Yichang, just below the dam site (**B**), has become a boomtown, with a new international airport and rapid economic growth.
- It is a sign of China's economic development – a symbol of modernization.

Against the scheme

- It will flood an area the size of Singapore and submerge 13 cities, 140 towns and 4,500 villages.
- 1.2 million people and 1,600 factories will be relocated.
- The landscape will be changed forever, drowning the famous Three Gorges scenery (**D**).
- 7,000ha of forest will be lost and there are fears that the river's fragile ecosystem will be disturbed and the biodiversity reduced downstream.
- The reservoir is expected to trap huge amounts of human and industrial waste.
- 28,400ha of farmland will be lost and farmers below the dam will be deprived of an estimated 530 million tonnes of silt.
- There are worries about sedimentation and the dam's location in an earthquake region.

The Three Gorges Dam is the biggest building site in the world and will be the world's largest dam when completed around 2009. Although it will undoubtedly control flooding, it is an extreme solution to the hazard. There are, of course, other benefits (**C**). However, **C** also reveals that great doubts exist about the project. The cost of the dam is put at £15 billion (and rising), but what about its long-term economic, social and environmental costs? China is a communist country though and the scope for political protest is limited. The changes will be colossal, and all to tame a river.

D The Three Gorges, before work started on the dam

Decision making exercise

Use information from pages 90-95, as well as your own resources, to help you answer this question.

Choose **three** of the five options. For **each** one you choose:

a) explain its advantages and disadvantages

b) state, with reasons, a group of people or organization that might be in favour of it.

(7, 7, 6)
Total: 20 marks

Here are five options on how to reduce the impact of flooding:

Option 1 Devise a small-scale scheme to improve people's behaviour when reacting to flooding (as illustrated on page 93, **C**, point 1). Make no structural improvements.

Option 2 Improve and build new embankments (as in Bangladesh, the Netherlands and China).

Option 3 Plan an international scheme where the flood prevention measures are in a different country to where they will be effective (as on the Rhine).

Option 4 Change the land use on the floodplain to uses that can exist despite occasional flooding (as on the forelands of the Netherlands).

Option 5 Build a large structure, such as a major dam (as in China).

Drought

What is drought?

A drought, in meteorological terms, is a continuous or lengthy period without a significant amount of rain recorded. The precise definition varies with the climate of the region.

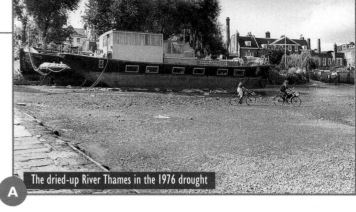

A The dried-up River Thames in the 1976 drought

DEFINITION

In the UK, an **official drought** is defined as a period of at least 15 consecutive days without more than 0.2mm of rain. A **partial drought** is a spell of at least 29 days, some of which may experience slight rain, but during which the average daily rainfall does not exceed 0.2mm.

In areas where a dry season is a usual feature of the climate, such as over much of Africa, it is defined as a period of two years or more with below average rainfall.

Factors affecting drought

A drought is a serious matter wherever it occurs in the world, but the severity of the effects will vary according to:

- temperature – affects evaporation and demand
- previous rainfall – affects the amount of water in ground and surface stores
- run-off rates – determines what water reaches stores or is quickly lost from the system
- wealth – may determine how well people cope with drought
- population (number of people) – affects the amount of water needed
- land use – affects how much water is needed, i.e. urban or rural; farming or industry?

Q

1 What is the difference between the definition of a drought in the UK and of a drought in Africa?

2 Show how **each** of the **six** factors above affects the extent to which drought causes hardship at a particular location. Give examples where possible.

How does drought affect MEDCs?

Drought in developed countries may seem fairly severe at the time, but compared to those in developing countries they are no more than a 'dry spell'. On average, south-east England experiences a drought once a year, but compared to the hardships of a drought in Africa, where it can cause mass starvation and large-scale migration, the effects are relatively small. They include:

- Falling river levels, as with the Thames in 1976 when the UK suffered its worst drought on record (**A**).

- Reduced water supply. Both ground and surface stores were affected in 1976 (**B**).

- Hosepipe bans, affecting gardeners and the washing of cars. In bad droughts, rationing or standpipes in the street are introduced.

- Damage to houses, which can subside if clay soils dry out and shrink, disturbing the foundations.

- Increased fire-risk, both in forests and on grassland.

- Reduced crop yields, increasing food prices if farming is badly hit as crops and grass stop growing.

- Reduced water supply for industry, which depends on water for cooling and processing.

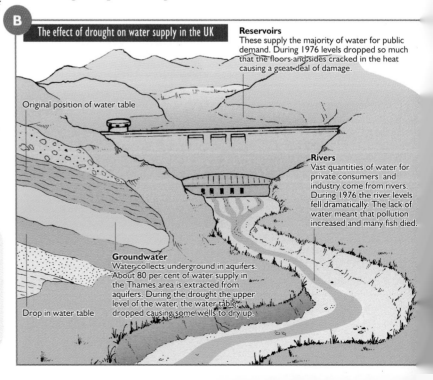

B The effect of drought on water supply in the UK

Reservoirs
These supply the majority of water for public demand. During 1976 levels dropped so much that the floors and sides cracked in the heat causing a great deal of damage.

Original position of water table

Rivers
Vast quantities of water for private consumers and industry come from rivers. During 1976 the river levels fell dramatically. The lack of water meant that pollution increased and many fish died.

Groundwater
Water collects underground in aquifers. About 80 per cent of water supply in the Thames area is extracted from aquifers. During the drought the upper level of the water, the water table, dropped causing some wells to dry up.

Drop in water table

In 1998 there was a five-month drought in Texas. This reached a climax in late July/early August. For 29 consecutive days temperatures were well above 100°F (38°C) (**C**), making the problem worse. The elderly and sick were most at risk – 150 died. Forty illegal immigrants from Mexico also died. Hospitals were under great pressure and sporting activities restricted. Fires broke out and sales of bottled water rapidly increased.

Causes

A lack of rain, combined with high temperatures, is usually the cause of drought. The Texas drought was no different after five months without significant rain and a dry winter. The heatwave that then hit southern USA (**C**), with maximum daily temperatures of 102-105°F (39-41°C) recorded at both Dallas and Houston, caused rapid evaporation of surface water and drying out of the ground. Reservoirs lost vast amounts of water. The drought was made worse by the rapid rise in demand for water, both in the home and by industry, over recent decades. Water wastage and leaks did not help. The US Vice-President, Al Gore, suggested that global warming (chapter 1, page 55) may have contributed to the unusually high temperatures.

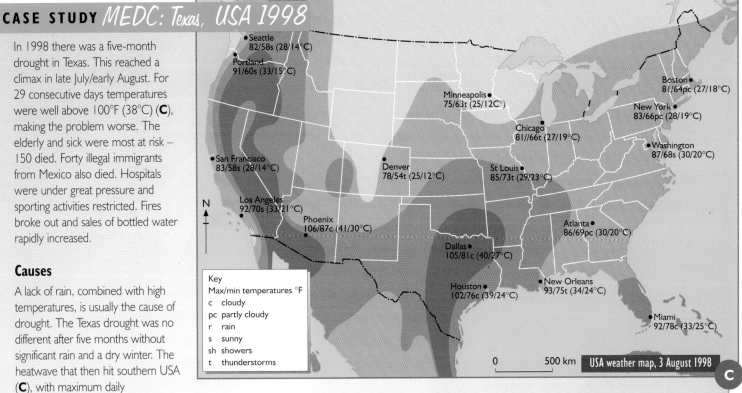

Key
Max/min temperatures °F
c   cloudy
pc partly cloudy
r   rain
s   sunny
sh showers
t   thunderstorms

0   500 km   USA weather map, 3 August 1998   **C**

Coping with drought

Drought cannot be prevented, but its effects can be reduced. Users can be encouraged to conserve water by reducing demand so that existing supplies last longer. Water restrictions, such as banning washing of cars, filling private swimming pools and watering gardens, all help. In Dallas charities issued free fans to cope with the heat, while some workers switched to night shifts and children were kept indoors.

In the longer term, drought can be prepared for by increasing water supply and decreasing demand. New reservoirs and the transfer of water from areas of excess water to those with a shortage can all help, but at a price. The question is can we afford to prepare in this way for events that occur only rarely?

1 If you experienced a drought, how could you save water where you live? Think of **five** ways.

2 **D** gives some newspaper headlines about the July 1989 UK drought. Use these, and the information in the text, to list **five** groups who benefit, and **five** who do not, from drought. Give brief reasons for each choice.

D

Cyclist dies after road lines melt

A cyclist who died when he rode into the path of a van may have thought he had the right of way after heat melted the tarmac, wiping out road markings.

Ice cream consumption is going at a remarkable lick

Price of bread and beer likely to rise

IF the heatwave is driving you to drink, make the most of it, for the chances are the price of beer will be going up, partly because barley and other cereal crops are suffering from the prolonged hot, dry weather. The price of bread may also rise, perhaps by 2p for a standard loaf.

Water crisis for 500,000 homes because of drought

ABOUT 500,000 homes in south-east London and north Kent are without water or are experiencing very low pressure, Thames Water said yesterday.

Medical tips for people most at risk

THE HEATWAVE should pose no risk to most people, but precautions should be taken by the old, the very young, the obese and those with serious illnesses such as heart or kidney disease.

Those taking diuretics (water pills) prescribed for high blood pressure, may have to take care. Dehydration and heat exhaustion may result from the loss of fluid and salt due to excessive sweating. This is prevented by making good the loss of both.

BUBBLING AWAY IN BUXTON

THE weather, combined with scares about the purity of tap water, has brought booming business to one of Britain's best known spa towns.

The Buxton Mineral Water Company was due to close for a fortnight next week for its annual staff holiday. That has been cancelled and the bottling factory has been put on continuous 24-hour working to cope with the surge in demand. The water, which comes from St Ann's Spring in the centre of the elegant Derbyshire town, is being bottled at the rate of nearly a million gallons a week but demand is still exceeding supply.

"It's incredible," says the plant manager, Nick Dege. "Six months ago we didn't think we'd have to work any overtime. Now I don't see how we'll cope without a 36-hour day."

Source: *The Daily Telegraph*, July 1989

How does drought affect LEDCs?

CASE STUDY *The Sahel*

One of the most vulnerable areas in the world to drought is the Sahel (**A**). Meaning literally 'edge of desert', this is a narrow belt of semi-arid land south of the Sahara Desert. It extends across Africa between latitudes 13°N and 17°N.

Causes of drought disasters

Drought in the Sahel occurs when the normal short rainy season is delayed or postponed. This happens when the Inter Tropical Convergence Zone (ITCZ) (chapter 1, page 50) cannot follow its normal northerly migration pattern (**B**). This prevents south-westerly winds from the South Atlantic bringing the annual rain. Higher sea temperatures south of West Africa since the 1960s are thought to be partly responsible. The loss of much vegetation in the Sahel has made this worse by increasing the *albedo* effect (reflectivity of the land). More water vapour is lost from the system reducing the potential for rain.

Human activity has cleared the vegetation for firewood, shelter and farming. People's activities have clearly made the drought situation worse. Population pressure and poor farming practices, such as overgrazing, have caused the deserts to spread – **desertification**. It is a vicious circle for the increase in desert makes the climate drier and so increases the drought risk, and so on.

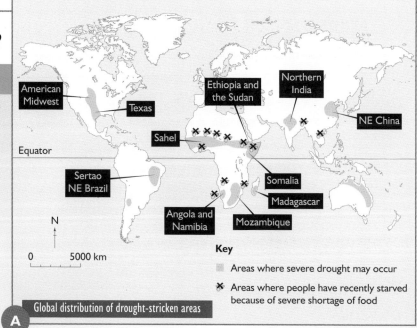

Key

🔲 Areas where severe drought may occur

✖ Areas where people have recently starved because of severe shortage of food

A Global distribution of drought-stricken areas

Effects

The fact file shows some of the effects of drought in the Sahel. You will also have seen pictures of the starving and dying on the television news. Diagram **C** shows other effects. People were forced to migrate south to wetter areas or towards refugee camps where water and food were available, as wells dried up, rivers failed to flood or the land was stripped of fodder. In 1973, 25 per cent of all cattle perished in the Sahel. In 1974, the drought caused 200,000 people in Niger to be totally dependent upon food aid. In 1983, bush fires destroyed 65 per cent of all crops on the Ivory Coast. Deserts have continued to spread as a result of the droughts.

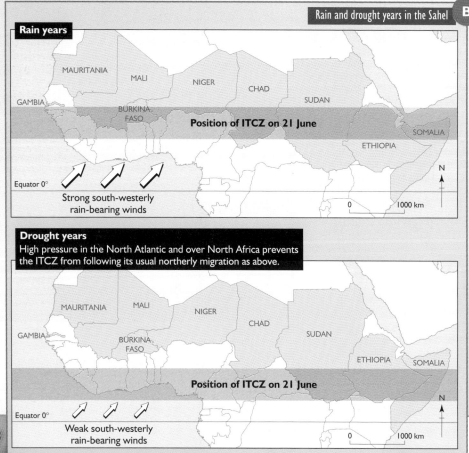

B Rain and drought years in the Sahel

```
FACT  FILE
Climate: dry with short rainy
season (July–Sept.)

Average annual precipitation:
250–500mm

Average daily temperature:
28–30°C

Population: doubling every
20–30 years

Agriculture: subsistence
agriculture and nomadic
pastoralists

Drought: continuing since 1968

● 1973–74: drought killed
  100,000 in Sahel

● 1983: 5 million in
  Ethiopia suffered from
  drought

● 1984–91: Sudan experienced
  three major droughts and
  famines

● 1991: Sahel rains failed
  again, leaving 4.28
  million facing starvation

● 1998: problem returns to
  Sudan.
```

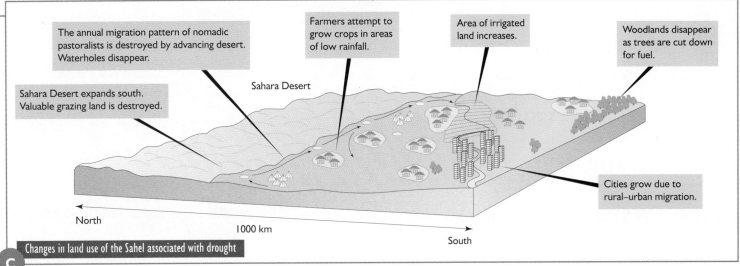

The annual migration pattern of nomadic pastoralists is destroyed by advancing desert. Waterholes disappear.

Farmers attempt to grow crops in areas of low rainfall.

Area of irrigated land increases.

Woodlands disappear as trees are cut down for fuel.

Sahara Desert expands south. Valuable grazing land is destroyed.

Sahara Desert

Cities grow due to rural–urban migration.

North

1000 km

South

C Changes in land use of the Sahel associated with drought

Can drought be controlled?

Are there any solutions? There are three strategies for reducing the impact of drought:

1 Reduce the causes of drought

Global conferences seek to reduce **deforestation**, pollutants and to understand climatic change. However, until more is known about the global system and causes of drought, it is all too easy for governments to avoid doing much.

2 Cope with drought

- Improve methods of prediction. Early warning systems, such as satellites, can observe vegetation changes and help people prepare for droughts.
- Provide food aid to help prevent effects such as starvation and migration developing. Changes in government policy have occurred to target aid at small-scale farmers.
- Improve water supply and irrigation by building large-scale water reservoirs, in places such as Senegal, and deeper wells.

3 Live with drought

- Improve farming methods. The AGRHYMET programme seeks to improve agriculture, hydrology and meteorology at a local level. Established by the World Meteorological Organization in Niamey, Niger, it trains locals to improve farming methods and drought response. Water harvesting is one such scheme. Small stone walls (**D**) are built across the slope to prevent the loss of surface water and soil. Drought-resistant crops, such as millet and sorghums, have become more widespread.
- Stop desertification. Mauritania is one of the countries to start a tree-planting programme to try and stop desertification.

Much progress has been made. However, there remain many obstacles to a solution. Population growth continues to outstrip better food production; civil wars stop aid getting through and themselves cause migrations; inappropriate high-tech solutions have at times been expensive and have not really benefited the people in most need. Then there is the sheer scale of the problem: 30 per cent of the world is at risk from this most devastating of hazards. Is there a solution?

D Building stone walls in Burkina Faso to trap water and soil, an example of a small-scale solution

E Starving boys eating soup at a relief centre

Questions

1 Use map **A** to describe the global distribution of drought. (5)

2 Make a list of natural causes that contribute to droughts in the Sahel. (5)

3 Diagram **C** shows changes in land use associated with drought in the Sahel. Choose **four** of these changes and, for each of these, explain how drought might have caused the change. (9)

4 How does drought affect people in LEDCs differently to those in MEDCs? (6)

Total: 25 marks

Fire

How do people's activities cause fires?

Large fires can be a major hazard, and have an enormous impact on the communities affected, particularly where they burn out of control. Some recent examples are shown in **A**.

In 1997 the worst hit countries were Indonesia, Brazil, Papua New Guinea, Colombia, Peru, Tanzania, Kenya, Australia, China and Russia. In Europe, France, Greece, Italy, Portugal and Spain lost large areas of scarce temperate forest.

Some fires, such as the Indonesian forest fires of 1997, have an international impact. Their smoke created air pollution that severely disrupted life in nearby Malaysia, Singapore and Thailand.

Fire, however, is a hazard that is not necessarily a *natural* hazard. Many fires are started deliberately as part of a controlled system of farming or land management (**D**). **B** shows some of the main causes of fire. Naturally occurring fire is likely only in areas where there is a long, dry period or where lightning is common. Not surprisingly therefore, most major fires are found in the hotter and drier parts of the world. Semi-arid, savanna and forest areas (with a distinct dry season) are most prone.

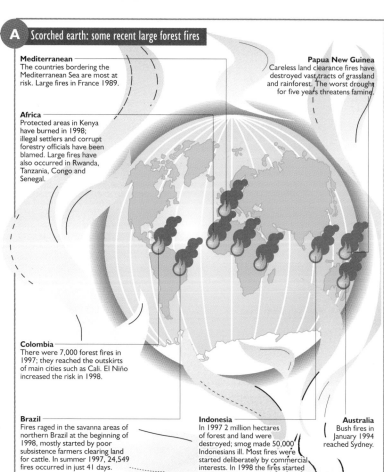

A Scorched earth: some recent large forest fires

Mediterranean
The countries bordering the Mediterranean Sea are most at risk. Large fires in France 1989.

Papua New Guinea
Careless land clearance fires have destroyed vast tracts of grassland and rainforest. The worst drought for five years threatens famine.

Africa
Protected areas in Kenya have burned in 1998; illegal settlers and corrupt forestry officials have been blamed. Large fires have also occurred in Rwanda, Tanzania, Congo and Senegal.

Colombia
There were 7,000 forest fires in 1997; they reached the outskirts of main cities such as Cali. El Niño increased the risk in 1998.

Brazil
Fires raged in the savanna areas of northern Brazil at the beginning of 1998, mostly started by poor subsistence farmers clearing land for cattle. In summer 1997, 24,549 fires occurred in just 41 days.

Indonesia
In 1997 2 million hectares of forest and land were destroyed; smog made 50,000 Indonesians ill. Most fires were started deliberately by commercial interests. In 1998 the fires started up again after the rains had gone.

Australia
Bush fires in January 1994 reached Sydney.

Q

1 Make a list of causes of forest and bush fires. Indicate next to each, whether it is a 'natural' or 'man-made' cause.

2 Are most fires due to 'natural' or 'man-made' causes?

B Forest fires: how they start

Drought
Not a direct cause, but the number of fires peak in drought or very dry years.

Drainage
Even wetlands (including peat) become susceptible after drainage.

Climate change
The El Niño phenomenon can cause drought. An upsurge of warm water in the Pacific Ocean causes a change in weather patterns and delays the rainy season. Therefore, fire risk increases.

People
Arson and the careless throwing away of cigarette ends are just two ways people start fires.

Timber speculation
Deliberate forest fires are used to overcome laws about clearing timber for sale, or to create a source of damaged, and thus cheap, timber.

Selective logging
This can create artificially dry forests by opening up the canopy. Tropical moist forests are most affected.

Intense heat
Temperatures of over 40°C can cause plant litter to ignite

Artificial fire suppression
Stopping minor fires allows the build up of flammable material. This increases the likelihood of intense fires.

Lightning
With 100 strikes to Earth per second, lightning is the main natural cause of forest fire.

Land clearing
The quest for increased pasture, particularly for ranching, is a major cause of fire. The fires in Indonesia were the result of traditional 'slash and burn' agriculture during dry and windy conditions.

MEDC: Australian bush fires, January 1994

Causes

These were the result of a combination of factors:

- a very dry early summer between October and January – plant litter was dry
- intense daytime heating (over 40°C), causing litter to ignite
- lightning
- accidental littering of cigarettes
- arson.

Effects

The fires were in south-east Australia, in the area around Sydney. The worst affected area was the Royal National Park, where 98 per cent of the land was burned. Vegetation was completely destroyed, air polluted, water supplies reduced, communication lines disrupted and electricity supplies cut.

In parts of western Sydney visibility was down to 3.5km; in Gosford, to the north of the city, hundreds of people had to be evacuated from their homes; 200 houses were destroyed and four people were killed.

C Sydney, January 1994: sunset obscured by smoke from bush fires

Forest fires in Europe

The greatest risk of fires is in the countries bordering the Mediterranean, but the hazard is also found in other areas. Cannock Chase and the Malvern Hills are just two areas in the UK that quite regularly experience bracken fires.

Up to 60,000 fires a year damage an estimated 700,000 hectares of forest in Europe. Most are relatively small fires and can be controlled. It is large fires, such as those in southern France in 1989, which create considerable problems.

In Europe, natural causes are relatively insignificant in starting fires – about 5 per cent. Most fires are due to arson (32 per cent) and negligence (23 per cent). Unknown factors account for the rest.

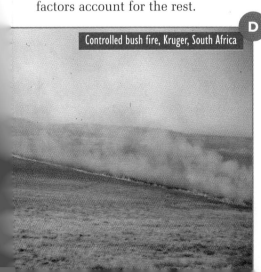

D Controlled bush fire, Kruger, South Africa

The effects of fires – environmental conflict?

- **Ecosystems** The consequences of fires can be positive. Fire creates rich soils by releasing nutrients. This is the main reason why many subsistence farmers deliberately start fires. Fire can also control many insects, parasites and fungi that are not wanted, while increased soil temperatures assist seed germination (**D**). On the other hand, fires can clear vegetation and lead to increased soil erosion.

- **Animal loss** Many orang-utans have died from the Indonesian fires in Borneo. Fires have also led to the loss of large numbers of red deer, wild boar and badgers from Mediterranean forests.

- **Cost** Large fires are expensive to deal with. Indonesia lost 75,000 hectares of tropical forest in 1998, the cost of which was estimated at £2 million. The cost includes prevention, as well as the cost of control and rehabilitation afterwards. In Brazil there is no airborne fire service and so many fires in remote areas are left to burn until the rains come.

- **Settlement** Many are forced to flee leaving their crops and animals to be destroyed, if not their settlement. In 1998 raging fires forced the Yanomami Indians of northern Brazil to retreat deeper into the forest as fires affected an area of up to 32,000 sq km.

- **Pollution** Smog and breathing difficulties often result. 50,000 had to be treated in Indonesian hospitals as a result of the 1997 fires. Airports were closed due to poor visibility.

- **Tourism** Not only do many fires reduce the scenic value of vast areas, but the publicity can also deter tourists. Thailand threatened to sue Indonesia because of lost tourist income in 1997. Tourists also rapidly left Malaysia as the smog moved in from the same fires.

Q

1 What were the effects of the Indonesian forest fires of 1997?
2 What benefits can fire bring to an area? Give named examples.
3 Is fire as serious a natural hazard as other hazards covered in this chapter?

Why live in hazardous areas?

Each year sees numerous natural hazards, many of them disasters, all around the world. They appear in the media with seemingly endless regularity and yet, despite all the dangers outlined in this chapter, people still continue to live in the very areas most likely to be affected by future natural hazards.

- It is estimated that 360 million people live on the slopes of volcanoes.
- 450 million people (40 per cent of China's vast population) live in areas at risk from flooding from the main rivers of China.

- Coastal regions now have some of the highest population densities and yet many are at risk from tropical storms, tsunamis or possibly global warming.
- Over a third of the fastest-growing cities in the world are within areas at risk from earthquakes or volcanoes.

So why do wealthy Californians continue to live and invest in areas near the San Andreas fault? Why do millions live in the disaster-prone coastal and delta areas of Bangladesh?

Scottish coast rocked by quake

AN EARTHQUAKE rocked the west coast of Scotland yesterday. Measuring 2.7 on the Richter scale, the tremor was described by experts as 'significant'.

Lisa Clarke, manager of the Argyll town's Royal Hotel, was watching television when she felt the quake.

'At first I thought it was a heavy lorry going past,' she said. 'My dog started going crazy, but it didn't make the ornaments shake or anything like that.'

Police said there were no reports of injuries or damage to property.

Glenn Ford, seismologist at the British Geological Survey in Edinburgh, said: 'There are 300 earthquakes in the UK every year, but only about 30 are felt by the public so this was significant in those terms.'

The biggest British earthquake on record – 5.4 on the Richter scale – was in North Wales in July 1984. The whole of Wales felt it and some buildings were damaged.

Newspaper extract, 1998 **A**

Reasons

No choice For many this is the main reason. They may be poor, landless inhabitants of the delta area of Bangladesh. Fishing and farming may be the only way of life that they know.

Fertile land Fire, flooding and volcanoes can each increase the fertility of soils. Many river valleys in Asia depend upon the annual flooding to provide the water and silt for their rice crops. Such areas often support high population densities.

Economic activities The hazardous area may possess precious minerals; geothermal energy generation may be possible, as in Iceland; or the hazard may be the focus for tourism, bringing valuable revenue to the local economy. Mount Etna (Sicily), one of the most active volcanoes in Europe, is a popular destination with tourists. Holiday villas, hotels, restaurants and shops have all been built around its lower slopes.

Investment Large cities, such as Los Angeles and San Francisco, have vast amounts of money already invested in them.

Risk not great enough Some areas experience hazards, but they are either not severe or frequent enough to deter habitation. **A** shows this is clearly the case for the UK for earthquakes.

Forecasting is improving Satellite monitoring has meant that hazards, such as tornadoes in the American Midwest, can be predicted and the worst effects avoided.

B Flooding is a regular problem in Worcester

Management schemes B and **C** provide examples of coping with hazards in both MEDCs and LEDCs. In Worcester, the floors of the houses are to be raised 40cm to reduce the flood-risk from once every two and a half years to every fifty years. In Bangladesh, cyclone shelters and other measures have already reduced casualties to hundreds rather than thousands.

Geographical inertia Many stay because that is where they, and perhaps their families, have always lived. It is after all often easiest to do nothing!

C A cyclone shelter and school near Cox's Bazar, Bangladesh

CASE STUDY *LEDC: Why do people continue to live on Montserrat?*

In July 1995, after nearly 400 years of being dormant, the Soufrière Hills volcano on Montserrat unexpectedly became active again. Located on a destructive plate boundary where the Atlantic and Caribbean plates meet, this British-run island forms part of an island arc in the West Indies (**E**). It is a sparsely populated LEDC.

By April 1996, most of the population of Plymouth, the capital, and the southern half of the island had been evacuated (**F**). At this stage only minor eruptions had occurred. No major volcanic activity took place until 25 June 1997. Then a large part of the dome collapsed, exploding material 9000m into the sky and sending a major *pyroclastic flow* (rivers of hot gas, ash, mud and rock) to the north east. The airport (the only one on the island) was almost reached, 19 people died, 7 villages, including Harris, and 175 homes were destroyed. August 1997 finally saw the destruction of Plymouth, the only town of any size, and the evacuation zone was extended.

Years after the start of the volcanic activity the hazard still continues. The island's population which was 11,000 is down to 4,000. Why do some still stay?

- For many this island was an 'idyllic tropical paradise' (pop stars had set up a recording studio here). Many had invested all their savings to come here.

- The weathered volcanic material formed fertile soils and, together with the hot, wet climate, is excellent for farming. Many farmers stay, hoping to return to their productive land.

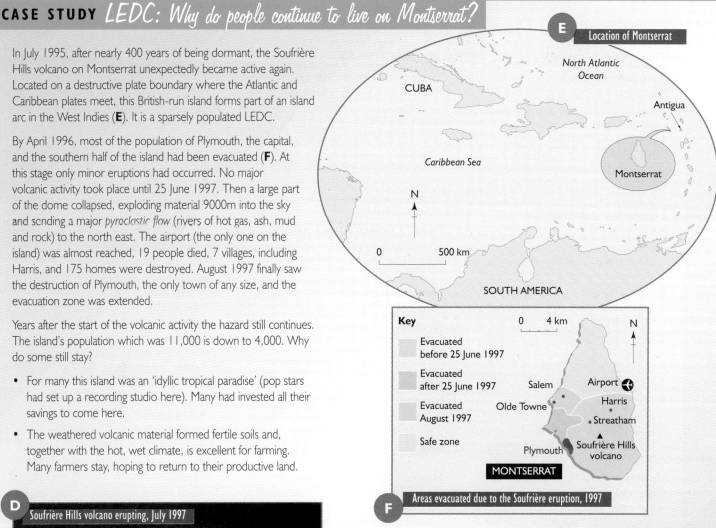

E Location of Montserrat

F Areas evacuated due to the Soufrière eruption, 1997

Key
- Evacuated before 25 June 1997
- Evacuated after 25 June 1997
- Evacuated August 1997
- Safe zone

MONTSERRAT

D Soufrière Hills volcano erupting, July 1997

- Initially, the British Government offered 'assistance packages' to encourage residents to stay and keep Montserrat economically viable.

- Many cannot afford to go. They claimed that the £2,500 offered in 1997 was insufficient to pay to relocate on nearby Antigua or to emigrate to Britain.

- Some said they were too old to move and they preferred to stay.

Even those who have relocated to other Caribbean islands say that as soon as volcanic activity has ceased they will return. Montserrat will always be 'home' to them.

Questions

1. Describe the location of Montserrat. (2)
2. Why were people originally attracted to the island? (2)
3. Use your knowledge of plate tectonics to produce an annotated diagram to show how Montserrat was formed. (6)
4. Imagine that you were living on Montserrat during the volcanic activity. Would you leave the island? Give reasons for your decision. (6)
5. Specify another natural hazard that you have studied. With reference to specific detail explain why people choose to live so close to this potential or actual danger. (9)

Total: 25 marks

GLOSSARY

Active volcano A volcano that has erupted recently.

Avalanche The sudden and rapid movement of snow and ice down steep slopes.

Collision zone Areas where two plates, both with continental crust, meet and form fold mountains.

Conservative margin A boundary between two plates moving alongside each other.

Constructive margin A boundary between two plates where new crust is created as they move away from each other.

Continental drift A theory that continents move over the surface of the Earth.

Crust The thin outer layer of the Earth.

Cyclone Tropical storm in the Indian Ocean

Deforestation The complete clearance of forested land.

Desertification The spread of desert-like conditions in arid or semi-arid areas, due to human influence or climatic change.

Destructive margin A boundary between two plates where plate is destroyed as they move together.

Dormant volcano A volcano that has not erupted for a long time but is not extinct as it may do so in the future.

Drought A lengthy period without precipitation.

Earthquake A shaking or trembling of the Earth's crust.

Epicentre The place on the Earth's surface that is directly above the centre (focus) of an earthquake.

Extinct volcano A volcano that has not erupted since records began and is no longer in an area of volcanic activity.

Eye of the storm The centre of a storm. An area of calm where air descends, around which winds rotate.

Flash flood A short-lived but rapid rise of water in a river due to heavy rainfall.

Flood A high water level in a river or on a coast that leads to the submerging of land not normally covered by water.

Focus The centre or source of an earthquake.

Gale A strong wind likely to cause damage.

Geothermal energy Heat energy from the hot rocks in the Earth's crust.

Hot spot An area of volcanic activity usually away from a plate margin.

Hurricane Tropical storms in the area around the Caribbean and Atlantic Ocean.

Island arc A chain of islands formed as the result of volcanic activity above a subduction zone.

Lava Molten rock flowing away from a volcano.

Magma Molten rock beneath the surface of the Earth which forms igneous rocks when it solidifies. Magma that reaches the surface flows out as lava.

Mantle The layer of the Earth between the crust and the core.

Mid-oceanic ridge A ridge of cooled magma on the ocean floor where two plates are moving apart.

Monsoon A seasonal wind that brings dry weather for part of the year and heavy rainfall for the rest.

Mudslide A rapid form of mass movement consisting mainly of mud and water.

Natural hazard A natural event which is perceived by people as a threat to life and property.

Ocean trench A deep trench associated with the subduction zone at the margins of two plates.

Plate The Earth's crust is made up of seven large pieces and twelve smaller ones. These are known as plates.

Plate margins The boundary between two plates.

Plate tectonics The theory that the Earth's surface is made up of a number of moving plates.

Richter scale A scale used to measure the magnitude of earthquakes.

Seismograph A machine which records and measures the Earth's tremors.

Storm surge A rapid rise of sea level caused by storm winds forcing sea water on to a coast.

Subduction zone The area where plate descends into the mantle and is destroyed.

Tectonic processes Movements within the Earth's crust.

Tornado A rapidly rotating column of air with extremely violent winds.

Tropical storm A storm at low latitudes associated with low pressure and characterized by very strong winds and heavy rainfall.

Typhoon Tropical storm in the west Pacific.

Volcano A mountain or hill through which lava, gas, steam and ash are ejected at irregular intervals.

Willy-willy Tropical storm off north-west Australia.

3

Economic systems and development

Introduction

Why study economic systems and development?

What was the last major purchase your family made – a new car, a washing machine, a computer, or a television? Have you ever stopped to think how and where this product was made? The television, for example, may be Japanese, made with components from Taiwan, assembled in Ireland and sold in the UK. This system of production, which is spread across the world, is called **globalization**. Large **multinational** firms can take advantage of cheap production and marketing costs, maximizing their profits by minimizing their costs in this way. LEDCs sometimes benefit from multinational industries, but most profits go back to the MEDCs.

An economic system brings physical, human and economic resources together to produce a marketable product. Generally, the location of economic activities depends on, for example, labour supplies, raw materials and energy. In this chapter you will learn about economic systems and factors that decide the location of economic activities.

Sometimes other factors determine the location of industries as in, for example, the tourist industry. Cheaper and quicker air transport, improved technology and marketing have determined the success or failure of many tourist destinations. Rapid growth and decline may cause widespread economic and environmental damage to host countries. In this chapter you will learn about the impact of economic change.

Few countries are able to provide all the resources they need, this leads to trade between countries. In this chapter you will learn that not all trade is fair and equal, sometimes less well off countries need more support than others. Fair trade policies can help to narrow the development gap between countries.

We are all aware of how economic development can use up valuable finite resources and damage fragile environments. In this chapter you will learn how economic development can be **sustainable**.

Questions for enquiry

To give a better understanding of economic systems and development, the following key questions will be investigated in this chapter:

- How can systems' ideas help the study of economic activity?
- Where are different economic activities located and why?
- How and why is economic activity changing?
- Why do some places experience growth while others decline?
- What are the effects of economic change on the quality of life in different places?
- What variations in levels of development exist between countries?
- How and why do living standards vary?
- What links exist between countries in terms of trade, investment, and aid?
- How can the use of resources and environments best be developed and managed?
- Can sustainable development be achieved?

Themes

The answers to these questions will be explored by examining the following economic areas:

- farming
- the iron and steel industry
- high-tech industry
- tourism
- levels of development
- trade and aid.

People and places

Economic activities involve all people in some way at every level of development. The type of economic activity in a country is linked to its level of development. With relatively cheaper and quicker transport and communication links it seems the world is shrinking and the development gap between countries is getting smaller. However, there are still marked differences in the quality of life for people in different countries and regions. By studying countries such as Brazil, Japan and Bangladesh this will become clearer.

Inequalities in economic development are also found within countries and regions. Within the EU and the UK, financial support from the government is used to try and balance out the gaps in economic development between regions. Examples of this include areas of industrial decline such as South Wales and an area such as southern Italy which has been slow to develop its economy.

Economic activities

Q

1 These photographs show different types of economic activity. Using the numbers to identify the photographs give a 'job title' for each activity.

2 Identify similar types of activities and group these together giving titles to your sections. You may find that one activity fits into more than one group.

3 Write a sentence explaining or defining an 'economic activity'.

Economic systems

Inputs	Processes	Outputs
What goes in	What goes on	What comes out

An economic system

What is a system?

This book has already looked at physical systems, such as a river basin where there are 'inputs' (energy and water), 'stores' (ground, or channel) and 'processes' (erosion) and then an 'output' of water (channel flow or evaporation). An economic system works on the same basis.

An economic system is a process where human, physical and economic resources are put into a system of production to make a saleable product. For an economic system to be successful the costs of the inputs and processes must be less than the income received from the sale of the outputs.

Closed systems

Some systems may be described as **'closed systems'**. The outputs are all put back into the system as inputs. Subsistence farming is a good example of this where the outputs in the form of food energy, seeds and manure become the inputs. Farmers grow just enough to feed themselves with little surplus for sale.

A subsistence farmer in Mozambique **A**

A closed system, e.g. subsistence farming

Inputs	Processes	Output
Labour	Planting	Food
Seed	Weeding	Seed
Animals	Harvesting	Manure
Manure	Tending stock	
Soil		
Rain		
Sunshine		

Seed, manure and food energy back into the system as inputs

Q Write a short definition of the term 'economic system'.

Open systems

Most economic systems are **'open'**. The outputs are sold and only part of the income from the sale goes to pay for the inputs and processes. The remainder goes out of the system or part of it is used to re-invest in the industry to make it more efficient.

An open system, e.g. manufacturing industry

Inputs	Processes	Outputs
What has to be paid for?	Processing	The sale of which leads to profit or loss
Raw materials	Packaging and assembly	Finished products
Labour supply/knowledge and experience	Distribution	Waste products (disposal will have to be paid for)
Energy/power		
Site		
Finance (sometimes loans that need to be repaid)		
Machinery/technology		

Profits

Income from sales used to pay for inputs and re-investment

B

Manufacturing industry

What factors affect the location of different types of economic activity?

There are three main groups of economic activity – primary, secondary and tertiary. The term **quaternary** industry is also sometimes used for activities concerned with research and development or information technology and in the control of other business enterprises. Each type of activity has particular **location factors** or a group of reasons to explain its location. The economic system works by making enough money from the sale of the finished product to pay for all the running costs. The major costs of economic systems are raw materials, transport, labour, power and water supplies, land, and the disposal of waste materials. Industries usually locate where they can keep their costs as low as possible while still ensuring a supply of their needs.

Primary industries		Examples	Location factors
Economic activities that extract natural resources directly from the sea or ground.		Coal mining Oil drilling Farming Fishing Forestry	Only located where there are natural resources, e.g. coal mining can only be where there is coal! They often influence the location of secondary industries, e.g. fruit canning. The type of farming, fishing and forestry is dependent on different physical factors such as the climate. Governments also have a major influence on the location of these primary industries, e.g. the Common Agricultural Policy.
Secondary industries			
Also called manufacturing industries. Process natural resources or make products from raw materials. These are either finished products or components used in the assembly of items such as cars, computers, etc.		Steel production from iron ore Car assembly from components Wood products from timber Food products from farmed crops	Very variable and dependent on many different facts: • Some, such as iron and steel, need to be located near a supply of bulky raw materials. • Others need a source of cheap energy, e.g. aluminium smelting needs heat. • A skilled or cheap and plentiful labour supply may be the locating force for a lot of assembly industries. • Cheap, flat land has been a major reason for large space-using industries locating on the edge of towns and reclaimed tidal flats. • Quick, accessible and cheap forms of transport are important for assembly industries. (The typical car is made up of 20,000 components made in different places.) • Governments also have control over the location of manufacturing industry by offering incentives for some areas and penalties for locating in others.
Tertiary industries			
Huge range of economic activities involved in providing a service (often called 'service industries')		Doctor Teacher Shop assistant Plumber Computer operator Entertainer Tour operator	Need to be near people and settlements. Some depend on technology to communicate with people (fax, e-mail or telephone) and can be more **footloose**, e.g. telephone banking.

Questions

1 Conduct a class survey to find out what types of economic activity there are in the local area. Ask each class member to select two people who they know who work in the local area and give their job description and the company they work for.

2 Use the information collected to draw a graph showing in which sectors of industry the people in your survey work. Write a comment on which industries employ most people locally and how important they are to the local economy. (10)

3 Select a local primary or manufacturing industry. Complete an investigation into the industry by finding out information about its system, in terms of inputs, processes and outputs; its market; its location factors. Use maps and graphs when presenting your investigation. (15)

Total: 25 marks

Primary industry: farming

What impact does farming have on the environment?

A — Natural ecosystems

C — Desertification

B — Agro-ecosystems

D — Agroforestry

Primary industries extract natural resources from the Earth or sea. Farming is a primary activity and one of the most important because it provides us with our essential supplies of food and many other raw materials. Farming takes up more land than any other human activity and has a great impact on natural environments. Soils, water, plants and other natural elements are important inputs into the farming system. Farming makes use of these natural inputs and changes natural ecosystems controlled by nature into agro-ecosystems controlled by the farmer (**A** and **B**).

Some farming systems have more impact on natural environments than others. The more commercial farming becomes, the more technology and chemicals are used. In most LEDCs less technology is used, productivity rates are lower and more people are dependent on farming for a source of food supply and employment. Overuse of the land due to growing populations and low crop yields cause major environmental problems such as **deforestation**, soil erosion and **desertification** (**C**). Where population densities are lower and ecosystems are less vulnerable, farmers can farm in a more **sustainable** way causing minimal damage to the environment. **Agroforestry** (**D**) is a sustainable type of agriculture practised in some LEDCs.

In the EU and many other MEDCs, governments are now encouraging more environmentally friendly ways of farming (see page 100).

Q

1 Study **A** and **B**. Using the headings 'Semi-natural ecosystems' and 'Agro-ecosystems' sort out the following list into two columns:

many different plant and animal species; only limited species of plants and animals; chemical nutrients used; dead plants and animals provide the nutrients; weeds and pests are a problem; no weeds or pests; plants at different stages of growth; most plants at the same stage of growth.

2 Make a sketch of **C**. Annotate the sketch to show how desertification causes long-term damage to the natural environment. Use the following list of words to help you:

soil erosion; ground cover; nutrient cycle; surface run-off; interception; soil exhaustion; exposure to strong sunlight; moisture in atmosphere. (Some of these words are in the glossary, page 162.) Add brief but detailed explanations to these labels.

3 Using **D** explain why agroforestry is a sustainable method of farming.

TYPES OF FARMING

Farming is an industry practised in practically every country in the world at different levels of development. The type of farming depends on physical, human and economic factors.

E

Farming types

Arable	Growing crops, such as sugar beet, potatoes or cereals.
Pastoral	Rearing animals such as sheep and cattle.
Mixed	Combination of crops and animals on the same farm.
Horticulture	Growing flowers, fruit and vegetables, often in climate-controlled conditions such as greenhouses.
Commercial	Farming to sell the produce. Most farmers sell most of what they grow — cash crop farming.
Subsistence	Farming just to provide a supply of food for the farmer and family. This type of farming is usually found in developing countries where people have to live off what they grow.
Sustainable	Farming that causes minimal impact on the environment by not using damaging practices.
Extensive	Either a large area farmed with limited inputs of labour and capital (e.g. hill sheep farming); or a large area with limited labour and a high investment of capital and technology (e.g. Canadian wheat farms).
Intensive	Either a small amount of land farmed by a large labour supply with limited technology and investment (e.g. rice farmers in the Ganges valley); a large amount of capital. labour and technology is used in a relatively small area as in horticulture.

G Ranching in rainforests. The growing demand for beef has led to large areas of rainforest being cleared for cattle ranching. However, as the soils rapidly lose their fertility and the grasses fail to grow, ranchers move on to clear a new plot.

Coffee plantations in Hawaii. Farmland in many tropical countries is used for plantation crops, e.g. rubber or palm oil. These are usually owned by large multinational companies such as Unilever.

H

Q

1 Using the terms from **E**, give a brief description of each type of farming shown in the photographs above.
2 Select two of the farming types in **F–H** and make a list of the ways in which the methods used may have an impact on the environment. Use some of the terms on the previous page.

Hill sheep farming in Wales. Hill farms often have poor soils and suffer high rainfall and heavy snows in winter. The land has limited value for growing crops or rich pasture. Sheep are hardy animals and can withstand the unfavourable conditions.

F

THE FARMING SYSTEM

A farmer has to weigh up all the costs and benefits before deciding which crops to grow or animals to rear. Most farmers in LEDCs have less choice and have to depend more on the physical inputs into the system. The farm system shown in **A** is similar to all economic systems: *inputs* (what goes into the system and are usually paid for) are processed (by farming activities) and come out as *outputs* (products which come out).

The 'decision makers' in the farming system may be individual farmers, large agricultural companies or government ministers. Farming is an economic activity and the costs have to be considered carefully

Farming takes up more land than any other human activity. The decision makers weigh up all the inputs available and the costs involved, then they make a decision on the most cost effective or efficient type of farming for them. However, there are always exceptions; many farmers are influenced by personal as well as economic factors.

Q

Look at the photographs on the previous page showing types of farming in different locations and read through the farm system in **A**. Using the example of the 'Hill sheep farming in Wales' (**F** on page 111), list the main physical and human factors that would have influenced the farmer's decision to keep sheep.

A

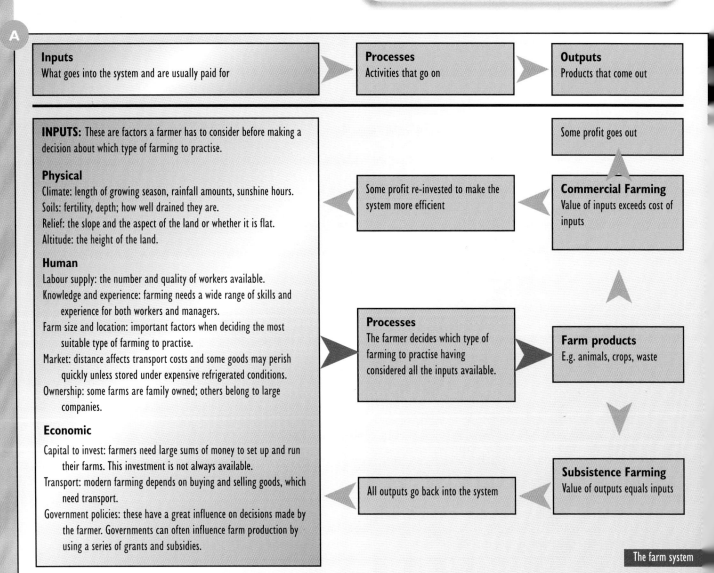

Inputs	Processes	Outputs
What goes into the system and are usually paid for	Activities that go on	Products that come out

INPUTS: These are factors a farmer has to consider before making a decision about which type of farming to practise.

Physical
Climate: length of growing season, rainfall amounts, sunshine hours.
Soils: fertility, depth; how well drained they are.
Relief: the slope and the aspect of the land or whether it is flat.
Altitude: the height of the land.

Human
Labour supply: the number and quality of workers available.
Knowledge and experience: farming needs a wide range of skills and experience for both workers and managers.
Farm size and location: important factors when deciding the most suitable type of farming to practise.
Market: distance affects transport costs and some goods may perish quickly unless stored under expensive refrigerated conditions.
Ownership: some farms are family owned; others belong to large companies.

Economic
Capital to invest: farmers need large sums of money to set up and run their farms. This investment is not always available.
Transport: modern farming depends on buying and selling goods, which need transport.
Government policies: these have a great influence on decisions made by the farmer. Governments can often influence farm production by using a series of grants and subsidies.

Some profit goes out

Some profit re-invested to make the system more efficient

Commercial Farming
Value of inputs exceeds cost of inputs

Processes
The farmer decides which type of farming to practise having considered all the inputs available.

Farm products
E.g. animals, crops, waste

All outputs go back into the system

Subsistence Farming
Value of outputs equals inputs

The farm system

Farming – a risky business?

If a farmer makes an informed decision about the options available then the business should be a success. Unfortunately, this is not always the case. In any economic activity there are factors beyond the control of the decision makers. Most types of farming are dependent on the climate – sunshine, rainfall, temperatures. Look at **C** and **D**, which show how unpredictable weather conditions can ruin farm crops.

C Farmland ruined by floods in Bangladesh

D Farmland in the UK ruined by bad weather

B

Physical

Floods: sea or river flooding caused by storms and heavy rain can wash away soils or ruin crops. Sea flooding causes soil to become saline (salty).

Droughts: long periods without rainfall dry out soils and kill plants; animals may die of thirst.

Earthquakes: ruin valuable farmland, crops and animals.

Diseases: affect both plants and animals. Farmers cannot always protect against these.

Economic

Loss of markets: competition or a change in demand for a product may cause loss of business.

Quotas: governments sometimes put a limit on the amount of certain products, such as milk, to control the market price.

New technology: introducing computer-aided farming or even basic machinery in developing countries may improve output but also increase costs and cause unemployment.

Unpredictable factors affecting the farming system

E 'Bad harvests' in MEDCs and LEDCs

Farming in more developed countries

The poverty line

Bad harvest

Why can a farmer in a developed country survive a bad harvest better than one in a less developed country?

Farming in less developed countries

The poverty line

Bad harvest

Questions

1 Arrange the following terms into a systems diagram under the headings 'Inputs', 'Processes' and 'Outputs':

   warm wet climate; rich soils; planting; fuel; machinery; cattle; silage; milking; potatoes; barley; machinery; milk; ploughing; weeding; harvesting; seeds; fertilizers; cutting; labour; finance; subsidies; manure. (5)

2 Look at the cartoon in **E**. What is it trying to show and why does this happen? (5)

3 Read the definition of 'costs and benefits'. Explain how the costs and benefits for a farmer may be affected by **each** of these unpredicted events:

   • a particularly dry summer causing drought conditions for six weeks
   • the introduction of milk quotas to limit milk production
   • extra subsidies and guaranteed prices given for barley
   • an increase in the price of oil
   • BSE causes the government to ban beef sales. (15)

   Total: 25 marks

DEFINITIONS

The **costs** are what the farmer has to pay for – usually the inputs. The **benefits** are the profits or the advantages gained – usually from the sale of the outputs.

What factors affect what is grown?

Vine House Farm is located in the Fens of East Anglia (**A**) – one of the richest arable farming areas in the UK. The soil is a mixture of peat and clay **loam** and the land is flat, low lying and well drained (**B**). The climate in this area is suited to arable farming with generally less rainfall than most of the UK and longer sunshine hours for ripening crops (**C**).

Vine House Farm belongs to Nicholas Watts and has been in the family for three generations. There have been many changes on the farm during the past fifty years mainly due to changes in transport systems, technology and government policies.

A Farming types by region in the UK

Key
- Arable
- Livestock rearing
- Dairying
- Horticulture
- Mixed farming

N

0   100   200 km

B Flat fen landscape

The farming year on Vine House Farm

January/February Maintenance of machinery and buildings. Stored crops loaded onto lorries to sell. Land drains cleared.

March Drilling/sowing of Spring crops – peas, sugar beet, potatoes (very dependent on weather).

April Planting continued. Nitrates, herbicides and fungicides added.

May All crops in ground by now. Spraying of chemicals continued. Machinery used to cultivate some crops.

June Some weed control. Grass verges trimmed. Wild oats gathered from some fields by hand. Machinery prepared for harvesting. Fungicides and pesticides applies to crops where necessary.

July Grain stores cleaned out. Spraying of crops continued. Machinery prepared for harvesting.

August Oil seed rape and early potatoes harvested. Wheat harvesting started.

September Harvesting of wheat and potatoes continued. Oil seed rape sown. Remains of harvested crop ploughed in to provide humus in the soil. Winter wheat sowing started.

October Potatoes and sugar beet harvested. Transported to processing plant. Winter wheat sowing continues.

November Sugar beet harvested. Ploughing and drilling for new crops. Herbicides applied to winter wheat.

December Ploughing and drilling finished off. Seed potatoes put into trays to start sprouting.

C

The Fens of East Anglia
Table of temperatures, rainfall and sunshine hours

	J	F	M	A	M	J	J	A	S	O	N	D
Temperature (°C)	3	4	6	8	12	15	17	16	13	10	7	4
Rainfall (mm)	45	30	30	45	45	36	60	45	50	45	40	35
Sunshine hours	1.6	2.3	3.8	4.8	6.1	6.8	6.1	5.8	4.6	3.3	1.9	1.3

Q

1 Study the map of the UK in **A**. Briefly describe where each farming type is located.

2 Draw a temperature and rainfall graph for Vine House Farm using the figures in table **C** and a separate graph for sunshine hours. Use an atlas to draw a similar graph for a weather station in the Lake District or another location in the UK where sheep farming is important.

3 Compare the graphs and explain why the different farming types are suited to the different climates.

How has the farm changed?
Vine House Farm, 1950

The farm was 118ha split into fifteen fields of approximately 7.8ha each. Nine men were employed on the farm in addition to Mr Watts' father. Four men were labourers, four were horsemen and one was a tractor driver. It was normal to have a ratio of one man to 12ha at that time. The farm had only one tractor as most of the implements were still pulled by horses. Eighty cattle were kept on the farm during the winter; this was reduced to twenty during the summer. All the farm buildings, apart from the one used to keep the farm implements in, were for housing the livestock. The animals were used to fertilize the land. Agro-chemicals were not used and farmyard manure was essential to grow good crops. Potatoes, sugar beet, wheat, peas, ley grass and oats were all grown. Some of these were marketed locally, but the potatoes were taken to South Wales or the Midlands by lorry and train.

Vine House Farm, 1998

Mr Watts now farms an extra 640ha (located on another site) in addition to the original 118ha. He employs just one man to manage the original land and seven full-time workers on the additional hectares. Casual labour is also brought in at harvest time. Potatoes require more workers than wheat. If Mr Watts only farmed cereals, he could manage the whole farm on just two or three workers. Skilled office staff, including Mr Watts' daughter, are employed for the paperwork and accounting. Fields have increased in size; there are now fewer fields.

The farm has a range of machinery including tractors that are three times as powerful as the 1950 versions. He invests a lot of the farm income back into the system by regularly changing and updating his machinery and other technology to improve efficiency and production. A large combine harvester costs £150,000 and he changes it every three years. Mr Watts now grows crops that are subsidized by the EU, such as oil seed rape and linseed. He also grows wheat, sugar beet and peas at Vine House Farm and potatoes at his other farm. Potatoes are no longer grown at Vine House Farm because the soil has become too heavy. Mr Watts rents 50ha from another farmer to grow potatoes. He stores his potatoes and waits for the best market price. There are two other buildings; these are used for storing grain. All the livestock buildings have gone. With no livestock to produce manure, chemical fertilizers are used on the land. Chemical pesticides, fungicides and herbicides are also used. All these are inorganic and if not carefully used may cause environmental problems.

Questions

1 Explain how physical factors make Vine House Farm suitable for arable farming. Table **C** and photo **B** will help you. (9)

2 Describe the changes on the farm between 1950 and 1998. Include details on the size of the farm, size of fields, numbers employed, farm buildings, soil and fertilizers. (6)

3 Using specific detail; draw a systems diagram for Vine House Farm in 1998. (10)

Total 25 marks

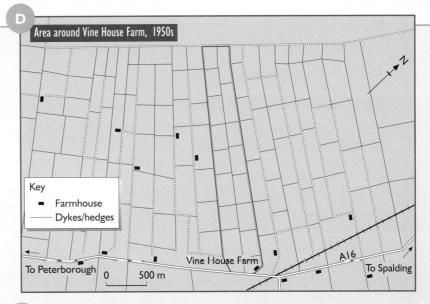

D Area around Vine House Farm, 1950s

Key
■ Farmhouse
— Dykes/hedges

To Peterborough   0   500 m   Vine House Farm   A16   To Spalding

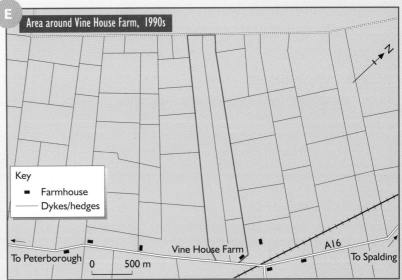

E Area around Vine House Farm, 1990s

Key
■ Farmhouse
— Dykes/hedges

To Peterborough   0   500 m   Vine House Farm   A16   To Spalding

F "Farming has become much more market led. With all the chemicals at our disposal we no longer need traditional farms with various crops and a range of animals. Farmers grow whatever will bring in the best price. Farming has become big business and there is a lot of competition. With improved transport networks the market is less localized. Many of our local food processing industries are supplied with produce from Spain and other European countries. Vegetables that we can't produce are brought in by road from Spain and France. The Channel Tunnel and new motorways have speeded things up, but roads are becoming overloaded with large lorries coming from the Continent. Farming has become a big industry. Farms are getting bigger and the small traditional farmer is being taken over by large agricultural companies. They are experts at getting maximum yields and maximum profits. This leaves less room for wildlife. Wildlife will continue to decrease on our farms unless the government gives incentives to save it. Over the years I have been careful not to fill in the dykes because this destroys habitats. I have grown crops for birds on set-aside land to keep them fed in winter. It would be better if I farmed organically, then a wider variety of plants would grow; there would be more insects and a better biodiversity. Losing the livestock and having to store all crops under cover now, instead of out in the open, has meant a further loss of food supply for wildlife."

How is EU farming changing?

The Common Agricultural Policy

Most of the changes to farming in the European Union countries are the result of the Common Agricultural Policy. This was introduced in the member countries (six of them then) in 1962.

The CAP regulates farming practices in the fifteen member countries of the European Union. It replaced all existing national agricultural policies. All EU countries use the ECU (European Currency Unit) for trading agricultural produce. Each country adjusts their own currency to the ECU. This makes trade between individual countries easier by avoiding changing currency exchange rates.

Aims

The CAP's initial aims were:

- to increase food supplies at a reasonable price to all EU members
- to make sure farmers maintained their jobs on the land and had a fair income in return.

These aims were achieved through a variety of measures including:

- increasing and guaranteeing prices for selected farm produce, e.g. wheat
- making farming more intensive (**F**) by encouraging the use of agro-chemicals such as nitrates and pesticides, and increasing technology
- using subsidies for certain crops to protect against cheaper imports.

Impacts

This brought a mixture of both positive and negative impacts to the farming environment. The initial aims were achieved:

- food supplies and jobs were secured
- farm incomes were increased
- many other indirect jobs were created in the food processing, chemical and other related industries.

However,

- food surpluses were produced (**A**)
- hedgerow loss in the UK was accelerated (**B**) as farmers enlarged their fields to take advantage of guaranteed prices
- the more intensive farming methods led to more nitrates and pesticides entering the water cycle (**C**).

CAP controls

Subsidies Farmers are given more money to grow certain crops and farm particular animals in order to increase production where there is a shortage, e.g. wheat, oil seed rape.

Grants Farmers are given extra money to help them on major projects, which would lead to an increase in production, e.g. new buildings, purchase of machinery.

Quotas The rates of production are controlled by giving farmers a set amount that they can produce. If they exceed this quota there are penalties.

A

Mountain madness!

In 1985 thousands of tonnes of beef, butter, cereals and skimmed milk were stored in 200 warehouses in Britain at the tax payers' expense. These surplus amounts were the result of over-production encouraged by subsidies paid to farmers.

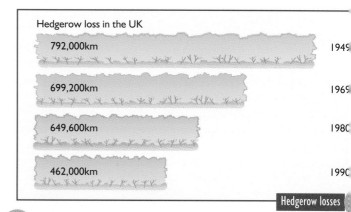

Hedgerow loss in the UK

792,000km	1949
699,200km	1969
649,600km	1980
462,000km	1990

Hedgerow losses

C

Effects of pesticides and nitrates

Changes made to the CAP

The policy is constantly being reviewed and updated. In the 1980s there was increasing pressure from farmers, environmental groups and the tax-paying public to make changes to the CAP. There were growing concerns about the environment and the expense – 70 per cent of the total EU budget was being used to support agriculture. Changes were made and included:

- a **set-aside** policy – some farmers paid not to farm the land
- cutting subsidies on cereals and beef
- supporting farmers who use fewer chemicals and plant more trees and hedgerows
- giving financial support to farmers in less favourable or **peripheral** areas
- encouraging farmers to **diversify** (e.g. setting up farm shops (**D**), golf courses (**E**)).

Q

Farm shops and golf courses are just two examples of ways in which farmers have diversified. What other methods of farm diversification are there?

In 1992 further reforms were introduced to increase the diversification of land and to encourage farmers to become 'stewards of the countryside'. Farmers were given incentives to take greater care of the natural environment and cause less environmental destruction.

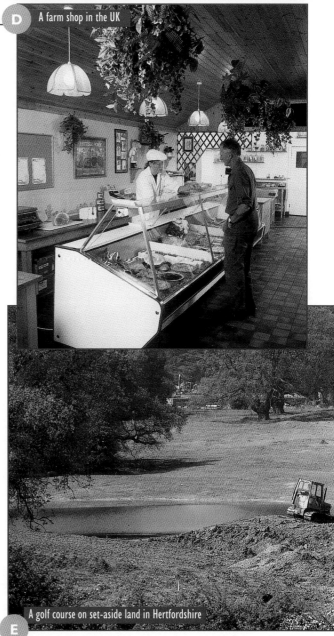

D A farm shop in the UK

E A golf course on set-aside land in Hertfordshire

F Intensive arable farm landscape in Grampian, Scotland

Q

1 Draw a sketch of **F** and annotate it fully to show the impact of the early CAP measures on the environment. Use the following descriptions to help you and add explanations of the damage they cause to the environment:

Hedgerows removed; ponds and dykes filled in; agro-chemicals used; large, heavy machinery used; one crop planted on large expanses (**monoculture**); large areas left without a crop cover.

2 Set-aside was brought in to reduce the surplus amount of food being produced and to limit further damage to natural environments. Not everyone agreed with set-aside. Why do you think it would be unpopular with some people? List your reasons.

How and why is Japanese farming changing?

CASE STUDY *MEDC: Japan*

There has been rapid industrial growth in Japan since World War II and in the 1990s Japan overtook the USA as the richest country in the world. The farming industry has had to compete with a growing manufacturing industry for space and workers.

- **Competition for space** Only one-fifth of Japan is suitable for farming – 80 per cent of the country is made up of high land (**A**). Other large space users of flat land such as manufacturing industry can often be a far more profitable use of land.

- **Loss of workers** Farming is traditionally a family-based industry with children working alongside grandparents. Japanese farms are typically small – usually only 1.5ha compared with the average 100ha in Britain. This means the income from farming is limited and has to be spread thinly. It is becoming increasingly difficult to keep young people in the farming industry: they are drawn into other industries by higher wages and more attractive working conditions.

Pressures from outside Japan

Until recently, the Japanese government has supported its farmers with subsidies (in the same way that farmers in the USA and the EU have been protected against imports of cheap foodstuffs) (**E**). The Uruguay Round's Agreement of 1995 gave LEDCs a fairer chance of trading their foodstuffs by encouraging MEDCs, such as Japan, to drop government subsidies and support for their farmers. This means farmers will receive less income as more people will buy the cheaper imports from LEDCs such as rice from Thailand and the Philippines. This will put further pressure on the Japanese farming industry.

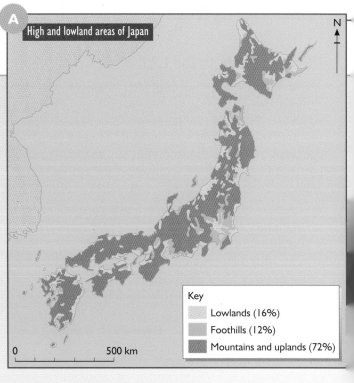

A High and lowland areas of Japan

N

Key
- Lowlands (16%)
- Foothills (12%)
- Mountains and uplands (72%)

0   500 km

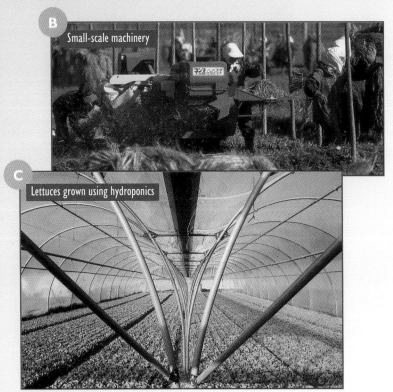

B Small-scale machinery

C Lettuces grown using hydroponics

Changes in technology

The Japanese have applied their expertise in high technology to the farming industry to make small-scale farm machinery (**B**). This makes the industry more efficient and speeds up production by being less **labour intensive** and more **technology intensive**. Technology has also been applied to the production of fresh vegetables in a completely artificial environment by using hydroponics (**C**). Vegetables are grown without soil, on a bed of artificial material; water and plant foods are fed in exact amounts; light and heat levels are carefully controlled. Between 500 and 600 lettuces can be grown in 24 hours in a small factory. This means that far less space is needed and the land can be used for other purposes.

Q

1 Consider the field size and machinery used on a UK farm, such as Vine House Farm. Why is small-scale machinery more suitable for Japanese farms?

2 Read over the section on 'hydroponics' again. Discuss the advantages and disadvantages of this method of farming as a replacement for the traditional way of growing vegetables in fields on small family farms. Japan is short of flat land. Could the farmland be more profitably used? With a partner construct a spider diagram listing the advantages and disadvantages of the hydroponics method of farming.

What are the impacts of change?

The Japanese Ministry of Agriculture, Food and Fisheries (MAFF)

The Japanese government is concerned about:

- the number of young people moving into non-agricultural employment (**D**)
- the breakdown of balanced rural communities: young people moving away leaving an ageing population. This is a particular problem in mountainous areas which account for 40 per cent of the cultivated land in Japan and 40 per cent of the farmers.
- most farmers take on additional jobs to keep their incomes up. But this can only be in areas where there are other jobs available. The large industrial areas in the south of Honshu Island continue to attract people from less well-paid farming jobs.
- competition from imported foodstuffs.

Changes planned by MAFF

To address these concerns, the Japanese MAFF has taken the following measures. It has:

- provided farmers and businesses in rural areas with 'start-up' loans to improve services and amenities and financed new farm roads to improve links between urban and rural areas (**F**).
- encouraged environmentally friendly methods of agriculture so the industry will be sustainable in the future. Farming is to become more organic and use fewer chemicals.
- invested in research and development of new crops and introduced information technology into farming areas to keep farmers up to date.
- planned on strengthening the competitiveness of the industry by producing high quality foods checked and labelled by government inspectors.
- encouraged the education of young people in modern farm management.
- guaranteed farmers the same working hours and conditions as in other industries in Japan.
- set up financial aid packages for industries to relocate or set up in rural areas to provide farmers with a second income.

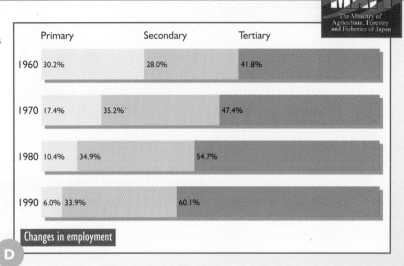

	Primary	Secondary	Tertiary
1960	30.2%	28.0%	41.8%
1970	17.4%	35.2%	47.4%
1980	10.4%	34.9%	54.7%
1990	6.0%	33.9%	60.1%

D Changes in employment

F Road building next to rice field, Nagano, Japan

E Governments protecting farmers

Questions

1 Define the terms – labour intensive and hydroponics. (4)

2 With reference to specific detail, describe the main changes in Japanese farming. (8)

3 How might changes in transport affect Japanese farming? (4)

4 For technological changes in Japanese farming:

a) explain the effects on the farms

b) show how the quality of life of the farmers is affected. (9)

Total: 25 marks

Secondary industry: changing locations

Secondary industries, often called manufacturing industries, process raw materials from primary industries to produce finished or semi-finished products. The semi-finished products, such as sheets of steel, become the raw materials of other manufacturing processes.

The UK was a world leader in manufacturing industries in the nineteenth and early twentieth centuries. Today, manufacturing industry in the UK has changed considerably. Many of the old heavy industries such as coal, iron and steel and ship building have declined due to exhaustion of raw materials and competition from overseas. The Newly Industrializing Countries, such as South Korea, have now become the world leaders in ship building. **A**, **B**, and **C** show some of the main changes in the location and structure of manufacturing industries in the UK.

Key changes in UK manufacturing industries

- Changes in location away from the old coalfield sites where coal was used to power traditional industries. Other location factors are now more important (see page 109).

- Many of the traditional 'heavy' manufacturing industries, such as iron and steel, have declined in importance and been replaced with 'light' assembly manufacturing industries, such as electronics. These newer industries favour locations near fast and efficient transport links, such as motorways. They build away from the old inner-city areas on spacious **greenfield** sites on the edge of built-up areas.

- Changes in technology have resulted in many of the old traditional methods of production being overtaken by robots and computer-controlled production. This has resulted in a reduction in the labour force in manufacturing industries. Many industries have not been able to finance the new investment needed to update their technology – they are then open to competition from other producers. Many of the new manufacturers are from the **Newly Industrializing Countries**, e.g. South Korea, now the world's largest steel producer.

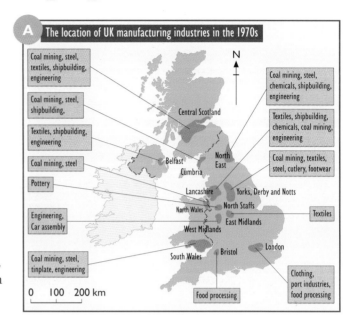

A The location of UK manufacturing industries in the 1970s

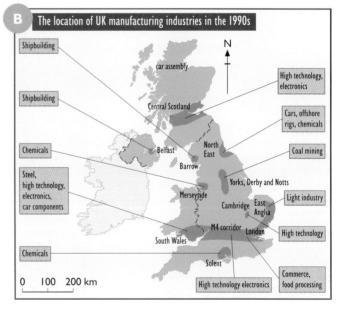

B The location of UK manufacturing industries in the 1990s

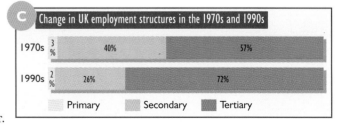

C Change in UK employment structures in the 1970s and 1990s

| 1970s | 3% | 40% | 57% |
| 1990s | 2% | 26% | 72% |

Primary   Secondary   Tertiary

- A large number of overseas manufacturers have been attracted to the UK, particularly in areas offering government assistance. This has added considerably to the changing manufacturing industry structure in the UK.

- There has been an overall decline in the numbers employed in manufacturing as the UK moves to a more tertiary-based economy.

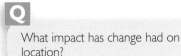

Q

What impact has change had on location?

CASE STUDY EU: Nissan Motor Corporation, Sunderland

The Nissan Motor Corporation is a Japanese **multinational** car producer which set up an assembly plant in 1986 on a **greenfield** site just outside Sunderland, Tyne and Wear. By 1993 Nissan was the UK's largest car exporter ahead of Rover and Ford, exporting a total of 182,207 cars. Nissan is typical of so many Japanese companies which start as small-scale concerns in Japan and then expand into producing a range of different products and move their manufacturing base to several overseas locations. In August 1998, the Nissan plant in Sunderland topped Europe's productivity league table by making almost 100 cars per employee per year. Second in the league table was the General Motors plant in Germany which made 77 cars per employee.

These records of production are achieved by Nissan's efficient manufacturing methods which are constantly being updated in response to new technology and improved working practices. Using a computer controlled system of 'synchronous supply', components are delivered to the assembly line just when they are needed (just in time – JIT). This cuts down considerably the component supply time to as little as 10 minutes from the request time.

Components from the UK mainland arrive by lorries delivering up to four times a day. Nissan makes a regular tour of suppliers with a single haulier collecting from each one before heading to the Sunderland plant. It calls this its 'milk-round collection'. This has reduced the number of road miles required for the delivery of the 'Micra' car components by 2.3 million miles a year. Previously, each supplier made individual journeys wasting time and resources.

Newcastle upon Tyne
• Sunderland
Teesside

FACT FILE

- By 1995 Nissan had invested £900 million in its UK production including its research and design centre at Cranfield.

- It has created thousands of jobs in an area with high unemployment.

- It is a major market for UK component suppliers and British Steel.

- It has attracted other Japanese component firms to the north east, such as TI Nihon and SP Tyres.

Why Japanese companies locate in the UK

- To cut down on the cost of transporting the finished products to local markets.

- The EU has a market of over 360 million people.

- Goods produced within a country will not have to pay import duties and are not counted within an import quota system.

- Cheaper and faster to build a new plant in the UK with government support.

- Wage costs are higher in Japan which makes the finished product more expensive.

D

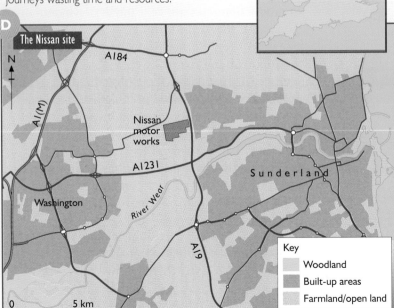

The Nissan site

N

A1(M)

A184

Nissan motor works

A1231

Sunderland

Washington

River Wear

A19

Key
Woodland
Built-up areas
Farmland/open land

0   5 km

Questions

1 Use **D** to give **four** advantages of this site for a motor manufacturer. (6)

2 Suggest why the port of Teesside was important in the decision to locate near Sunderland. (2)

3 Explain what other factors influenced Nissan to locate near Sunderland. (8)

4 What evidence is there in the description of the Nissan Company that it is an industry which has kept up with changes in transport and technology? (9)

Total: 25 marks

THE UK IRON AND STEEL INDUSTRY

Steel is used in all types of manufacturing and engineering. Nearly all machinery has steel as a main component. Iron and steel is made from processing three raw materials, iron ore, coal and limestone. The supply and the cost of transporting these raw materials influence the location of iron and steel plants. Using these raw materials in such large quantities has resulted in the exhaustion of many of the supplies in both the UK and the EU. Improved technology means less raw materials are now needed in the process (**B**). However, there are still not sufficient accessible supplies locally. Coal and iron ore are now imported in large quantities from Australia, Sweden, Canada and Colombia.

The main location factors are still based on the supply of the heavy raw materials, but as most of the materials are now imported by bulk carrier ships, the most favoured locations are at **break of bulk points** (**C**). These are the deep water ports where the heavy imported raw materials are unloaded, such as at Port Talbot. If there is further transport then further costs are incurred.

Advances in steel-making technology have speeded up production and led to larger, more efficient **integrated** works, where all the manufacturing from raw materials to the finished steel is concentrated on one site. Large areas of flat land are needed for these integrated works. Again coastal sites such as Port Talbot and Llanwern have large expanses of coastal dunes and mudflats available for development.

'Steel is a vital material at the heart of the modern world. Essential in industry, agriculture and transport, in the home, in sport and in building, packaging and engineering, steel products are everywhere. Steel also forms the basis of the machinery for making nearly every product we possess. Without it, wood and glass cannot be shaped, stone cannot be mixed, other metals cannot be melted and formed and plastics cannot be manufactured. Without steel our modern world would not exist.'

Chairman of British Steel (now Corus)

Extract from British Steel's annual report, 1996

B

Changing quantities of raw materials needed to produce one tonne of iron			
Date	Iron ore	Coal	Limestone
1880	2 tonnes	10 tonnes	0.1 tonnes
1960	2 tonnes	4 tonnes	0.1 tonnes
1990	2 tonnes	0.5 tonnes	0.1 tonnes

Q

Draw a divided bar graph to show the figures for the changing quantities of raw materials used in the manufacture of iron and steel.

Additional factors affecting iron and steel production

Not only has the location of the industry changed, the number of iron and steelworks has decreased considerably in response to other factors:

- **Other industries** The steel industry is a key provider of raw materials for all other industries so production rates are very much dependent on demand. If the car industry goes through a recession, then the steel industry also suffers!
- **Rationalization** Privatizing the UK steel industry in 1986 led to the **rationalization** of production. This resulted in the closure of large steel works such as Corby, which were less well placed to receive imports of heavy bulky materials. The European Steel industry had an over capacity of 30 million tonnes in the early 1990s which led to further closures of plants in the UK (Ravenscraig and Consett), and older plants in Northern France and the Ruhr in Germany.
- **Globalization** of industry (see page 106) has led to imports of cheaper, high-quality steel from Latin America, Korea and other countries in the Far East, making it harder to remain competitive.

C

The changing location of iron and steel works in the UK (excluding N. Ireland)

1967

1995

N

Ravenscraig
Consett
Cleveland
Sheffield
Irlam
Scunthorpe
Shotton
Shelton
Bilston
Ebbw Vale
Corby
Newport
Port Talbot

Redcar
Scunthorpe
Sheffield
Newport
Port Talbot

Key
■ Steelworks not integrated
● Integrated works

0   200 km

Using new technology in the UK

The UK steel making industry has had to become much more competitive to survive. One of the biggest problems with early UK industries was the lack of new investment to keep up with new technologies. Corus (formerly British Steel), an Anglo-Dutch company, responded to many new initiatives to keep its manufacturing processes up-to-date and more environmentally friendly. Team training programmes have also dramatically improved production by making steel workers more adept at tackling technical problems on the spot. It has made significant advances in making full use of information technology allowing customers to order directly from Corus through a computerized network covering Europe and the UK Corus has also invested in new research and development methods; it believes in sharing ideas with customers.

Corus reuses four million tonnes of steel a year. Iron ore will run out so recycling is crucial. Most waste products, from dust to heat energy, are recycled. The amount of energy used in making a tonne of steel has been reduced by 25 per cent in the last fifteen years.

In spite of all these initiatives rationalization continues. In January 2001 Corus made 6050 people redundant leaving a workforce of 22,000 at plants throughout the UK. Ebbw Vale, Llanwern and Port Talbot were some of the plants the worst hit. Corus blamed 'excess capacity' for the loss in jobs. There is less of a market for British steel abroad. This is largely due to the pound's strength against the euro, which has undermined the competitiveness of steel exports from the UK. There have been talks of retraining steel workers for the growing telecommunications industry.

How and why is the German iron and steel industry changing?

CASE STUDY *EU: The Ruhr region, Germany*

Changing fortunes of the German iron and steel industry

The Ruhr region of Germany (**D**) built up its heavy manufacturing base of steel, chemicals and textiles using local resources of coal and iron ore. This region still produces 20 per cent of all the steel made in the EU, but it is nowhere near as important as it was when it supplied the huge arms industry based there in the 1940s.

Since 1960, 300,000 jobs have been lost in the local steel plants such as Krupp-Hoesch in the old centres of Dortmund and Bochum. The problems facing this area are similar to those in the UK:

- Many of the local raw materials have become exhausted and imports from overseas are brought inland via Rotterdam along the Rhine. This adds to transport costs.
- Many of the industries are old and technology is outdated.
- The high labour costs in Germany makes German steel far more expensive than imported steel from Taiwan and South Korea.

The German government has been subsidizing the steel industry heavily, which has helped it survive and remain one of the largest employers in the region. However, many of the old heavy industries of the Ruhr (**E**) are now being replaced by newer industries, such as electronics, telecommunications and media. These demand different skills and new investment. This is attracting many of the multinational firms, such as Hitachi and Mitsubishi, which favour the location because the Ruhr is located at the centre of the large European market.

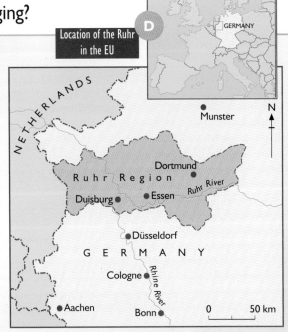
Location of the Ruhr in the EU **D** GERMANY

Ruhr Region — Munster, Dortmund, Duisburg, Essen, Ruhr River, Düsseldorf, GERMANY, Cologne, Rhine River, Aachen, Bonn 0 50 km N NETHERLANDS

E The Ruhr region

Questions

1 What is meant by the globalization of industry and rationalization of industry? (4)

2 Using map **C**, describe the changes in the location of the UK iron and steel industry. (6)

3 In what ways are the changes in the German iron and steel industry similar to those in the UK? (6)

4 Using examples wherever possible, explain the factors influencing the location of a modern integrated steelworks. Page 124 may also help you. (9)

Total: 25 marks

The Llanwern works **A**

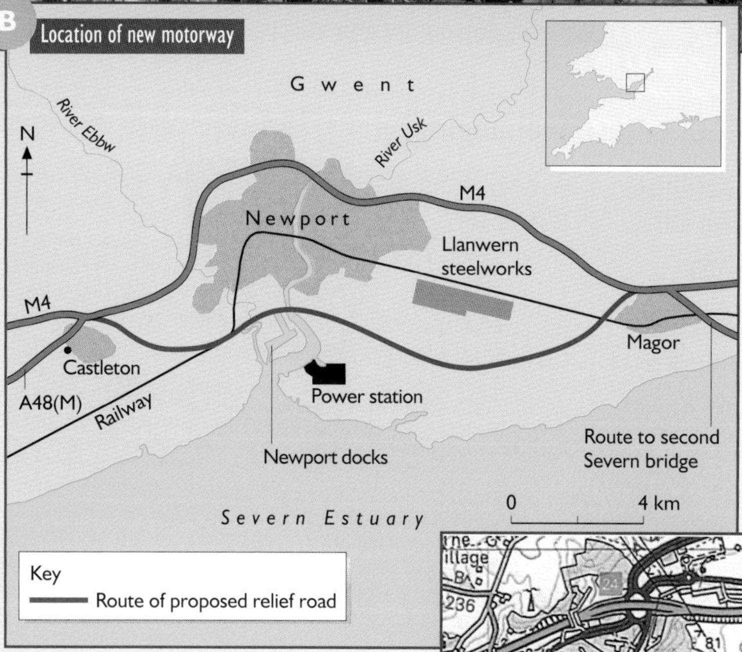

B Location of new motorway

G w e n t

River Ebbw

River Usk

N

Newport

M4

Llanwern steelworks

M4

Castleton

A48(M)

Railway

Power station

Newport docks

Magor

Route to second Severn bridge

0   4 km

S e v e r n   E s t u a r y

Key
——— Route of proposed relief road

Why is Llanwern an ideal location for a modern integrated steelworks? Notice how flat the area is in **A**. It is built on reclaimed marshland, approximately 12 sq km on the edge of the Severn Estuary in South Wales. The marshland site has been 'under-piled' to give the huge works (994ha) a solid foundation. This has made good use of otherwise redundant land. On the land-ward side, the M4 motorway (**B**) runs parallel with the steelworks to take finished steel to the car manufacturers and other steel-using industries in the Midlands. **B** also shows an extension of the motorway that is planned to run south of the steelworks. This will link up with the second Severn Bridge crossing and improve the transport links of the steelworks.

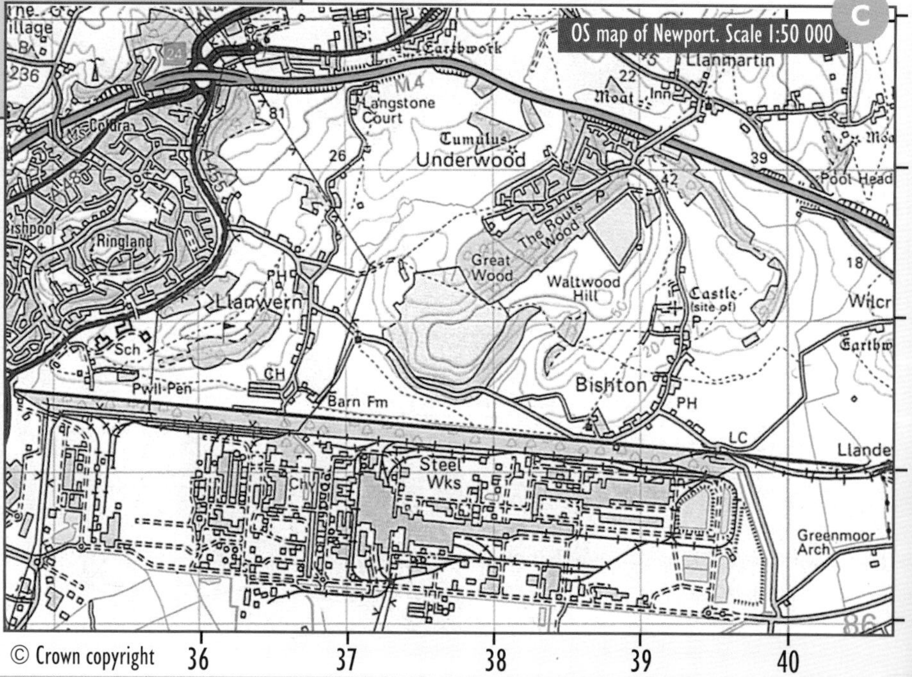

C

OS map of Newport. Scale 1:50 000

© Crown copyright

36   37   38   39   40

Q

Using **B** and **C**, draw an annotated sketch map showing the location of the Llanwern steelworks. Mark in the following features:

- the coastline and the site of the steelworks
- the major roads and the position of the proposed M4 extension using a dashed line
- the land over 50 metres
- the position of Newport
- annotate the map with details of raw material supplies and the direction of movement of the finished products.

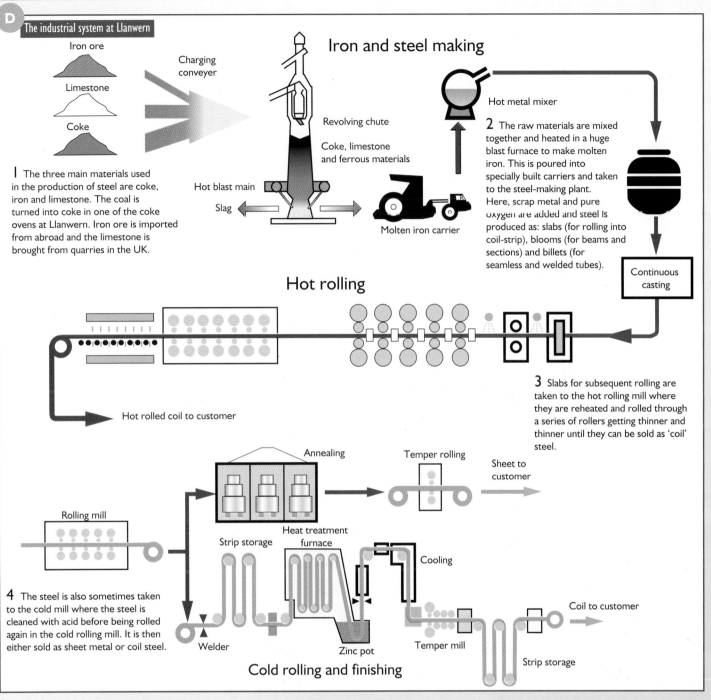

D The industrial system at Llanwern

Iron and steel making

Iron ore

Limestone

Coke

Charging conveyer

1 The three main materials used in the production of steel are coke, iron and limestone. The coal is turned into coke in one of the coke ovens at Llanwern. Iron ore is imported from abroad and the limestone is brought from quarries in the UK.

Revolving chute

Coke, limestone and ferrous materials

Hot blast main

Slag

Molten iron carrier

Hot metal mixer

2 The raw materials are mixed together and heated in a huge blast furnace to make molten iron. This is poured into specially built carriers and taken to the steel-making plant. Here, scrap metal and pure oxygen are added and steel is produced as: slabs (for rolling into coil-strip), blooms (for beams and sections) and billets (for seamless and welded tubes).

Continuous casting

Hot rolling

Hot rolled coil to customer

3 Slabs for subsequent rolling are taken to the hot rolling mill where they are reheated and rolled through a series of rollers getting thinner and thinner until they can be sold as 'coil' steel.

Annealing

Temper rolling

Sheet to customer

Rolling mill

Strip storage

Heat treatment furnace

Cooling

4 The steel is also sometimes taken to the cold mill where the steel is cleaned with acid before being rolled again in the cold rolling mill. It is then either sold as sheet metal or coil steel.

Welder

Zinc pot

Temper mill

Coil to customer

Strip storage

Cold rolling and finishing

D is a systems diagram for the Llanwern steelworks. The site at Llanwern is fully integrated, i.e. all the processes from bringing in the raw materials to rolling off the finished steel are completed on the one site. The coking coal and iron ore are imported to Llanwern's 'sister' works at Port Talbot, located further west along the coast. Port Talbot has a deep water harbour where coal is brought in from the USA and Poland, and iron ore from Australia, Canada and Sweden. Limestone comes from the UK. The raw materials are then brought to Llanwern by train, which adds £7 to the cost of each tonne of finished steel at Llanwern.

New technology allows scrap steel to be used as a 'raw material' at Llanwern. This is brought in from suppliers outside and any waste scrap from the production line is recycled into the blast furnaces. Twenty five per cent of British steel is now produced from scrap. There is very limited 'waste': exhaust gases, water and solids are all recycled.

The plants at the Llanwern site and Port Talbot generate a lot of indirect employment in the local economy. Local shops, services and transport systems all depend on employees from the steelworks to bring in custom. This is known as the **multiplier effect**.

Regional economic change

How do governments affect location?

The industrial scene in the traditional manufacturing areas of the UK and the EU is very different from what it was 50 years ago. These areas have suffered from the decline of the old heavy **sunset** industries (coal, steel, shipbuilding and textiles). These changes had a significant impact on the socio-economic and natural environments of these areas. Some argue that industry has become 'leaner and fitter'; others who live in the areas where the industries have closed may not agree. When a major employer closes, it is not only the people who were directly employed who suffer, much of the indirect employment in the area also goes (**A**). Retail services in an area, for example, suffer if there is less money to be spent. Property values are depressed and many of the old industrial premises fall into disrepair.

However, many of these depressed industrial areas have become thriving centres of new industry. South Wales, Central Scotland, and north-east England have all attracted new industries with the help of government financial aid. This aid is nothing new and has existed in various forms since 1934. However, when the economic recession hit the UK in the mid-1970s the government renewed attempts to combat the problems of economic decline and unemployment. They decided to:

- institute strict planning controls on the location of industry to limit the number of industries that were setting up in more favourable areas.
- redistribute industries, especially service activities, from thriving areas to areas of high unemployment, e.g. the British government **decentralized** many of its offices from Central London, such as the DVLC to Swansea.
- target areas of high unemployment as 'Assisted Areas'. **B** shows the three types. The aim was to attract new industry by giving a range of financial incentives and create an upward spiral of improvement so that new jobs could bring a multiplier effect to the local economy.
- set up Enterprise Zones (**B**) in 1981 to focus aid on specific areas of decline. Many of these were in old inner-city areas such as the Isle of Dogs in London Docklands.
- create Urban Development Corporations (UDCs) (**B**) to rejuvenate areas of decline. The aim was to make these areas more attractive for economic activity. London Docklands was the first and most notable example, but by 1999 thirteen UDCs had been created.
- attract investment from overseas. In 1998, 20 per cent of industry in the UK was owned by large foreign multinational companies.

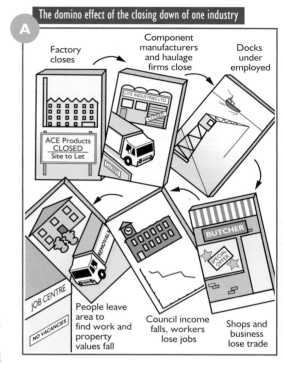

A The domino effect of the closing down of one industry

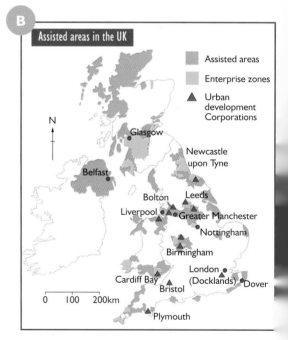

B Assisted areas in the UK

Q

1 What is meant by the terms decentralization and the multiplier effect.

2 Why do some areas attract more financial support from the government than others?

High-technology industries in South Wales

From 'Soot to Sony'

South Wales was once famous for its coal and steelworks in valleys such as the Rhondda, using the large reserves of local iron ore and coal. The industrial scene today is very different. Gone are many of the 'old' heavy industries and instead South Wales has been able to attract a lot of new industry from overseas by using a policy of 'inward investment'. This is where a government office, in this case the Welsh Development Agency, has offered financial incentives to companies to set up in the area. This area also qualifies for financial support from the central UK Government under the Assisted Areas programme. Much of the new industry is **high-tech industry**. This is a general term to describe a range of recently developed information technology industries involving micro-electronics and related activities. It is also sometimes extended to include **sunrise** industries which use high technology in their industrial system. These industries in South Wales are mainly concerned with electrical components, electronic equipment and consumer electronics and have taken the area away from its heavy industrial base into light manufacturing (**C**).

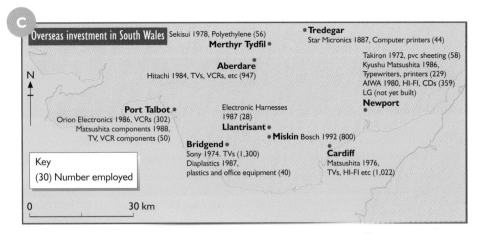

C Overseas investment in South Wales

- Sekisui 1978, Polyethylene (56) — **Merthyr Tydfil**
- **Tredegar** Star Micronics 1887, Computer printers (44)
- **Aberdare** Hitachi 1984, TVs, VCRs, etc (947)
- Takiron 1972, pvc sheeting (58)
- Kyushu Matsushita 1986, Typewriters, printers (229)
- AIWA 1980, HI-FI, CDs (359)
- LG (not yet built)
- **Newport**
- **Port Talbot** Orion Electronics 1986, VCRs (302); Matsushita components 1988, TV, VCR components (50)
- Electronic Harnesses 1987 (28)
- **Llantrisant**
- **Miskin** Bosch 1992 (800)
- **Bridgend** Sony 1974. TVs (1,300); Diaplastics 1987, plastics and office equipment (40)
- **Cardiff** Matsushita 1976, TVs, HI-FI etc (1,022)

Key
(30) Number employed

0 — 30 km

A choice location

- Over 200 electronics companies operate from South Wales and employ over 29,000 people. South Wales has gained world-wide recognition in establishing itself as a choice location in the semi-conductor industry.
- Japanese TV and HI-FI companies, such as Sony, Panasonic, Hitachi and Technics, have been established in South Wales for over twenty years.
- Over 300 international companies have chosen South Wales as the best location in Europe (**D** and **E**).
- There are over 150 automotive companies in South Wales including Ford and Bosch.

The advantage of assembly industries is that they create a multiplier effect by attracting component manufacturers, such as Ocean Technical Glass a joint German/Japanese company, making TV and VDU screens (**F**).

One of the greatest advantages South Wales offers new high-tech companies is its position on the M4 motorway, which runs from Swansea to London.

Q The high-tech industries are often referred to as the 'sunrise' industries. Why?

D High-tech companies along the M4 corridor

Apple
Dell
Hewlett Packard
IBM
LG
Mitel
Matsushita
Sony
Dec
Compaq
Motorola
Toshiba
Sun
Silicon Graphics
Hitachi
Philips
Thompson
Bosch
AT&T
Nortel
Fujitsu
Ericsson

Japan
USA
Canada
Germany
France
Irish Republic
Sweden
Switzerland
Denmark
Italy
South Korea
Taiwan

E Overseas investors in South Wales, 1996 (in order of greatest number of companies)

Why has high-tech industry been attracted to South Wales?

- The Welsh Development Agency set up in 1976 has spent £2,228 million through grants and loans to attract inward investment.
- The UK Government gave the area 'Assisted Area' status, which attracted more funds from central government.
- EU regional development funded a new road to open up the valleys and extended the M4 west. The M4 runs from Swansea to London.
- Skilled labour is available.

F Ocean Glass, a high-tech company in South Wales

Why do some places experience growth?

What is Bosch?

Bosch is the world's largest independent manufacturer of automotive equipment and is one of the ten largest industrial groups in Germany. This precision mechanics and electrical engineering company was started in 1886 by Robert Bosch in Stuttgart, Germany. Bosch became one of the earliest multinationals, setting up its first overseas office in the UK in 1898. The company now employs a world-wide workforce of 180,000 in 32 countries, including Brazil, Mexico, Spain, South Africa, China, Australia, India and Venezuela at 175 different sites (**A**); 42 of these sites are located in Germany. Bosch has maintained a world-wide reputation for quality engineering and excellent employment practices. The annual sales turnover of the company in 1997 was £16 billion (65 per cent of these sales were outside Germany).

Where is it?

Bosch is a typical example of the type of multinational high-tech company that has brought new skills, investment and employment opportunities to regions like South Wales. The Bosch site at Miskin (**B**) in Wales produces a range of advanced compact alternators for the automotive industry. This was the company's first manufacturing venture in the UK. A total of £120 million was invested between 1991–95 to set up the 80ha plant.

Bosch was attracted to this greenfield site in South Wales (**B**) for the following reasons:

B Bosch, Miskin, South Wales

- **Transport** Close to the M4 motorway and railway network. Airports at Cardiff and Manchester are also close by and the ports at Cardiff and Dover offer international links (**C**).
- **Space** Ample room to expand on the site.
- **Labour** High quality local workforce. Good training facilities in local colleges and universities.
- **Grants** Government support from the Welsh Development Agency.

Workforce

Some 950 people are employed at the site. The company invests heavily in comprehensive training programmes to maintain high-quality production levels. Employees involved in the production line visit the parent company at Stuttgart where they are taught specific technical information by experts.

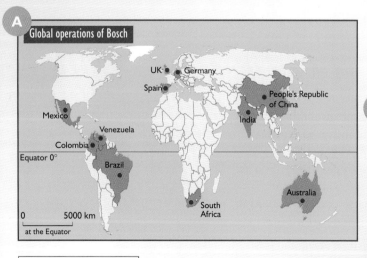

A Global operations of Bosch

Key
- Factory
- Production under license

C Cardiff — the ideal location

D Bosch products

Power tools

Domestic appliances

Fuel pumps

Ignition systems

Alternators

Antilock breaking systems

Car radios (Blaupunkt)

Lawnmowers

Navigation equipment

Mobile telephones

... and others decline?

Not all areas of South Wales have benefited from the growth of new industry. The narrow, steep-sided valleys of the Rhondda lined with terraced houses (**E**) have been less attractive to the large new assembly industries. They have taken up large flat sites positioned along the M4 corridor. The valley floors are often too narrow and the landscape is scarred from years of coal mining and steelworks (**F**). An adequate flat site and access to an efficient transport network is essential for modern component-based industries. Uneven industrial development has meant that some areas have suffered as shown by local opinions (**G**).

In the late 1990s government policies began steering development away from greenfield sites and onto brownfield sites. This was intended to help development on the former industrial sites in the valleys and bring employment back to these neglected areas.

E Terraced housing in Rhondda valley

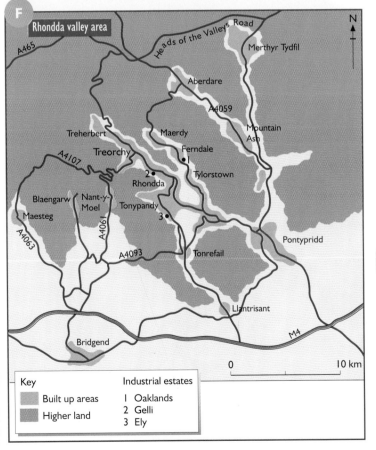

F Rhondda valley area

Key

Built up areas

Higher land

Industrial estates
1 Oaklands
2 Gelli
3 Ely

G Differences in employment opportunities in the same region cause social problems and, as with many areas of high youth unemployment, the Rhondda valleys are suffering from a growing level of crime and drug abuse. The strong community ties are being broken down.

'We desperately need more companies to take up factory space in the valleys. The likes of me in my late forties feel we may never work again. What's worse, there's nothing for the youngsters either. They'll just leave and the valley will become a ghost community. Crime levels are getting worse too: I see in the papers that people over at Abergwynfi have formed their own vigilante patrols – we'll have to think about it soon too. Two or three cars a night are being stolen or broken into.'

An ex-miner from the Rhondda

'How can they expect industrialists to take up options in Ferndale, or Gelli, for that matter? Driving HGVs through these narrow congested streets is an absolute nightmare. My drivers always moan when they have a delivery job up there.'

Local contract haulier

Many people commute from the valleys to the new industries in the Cardiff area, but this takes people out of the communities in an area that has been established on close community ties.

'I'll be only too glad to see more companies come into the valleys. My wife works for a Japanese company on an estate the other side of Cardiff. The money's good, but I hardly see her in the week. The long hours commuting don't do much for family life and the car's not getting any younger either!'

Ex-steel worker from Treorchy

Questions

1 Give examples of the new sunrise industries. (3)

2 Describe the main changes in the location of industry within South Wales. (5)

3 How have changes in transport influenced the location of firms such as Bosch in South Wales? (6)

4 Explain why coastal South Wales has had more success than the valleys in attracting new business. (6)

5 What effects might economic decline have on the quality of life in parts of South Wales? (5)

Total: 25 marks

Regional economic change: the EU

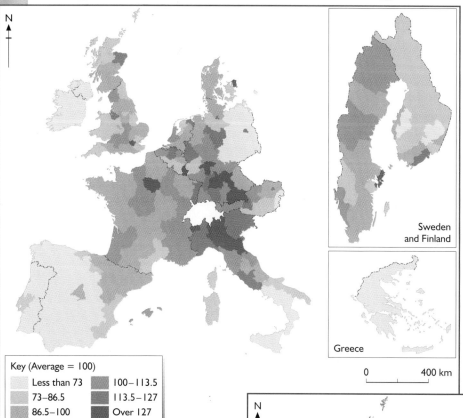

Key (Average = 100)

Less than 73	100–113.5
73–86.5	113.5–127
86.5–100	Over 127

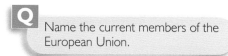

A GDP for different regions of the EU

Differences in regional economies

Of the fifteen member countries of the EU, Greece, Portugal and Spain to the south and the former East Germany have very different economies and lifestyles compared to the more recent members – Austria, Finland and Sweden. The contrasts become very clear when trying to get all fifteen to agree to the same economic and social policies.

The maps **A** and **B** show some of the regional economic differences in the European Union.

Q Name the current members of the European Union.

- The areas with the highest GDP are concentrated in the centre of the EU in a line extending from the North Italian Plain to the South east of England.

- The less well-off regions with the highest rate of unemployment are on the edges of the EU, for example Greece, Spain, Eire and Finland.

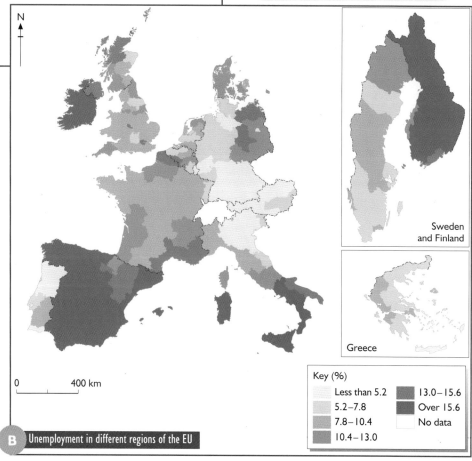

Key (%)

Less than 5.2	13.0–15.6
5.2–7.8	Over 15.6
7.8–10.4	No data
10.4–13.0	

B Unemployment in different regions of the EU

Which areas experienced decline?

The section on secondary industry (3.3) in this chapter explains how many heavy industrial regions of the EU have experienced economic decline because of exhaustion of raw materials and competition from overseas producers. Map **C** shows the main industrial regions of Western Europe. Some of these are the areas where the former coal and steel industries were located. These areas of industrial decline now qualify for EU grants and subsidies to try and attract new economic growth and improve the environments scarred by the former heavy industries.

The EU's economic **core**, i.e. its rich economic centre, is sometimes referred to as Europe's 'hot banana' (**D**). The areas away from the core, i.e. the economically less well developed centres are said to be on the **periphery**. Look at map (**C**) and identify five regions at the EU's economic core and five on the periphery.

C
Major industrial areas of Western Europe

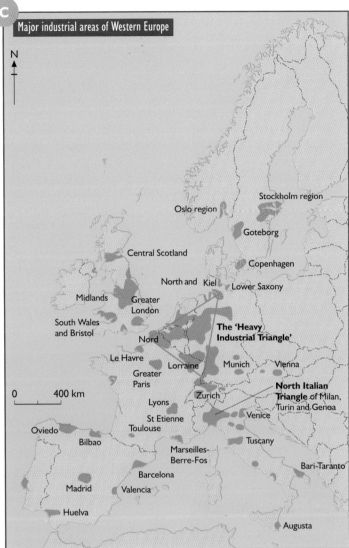

D
Europe's 'hot banana'

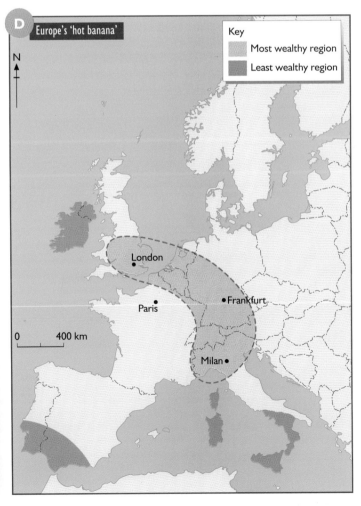

Key
- Most wealthy region
- Least wealthy region

Questions

1 Using the maps **A** and **B,** identify two regions that have both a low GDP and a high unemployment rate. (2)

2 Identify two regions that have both a high GDP and a low unemployment rate. (2)

3 Which type of region do you think may need financial help from the EU? Why? (3)

4 Look at **D**. Why do you think the term 'hot banana' has been used? (2)

5 Choose **one** area in **each** of the EU 'core' and 'periphery'. For **each** area use an atlas and other sources of information to help explain its economic position. You should refer to both economic and physical reasons. (8,8)

Total: 25 marks

From textiles to TGV

Lille is in north-east France (**A**). Forty years ago Lille was at the centre of one of Europe's heavy industrial manufacturing areas. Its main industries were coal, steel and textiles. These developed because of a rich local supply of raw materials. Lille was well positioned on the Franco-Belgian coalfield. However, as with other old industrial centres in Europe, such as South Wales and the Ruhr area, the supplies of raw materials began to run out after the Second World War. Lille could no longer depend on local supplies of coal and iron ore. The textile industry, which the region was famous for, suffered badly from competition with cheaply produced textiles imported from overseas. The Lille area fell into deep recession in the 1980s and unemployment was worse than in any other area of France.

Today, the economic outlook for Lille region has changed. It has been transformed into a thriving area with an expanding economy. Most of the old heavy industries have now gone; they have been replaced by modern service industries, such as banking, insurance, retailing and telecommunications. There is still a strong link with the textile industry, but the modern manufacturers specialize in retailing high quality clothing products such as Damart thermal wear, which have earned an international reputation.

Why has Lille been so successful?

There are two main reasons for this success:

- **Financial aid** The region has received over £28 million in financial aid since 1985. Some has come from the French government and, as has South Wales, the region has also received help from the EU regional aid programme. This totalled £5.7million up to 1996. The money was used for renovation and building development, for example the Eurolille centre in Lille. This covers an area of 70ha and is a city within a city. It is a huge construction of glass and steel housing offices, shops, apartments and the two TGV (*Trains Grande Vitesse*) stations – Lille Europe and Lille Flanders. A huge urban park is also being constructed to give the downtown area of Lille a greener, more open look. The urban park will be the 'great lungs' of this new area. The Eurolille centre is connected to the Centre of Exchange and Advanced Telecommunication – Euroteleport of Roubaix.

- **Transport improvements** Transport links are essential to a region trying to develop new service-based industries. The two most important recent developments are the new autoroute system and the improved rail network. Both of these developments have placed Lille at the centre of a rapid transport system serving most other European capitals (**A**). The Lille-Losquin airport was extended and improved in 1996 to accommodate up to a million passengers. Lille is also served by a large canal, which makes the city the third largest river port in France.

New industry in the Lille region

There has been a dramatic change in the employment structure in the Lille region (**B**). It has moved from being a predominantly mining and heavy industrial area to mainly service-based employment. One of the major employers in Lille is *La Redoute*, the largest mail order company in France (**E**). The company started as a small textile company some years ago but expanded into mail order as the road transport facilities serving Lille improved.

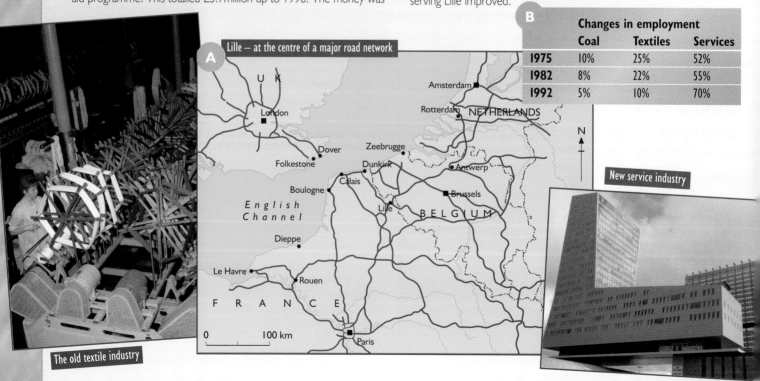

The old textile industry

Lille — at the centre of a major road network

New service industry

B | Changes in employment
	Coal	Textiles	Services
1975	10%	25%	52%
1982	8%	22%	55%
1992	5%	10%	70%

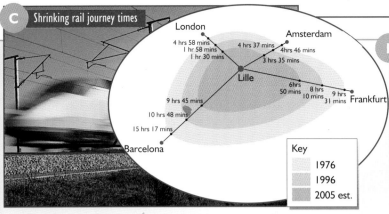

C Shrinking rail journey times

London
4 hrs 58 mins
1 hr 58 mins
1 hr 30 mins

Amsterdam
4 hrs 37 mins
4hrs 46 mins
3 hrs 35 mins

Lille

6hrs 50 mins
8 hrs 10 mins
9 hrs 31 mins
Frankfurt

9 hrs 45 mins
10 hrs 48 mins
15 hrs 17 mins

Barcelona

Key
- 1976
- 1996
- 2005 est.

How have transport changes attracted industry?

Improved rail connections

The Lille TGV rail link in 1993 significantly reduced journey times between other regional capitals of France and surrounding countries. The high speed train is a major location factor for new industries coming into the Lille region. An added bonus for the city was its successful bid to become a 'Eurostar' station connecting Lille to Paris, Brussels and Lyons, and London via the Channel Tunnel. The Eurostar connection has also made travelling time between international airports quicker. The Charles de Gaulle airport in Paris is only 57 minutes away and Brussels airport, connected in 1998, is only 25 minutes from Lille. **C** shows the effect of all these improvements.

D

Road distances from Lille			
To Paris	231 km	To Strasbourg	544 km
To Brussels	112 km	To Lyons	663 km
To Amsterdam	291 km	To Bordeaux	747 km
To Luxembourg	303 km	To Nantes	603 km
To London	224 km	To Toulouse	902 km
To Cologne	305 km	To Marseilles	994 km

E Delivery roads feeding areas of France

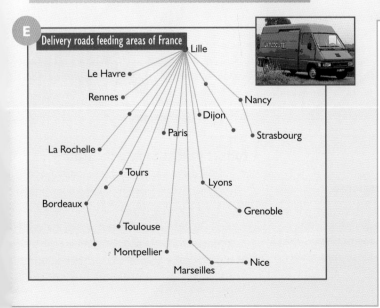

Lille
Le Havre
Rennes
Nancy
Dijon
Paris
Strasbourg
La Rochelle
Tours
Lyons
Bordeaux
Grenoble
Toulouse
Montpellier
Nice
Marseilles

F

Typical travel times from Lille to European destinations			
From	**Flight time**	**From**	**Flight time**
Mendrisio, Switzerland	1 hr 15 mins	Dublin, Ireland	1 hr 20 mins
Athens, Greece	3 hrs 40 mins	Lisbon, Portugal	2 hrs 50 mins
Berlin, Germany	1 hr 25 mins	Madrid, Spain	2 hrs 15 mins
Copenhagen, Denmark	1 hr 35 mins	Rome, Italy	2 hrs 10 mins

Improved road network

There are six main autoroutes connecting Lille with six European capitals (**D**). The new road building programme has put Lille at the 'hub' of Europe and brought a potential market of 300 million people within a radius of 300km of the city. Travel between the EU countries has also been made far easier by the lowering of border controls in 1992. This was particularly important to Lille as it is so close to the Belgian border.

APIM

Lille's International Agency for the Promotion of the Lille area (APIM) is similar to the Welsh development agency. This is a marketing agency which sells Lille as a location to potential new industries moving into the area. The transport network is one of the most important selling points for Lille, which is at the centre of the European market. APIM attracted over 93 new industries to the region between 1993 and 1995.

Pie chart:
- Japan (3%)
- USA (11%)
- France (38%)
- UK (14%)
- Other (12%)
- Belgium (22%)

G Source country of new industries

Questions

1 What were the most important industries in the Lille region 40 years ago? (2)

2 Why did these industries decline? (4)

3 Use table **B** to describe the changes in employment in the Lille region. (3)

4 'Lille is at the centre or "hub" of the European transport network.' Use evidence from the resources to explain this statement. (6)

5 **Either**:
   a) Describe the recent changes to the transport network in the Lille region, and (4)
   b) Explain how these changes have affected the economic development of the region. (6)

   Or: Explain how improved transport facilities have led to the economic regeneration of the Lille region. (10)

   Total: 25 marks

The North–South contrast

The information on pages 130–133 gives an understanding of regional economic differences in the EU and why some areas have experienced growth and others decline. Can you identify a distinct regional **disparity** in Italy? It has a rich northern plain and a poor south or Mezzogiorno (the land of the midday sun). When Italy joined the EU (it was then called the Common Market) the Mezzogiorno was the poorest region within the union. Despite many attempts since to improve the area parts of it still remain poor by relative standards in the EU. However, remember that compared to LEDCs it is developed.

A Milan

The North Italian Plain

This region contains the 'industrial heartland' of Italy. The large cities of Turin, Genoa and Milan enclose a rich industrial triangle containing over ten million people.

Famous names such as Benetton, Fiat, Alfa Romeo, Zanussi and many more have their headquarters here. Motor manufacturers alone employ over 14,000 people. Large space-using industries have found room to spread out on the flat Italian plain. A good network of communications has made movement between cities easy. The markets in other European regions to the north are easily accessed via a system of road and rail tunnels through the Alps (e.g. Simplon tunnel).

The rich silt soils and plentiful supply of water on the flood plain of the river Po have provided an excellent base for agriculture. The wetter climate with less extreme temperatures than in the dry, hot south favours the growth of rice, cereals and vegetable crops.

The quality of life in the North compares very favourably with the South.

The South – Mezzogiorno

Southern Italy lies on the 'periphery' of Europe in terms of economic development. The steep slopes of the Apennine mountains have limited the building of a network of good quality roads and railways connecting the South with the wealthy markets to the North. Added to these poor communications a lack of raw materials and local supply of energy have limited industrial development in the South.

There are only a few large settlements such as Naples, but there are many isolated villages perched high up on the barren slopes of the Apennines which have relatively few modern amenities. Agriculture is the main employer but this usually brings in a poor level of income. The soils are thin and dry on the slopes of the Apennines. Soil erosion is a major problem. With six months of near drought conditions and high summer temperatures, farming is more difficult. Vines, olives and some cereals are grown in lower areas. Farmers cannot afford to invest in expensive machinery and technology, although EU grants have brought some improvements.

Tourism is important in some areas, but most holiday makers prefer to go to the more developed resorts in the North.

Out-migration has always been a problem in the South. In the immediate post-1945 period southern Italians migrated to the richer European countries of the north, such as Switzerland and Germany to work. Since 1950 over four million southern Italians have migrated to the North looking for work. Fewer migrate now though.

B Italy's North–South divide

Map labels: Val d'Aosta, Trentino-Alto Adige, Friuli-Venezia, Milan, Lombardy, Veneto, Turin, Piedmont, Genoa, Liguria, Emilia-Romagna, The 'North', Tuscany, Marche, Umbria, Latium, Abruzzi, Rome, Molise, Naples, Campania, Apulia, Basilicata, Sardinia, The 'Mezzogiorno', Calabria, Sicily, 0 200 km, N

C Naples

Regional aid for the Mezzogiorno

The Mezzogiorno has attracted different forms of aid and investment for a long time. Study the details opposite to understand why economic change has not made a huge impact on the Mezzogiorno and it is still one of Europe's poorest regions.

Further policies to help the south

• In 1986 a law was passed to encourage private investment in the South by offering loans, grants and tax incentives. Fiat took advantage of these offers and set up several new factories in the South at Melfi, Cassino, Avalino and Pomigliano. Fiat now produces more from its southern plants than from the North.

- EU funds for agriculture, industry and other projects are being pumped into the area regularly in addition to the regional aid funds. Irrigation has helped grow new crops such as peaches and pears. Coastal marshes have also been drained.

- More recently European Business Innovation centres have been set up to encourage small-scale businesses that are protected by strict security. One of the major drawbacks to development of the South is crime and corruption (the Mafia).

- Tourism has also become a focus for new investment (**E**).

Cassa per il Mezzogiorno (Cash for the South)

This package was launched as far back as the 1950s and was jointly funded by the Italian government and the Common Market (former EU). It was set up to raise living standards in the South to the level of those in the North. The three main reforms were aimed at agriculture and industry.

- The large estates of land that had been owned by 'absentee landlords' were split up, which created about 120,000 new farms. This was to give local people more independence.
- Huge government-owned steel and chemical plants were set up as **growth poles** in the South (**E**); 60 per cent of all state investment was to go to the South. It was hoped these industries would create a multiplier effect.
- Roads and motorways were built to improve communications, so that industries needing to bring in raw materials or to market finished goods would be able to make use of an efficient transport network. In particular the Autostrada del Sol, a motorway from North to South Italy, helped.

What success?

The Mezzogiorno continues to lag behind the rest of Italy and remains on the periphery of development in the EU. Over fifty years of targeting funds into the region has brought limited success. The regional disparities between the North and South are in fact gradually widening. The quality of life has improved for many people in the South. There is a wider range of industries, services and amenities in most settlements, but the rate of change is very slow. Many people from southern Italy continue to migrate to the North or other EU countries in search of work and a better lifestyle.

Why the failures?

- Southern Italy is relatively isolated from the rest of Europe in terms of trade and communications.
- The major industries — steel and chemicals — that were set up were affected by the rise in oil prices in 1974, and the rationalization measures that took place in European steel production have affected the Toranto plant (**E**).
- The industry in the South is either large state or foreign-owned companies at one end of the scale or small family-owned workshops at the other end. There has been little growth in between.
- The physical environment of steep slopes, thin soils and hot, dry summers is not favourable to agriculture.
- Administration from central government has been poor; loans are expensive and the area continues to be dogged by corruption and organized crime.

D

Regional contrasts in Italy 1990

	Population (000)	Unemployment (%)	Agriculture	Industry	Services	GDP (Eu=100)
			Employment by sector (%)			
Piedmont	4358	6	7	41	52	121
Val d'Aosta	115	2.4	10	28	62	128
Liguria	1727	8.5	6	22	72	117
Lombardy	8912	3.4	3	44	53	139
Trentino-Alto Adige	887	2.7	11	26	63	119
Veneto	4385	3.9	7	42	51	118
Friuli-Venezia	1203	5.7	9	47	59	104
Emilia-Romagna	3925	4.3	10	36	54	130
Tuscany	3561	7.6	6	34	60	114
Umbria	800	8.2	9	32	59	99
Marche	1431	6.3	10	37	53	104
Latium	5171	10.9	5	20	75	117
Campania	5809	19.8	12	24	64	67
Abruzzi	1267	10.2	12	28	60	89
Molise	335	12.1	20	25	55	79
Apulia	4069	14.4	17	25	58	73
Basilicata	623	21.5	21	27	52	62
Calabria	2153	22.6	22	18	60	57
Sicily	5173	22.6	15	20	65	69
Sardinia	1658	18.9	14	23	63	75
Italy	57 576	10.2	9	32	59	104

Key: North ▨   South ▨

E

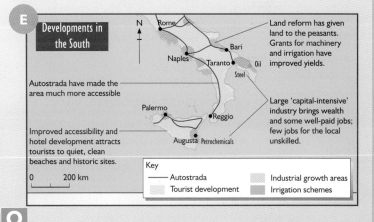

Developments in the South

- Autostrada have made the area much more accessible
- Improved accessibility and hotel development attracts tourists to quiet, clean beaches and historic sites.
- Land reform has given land to the peasants. Grants for machinery and irrigation have improved yields.
- Large 'capital-intensive' industry brings wealth and some well-paid jobs; few jobs for the local unskilled.

0   200 km

Key
— Autostrada
▨ Tourist development
▨ Industrial growth areas
▨ Irrigation schemes

Q

1 On an outline map of the regions of Italy, use the GDP figures (**D**) to construct a choropleth map (density shaded) to show the regional differences. Write a comment on what the map shows.

2 Draw an annotated map of Italy showing the main features of the North Italian Plain and the Mezzogiorno. Use the information given on these pages and your own research. Make your map informative but clear; it must not be too cluttered.

Tertiary industry

Factors which influence employment structures include:

- tourist potential
- industrial history
- proportion of cash vs subsistence farming
- amounts of natural resources
- income per head (more wealth means more spending money.

Tertiary industries are the economic activities that provide a service. They depend on people and governments having funds to spend, so the more economically developed a country is, the more service industries it usually has. When people earn increasing amounts of money they have more disposable income and demand more services.

A

Employment sectors for a range of countries (1992)

Country	Primary (%)	Secondary (%)	Tertiary (%)
UK	2	26	72
USA	3	23	74
Germany	4	37	59
Japan	8	33	59
Italy	10	31	59
South Korea	10	42	48
Brazil	23	27	50
Bangladesh	60	14	26
India	62	11	27
Kenya	81	7	11

MEDCs / LEDCs

How do employment structures vary?

There are also differences in employment structures within different countries and regions as shown in **C** for selected areas of the EU.

C

Employment structures within countries

Country/region	Primary (%)	Secondary (%)	Tertiary (%)
North Rhine, Westphalia and Ruhr, Germany	0.9	40.5	57.6
Hamburg, Germany	0.2	25.6	74.2
Brussels, Belgium	0	19	81
Central Greece	28.3	30.3	41.4
North-east Spain	3.5	41.8	54.7

B Comparison of countries' employment sectors

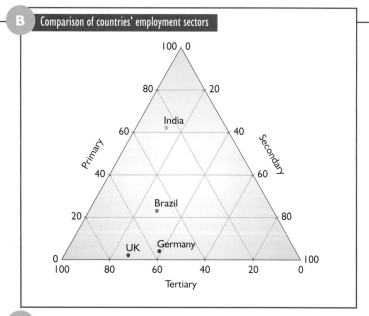

D Changing employment structure in the UK

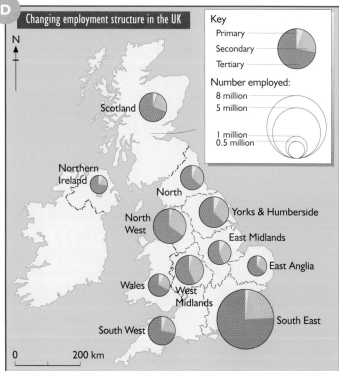

Q

1 Using the figures in **A** construct a triangular graph (as in **B**) to show the percentage of primary, secondary and tertiary employment in each country. The UK, Germany, Brazil and India have been completed (**B**) for you.

2 What is the relationship between the economic development of a country and the numbers employed in each sector? Support your answer with examples and GNP data.

3 Select two regions with contrasting employment structures from **D**. Research these regions and find out what type of industries make up each employment sector. Find out why their structures are different.

CASE STUDY EU: Pearl Assurance, Peterborough

The tertiary sector of employment in the UK has shown considerable growth within the past few decades. One of the fastest growing industries in this sector is the finance industry, which includes banking, insurance, credit cards and investments. As information technology becomes more sophisticated, there is less need for direct contact with the public, therefore less need for a central location in crowded city centres. Most customer contact is by telephone, e-mail, fax or the postal system. These new industries are footloose and there is a growing trend for them to locate in new business parks in pleasant locations on the outskirts of towns and cities near major transport routes.

E Pearl Assurance

DEFINITION

Footloose industries are those with a free choice of location as they are not tied to particular sources of materials or 'markets'.

Why locate in Peterborough?

Peterborough was designated a new town in 1968 and part of the overall planning process was to attract new industry to the city. Pearl Assurance (**E**) is an example of one of these new industries which has relocated from its city centre site in London to a new business park in Peterborough (**F**). It chose to relocate as the company's computer operations were developing rapidly and outgrowing their London headquarters. Peterborough offered a prestigious office park site; a plentiful supply of young high-quality staff, excellent communications with London and a good range of housing and additional services to attract a stable workforce.

In 1989 Pearl Assurance was taken over by a multinational finance corporation. At this time a decision was made to move again. Pearl invested over £80 million in building a huge new office complex to house its UK headquarters on the new Lynchwood Business Park, 4km west of Peterborough's city centre. Among the other well known companies located on the 50ha site are Royal Insurance, Barclays Bank, Norwich and Peterborough Building Society and Eastern Electricity. Pearl employs almost 4,000 staff at the site including 2,700 sales staff, most of which work in telephone sales. The new site offers many advantages:

- It is within 3km of the A1(M) which means a journey of just 136km to London.
- It is in a pleasant rural setting on the outskirts of the city.
- There is ample parking space for employees and visitors.
- The company has a shop on-site selling convenience goods, banking facilities, a resource library and information centre, crèche facilities, a top quality restaurant providing free meals to employees, a discount travel shop and a purpose-built leisure centre.

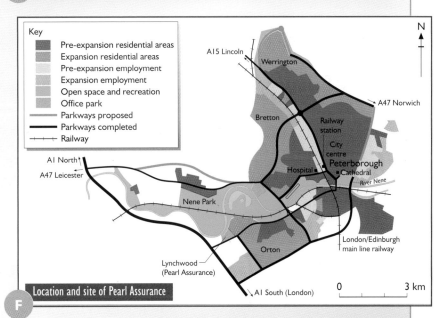

F Location and site of Pearl Assurance

Key
- Pre-expansion residential areas
- Expansion residential areas
- Pre-expansion employment
- Expansion employment
- Open space and recreation
- Office park
- Parkways proposed
- Parkways completed
- Railway

Companies like Pearl have generated a lot of direct and indirect employment in Peterborough and have helped turn the city into an economic growth pole.

Questions

1 In what ways is Pearl Assurance a footloose industry? (2)
2 Give **two** other examples of footloose industry? (2)
3 How have developments in technology allowed Pearl Assurance to move to Peterborough? (4)
4 Explain why Pearl Assurance moved from London to Peterborough. (9)
5 What evidence is there of the multiplier effect in this case study? (4)
6 Use map **F** to help show how a pleasant environment has been created at Pearl Assurance. (4)

Total: 25 marks

THE TOURIST INDUSTRY

How important is the tourist industry?

FACT FILE

- Tourism is the world's fastest growing industry.
- There is some form of tourism in practically every country in the world.
- Tourism has given many LEDCs an opportunity to improve their economies very rapidly.
- An increase in personal income and leisure time have led to an increase in tourism.
- Faster, more efficient transport networks have opened up the world.
- The number of international tourists doubles every four years. Most of them come from developed countries.
- Over 400 million people from MEDCs took holidays abroad each year in the early 1990s.

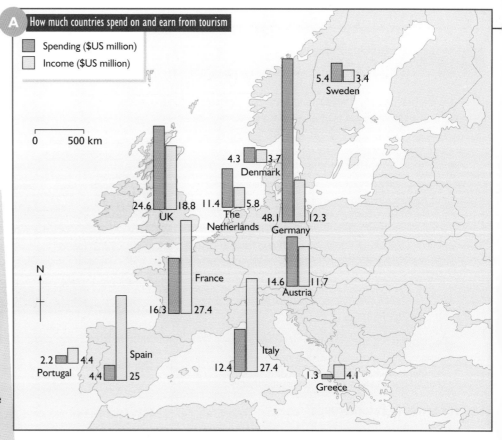

A How much countries spend on and earn from tourism

Spending ($US million)
Income ($US million)

5.4 / 3.4 Sweden
4.3 / 3.7 Denmark
24.6 UK 18.8
11.4 The Netherlands 5.8
48.1 Germany 12.3
France 16.3 / 27.4
14.6 Austria 11.7
2.2 Portugal 4.4
4.4 / 25 Spain
Italy 12.4 / 27.4
1.3 / 4.1 Greece

Holidays 'abroad' are becoming more and more popular and falling prices are putting them within the financial reach of more people. European destinations are still a first choice for many holiday makers. Some of the less well off regions on the economic periphery of Europe depend heavily on income from tourism (see **A**).

The 'traditional' European tourist tends to go for the 'sun, sea and sand' holiday that is fairly close to home. This has brought great wealth to the Mediterranean coastal resorts of southern Europe over the past thirty years. As time goes on tourists are becoming more adventurous in their choice of destination. They want to travel further and try different experiences. Resorts in LEDCs, such as Kenya, India, The Gambia and Tunisia, offer something more exotic. A significant number are also taking more than one holiday a year. It is becoming less of a seasonal industry. You can find the sun somewhere at any time of the year!

How can tourism help economic growth?

The growth of the tourist industry brings many advantages to countries in need of economic development. Tourism not only creates employment, it also encourages regional development. Airports may have to be built or improved, road networks improved and electricity and water laid on. A lot of indirect employment is created, such as farmers supplying food, taxi drivers, builders, as well as the huge numbers of people directly employed in hotels, gift shops and wine bars. **B** shows how this forms a multiplier effect.

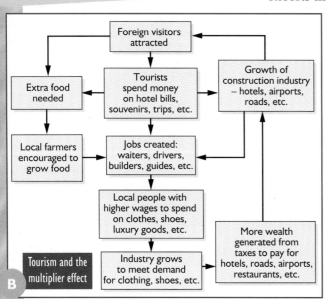

B Tourism and the multiplier effect

Foreign visitors attracted → Tourists spend money on hotel bills, souvenirs, trips, etc. → Growth of construction industry – hotels, airports, roads, etc. → Extra food needed → Local farmers encouraged to grow food → Jobs created: waiters, drivers, builders, guides, etc. → Local people with higher wages to spend on clothes, shoes, luxury goods, etc. → Industry grows to meet demand for clothing, shoes, etc. → More wealth generated from taxes to pay for hotels, roads, airports, restaurants, etc.

Is there a negative side to tourism?

Many countries have seen a huge rise in their GNP levels due to tourism. There are many examples of countries such as Kenya, which were economically dependent on producing raw materials such as coffee, tea or timber for export. Prices for raw materials on the world market fluctuate and are usually determined by the MEDC that buys the products. These countries have now developed their economies and improved the quality of life for many of their people with the income from tourism. The tourist industry opens up all sorts of new opportunities for LEDCs. However, is tourism as beneficial to these countries as it might seem?

- The World Bank estimates that only 45 per cent of revenue from tourism reaches the host country. In less developed areas it is often lower. In the Annapurna area of Nepal, only ten cents out of every hundred spent by tourists stays in the local economy (**D**).
- Many of the products for tourists come from abroad.
- What happens if the area ceases to attract tourists (**E**)?
- Tourists can damage the environments that they come to see, as **F** suggests.

C Exploitative tourism

Aw, come on darlings – say cheese…

E Cycles and stages of tourism

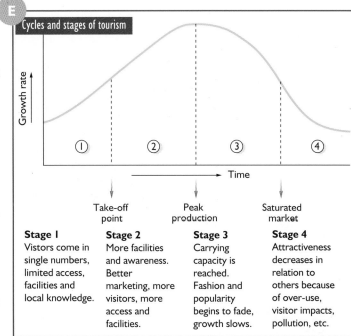

Growth rate / Time

Take-off point / Peak production / Saturated market

Stage 1
Vistors come in single numbers, limited access, facilities and local knowledge.

Stage 2
More facilities and awareness. Better marketing, more visitors, more access and facilities.

Stage 3
Carrying capacity is reached. Fashion and popularity begins to fade, growth slows.

Stage 4
Attractiveness decreases in relation to others because of over-use, visitor impacts, pollution, etc.

The closure of the Taj Mahal would add one more name to a growing list of World Heritage Sites where access is restricted or impossible. As world tourism increases, the number of ancient monuments that have to be protected from the pounding of human feet and the humidity of human breath is growing.

The prehistoric paintings of the Lascaux caves in the Dordogne, France, have been visible only in reproduction since the 1970s, when the caves were closed to visitors because their breath was promoting the growth of damaging moulds.

In Egypt, several tombs in the Valley of the Kings are permanently closed, while the three giant Pyramids of Giza are being closed in turn this year and next to give them some respite. In Italy, the basilica at Assisi is closed while restoration work continues on frescoes smashed in the earthquake of 1997, while in Pisa people are no longer permitted to scale the Leaning Tower in case they bring about its downfall.

Robin Young, The Times, 17 November 1998

F Negative impacts of tourism

D Some of the ways in which money leaks out of a country

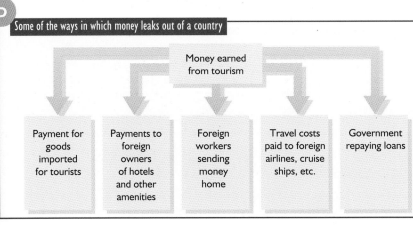

Money earned from tourism

| Payment for goods imported for tourists | Payments to foreign owners of hotels and other amenities | Foreign workers sending money home | Travel costs paid to foreign airlines, cruise ships, etc. | Government repaying loans |

Q

1 What examples of direct and indirect employment connected with tourism are there?

2 What is a 'seasonal' industry? Give some examples apart from tourism.

3 Study map **A** and make a list of the countries in rank order according to their income from tourism. Write a comment on what this list shows.

4 Study the resources and make a list of the ways in which tourism may have a negative impact on a developing country. Include 'Human', 'Economic' and 'Environmental' impacts.

Economic development in an LEDC

Brazil is a country of many regional contrasts. With its huge wealth of natural resources it has the potential to be one of the richest countries in the world. Unfortunately, by the mid 1990s Brazil was the largest debtor nation in the world. Its vast natural forests and mineral resources have been exploited and poorly developed. The greatest wealth lies in the south-east region.

South East Brazil

The cities of Belo Horizonte, Rio de Janeiro and São Paulo in the South East region (**A**) form a triangle of economic wealth often referred to as the 'golden triangle'. The past thirty years of economic development in this region has led to Brazil being one of the fastest industrializing LEDCs in the world. It has moved from an economic dependence on the primary product coffee, to a manufacturing and service-based economy. The region is home to 60 per cent of Brazil's population and accounts for 90 per cent of the country's economic wealth. A large young and skilled workforce has provided the human resource needed for rapid economic growth.

São Paulo

Most of the economic development is focused on São Paulo, the largest city in Brazil with a population of over 23 million. The rapid economic growth has attracted many migrants to the city. At one point during its period of greatest economic growth the city was attracting over half a million migrants a year. Many of the newcomers live in the sprawling shanty town settlements such as Edith Gardens built on the edge of the city. Street vendors, car repairers and shoe cleaners from these areas all play their part in the **informal sector** economy. Central São Paulo has become densely packed with skyscraper buildings as property prices have risen. Well-known multinational companies such as Phillips, Sanyo and Nestlé are all in the Barrina business district. Vehicle manufacturers have come to São Paulo to take advantage of the cheaper production costs, the growing Brazilian car market and the rich local supply of raw materials. Mercedes, Fiat, VW, General Motors and Ford are large employers in the area. Brazil is now the ninth largest car producer in the world. Most production goes for export through the Atlantic coast ports, especially Santos (**A**). The excellent system of roads has encouraged a move of many companies away from the high land values in the centre of the city. São Paulo is spreading along these roads as new building continues. As the south east grows, its demand for electricity rises. The area is supplied by the largest HEP station in the world at Itaipu on the border with Paraguay (**A**). Nearer São Paulo there is a large nuclear power station at Angra dos Reis.

FACT FILE		
	Brazil	UK
Population (million)	159.1	58.3
Population density (per sq km)	19	241
Area	8,511,965	244,100
Capital city	Brasilia	London
GNP per person ($US)	$2,920	$17,970

Key
- Lowland swamp
- Lowland
- Hills and low plateaus
- Plateaus and mountains
- Cities with more than 1 million people

The Amazon Basin

This is a thickly forested river basin with an equatorial, humid climate. The Amazon has the largest remaining area of rainforest in the world, but it is being destroyed at an increasingly rapid rate. **B** shows a satellite image of the area around Manaus, its largest settlement. Large areas of the land have been cleared by farmers. Poor farmers from the north-east region suffering the effects of drought were encouraged by the government to move to the rainforest areas and start farming there. They soon found the land unsuitable for farming. The soils lose their limited nutrient content and are rapidly eroded and leached by heavy rains once the forests are removed. Commercial farmers have merely moved on using up more and more land once the soil has been exhausted.

Poor roads

The limited transport network has done little to encourage large-scale economic development. The Brazilians started a major road building programme in the 1970s to open up the forest. 12,000km of roads were built including the very expensive 6,000 Trans-Amazonian Highway, but they did little to attract industry and settlement. The main problem was that the roads were not surfaced and impossible to drive on in the frequent heavy rains.

Indigenous tribes

There are a few larger settlements like Manaus (population 650,000), but most are small primitive villages with very limited services and amenities. Many of the traditional tribal villages that practised shifting cultivation have been abandoned. Tribal people have moved on or been exploited for their cheap labour by mining and timber companies moving into the area. The rainforest holds a wealth of mineral resources such as iron ore, bauxite, copper and gold.

Mining

Iron ore is mined in the Amazon basin. The Carajas mine (**A**), 690km inland from the Atlantic coast and situated on a tributary of the Tocantins river, is sited on one of the largest known deposits of high-grade iron ore in the world. Most of the ore is taken from the mine to the port of São Luis by rail where it is exported to countries such as Japan, Korea and

Germany. The remainder is used in Brazilian steelworks, one at Maraba close by and the others in the South East region. These provide finished steel for the home market. To the north-west of Carajas, on the south bank of the Amazon, is the large bauxite mine at Trombetas. Again most of this ore is exported to developed countries. Mining and refining these valuable metals need large amounts of electricity. This has been provided by the Tucurui HEP scheme close by (**A**). These new mining companies are more aware of protecting the rainforest but it is clear that economic development in the Amazon region has been limited. This is mainly due to exploitation and mismanagement of valuable resources.

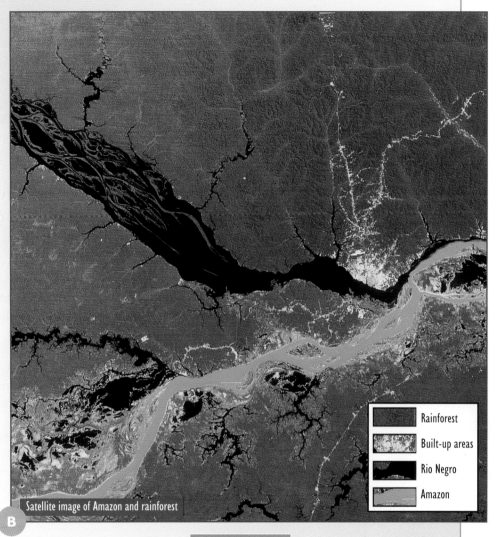

	Rainforest
	Built-up areas
	Rio Negro
	Amazon

Satellite image of Amazon and rainforest

B

Questions

Study the satellite image of the Amazon rainforest **(B)**.

1 Use evidence from the image to describe
   a) the pattern of settlement, and
   b) the location of the main areas of forest clearance for agriculture and settlement. (6)

2 Explain why these areas have been cleared of forest, rather than other areas shown on the image. (4)

3 Why is it difficult to develop a transport system in LEDC countries, such as Brazil? (6)

4 For the South East and Amazon regions:
   a) describe the differences in economic development, and
   b) explain why the South East has developed more quickly. (9)

Total: 25 marks

Economic development in Brazil

The previous pages highlighted the regional contrasts in economic development in Brazil. The Amazon region is remote from the coast of Brazil and economic development there has mainly focused on extracting natural resources such as timber and ores. This type of industry has brought little economic gain to the people of the rainforest and in fact has resulted in larger-scale human and environmental damage.

The south-east region has seen rapid economic growth in both the manufacturing and service sectors. Multinational companies have been largely responsible for this growth. However, there are disadvantages.

Multinational companies:

- often operate on a global scale and a large proportion of the profits go out of Brazil
- can exploit cheap labour available in Brazil
- may pull their operations out of the country as soon as production costs rise or cheaper locations are found elsewhere
- may cause environmental damage as pollution laws are usually more relaxed in developing countries.

Can development be sustainable?

The Rio Earth Summit, a meeting of over 160 of the world's countries, was held in Rio de Janeiro in 1992. The Summit called for:

- a stop to environmental destruction
- the development of **sustainable** economic activities
- the recognition of human rights in employment.

More detail is given in **A**.

The big project

Some more recent economic and industrial developments in Brazil are shown to have improved the quality of life for Brazilians and their environment. The Grand Carajas Plan, the largest iron ore mine in the world employing over 7,000 people, has aimed to restrict destruction of the rainforest. It has only cut down trees on 1.6 per cent of the area it occupies. The area is estimated to hold enough reserves to carry on mining for the next 400 years. It is obviously planning for long-term development. The Carajas mine depends on overseas markets to purchase much of its iron ore.

A

Selected targets from Rio Earth Summit

- 'Conserving biodiversity and promoting environmentally sound management.'

- 'Promoting sustainable agriculture and rural development…'

- 'Allowing a commitment and genuine involvement from all social groups, giving the community a greater degree of control over decision making…'

- 'Raising public awareness to promote sustainable development…'

- 'Enabling the poor to achieve sustainable livelihoods and changing unsustainable patterns of production and consumption.'

- 'Developing international cooperation and trade patterns which promote sustainable development.'

B

Why protect rainforests?

Rainforests cover only 2 per cent of the Earth's surface. They are also the oldest and richest ecosystem. They:

- contain over 50 per cent of all living species; by destroying rainforests we destroy habitats.

- act as 'gene pools'; over 40 per cent of our prescribed medicines come from rainforests. There may be a cure for cancer or Aids growing undiscovered.

- prevent flooding and maintain moisture levels in the atmosphere. They absorb 50 per cent of the water that falls on them then slowly release it by transpiration.

- are 'gas exchangers' and regulate the balance of gases in the atmosphere. Cutting down rainforests would increase greenhouse gases by 25 per cent.

- prevent soil erosion by anchoring the soils with their roots and intercepting eight out of every ten raindrops.

- protect the soils from sunlight: only 1 per cent of solar radiation passes through the canopy to ground level

- are the home of many indigenous tribes which have very distinctive lifestyles which need to be protected.

Types of development

1 The multinational solution

CASE STUDY *LEDC: The Pepsi Cola Corporation*

The Pepsi Cola Corporation is a multinational company with its head-quarters in the USA. As with many other multinationals, it has set up production in Brazil. It has three production sites and markets two thirds of Brazil's soft drinks. The Pepsi bottling plant at Jundiai is about 100km outside São Paulo on one of the main roads leading out of the city (**C**). The company provides 350 jobs bringing an improved quality of life to its employees. Most ordinary Brazilians do not have working conditions that offer regular work, regular wages, free meals and health care. There is a huge gap between the rich and poor in Brazil. Companies like Pepsi Cola are helping to close the gap in standards of living between the few rich and majority of poor.

The company opened its Jundiai plant in 1991 and Luis dos Santos was one of its first employees. His wife and children live in a modern three-bedroom flat close to the factory. There are shops, restaurants and play areas close by. It is a safe residential area unlike many of the shanty town areas around the large cities of Brazil. Luis enjoys the friendly and caring atmosphere in work. He can see opportunities for promotion within the firm in the future. Working for a multinational company has improved his quality of life.

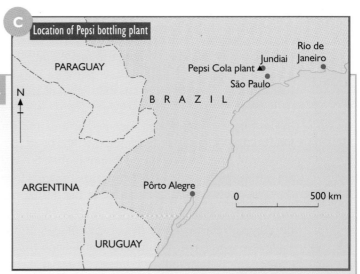

C Location of Pepsi bottling plant

PARAGUAY

ARGENTINA

URUGUAY

B R A Z I L

Pepsi Cola plant ▲
Jundiai

Rio de Janeiro

São Paulo

Pôrto Alegre

N

0   500 km

Q How have each of these two projects improved the quality of life of those involved?

2 The sustainable solution

CASE STUDY *LEDC: The Liana project*

The Liana project is run by the Rainforest Action Network (RAN). This is a non-governmental charity set up in 1985 to protect the Earth's rainforests and support the rights of their inhabitants. The Liana project offers an economic alternative to destructive land uses of the rainforest. It aims to develop rural community **micro-enterprises** that sell liana vines and its products. These enterprises will cultivate and collect the vines in a sustainable, ecologically sensitive way and produce finished and semi-finished goods locally (these add value to the vines).

The Liana project recognizes that the key to the preservation of the rainforest and its people lies within the local communities. They have the potential to act as destroyers or preservers of the forest. Indigenous (local) people have increased the rate of deforestation because they are poor and can only plan for the short term. Communities clear land for low value, short-term agricultural uses that eventually leave the land non-productive and unable to regenerate forests. Through sustainable projects like this one indigenous people can become stewards of the forest.

The project has developed a wicker furniture industry (**D**) in Brazil using the rattan-like lianas that grow in the rainforests. Project staff have found

D Wickerwork products

markets for the finished products in Brazil and the USA. They have funded start-up capital, technical knowledge and equipment for the local communities who will then run their own businesses. At present the vines are harvested in the wild but RAN is working with local communities in developing methods of cultivation. The industry is using the forest in a sustainable way and giving indigenous people the opportunity to use the forest resources for economic development.

3 The role of tourism

Tourism can bring a much needed boost to economies in LEDCs, but it can also bring many social and environmental problems. Tourism plays an important role in the economy of the coastal region of Brazil, with its beautiful beaches, such as Copacabana, Rio de Janeiro (**A**) and its attractive cities such as Salvado and Rio de Janeiro. Less attractive to the tourists has been the interior of Brazil with its impenetrable forests, limited amenities and uncomfortable humid climate. However, there is a new fast-growing sector of the tourist industry, which may bring a new, sustainable type of tourism to the Amazon Basin. There has always been a minority of travellers who have ventured off the 'beaten track' to explore the inhospitable wilderness areas of the world. They are also often concerned about the environment. A new tourist industry that caters to these people – ecotourism – is becoming very popular. In 1995 the industry was worth over £100 billion, this figure is set to double by the year 2000.

A Copacabana beach

What is ecotourism?

'Purposeful travel to natural areas to understand the culture and natural history of the environment, taking care not to alter the integrity of the ecosystem, while producing economic opportunities that make the conservation of natural resources beneficial to local people...' *Ecotourism society*.

If managed properly, ecotourism could mean the development of areas of the Amazon Basin in a sustainable, non-exploitative way in keeping with the development policy agreed at the Rio Summit.

Ecotourism can protect and benefit areas in three main ways:

1 Money can be generated to protect natural habitats and endangered species.
2 Local people may gain economically and socially from the income and protection provided.
3 Awareness of the importance of conservation is raised.

Can tourism harm the rainforest?

Because so little is known about rainforests, it is difficult to say how many people can visit in a day without disrupting the forest people and the ecology. Accommodating the physical needs of tourists, such as providing wood for fuel, living accommodation, access and communication routes, plus the disposal of waste all create stress on the environment. There must be a limit to the number of visitors if the area is not going to be adversely affected.

CASE STUDY LEDC: The Alta Floresta tourist project

The Alta Floresta tourist project

'Alta Floresta, a town in the highlands of the Amazon rainforest, is the home of an innovative research centre and ecotourist project (**B**). The research centre was set up to study sustainable ways of using the forest and to teach people in the area how to use these new practices. The project is centred on community involvement, setting up schools, hospitals and training programmes. Local people are trained in sustainable farming practices and the harvesting of non-timber forest products. In addition, instead of being forced out of the economy, they are trained to work at the tourist centre, thereby becoming an integral part of the whole project. The tourist centre also educates travellers on the ecology of the rainforest and causes and effects of its destruction. This project is a positive example of how an ecotourism centre can be set up.'

Rainforest Action Network

N

Alta Floresta

BRAZIL

0   1000 km

B Location map of project

C

FACT FILE

The Cistaline Jungle Lod

- Forest reserve
- Brazilian natural heritage site
- Ecologically sustainabl lodge accessible only by boat
- Internationally renowne for rare birds
- Opportunities for bird watching, trekking, swimming, canoeing, fishing

Decision making exercise

This section has covered details on some of the different types of economic development in Brazil. These include:

- Exploitative development, using up valuable resources for short-term gain.

- Multinational manufacturing companies have brought many new skills and opportunities to Brazilians. The companies themselves have also gained access to more markets and lower production costs.

- Sustainable development projects, where natural resources are used in a sustainable way for the benefit of the local people without jeopardizing resource supply for future generations.

Complete the following tasks using your own knowledge, opinions and the resources on pages 140–144. Make sure you use evidence from the resources in the form of facts, figures and quotations when giving your answers.

The background

1 a) Why have such large areas of rainforest been removed?

   b) What do the graphs **D** and **E** show about the rate of loss of the forests in Latin America (includes Brazil)? (8)

2 Rainforests are a valuable resource for the people who live in them and others in different parts of the world. State **four** ways in which rainforests are valuable and explain why they are so important. (8)

3 Here are two statements about the environmental damage which may be caused by the removal of rainforests:

'The soil quickly lost its nutrients once the trees were removed. With no plant cover the soils were exposed to the heavy rains which washed away the loose top layers into the fast-flowing rivers. This caused serious flooding downstream in our village'.

'The sea level is rising rapidly on this small low-lying Pacific island. We have had three major floods this year covering our crops with seawater which kills them. The experts say it is something to do with cutting down the rainforest in Brazil'.

Select one of these quotes and use diagrams and notes to explain how removing the forests might cause such environmental problems. (6)

The options

4 Consider the statements at the top of this page which recommend sustainable forms of development. For each of the three case studies on pages 143 and 144 assess how well they match up to the recommendations. (6,6,6)

The decision

5 Brazil needs to develop its resources to its economic advantage. It is the nation with the largest financial debt in the world and needs to become financially stable. Three different development options have been put to the Brazilian government for the same area of rainforest alongside the Amazon river.

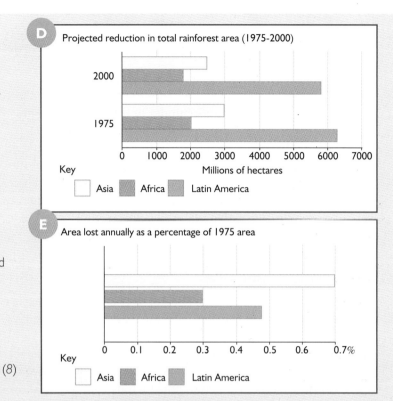

D Projected reduction in total rainforest area (1975-2000)

Millions of hectares

Key: Asia | Africa | Latin America

E Area lost annually as a percentage of 1975 area

Key: Asia | Africa | Latin America

a) **Small-scale village enterprises** providing oils and perfumes from the forest plants to sell in beauty salons and shops all over the world. The products would be manufactured in the village using appropriate technology and employ mainly local people. An international aid charity would market the goods through a 'Fair trade' policy. The wages would not be very high but certainly they would be an improvement on the limited income the village people have at present. They would also have a long-term and reliable source of employment.

b) **A multinational drug company** wants to increase their research of the medicinal properties of rainforest plants. They would set up a well resourced laboratory using up-to-date equipment in the forest. There would be some local employment but it would be limited to people gathering the plants and possibly cleaners, maids, etc. The company would pay the government a set fee for as long as they were there.

c) **A forest reserve** set up by an international conservation body. This would involve setting up a reserve with a 'core' area in the centre surrounded a 'buffer' zone where the local people would live and practise sustainable forms of agriculture, fishing and hunting. They would also develop craft industries and market their goods through aid agencies.

What would be the best choice for the Brazilian government to make in terms of improving its economic development in a sustainable way? Write a letter of recommendation justifying your choice to the government. You should give advantages and disadvantages of the projects you have rejected. (20)

Total: 60 marks

Development differences

How can development be measured?

Images such as **A** are a reminder of the huge gap in the quality of life experiences by different peoples of the world. These images often give us the impression that all people in the same country have the same quality of life. There are, of course, rich and poor in all societies. Their quality of life is usually linked to income: the problem in some countries is that higher incomes are restricted to a small minority whereas the majority of people have a very low income and quality of life.

Contrasts in GDP

The Brandt report of the late 1970s used the GDP levels of individual countries to divide the world into a 'rich developed north' and a 'poor developing south'. Development was judged by the amount of money a country earned. This was easy to calculate and allowed countries to be compared quickly. But GDP fails to show many important facts, for example:

Inequalities In many LEDCs the wealth remains with a few people in control of government and industry.

Informal employment In LEDCs many people work in informal employment such as street vending. Money is exchanged without record and does not appear as GDP.

Subsistence lifestyles Many LEDC farmers have a subsistence lifestyle.

A Mukuru, a shanty town area of Nairobi, Kenya

> **DEFINITIONS**
>
> **Gross Domestic Product (GDP)** or **Gross National Product (GNP)** is the total income of a country per year in US$ divided by the number of people in the country (GNP includes income earned from overseas investment as well).
>
> **Human Development Index (HDI)** – an average score of three variables (purchasing power of individuals, educational attainment and life expectancy).

Social development GDP assumes that this should be measured against 'Western' societies, where income and possessions, such as cars and property, are often seen as indicators of social status.

Changing standards of development MEDCs are often the main producers of pollution. Increasing cleaner industries may be considered a better measure of development than increasing a country's GDP by developing successful but polluting industries.

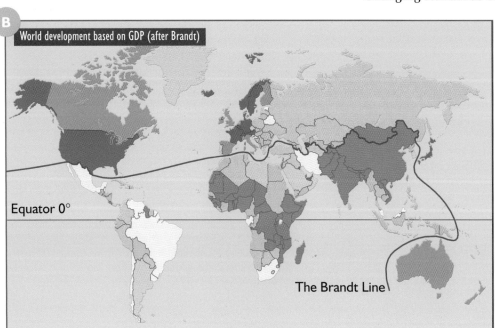

B World development based on GDP (after Brandt)

Equator 0°

The Brandt Line

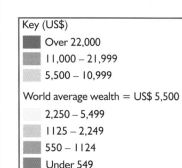

Key (US$)
- Over 22,000
- 11,000 – 21,999
- 5,500 – 10,999

World average wealth = US$ 5,500
- 2,250 – 5,499
- 1125 – 2,249
- 550 – 1124
- Under 549

Key

■	0.90 and over (32 countries)
■	0.75 – 0.899 (32 countries)
■	0.5 – 0.749 (33 countries)
■	0.25 – 0.049 (30 countries)
■	0.249 and under (31 countries)

Equator 0°

0   5000 km
at the Equator

C World development based on the Human Development Index

Is there a better measure of development?

Some of the problems of comparing places by GDP have been solved by using the Human Development Index as a measure of development (**C**). This index was drawn up by the United Nations Development Programme (UNDP). The index is **composite**, which means it takes more than one measure of development into account, not just income. The three measures included are:

1 **Adjusted income per capita** This is really a measure of the local value of currency – how much can be bought with a set amount of money in different countries. For example a dollar in the USA will buy considerably less than a dollar in India.

2 **Educational attainment** This measure combines adult literacy level and the average number of years of schooling.

3 **Life expectancy at birth** This figure will give an indication of the quality of health care, diet and quality of life.

GDP is measured in US dollars to give a common scale for comparing different countries. The Human Development Index is also measured on a common scale and countries are given a development score. The highest and lowest values are 1 (highest) and 0 (lowest). The values in between are then given proportional scores. For example, when comparing life expectancy rates, Japan, with the highest level at 79 years, would score 1 whereas Bangladesh with a life expectancy of 53 would score 0.67.

The HDI is the average score of the three variables expressed as a value between 1 and 0. It tells you how a country stands in relation to the best conditions. This makes it easier to identify where a country is in terms of development (**D**).

There are many other ways of measuring social development, such as the 'Human Suffering Index' which includes political freedom and women's access to education.

D

	Country	Life expectancy	Adult literacy	GNP per capita (US$)	HDI
	**The five wealthiest and five poorest countries (1995)**
1	Japan	F83 M77	99%	37,640	0.937
2	Canada	F83 M76	99%	19,380	0.95
3	Iceland	F83 M76	99%	24,950	0.933
4	Sweden	F81 M76	99%	23,750	0.929
5	Switzerland	F81 M75	99%	40,630	0.925
11	UK*	F81 M74	99%	19,260	0.916
156	Guinea	F48 M43	33%	550	0.23
157	Gambia	F56 M51	36%	320	0.57
158	Afghanistan	F46 M47	29%	300	0.22
159	Mali	F49 M46	27%	250	0.22
160	Sierra Leone	F51 M45	29%	180	0.34

Q

1 Use **D** to draw a scattergraph to see if there is a link between GDP and the HDI ranks for the different countries listed.

2 What does the graph show?

3 What are the advantages of using the HDI as a measure of development rather than GDP? What other measures of development could be included in the human development index?

* for comparison

HOW DO LIVING STANDARDS VARY?

The quality of life is variable and should not always be assessed by Western standards; however, access to food, shelter and equal opportunity should be a basic right of all people. The Human Development Index (HDI) gave a measure of development using three basic values. Table **A** shows a wider range of values that could be considered when comparing living standards.

There is an obvious gap in the opportunities and quality of life for people in countries at different levels of economic development and the gap is widening (**B**). Of the world's population 20 per cent now lives in a state of poverty. The richest 25 per cent, as shown in the diagram below, have incomes sixty times greater than the poorest 20 per cent. This is twice the gap of thirty years ago.

A

Development indices of selected countries								
	Japan	**USA**	**UK**	**Italy**	**S. Korea**	**Brazil**	**India**	**Bangladesh**
GNP (US $ per capita)	36,640	26,980	18,700	19,020	9,700	3,640	340	240
Life expectancy	77M 83F	73M 79F	74M 79F	75M 82F	70M 78F	57M 66F	60M 61F	56M 56F
Birth rate (per 1000)	10	15	13	10	16	20	25	30
Death rate (per 1000)	8	9	11	10	6	9	9	11
Infant mortality (per 1000 live births)	4	7	6	7	8	53	69	100
Adult literacy	99%	99%	99%	97%	97%	81%	50%	36%

Q

1 Construct a table based on **A** with extra columns so that you can rank the eight countries for **each** of the development indices. Rank **one** should indicate the greatest development. **Take care**: the highest value is not always the best, e.g. infant mortality.

2 Add up the ranks for each country to give you a total Development Index and write the answer in an extra column. Finally, rank the countries based on their Development Index.

B

Global distribution of wealth and economic activity

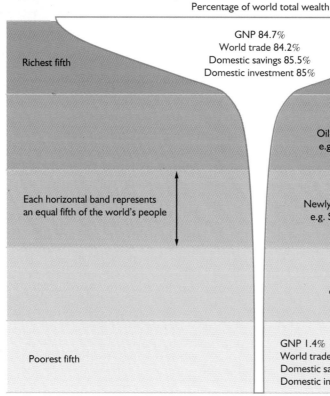

Percentage of world total wealth

Richest fifth

GNP 84.7%
World trade 84.2%
Domestic savings 85.5%
Domestic investment 85%

More developed countries, e.g., USA, Japan

Oil-exporting countries, e.g. Saudi Arabia, Libya

Each horizontal band represents an equal fifth of the world's people

Newly industrialized countries, e.g. Singapore, South Korea

Debtor countries, e.g. Mexico, Ghana

Poorest fifth

GNP 1.4%
World trade 0.9%
Domestic savings 0.7%
Domestic investment 0.9%

Low income countries, e.g. Chad, Malawi, Bangladesh

CASE STUDY *1* LEDC: Bangladesh

Minal Chandra (**C**) is ten years old. He is from Bangladesh, one of the poorest countries in the world by GDP standards.

Schooling is open to everyone in Bangladesh, but not all children can go. Even though schools are free, parents often cannot afford to buy the uniforms, textbooks, paper and pencils that the child would need at school; and not all villages have primary schools where young children can start to learn. Most children are needed to work at home; many families would not survive without the help of children to tend and harvest the crops. More boys attend school than girls because girls are usually kept at home to work.

Minal Chandra travels 22km every day to work in a cycle repair shop – mending tyres, welding and running errands. For a day's work he is given food and earns a small amount of money. Minal wanted to keep going to school but his mother and father do not earn enough money. His aim is to earn enough money so that he can finish his studies and fulfil his dream to become a school teacher.

CASE STUDY *2* LEDC: Brazil

Julio Santos, 15, used to hang around street corners wielding a machine gun as he peddled cocaine in some of Brazil's most crime-ridden slums. Now he has discarded his weapon in favour of a PC (**D**). "I am much better off armed with my computer skills. This way I may have a future," he says. He is among thousands of youths to find an alternative via computing schools set up by a Brazilian non-governmental organisation in some of Rio's most precarious urban sprawls. He came off the streets in April to attend daily class in a makeshift shack crammed with top-line Pentiums. The schools offer four-month courses in basic PC skills and only those who can afford the $10 charge have to pay.

The idea came from Rodrigo Baggio, a computer science teacher in Rio. Baggio gave up his job to lobby businesses to donate computers for the favelas. By 1995, he had set up the Committee for the Democratisation of Computer Technology (CDI) with fellow computer buffs. Relying on donated equipment and dozens of voluntary workers, they began to install PCs in classrooms. "The idea was to teach computing from a technical point of view but also deal with important issues for favela inhabitants such as citizenship rights, human rights, crime and segregation," says Baggio. "This way people would see that some of their problems could be dealt with at the same time as acquiring a skill."

Baggio now boasts 36 schools in as many favelas around Rio, catering for 190 pupils at a time. "We aim to take schools even to remote villages in the Amazon rainforest," he adds.

Gabriella Gamini,
Inter//face, The Times,
29 July, 1998,

Questions

1. Place the eight countries from table **A** in two groups depending on whether they belong to the 'rich economically developed north' or the 'poor economically developed south'. (2)

2. Use the information from table **A** to show that the countries of the 'South' are less well off than the countries of the 'North'. The results from the question on page 148 could help support your answer. (6)

3. Suggest **two** other measures of development not used in table **A**. Explain how you think these measures may indicate levels of development. (6)

4. Why is GDP not always a good measure of development? (6)

5. Case study 1 clearly suggests that the quality of life in the poorer LEDCs is worse than in the richer MEDCs. In what ways might the opposite be true, where the quality of life may be seen as better in LEDCs than MEDCs? (5)

Total: 25 marks

CLOSING THE DEVELOPMENT GAP

Trying to close the development gap is not an easy or a short-term challenge (**A**). If the issues of inequality between different countries is to be tackled, then it is important to try and understand why there is such a huge and growing gap in the levels of development.

A 'It is one thing to wish the world were a better place, and quite another to make it happen in the very near future. World leaders who proclaim that closing the gap between the rich and poor countries is the most urgent task of our times should ask themselves how this could be done. This alluring goal simply cannot be approached, much less attained, in the next 100 years.'

An economist, Khan, 1979

Why is there a gap?

The relationship between the rich and poor countries of the world is all too often like the one shown in **B**. Why is this?

Manufacturing first developed in the MEDCs often by using raw materials from LEDCs. LEDCs sold these cheaply to MEDCs, but the LEDCs soon became financially dependent on exporting their resources. Because the export of raw materials is often their only source of income it is economically very risky. The price paid for the exports is subject to changes in world market prices and many resources are limited making long-term planning impossible. Many hectares of valuable farmland are used to grow export

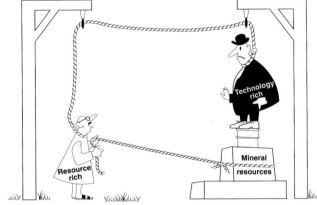

" Do you realise I have you under my control ? "

crops rather than local food supplies. Few LEDCs have developed their manufacturing industries successfully because they export their raw materials for processing. Resource **exploitation** still goes on. Multinational corporations have now set up factories in developing countries to take advantage of cheap labour, relaxed pollution laws and new marketing opportunities. Again, most of the profits are fed back to the MEDCs. LEDCs and MEDCs have become financially and resource dependent on one another. However, the MEDCs often take the largest share of profit.

D

Countries exporting raw materials				
Country	Value of exports	Commodities	Value of imports	Commodities
Ghana	$1.57 billion	Gold 39% Cocoa beans 35% Timber 9.4%	$1.84 billion	Machinery, petroleum, foodstuffs
Niger	$188 million	Uranium ore 67% Livestock (meat) 20%	$374 million	Machinery, vehicle parts, petroleum
Sudan	$620 million	Cotton 23% Sesame 22% Livestock 13% Gum 5%	$1.5 billion	Food, petroleum, manufactured goods, machinery, medicines
Zambia	$2.5 billion	Agricultural goods 38% Gold 12% Other metals 7% Textiles 4%	$2.2 billion	Machinery, foodstuffs, manufactured goods, chemicals

Q

1 Using the information in **D** explain why you think these countries have a problem closing the development gap?

2 Study the cartoons in **B** and **C**. Suggest what message **each** cartoon is trying to give.

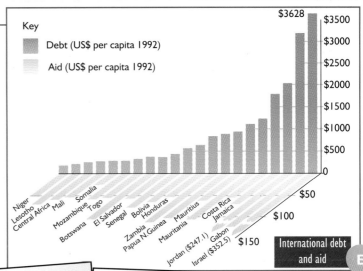

Heavy dependence on foreign loans has led to a build up of foreign debts (**E**). In the 1970s many LEDCs were encouraged to borrow heavily from banks in developed countries, often for large and inappropriate building projects. Examples of these include huge dams such as the one on the Volta in Ghana, which proved to be less successful than hoped because of the irregular flow of the river. There is very little water in the dry season. Projects like this often bring limited benefit to the majority of people in these countries, yet they are all burdened with the effects of the debt. During the 1980s interest charges rose rapidly adding millions of dollars to the repayments. Nigeria spends more money paying interest on its loans than it does on health care.

Some LEDCs are politically unstable and get caught up in civil wars. Financing these wars swallows up what limited resources are available and this also discourages investment from overseas. Sometimes LEDCs buy arms from MEDCs as part of a trade deal. This does little to help the economic development of the LEDC.

Tourism, the world's largest industry, is often affected by political unrest. Countries may lose a valuable source of income in this way.

Can the gap be closed?

Several different approaches have been tried, most of which fall into two categories:

Aid programmes

These are one way in which the MEDCs give help to improve the quality of life in LEDCs. This aid is usually in the form of money and can be a direct donation or a loan. The money is then used for a variety of different aid programmes. It may be used for disaster relief; to develop new industries, power supplies or transport links; to build new schools and hospitals or teach people new skills and invest in small-scale developments. By introducing appropriate technology and limited loans on a local scale, people can be helped to break out of poverty and the dependency trap. Aid programmes have to be carefully managed to be successful; depending on aid can become a major problem (**H**).

Investment programmes

In recent years some LEDCs have developed their economies rapidly through investment in and development of their manufacturing industries. The **Newly**

F 'The total owed by the poorer countries to the richer ones now stands at a staggering one trillion pounds.'
Friends of the Earth

G 'Third World countries want to pay the money back, it's just that they can't. If it were only a question of paying the initial loans, the Third World would have done this many times over. But repaying debt means paying off high interest charges. In 1982 the total amount that the Third World owed to the developed countries was $860 billion. Since then debtor countries have repaid thousands of billions, yet they still owe $2,000 billion.'
Oxfam

Q What are the good and bad points of the type of graph shown in E? Can you suggest a better way of showing this information?

Industrializing Countries of Asia (Hong Kong, Singapore, Taiwan, Malaysia and South Korea) now account for 10 per cent of world trade. The products from these countries have a world-wide reputation and include a wide range of electrical goods and motor vehicles. These countries have developed their economies using the 'top-down' route (**I**) (see South Korea, pages 154–155).

H ### The problems of depending on aid

- Aid encourages countries to become dependent on donations.
- Many government officials are corrupt and the money does not always reach those in most need
- Non governmental aid depends on charitable donations and it is difficult to rely on long-term solutions.
- Aid is only a 'sticking plaster' to cover something up temporarily. Countries need to develop their own trade and industries and become self-sufficient.

I ### Different routes to economic development

'**Top-down**' This is where a government or multinational company makes the decisions rather than involving local communities. Tend to be large-scale development projects which bring prestige and new sources of employment and income to the country but do not necessarily improve the quality of life for the majority of people.

'**Bottom-up**' This is where local communities develop small-scale projects which are appropriate to local needs.

'**Sustainable**' This type of development reaches the needs of local people but also does not affect resources for the future.

AID: IMPROVING THE QUALITY OF LIFE IN LEDCS?

A and **B** are examples of advertising used by charities to encourage us to donate money to people in LEDCs. Many people in the UK and other MEDCs donate money on a regular basis to help improve the quality of life of people in LEDCs. Others donate in response to national fund-raising activities such as 'Red Nose Day' or in response to a disaster appeal. 70 per cent of all natural disasters occur in LEDCs, yet these are the countries least able to cope with such events.

The money that individuals donate is often targeted at small-scale projects or is spread so thinly that it has little impact in closing the development gap. Most LEDCs receive much larger donations of aid from other sources (see below).

Different types of aid

Voluntary Aid This is aid that has nothing to do with government where well-known charities, such as ActionAid and Oxfam, provide money for use on special projects in poorer countries. They depend on voluntary contributions and active support and they usually have a range of fund-raising activities including sponsoring children, high street charity shops and donations from industries. ActionAid raised over £37 million in 1995.

Bilateral Aid This is a type of aid between two countries. It usually involves a loan or investment from an MEDC for a building project such as a dam in an LEDC. This type of aid does have its drawbacks because it often involves the LEDC taking out further loans to finance the project fully or it *ties* the LEDC into trading deals with the donor. Examples of this type of aid are often linked with guarantees of orders of defence weapons. There are major criticisms of this type of bilateral aid; the LEDC often loses out as in the example of the Pergau Dam in Malaysia (**C**).

Multilateral Aid This is when rich countries give money to the poorer countries through international banks such as the World Bank and the International Monetary Fund. The United Nations recommends that all MEDCs contribute 0.7 per cent of their GNP to aid. In 1998 the UK was falling short of this target. The Minister for Overseas Development pledged to raise the UK's contribution to the 0.7 per cent level by the year 2000.

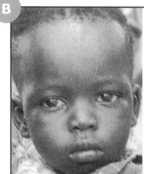

Imagine going hungry for a day, for a week, or for even longer. Yet in parts of the developing world there are people who, in between harvests, quite literally go hungry for months.

ACTIONAID

C

An example of bilateral aid: The Pergau Dam Project in Malaysia

A controversial bilateral aid project, involving the British government in 1988, was the construction of the Pergau Dam on the Pergau river in northern Malaysia. This project took up £234 million of British aid. The 600-megawatt Malaysian HEP project was originally planned to be a 200-megawatt dam. The plan was opposed by the local people who favoured a small gas-fired power station which would have cost a third as much. In the end it actually cost the Malaysian government £100 million more in electricity costs than using some cheaper alternatives.

Large areas of land were flooded and people were displaced. The water supply to the dam caused problems because of the irregular flow of the Pergau River so a regulating lake was built to ensure a smooth flow of water. Water has to be pumped up to the lake from a lower level. There were further additional costs as a ventilation unit had to be built to cool the hot rocks in the underground generating chamber. Critics saw a link between the huge loan offered for the dam at favourable interest rates and a £1 billion arms deal signed by the British defence minister and the Malaysian government. This was seen as an example of 'tied' aid. The British would supply the loan as long as the Malaysians continued to buy British arms.

'Critics note that there is an increasing amount of aid for countries that buy British arms; this means less aid for the very poorest countries of the world. With the aid budget already squeezed, there are fears that there will be increasing pressure to get 'good value' from the aid budget. The money that is spent on arms could be spent on human development.' (*Tearfund, Gunrunners Gold 1995*)

Bangladesh has some of the richest farmland in the world. It lies on the deltas of the rivers Ganges and Brahmaputra which have built up the land by depositing the vast amounts of silt they carry on their journey to the Bay of Bengal. Every year these rivers flood. It is normal for half of Bangladesh to be under water during the monsoon period.

Problems facing the people of Bangladesh

- **Over population** 118 million people live in an area half the size of the UK.
- **Poverty** 40 per cent of people live in absolute poverty. Bangladesh is ranked 143 on the Human Development Index (see page 148)
- **Small farms** Most people are subsistence farmers living off tiny plots rented from landowners.
- **Muslim law** Most people are Muslim (14 per cent are Hindu). Under the Muslim law land is always handed down from a father to be divided between his sons. Sometimes the land has been subdivided so many times that it becomes too small to work.
- **Female exploitation** Many girls have a very difficult life and few have the chance of independence or to develop their skills.
- **Natural hazards** Bangladesh suffers from heavy monsoon rains and cyclones (see page 88).

How has aid helped Bangladesh?

Bangladesh receives voluntary, bilateral and multilateral aid.

Aid from Oxfam

D   Tomiza Khatoon and a small village group asked a local Oxfam organization for a loan to set up a small business growing rice. As well as the loan, they were given training in all sorts of things, from setting up a small business, to learning to read, write and do sums. After their first harvest they were able to divide the profits between them. Next they asked for a loan to buy some cows, and then, along with another group, they were given loans to lease a pond and surrounding land to breed fish and plant banana trees

Tomiza also used her new skills to buy material, make dresses and sell them in her village, which has been a great addition to the family's income. Her life has greatly improved.

Oxfam

Aid for natural disasters

Relief agencies, such as Oxfam and other charities, plus the World Food Programme (an international aid programme) funded $726.2 million to help the 19 million people in most need after the 1998 floods. They estimated that the flood had destroyed over 300,000 million tonnes of rice. The UK government also gave £21 million to Bangladesh to help with the disaster relief. The UK and Bangladesh have close ties in terms of aid. Bangladesh received £45 million to spend on poverty-related programmes in 1997.

FACT FILE

	Bangladesh	UK
Population (million)	118	58
Population density (per sq km)	909	241
Land area (sq km)	130,000	244,000
Urban population	17%	89%
GNP per person (US$)	220	17,970
Life expectancy	53	76

Medical aid

Like many other LEDCs, the drift of people in search of a better life to large urban centres is creating major problems of overcrowding and increasing squalor. There are approximately 9 million people living in the slums of Dhaka. These slums lack access to the most basic of services including clean safe water, sanitation, primary health care and education. The Leprosy Mission (TLM) is a charity that works in countries such as Bangladesh to help people suffering from leprosy (**E**). Much of its work is based in slum areas of Dhaka, the capital city. The Dhaka Leprosy Control Project was set up in 1996 to provide medical relief and education to sufferers. TLM has also linked up with other charities such as ActionAid to provide better water facilities and informal education. Many leprosy sufferers have difficulty finding work because of their disability and the stigma connected with the disease. TLM has set up vocational training centres where young people are taught new and relevant trades such as vehicle maintenance and TV and radio repair. This means that a regular income is a real possibility.

E The Leprosy Mission

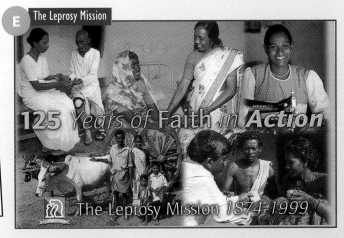

125 Years of Faith in Action
The Leprosy Mission 1874–1999

Questions

1 Use the fact file to explain why Bangladesh needs aid. (5)
2 State two differences between the types of aid given to Bangladesh and Malaysia (The Pergau Dam Project). (3)
3 Which type of aid, from question 2, is in your opinion best for an LEDC country? Give reasons for your choice. (5)
4 With reference to specific detail, describe how Oxfam has helped Bangladesh. (6)
5 How has the quality of life for Bangladeshi people been improved by foreign aid? (6)

Total: 25 marks

FACT FILE	South Korea (1995)
Area (sq km)	99,300 km
Population	45 million
Population density (per sq km)	457
GNP (per person)	$7,670
Capital city	Seoul
Language	Korean

South Korea is an LEDC that has developed its economy rapidly within the past fifty years. With very limited natural resources available for industrial development, like Japan, South Korea has been dependent on the import of most of its raw materials. The timeline in **B** shows how the country was helped by financial aid and investment from the USA. With this investment and strict government policies on trade and industrial development South Korea is now a lot wealthier than most LEDCs. Indicators of its success include:

- Ranked twelfth largest global trading country.
- World's largest producer of electronic parts in the mid-1990s and plans to be world's leading exporter of textiles.
- South Korean products have become household names in many countries including the UK. Samsung electronics company, for example, is ranked as one of the fifteen largest corporations in the world.
- Many South Korean companies have expanded their investment into manufacturing bases to other countries, including MEDCs such as the UK, globalizing its scale of production. Globalization is a major breakthrough for South Korea. It had been labelled the 'hermit kingdom' as it was so cut off from the outside world and overshadowed by its two powerful neighbours – China and Japan.
- The 1988 Olympics were staged in the capital Seoul. This event attracted a lot of investment in the infrastructure of the country and did much to improve its status.

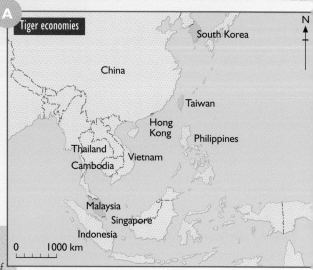

A   Tiger economies

B

Timeline of South Korean economic growth

1950s Through a policy of **import substitution**, South Korea banned the import of goods from overseas and developed its own manufacturing industries with financial aid and investment from the USA.

1960s Cheap labour costs meant that South Korea could export its manufactured products world-wide at a low cost. This opened up a huge trading market, bringing money into the country.

1970 Money was invested in education and training in South Korea. The manufacturing base was widened into large-scale iron and steel production. South Korea overtook Britain as the world's main shipbuilder.

1980 The heavy industries that developed in the 1970s continued to be very competitive on world markets. As the economy grew so did the standard of living and purchasing power of the South Koreans.
Quality of life for South Koreans was improving rapidly. Cheaper labour became available in countries such as Thailand and Malaysia, so much of the manufacturing production was switched to other countries. Labour costs in the 1990s were cheaper in Wales than in South Korea (the Korean company LG for example has located a new semi-conductor plant on the M4 motorway near Newport in South Wales).

1990 High-tech industries developing in South Korea: the economy has more of a service/tertiary base. One major problem with the rapid development of an economy based on trade and manufacturing on a global scale is the insecurity of currencies which affects the value of goods. In the late 1990s the 'Tiger' economies, including Japan, suffered currency collapses which affected production and sales both at home and abroad. Japan supports the single European currency to limit the insecurity of exchange rates. This support has affected its choice of location of European factories, favouring sites in countries that support the Euro.

C

Changes in employment in South Korea

Year	1963	1970	1980	1989
Agriculture	63.1%	50.5%	34%	19.5%
Manufacturing and mining	8.7%	14.3%	22.6%	28.2%
Services and other	28.2%	35.2%	43.4%	52.3%
Total workforce	7,6629,	745	13,706	17,510

D

Cars lined up ready for export

So successful has South Korea's policy on inward investment been that, among its many other industries, it has five car manufacturing companies which export to many countries of the world including the UK. Motor vehicle production began in South Korea in 1970 and this was based on imported designs and parts. Hyundai, the leading motor manufacturer, started off producing Fords as part of a joint investment programme with Ford Motors of America. The first real South Korean car was the 'Pony' which was designed in Italy and produced using former British Leyland machinery. The additional example of a joint investment policy led to the successful export of the 'Pony' in the early 1980s. Demand in the domestic market grew as the purchasing power of the South Koreans increased. South Korea is now a leading automobile producer and in 1993 overtook the UK in terms of total output (**D**).

E

South Korean motor vehicle production			
Year	Total	Passenger cars	Commercial vehicles
1970	28,819	14,487	14,332
1975	37,179	18,398	18,781
1980	123,135	57,225	65,910
1985	378,162	264,458	113,704
1990	1,321,630	986,751	334,879
1992	1,729,696	1,306,752	422,944

The Daewoo story

Daewoo is another success story for South Korea and again shows how the policy of inward investment and careful marketing has helped the South Korean economy to grow. Daewoo cars first appeared in the UK in 1994. It was the first company to sell cars directly to the public rather than using showroom outlets. Daewoo also manufactures pianos, ships, TV and HI-FI equipment, mobile phones and broadcasting systems. In South Korea the company is investing in the film and entertainment business and also financing new supermarkets, department stores and shopping malls. Daewoo has invested heavily in resource development overseas to secure a supply of coal, oil and other energy and natural resources. It is a typical success story of a small manufacturing firm starting in South Korea and growing into a world-wide multinational corporation (**F**).

F A Daewoo advertisement

The Daewoo company started in Seoul in 1967 with a capital of $10,000. It started as a textile company with five employees exporting nylon shirting material to south-east Asian countries. Its exports valued $58,000 in its first year. The money was reinvested in the company to improve and update the manufacturing process and production rates. By 1997, the company's total sales reached $16.89 billion and total exports $15 billion.

Daewoo has built up its powerful corporation by trading affordable and appealing products and ensuring a policy of continuing investment in the industry. It has kept up with market trends by being versatile and adjusting its range of products to consumer demand. The corporation now markets over 3,000 products to 165 nations around the world.

Has the quality of life improved?

South Korea is an economic success story, but, as with many 'top-down' models of economic development, success has been achieved at a price. There have been gains and losses in terms of the quality of life for the people of South Korea. There has certainly been a rise in income levels for those employed in the new industries which has led to a higher level of consumer demand and the growth of a thriving service sector. However, the rapid rate of industrial expansion has caused major damage to the environment and has not improved the quality of life for many South Koreans.

- South Korea has been labelled a 'sweatshop' with South Koreans working longer hours than workers in other countries. They spend an average of 52 hours per week at work, compared with 35 hours in Japan and 41 hours in the USA.

- Pollution has become a major side effect of rapid industrialization. Problems of air, water and land pollution have become a growing concern for the South Korean government.

- Most industrial development has been in the large city areas such as Seoul of South Korea. Rural depopulation has become a major problem and the numbers employed in agriculture are declining at a rapid rate as people flock to the better-paid manufacturing jobs in the cities.

- South Korea has built up an export-led economy, which is dependent on world market trends. As currency rates fluctuate and countries are developing more protectionist measures in their trading policies, economies such as South Korea's which depend on trading may suffer.

Q

1 Has investment in South Korea led to an overall improvement in the quality of life? Make a list of both positive and negative points.

2 How are living standards likely to have been affected by the economic collapse of the late-1990s?

Trade

Global patterns and trends

Many economists see trade rather than aid as the way forward towards economic development. Countries could be earning income through exporting their goods rather than just 'importing aid'. This certainly proved successful for South Korea and the oil states of the Middle East, but this does not mean any type of trade will bring rapid economic growth. Oil is the most traded commodity in the world and the Middle East countries hold the richest known reserves. The South Koreans combine cost effective production of manufactured goods, in demand on the world market, with successful trading strategies. Successful trading is not just exporting any type of goods; there has to be a real demand for the products.

Unfortunately, most LEDCs export low value raw materials which are then processed in the consumer, usually MEDC, countries. The profits made from processed or manufactured goods are much higher than from raw materials and so the MEDC benefits most. Not surprisingly MEDCs have a higher share of total world exports by value (**A**).

Trade is the movement of goods and services between different areas, usually between countries. Very few countries are **self sufficient** and can provide all they need; they have to buy in or import goods and services from other countries. This is trade. Some countries have a **comparative advantage** over others in terms of producing goods. Some advantages may be natural such as the climate or mineral resources. Other advantages could be human skills or a surplus of cheap labour. Brazil, for example, has a climate suited to growing coffee. Some countries have vast reserves of fossil fuels (South Africa) or metal ores (Brazil). The Philippines have plenty of cheap labour to produce inexpensive clothing. All this supply and demand of commodities leads to the import and export of goods.

Many countries are dependent on trade as a major source of their income (**B**). The '**export-led**' MEDCs are usually dependent on trading manufactured goods. The LEDC exporters are more likely to depend on trading raw materials.

A Share of world trade

Equator 0°

0   5000 km
at the Equator

Key
Percentage share of total world exports by value (1993)
- Over 10%
- 5 – 10%
- 1 – 5%
- 0.5 – 1%
- 0.25 – 0.5%
- Under 0.25%

B Dependence on trade

Equator 0°

0   5000 km
at the Equator

Key
Value of exports as a percentage of GNP (1993)
- Over 50%
- 40 – 50%
- 30 – 40%
- 20 – 30%
- 10 – 20%
- Under 10%

Is trade fair?

Looking at **C** it would seem that trade between countries can often be very unfair. Very little of the profit reaches the producer. Many LEDCs are worse off since they depend on the export of low value raw materials for the bulk of their income and are trapped into importing high value manufactured goods from MEDCs. This often happens when tropical developing countries allow their valuable farmland to be used for plantation crops, such as tea and coffee, grown for export to MEDCs. Processed foodstuffs and machinery then have to be imported at high prices. LEDCs become caught in a 'trade trap', where the cost of high priced imports exceeds the money earned from low value exports.

Between 1985 and 1993 a surplus of raw materials on the world market led to a 30 per cent fall in the price of many primary commodities. Unfortunately, the price of manufactured goods continued to rise. This gap between the value of imports and exports is referred to as a trade **deficit**. The ideal position to be in is to have a trade **surplus** where the value of the exports is greater than the cost of the imports.

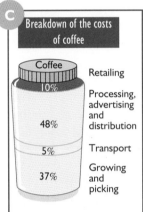

C Breakdown of the costs of coffee

- Retailing 10%
- Processing, advertising and distribution 48%
- Transport 5%
- Growing and picking 37%

6 sacks of Japanese rice cost the same as 24 sacks of Chinese rice

China

Japan

E Rice prices in Japan are protected

Free trade with no support or protection from governments would seem to be fairer. Then the countries which produce the goods at the best price or quality would be able to sell their produce through fair competition. There are already **free trade** agreements between some countries (**F**). This allows the lowering of trade barriers between countries.

D

Value of trade (US$ per person)		
1995	Imports	Exports
Brazil	345	298
China	106	122
Japan	2,684	3,540
Kenya	98	62
Mexico	508	520
Bangladesh	55	27
South Korea	3,013	2,788
UK	4,527	4,130
USA	2,929	2,222

The process of trade between countries is not always straightforward. South Korea built up its own industries by **import substitution**. They restricted imports into the country and manufactured the same goods themselves. This was good for South Korea, but not for the countries which used to export to them. They lost their trade.

Many countries, particularly the MEDCs, operate similar systems to South Korea to protect their own industries. Either they do not import goods that would compete with their own manufactured goods or they put import taxes on goods coming into the country. This makes them more expensive so people will be reluctant to buy them at the higher prices. In some cases, governments may pay subsidies to their own industries to protect them against cheap imports. This type of **protectionism** has been used in Japan. The Japanese government supported their rice farmers against cheap imports from China and the USA (**E**). However, the World Trade Organization are trying to change things to give all countries an equal opportunity to trade.

F

Examples of free trade agreements

EFTA European Free Trade Association
Members at present are Iceland, Liechtenstein, Norway and Switzerland. This trading group was set up in 1960 with seven members. Some of these original members have now joined the EU. EFTA countries have signed a free trade agreement with the EU abolishing import duties on industrial goods between the member countries.

NAFTA North American Free Trade Agreement
This is an agreement between the USA, Canada and Mexico to create an expanded and secure market for certain goods and services produced in their territories.

Q

1 Examine **D**. Which countries have a trade deficit and which a trade surplus? Suggest reasons for your answers.

2 What would the effects be of abolishing subsidies on Japanese rice production?

3 What are free trade agreements?

4 How could free trade agreements affect countries outside the agreement?

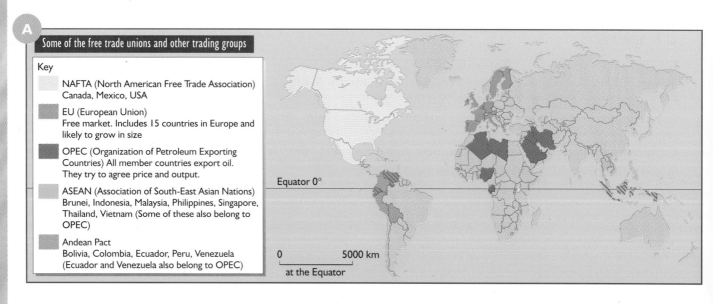

A Some of the free trade unions and other trading groups

Key

NAFTA (North American Free Trade Association)
Canada, Mexico, USA

EU (European Union)
Free market. Includes 15 countries in Europe and likely to grow in size

OPEC (Organization of Petroleum Exporting Countries) All member countries export oil. They try to agree price and output.

ASEAN (Association of South-East Asian Nations) Brunei, Indonesia, Malaysia, Philippines, Singapore, Thailand, Vietnam (Some of these also belong to OPEC)

Andean Pact
Bolivia, Colombia, Ecuador, Peru, Venezuela (Ecuador and Venezuela also belong to OPEC)

Equator 0°

0 — 5000 km
at the Equator

What links exist between states in terms of trade?

As map **A** shows, many of the countries of the world belong to free trade unions or other trading groups. The main aim of these unions is to encourage trade between particular groups of countries and to protect the industries of the member countries. These free trade agreements often give the MEDCs an unfair advantage compared with LEDCs. In 1994 the World Trade Organization was set up to encourage tariff-free trading between all countries of the world. This would give LEDCs a better chance to compete. By March 1999 there were 134 member countries in the World Trade Organization, including the UK. However, free trade agreements on such a large scale can lead to problems.

Problems arising from free trade

- World trade continues to be dominated by a few 'market-led' economies. Japan, the EU and the USA account for 60 per cent of world trade (1995), and the **Newly Industrializing Countries** (Singapore, Hong Kong, Taiwan, South Korea and Malaysia) account for a further 10 per cent.
- Trade and investment in LEDCs seems to be concentrated in a few areas. Of the remaining share of world trade (30 per cent), 60 per cent is shared by just eight countries which include Brazil and Mexico. However, even in those countries experiencing high rates of growth the benefits are not always trickling down to the poor.

- As barriers to trading in LEDCs are removed, world trade is increasingly becoming dominated by some large-scale multinational manufacturers. These have moved into LEDCs and pushed out small-scale local businesses and cooperatives. Much of the profits of these multinationals leave the LEDCs rather than being reinvested. According to World Bank figures, roughly half of the investment from multinational corporations located in LEDCs in 1992 left these countries as profits. Some multinationals have been accused of exploiting workers, particularly children (**B**). Many people are being paid below the minimum living wage and working in appalling conditions.
- In an attempt to keep prices down and compete on the world market many firms have ignored environ-mental protection measures. This has led to permanent environmental damage in many LEDCs.
- LEDCs continue to depend heavily on the export of raw materials for the bulk of their earnings. These raw materials continue to give a low return compared with imported manufactured goods and the trade gap widens.

B Child labour in a Nepalese carpet factory

Can trade be made more fair?

Fair trade is very different from free trade. Fair Trade Organizations aim to give people in LEDCs a chance to benefit from trade and investment rather than being exploited. Fair trade works to stop the abuse and poor working conditions of people by improving the economic and social development of individuals.

Fair trade works by:

- Reducing the number of 'middlemen' and overheads so that the profits go directly to the workers. Fair Trade Organizations (FTO) return up to 40 per cent of the profits to the workers.
- Working with co-operatives that provide safe and dignified working conditions.
- Encouraging producers to reinvest profits into their communities.
- Shifting processing and packing activities to LEDCs to boost incomes (often these activities take place in MEDCs at present).
- Publicizing human rights violations to consumers. This puts pressure on companies to do something about their working practices. As a result of publicity by the FTO, consumer pressure has forced many of the manufacturers of our top selling brands of fashion clothes to pass an internal code of conduct for its suppliers to ensure fair and humane treatment of its employers.

C *The Fair Trade Federation (FTF) is an association of fair trader wholesalers, retailers and producers whose members are committed to providing fair wages and good employment opportunities to economically disadvantaged artisans and farmers world-wide. FTF directly links low income producers with consumer markets and educates consumers about the importance of purchasing fairly traded products which support living wages and safe and healthy conditions for workers in the Third World.*

Fair Trade Federation, 1998

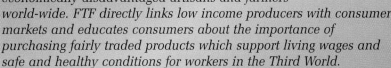

D Stories of hope

The following extracts give examples of how the Fair Trade Federation has given local craftsmen an opportunity to trade (do business) on an international scale. Retailers in the UK, especially those that are part of the Network of European World Shops, stock Fair Trade products.

The Association of Craft Producers in Nepal works with nearly 800 women, many of whom have been widowed or abandoned. The women involved with ACP create a wide variety of quality handcrafts including table linen, felted slippers, hand-painted wood trays, dolls, ceramics, and more. ACP provides a much needed earning opportunity for women and this work has raised the women's self esteem and communication skills.

Coffee farmers near Oaxaca, Mexico, barely eked out a living before Equal Exchange, a Fair Trade Organization, stepped in. Today, the villagers run a rural bus line, send their children to the only secondary school in the region and use a computer to track crop information and sales.

In Kenya, physically disabled people have few job opportunities because of the high unemployment rate and prejudice against them. At Bombolulu Workshop in Mombasa, Kenya, over 250 handicapped artisans design and create beautiful fabrics, wooden carvings and innovative jewellery. Bombolulu Workshop protects the environment by maintaining Kenya's forest resources. They plant ten trees to replace every one used for carving.

Following many years of war, Cambodia now has an overwhelming number of households headed by women. In the outskirts of Phnom Penh, such households make up 40 per cent of families. These families have little access to resources and are the poorest segment of society. Outside Phnom Penh, a Fair Trade Organization called Kemara gives these unskilled women access to credit and training. The women form small groups and start successful businesses such as orchid growing and silk weaving.

Fair Trade Federation, 1998

Q

1 What is meant by the term 'Fair Trade'? Read **C** and select one story from **D** to explain how the FTF has improved the quality of life for people.

2 Transfair International is a fair trade labelling initiative, which has been introduced in several European countries and Japan. It adds a seal to fairly traded products such as coffee, sugar and tea to show that they have been bought from co-operatives in developing countries that abide by fair trade rules. Design a poster to make consumers aware of the benefits of fair trade.

3 Read the following paragraph:

'Even though the stronger economies of the MEDCs would still be able to control a lot of the trade to their own advantage, the future is less certain. The economic growth rates of the LEDCs are racing ahead of the MEDCs, particularly the G7 countries (US, Japan, Italy, Germany, Canada, France and the UK). Asia has a growth rate of 8 per cent, South America 4.5 per cent and the G7 countries only 2 per cent (1998). For all but one of the past 33 years the world's developing economies have grown faster than the developed. The developing countries offer a growing market for the trade and sale of both manufactured goods and raw materials. This creates conflicting views in terms of world trade and aid. MEDCs want to help LEDCs towards economic development, but they do not want unnecessary competition to harm their own trade.'

Discuss in a group what you think this paragraph means and what the message is behind it.

TRADE IN THE EU

There are fifteen countries in the European Union (**A**). It is the world's largest single market with a combined population of over 370 million (larger than the USA). More trade involves the EU than anywhere else in the world: 38 per cent of all world trade is with the EU compared with 14 per cent for the USA and 8 per cent for Japan.

The EU was first set up as a trading union for coal and steel between six countries in 1951. In 1957 this was extended to all economic aspects for the six original members: France, West Germany, Italy, Netherlands, Belgium and Luxembourg. Since then it has continued to become a more powerful trading group as the six became nine, twelve and now fifteen countries. There are now plans to expand EU membership further as the countries of Eastern Europe arrange to join (**A**).

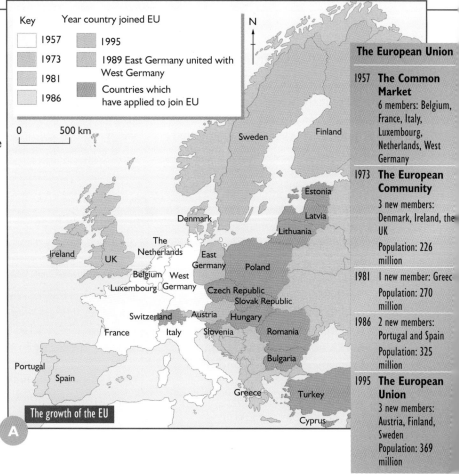

Key   Year country joined EU

□ 1957   ▨ 1995
▨ 1973   ▨ 1989 East Germany united with West Germany
▨ 1981
▨ 1986   ▨ Countries which have applied to join EU

0   500 km

A The growth of the EU

The European Union

1957	**The Common Market** 6 members: Belgium, France, Italy, Luxembourg, Netherlands, West Germany
1973	**The European Community** 3 new members: Denmark, Ireland, the UK. Population: 226 million
1981	1 new member: Greece Population: 270 million
1986	2 new members: Portugal and Spain Population: 325 million
1995	**The European Union** 3 new members: Austria, Finland, Sweden Population: 369 million

Internal trade

Not surprisingly there is a lot of internal trade between the member countries of the EU. **D** shows how extensive this trade is, with all except Finland having over 50 per cent of their trade with other EU members. Portugal has almost 75 per cent of its trade with fellow members. The formation of the Single European Market in 1992 saw a lowering of trade and employment barriers within the EU and particularly encouraged internal trade.

External trade

The EU has considerable trading links with other countries of the world. **B** shows the direction of its trade for both imports and exports. This pattern of trade is the result of a number of factors:

- **Former colonies** Many EU countries still trade heavily with former colonies as links continue long after independence. So the UK still has strong links with Kenya and France with Morocco.
- **The Commonwealth** The UK also used to trade a lot with fellow Commonwealth members. Since joining the EU in 1973, this has declined, but for example New Zealand lamb and bananas from the Caribbean are still prominent imports for the UK.

- **Distance** The EU has a lot of trade with other non-EU European countries, such as Switzerland. These countries are nearby and often have good transport links with EU members.
- **Development** The majority of EU trade is with other developed nations. These have the money to buy EU exports and produce many EU consumer products. EU trade with the USA and Japan is therefore quite extensive. Note, however, that the trade with NICs is rapidly increasing and that many primary products are imported from LEDCs.
- **Trading barriers** Quota or import duties have limited imports from non-EU countries. This makes it difficult for LEDCs to find new markets. However, countries such as Japan have overcome the barriers by setting up factories within the EU.

Q Discuss the advantages and disadvantages of granting EU membership to the countries which have applied for membership (**A**). Use the atlas to look up their GDP, employment structure, population, and other relevant information to consider their contribution to the EU.

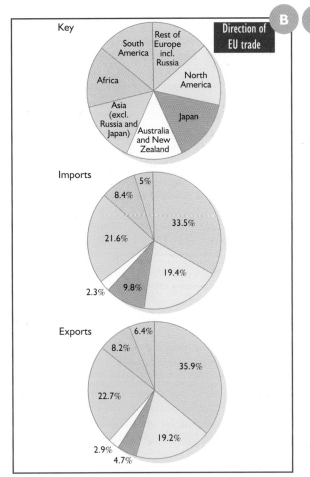

B Direction of EU trade

Key: Rest of Europe incl. Russia, North America, Japan, Australia and New Zealand, Asia (excl. Russia and Japan), Africa, South America

Imports: 33.5%, 19.4%, 9.8%, 2.3%, 21.6%, 8.4%, 5%

Exports: 35.9%, 19.2%, 4.7%, 2.9%, 22.7%, 8.2%, 6.4%

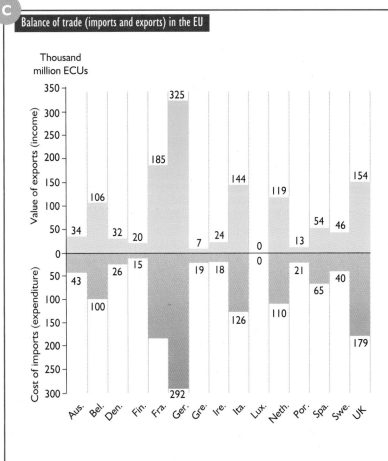

C Balance of trade (imports and exports) in the EU

Thousand million ECUs

Value of exports (income) / Cost of imports (expenditure)

	Aus.	Bel.	Den.	Fin.	Fra.	Ger.	Gre.	Ire.	Ita.	Lux.	Neth.	Por.	Spa.	Swe.	UK
Exports	34	106	32	20	185	325	7	24	144	0	119	13	54	46	154
Imports	43	100	26	15	292		19	18	126	0	110	21	65	40	179

D

Trade with other EU countries															
Country	Austria	Belgium	Denmark	Finland	France	Germany	Greece	Ireland	Italy	Luxembourg	Netherlands	Portugal	Spain	Sweden	UK
% imports	67	71	54	46	64	51	60	69	55	-	66	72	61	55	49
% exports	60	74	54	45	61	50	56	69	53	-	74	75	62	53	53

Questions

1 Describe how important the EU is as a trading group. (3)

2 Compare the main trends shown by the pie charts in **B** for the direction of EU imports and exports (5)

3 Use graph **C** to work out the trade balance for each EU country (to calculate the trade balance subtract imports from exports, e.g. the trade balance for Austria is –9). Briefly comment on your results. (5)

4 With reference to **D**, suggest reasons why some EU members depend on internal EU trade more than others. (6)

5 Explain the EU's pattern of trade with non-EU members. (6)

Total: 25 marks

GLOSSARY

Agroforestry   The combined use of land for agriculture and forestry wh e latter can benefit the former, e.g. as windbreaks and maintaining nutrient cycle.

Break of bulk point   A port or similar point where raw materials or goods being transported changes from one method of transport to another.

Closed system   An industrial or physical system where nothing leaves the system, i.e. the outputs become the next cycle of inputs.

Comparative advantage   When an area has an advantage over others in terms of industrial or agricultural production, e.g. its climate, resources, labour force, or access to good transport links.

Composite index   A measure of human development using a number of indicators rather than just one, e.g. adult literacy and life expectancy.

Core   An area of concentrated economic growth.

Decentralization   Movement of population or employment away from urban centres.

Deficit   A shortfall between the value of exports and the cost of imports.

Deforestation   Complete felling and clearance of forests.

Desertification   Spread of a desert.

Disparity   A difference in economic development between regions.

Diversification   Broadening of an economic activity, e.g. a farm offering bed and breakfast.

Exploitation   The use of resources or people at their expense affecting long-term supply or their well being.

Export-led   A country which is heavily dependent on the export of goods and materials for its economy.

Free trade   Not retricted by import, export duties, quotas or any form of protectionism.

Globalization   An industry or corporation acting on a global scale with manufacturing bases in several countries.

Greenfield site   An area of land used for development which has not been used before, usually in a rural area.

Growth pole   Locations where economic activities are planned in order to bring or encourage growth to the local economy, by setting off a chain reaction of expansions.

High-tech industry   Involving advanced technology, e.g. manufacture of semi-conductors, computers, or microchips.

Import substitution   The production of a good, which has been formerly imported, by the country itself.

Informal sector   Employment which is not registered with a government for tax purposes, e.g. street vending.

Interdependence   Countries/regions that are linked through trade are also dependent on each other. Each is affected by another's economic decisions and situations.

Integration   Bringing together the successive stages involved in the production of a particular good at the same location.

Labour intensive   An economic activity which involves a large labour force.

Location factor   A feature of a location which is an important requirement for an industry, e.g. flat land or near a motorway.

Micro-enterprise   Small-scale, local economic activity, usually based in LEDCs.

Multiplier effect   Direct or indirect consequences of an action, a knock-on effect, e.g. when an industry locates somewhere and others are attracted because of it.

Multinational company   A company or corporation which operates in several countries. Also transnational corporations (TNCs).

Newly Industrializing Country (NIC)   An LEDC which has industrialized and over the last 20 years has had a high rate of economic growth. Particularly used for the countries of South East Asia.

Open system   Where outputs leave the system of production, e.g. commercial farming of cereals.

Periphery   Areas outside or on the edge of the economic centre or core, which do not compare favourably in terms of economic development or standard of living.

Protectionism   Use of policies to discourage imports and protect country's own agriculture and industry from foreign competition.

Quaternary industry   Provide specialist information and expertise, e.g. the micro-electronics industries.

Rationalization   Reorganization of industry to achieve greater efficiency and economy.

Self sufficiency   Requiring nothing from the outside, e.g. a farm which grows all its own food.

Set-aside   Agricultural land that is set aside and not used. A policy introduced to reduce surplus food production within the EU.

Sunrise   Industries which are new, e.g. high-tech industries.

Sunset   Industries which are old and closing down.

Surplus   An excess of a product, e.g. the butter mountain in the EU.

Sustainable development   Use of resources and appropriate technology which does not damage the natural environment or affect the long-term supply of resources.

Technology intensive   Industry which uses mainly robots, machinery and computers in its production process.

CHAPTER

4

Population and settlement

Theme 4

Population, distribution, structure and change

The location and function of settlements

Land use within settlements

The growth and decline of settlements

Theme 5

Exploitation and management of natural resources

Resolving issues

Introduction

Why study population and settlement?

How many people are there alive today? Is it true that there are more people alive today than have died during the whole of history? Is there a problem over the estimated future size of the population? Where are people living? How have they come to live in this place? Have we any successful ways of reducing the problems of urban growth and improving the quality of life for people in cities? Why are people rushing towards cities in one place and away from them in another? Will cities still exist in the 21st century?

All of us follow a pattern of life, which includes some of the events described. They will be different for everyone but a pattern emerges. Birth rates are falling and life expectancy is increasing. More people are living in or close to cities. Too many people live in poor housing, cities are congested, crime is a threat and we are searching for a sustainable future.

This chapter explores the patterns of population change and the challenges it brings. There are too many people in some places and too few in others. Wealth is not equally divided so that the ability to meet the challenges of population and settlement growth is not equal. We explore the ways in which MEDCs meet one set of challenges and LEDCs a different set. For all people we look for ways to improve their quality of life.

Questions for enquiry

To gain a better understanding of population and settlement these key questions will be investigated in this chapter:

- 🌐 Where do people live?
- 🌐 Why do more people live in some places than in others?

- 🌐 How and why is the population of places changing?
- 🌐 How and why does the age structure of populations vary?
- 🌐 Why is the balance between the numbers of people living in rural and urban areas changing?
- 🌐 What affects the location of individual settlements?
- 🌐 Is there a link between the size and location of a settlement and its functions?
- 🌐 Where are different activities located within settlements?
- 🌐 How and why is land use within settlements changing?
- 🌐 What factors influence social and cultural patterns in towns and cities?
- 🌐 Why are some settlements growing while others are declining?
- 🌐 How are these changes affecting the quality of life?

Themes

The answers to these questions will be explored by looking at seven topics from population and settlement:

- Population distribution
- Population change
- Population structure
- Migration
- The location and function of settlements
- Land use patterns
- The growth and decline of settlements.

A People on a crowded beach, Europe

People and places

A lot of geography is about people. Suppose we were in a helicopter flying over a crowded beach. Look at **A**. How would geographers view the scene? A lifeguard would be concerned about the size of the surf and the danger of different users clashing. Two ice cream sellers would be searching for the best location. The local leisure officer would be interested in the size of the crowds and state of the beach. As a geographer we would be asking four questions:

1 Where are people and events *located* on the beach? Aerial photographs would help us observe and map this at different times of the day.

2 What *patterns* of people and activity can we see? We can pick out dense and deserted areas. We note groups of people doing different things.

3 Why are people and activities spread on the different parts of the beach in the way they are? We try to *explain* the patterns we have seen and mapped. We

could start by dividing the area into water and land and noting the people and activities in each. The area could be divided into regions such as the water, beach, sand dunes and car park. We wonder where the people have come from.

4 How is the scene *changing*? We are interested in the changes by the hour, day, season and year. Conditions change dramatically on the beach between winter and summer and very different patterns emerge.

If we explore these questions and understand what is happening we may be able to predict what will happen and suggest alternative ways to manage the beach. Predicting weather hazards, population totals, urban growth, traffic congestion and pollution make geographers very useful to society. Of course, it helps if our understanding is good and our predictions are accurate.

4.1

Population distribution and change

Where do people live?

People have argued for many years about the size of the population of the world. Some warn that the day will come when the world will not be able to support all the people. In 1998 the total population of the world was estimated to be just above 5.8 billion. Some estimates put the total as high as 8 billion by the year 2000AD.

People are not evenly spread. For example, in some parts of the UK the population is very dense in cities and their suburbs. Many fewer people live in the mountains of Wales or the highlands of Scotland. The spread of people is uneven throughout the world (**C**), with many parts of the world that are densely populated, such as Bangladesh, parts of India (**A**), south-east England and the Netherlands. Other areas, such as Antarctica, the Sahara Desert (**B**) and Central Australia are sparsely populated.

A Densely populated area of Bombay, India

B The Sahara Desert

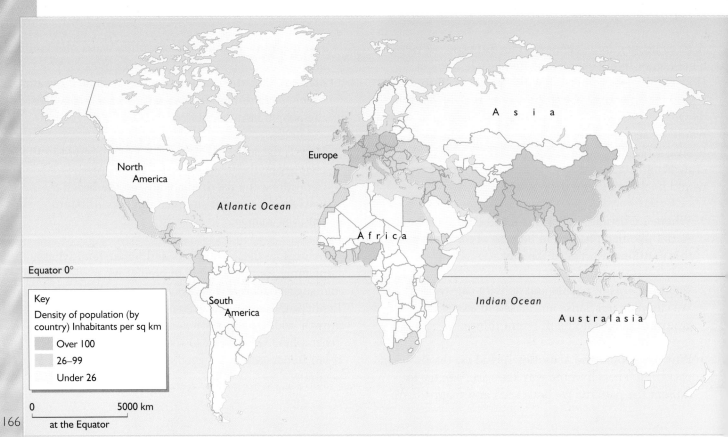

Asia

Europe

North America

Atlantic Ocean

Africa

Equator 0°

South America

Indian Ocean

Australasia

Key

Density of population (by country) Inhabitants per sq km

Over 100

26–99

Under 26

0   5000 km

at the Equator

Population density

Think of a large open space that you know well, say a park, school playing field or playground. Suppose you marked off a square 100m by 100m, then asked 50 people to stand in the square. You could calculate the population density for the square.

$$\text{Population density} = \frac{\text{Number of people}}{\text{Area}}$$

The square has a population density equal to 5000 people per sq km. The UK has a population density of 240 per sq km compared to Singapore with 4,600 people per sq km.

Population distribution

D shows three ways in which the people can be distributed in the square. They may be distributed evenly (uniform pattern) or clustered together (nucleated) or more usually somewhere between these two. Geographers search for the reasons for the distribution.

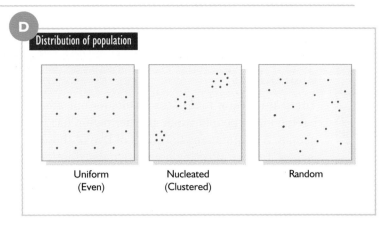

D

Distribution of population

Uniform (Even)   Nucleated (Clustered)   Random

Counting the people

Geographers help count the people by taking a **census**. Records of population counts have been discovered in 4,000 year-old graves in Mesopotamia (modern Iraq). The Ancient Greeks and Romans took censuses including the one at the time of the birth of Jesus Christ. Today, as well as counting people, information is needed on how people live, where they live, how they travel to work, their education, and the jobs that they do. If the make-up of a population is known, we can plan how to improve the quality of people's lives.

In the UK the Office of Population Censuses and Surveys organizes a census every ten years. In 2001 every house in the country will get a form to fill in. This has been happening since 1801. The data from this form is published as books, CDs and on the Internet.

With data from several censuses future population trends can be predicted. This is very helpful for planning, for example, housing development, transport needs and schools.

Q

Design a census or survey of a group in your class, school, club, village and/or neighbourhood. Include at least 25 people. The main purpose of the survey is to study their shopping habits. Collect information on age, sex, residence, car ownership, journey to work, shopping trips and leisure travel.

a) Describe the group to be included in the census.
b) Write a paragraph explaining the purpose of the census.
c) Design a census form to be filled in by the people.
d) Try out your form on a few friends and revise it if necessary.
e) Complete the census of 25 or more people.
f) Draw up tables to show the results.
g) Write a commentary to describe what each table shows.

Questions

1 Include these words in sentences to show their meaning:
  a) Population density
  b) Population distribution
  c) Densely populated
  d) Sparsely populated
  e) Uniform population distribution
  f) Nucleated population distribution.   (6)

2 Draw a table with two columns. Label the first column 'Densely populated' and the second 'Sparsely populated'. Write the names of **four** areas from around the world in each column.   (4)

3 Newspapers have individual ways of presenting news to their readers. Their headlines are very different in style. Some use long paragraphs to present a balanced account. Others use short, sharp sentences, focus on the sensational and tell their stories using the people involved.

Imagine a United Nations' report has been published today which has the following estimates:
• world population will continue to grow
• the highest rates of growth will be in LEDCs

• over 50 countries face population decline in the 21st century
• the average age of the world's population will continue to rise.

Imagine that you work for **one** of the following newspapers.

• A broadsheet with accurate headlines with the occasional twist or pun, such as *The Times*, *The Daily Telegraph*, *The Guardian* or *The Independent*

• A tabloid with sensationalist five-word headlines, such as *The Sun* or *Daily Star*.

• A tabloid with quiet headlines, such as *The Daily Mail*, *The Daily Mirror*, or *The Daily Express*.

Prepare a headline and 100-word front page column about population based upon the UN report.

Your column should be accurate and may use information from this book or other sources. You will find it helpful to have a look at two or three different newspapers before you begin.   (15)

Total: 25 marks

Why do more people live in some places than others?

There are several reasons or factors for one area having many people when another region has few people. **A** summarizes the effect of five of these factors. Factors affecting population distribution can be divided into two main groups:

- Physical factors: relief; climate; drainage; water supply; soils.
- Social and economic factors: mineral resources; employment; food supply; accessibility; politics; history.

Always remember there are exceptions to these factors. Dense populations can be found in Alaska, despite the cold climate, because of the rich oil fields. Hong Kong is very densely populated, despite having steep slopes, challenging temperatures, and little space for agriculture or mineral resources, because of its strategic position and the enterprise of its people.

Examples of factors affecting population density

Factor	Area	Dense population	Area	Sparse population
Relief		Lower, flatter land for easier development of agriculture, transport and manufacturing industry.		High, steep, rugged land hinders agriculture, transport and manufacturing industry.
Examples	LEDC	Bangladesh	LEDC	Himalayas; Andes
	MEDC	Netherlands	MEDC	Hokkaido, Japan
	UK	SE England	UK	North Wales
Climate		Moderate temperatures and rainfall make farming and living easier.		Very low or very high rainfall or temperatures make life difficult.
Examples	LEDC	SE Brazil	LEDC	Sahara Desert
	MEDC	SE Australia	MEDC	Northern Scandinavia
	UK	Devon and Cornwall	UK	Highlands of Scotland
Soil		Fertile soils, such as loams, help farming. Fertile river plains and deltas.		Poor infertile soils or soil erosion of exhausted soils do not help farming.
Examples	LEDC	Java, Indonesia	LEDC	Sahel, Africa
	MEDC	Paris Basin, France	MEDC	Central Massif, France
	UK	Fenlands	UK	Pennine moorland
Mineral reserves		Coal, oil, iron ore and gold attract people to settle and develop industry.		Lack of resources discourage investment.
Examples	LEDC	Zimbabwe	LEDC	Sahel, Africa
	MEDC	South Africa	MEDC	Some islands of Japan
	UK	East Midlands	UK	Southern uplands of Scotland
Accessibility		Communications help trade to develop.		Difficult communications or remote location cause difficulties.
Examples	LEDC	Rio de Janeiro, Brazil	LEDC	Zimbabwe (landlocked)
	MEDC	Singapore	MEDC	N Canada
	UK	M4 corridor	UK	Scottish islands

A

CASE STUDY *Population in an MEDC: Japan*

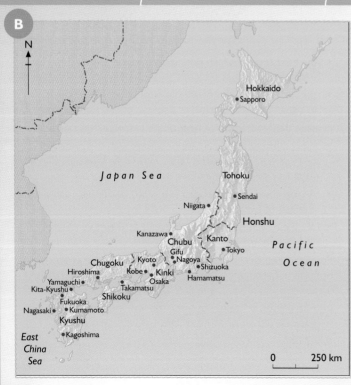

B

Japan Sea

Hokkaido
• Sapporo

Tohoku
• Sendai
Niigata •

Honshu

Kanazawa •
Chubu   Kanto
Gifu • • Tokyo
Kyoto • Nagoya
Chugoku • Kobe • Kinki • Shizuoka
Hiroshima • Osaka   Hamamatsu
Yamaguchi • Takamatsu
Kita-Kyushu • Shikoku
Fukuoka •
Nagasaki • Kumamoto
Kyushu
• Kagoshima

Pacific Ocean

East China Sea

0   250 km

FACT FILE

Area: 377,800 sq km (UK 244,100 sq km)
Coastline: 29,751km (1.5 times longer than USA)
Climate: Varies from tropical in south to cool temperate in north
Relief: Mostly rugged and mountainous
Natural resources: Negligible minerals, fish
Land use: Arable 13%; Grassland 2%; Forest 67%
Hazards: Volcanoes (1,500 seismic vibrations per year), tsunami, typhoons
Population: 125.9 million (half that of the USA; 2.2% of world)
Population density: 334 people per sq km (28 USA; 241 UK)
Birth rate: 10 births per 1000 (one of lowest in world)
Death rate: 7 deaths per 1000 (USA: 9)
Infant mortality: 4.3 deaths per 1000 live births (least in world)
Employment: 99% of workplaces employ fewer than 300.
Main companies: Toyota, Mitsubishi, Fuji
Products: Electrical appliances; cars; motor cycles; shipping.
Crime: One of the lowest rates in world.

Japan is made up of four main islands, Hokkaido, Honshu, Shikoku and Kyushu (**B**). There are many smaller islands. The islands have rugged mountains with smaller areas of plains near the coast, where most of the cities are found.

What factors affect the distribution of population?

From these maps, you could describe Japan's population distribution as follows: 'Japan has four main islands. To the north Hokkaido has a low population density. The largest island, Honshu, can be divided into two parts. The northern part has a lower population density than the south. In the south there is dense population on the coast including the large cities of Tokyo and Osaka. The two islands to the south have population densities similar to north Honshu except for the big cities of Takamatsu and Nagasaki.'

F Relief of Japan

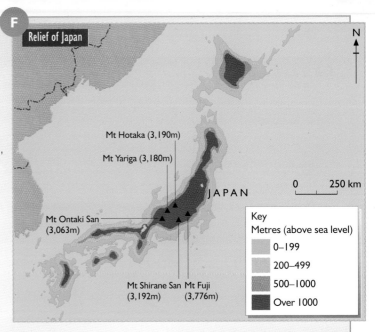

Mt Hotaka (3,190m)

Mt Yariga (3,180m)

JAPAN

0   250 km

Mt Ontaki San (3,063m)

Mt Shirane San (3,192m)   Mt Fuji (3,776m)

Key
Metres (above sea level)

- 0–199
- 200–499
- 500–1000
- Over 1000

C Population density

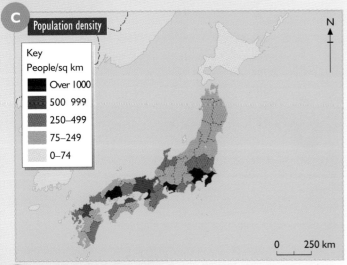

N

Key
People/sq km

- Over 1000
- 500 999
- 250–499
- 75–249
- 0–74

0   250 km

G Tokyo, Japan

Look at the map of relief land for Japan (**F**) and note the influence it has had on population density. The mountains are in the centre of the islands with the people and the cities along the coasts.

D Increase in population (1920–95)

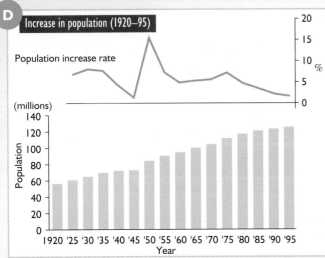

Population increase rate

E Change in age composition (1920–95)

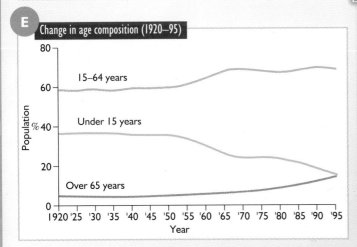

Questions

1 **D** shows the growth of population in Japan from 1920 to 1995.
   a) By how much has the total population increased between 1920 and 1995?   (2)
   b) Describe the changing rate of population increase in the period.   (4)

2 **E** shows the ages of people living in Japan between 1920 and 1995.
   a) Compare the situation in 1920 with 1995.   (4)
   b) Describe the problems likely to arise from these changes.   (6)

3 For Japan, or another named MEDC:
   a) Describe the distribution of population.
   b) What physical, economic and social factors have influenced the distribution you have described?   (9)

Total: 25 marks

Brazil has a rapidly increasing population (**A**). By 1990, half the people in South America lived in Brazil.

Six different factors affect rapid growth of population:

- **Birth rate** The rapid increase in Brazil's population is not because of more births. These have actually decreased.

- **Death rate** This is the main cause of the large population increase. The death rate has been falling because of better sanitation, health care and medicines, such as antibiotics.

- **Infant mortality** This has declined from 250 deaths per 1000 live births in 1900 to 65 in 1997.

- **Life expectancy:** Brazilians are living longer (men 62 years; women 68 years).

- **Immigration** Little effect

- **Emigration** Little effect (approximately 1.5 million have left since 1985)

Brazil is a large country and its population density is low at 19 per sq km (1998). The population is denser along the north-east and south-east Atlantic coasts (**B**). There are five regions whose population densities are shown in table (**C**).

Regions

The North

This region is mostly in the Amazon Basin and overall has a low population density. The Amazon River, however, has a slightly higher population density. It flows through lush tropical forests and contains one-fifth of the Earth's fresh water reserves.

The growth of Brazil's population (1776–1998)		
Brazil population	Population (millions)	Annual rate of growth (%)
1776	1.9	1.8
1876	10.9	1.9
1900	17.3	2.2
1940	41.2	2.3
1950	51.9	3.1
1960	70.1	2.9
1970	93.2	2.7
1980	121.3	1.8
1992	149.8	1.9
1998	165.9	1.8

A

The two main cities are Manaus and Bélem. Between 1850 and 1910 the population grew six-fold as a rubber industry developed. In the 1970s the government sponsored colonization by settlers from the north east of the region. During the 1980s there were fears of too rapid deforestation so colonization was stopped.

There are new signs of population growth as people migrate into the area to take advantage of iron ore at Carajas, bauxite at Trombetas and electricity produced by the Tucurui Hydro Electric Power Station. Manaus is a port on the River Amazon. It has been made a free port which means companies can import and export without paying local taxes. This should encourage economic growth in the area and attract more people to the area.

C

Changes in Brazil's population distribution and density (1970–92)				
	1970		1992	
Region	Population (millions)	Population density (people per sq km)	Population (millions)	Population density (people per sq km)
North	3.6	0.9	10.8	2.8
North East	28.1	18.1	43.2	27.8
South East	39.9	43.1	63.8	69.0
South	16.5	28.7	22.4	39.0
Centre West	5.1	3.2	9.6	6.0
Brazil	93.2	10.9	149.8	17.6

The North East

This area contains 30 per cent of the Brazilian population but it is suffering from drought. Birth rates are high and many people migrate from farms with poor soils to the cities of this area and the South East. The area is receiving aid from the central government and farms with palm oil fields are being developed. The two largest cities are Recife and Salvador. Salvador was the early capital of Brazil and first major port. This is because the Portuguese first landed here and developed this part of

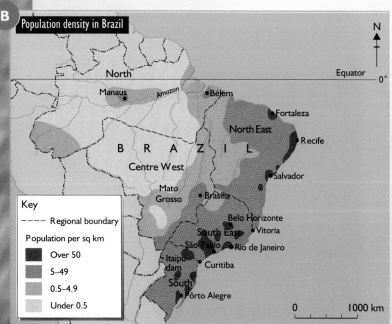

B
Population density in Brazil

Key
- – – – Regional boundary
- Population per sq km
  - Over 50
  - 5–49
  - 0.5–4.9
  - Under 0.5

Brazil. Sugar cane and diamonds were its main trade. Recife is also a port, exporting sugar, coffee and cotton. The city is growing rapidly due to people moving there from the surrounding countryside.

The South East

By far the highest population densities in Brazil are in this region. The area is highly industrialized around the cities of São Paulo, Rio de Janeiro and Belo Horizonte. This is the economic core of Brazil and most of the population is concentrated here. The area is rich in minerals and agriculture including coffee for export and meat and milk for home consumption. Rio de Janeiro is the second largest city in Brazil and was the capital from 1912–1960. It is the financial and service centre of the country. It also has famous beaches and spectacular rocky outcrops. São Paulo is 72km from the coast at a height of 760m. It grew because of coffee exports but today it has over 20,000 industrial plants employing 600,000 people. By the late 1990s the city had a population of 10 million and the wider metropolitan area had reached 17 million.

The South

The area with the second highest population densities is in the South. This is a highly developed region with good agriculture and manufacturing. The Itaipu Dam produces hydro-electricity for the region (the world's largest HEP scheme). The largest city is Pôrto Alegre. It is an important river port as well as the chief industrial centre of the region.

The Centre West

This is the sparsely populated grassland called the Mato Grosso. The present capital, Brasília, is located in this isolated area. Brasília was founded in 1960 on a plateau, 1100m above sea level and 1200km from Rio de Janeiro. Its population had reached 2 million by the mid-1990s, although many of the office workers return to the coast each weekend.

The changing distribution of population

Once much of the population was located in rural areas. Today most people live in cities. The movement to cities is called urbanization and has occurred mainly because:

- agricultural land has become overcrowded due to population increase
- people cannot make a living from their land
- people have moved to cities to look for jobs
- the North-East region has been hit by droughts
- better transport systems have allowed people to move
- radio and television have shown rural people urban life and they liked what they saw
- cities offer steady income, health care and clean running water.

This migration has caused cities to grow rapidly. Today many of the richer people are leaving the centres of cities to live in exclusive areas on the outskirts, such as in Barra outside Rio de Janeiro.

Questions

Below are data exercises on Brazil. Geographers need to analyse data and interpret the messages it contains. Data, however, can be twisted to affect the final message. You need to be aware of this. The third exercise shows some of the possible ways people use data to get their message across.

1   Draw a line graph to show the growth of population in Brazil since 1776. Describe the trend shown by your graph.   (5)

2   On a copy of **B** draw bar graphs or proportional circles to show the following city populations in 1991: São Paulo 9.6 million; Rio de Janeiro 5.5 million; Salvador 2.1 million; Belo Horizonte 2.0 million; Fortaleza 1.8 million; Brasília 1.6 million; Curtiba 1.3 million; Recife 1.3 million; Pôrto Alegre 1.3 million; Bélem 1.2 million.
Describe the pattern shown by your map.   (7)

3   Look at the figures for the annual rate of growth of population in **A**.

a) Write a sentence describing what you have found out.   (3)

b) Draw these axes and plot the data: (3)

c) Now repeat the exercise with these axes.   (3)

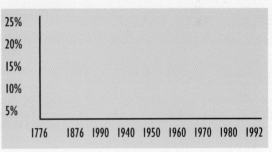

d) How does the message of population growth appear to change between the two graphs?   (4)

Total: 25 marks

POPULATION CHANGE
Trends in population growth

The population of the world continues to grow (**A**). The number more than doubled between 1950 and 1998 from 2.5 billion to 5.8 billion. Over 90 per cent of this growth was in LEDCs (**B**), which are least able to cope with increasing numbers. Why is the population total growing? What contributes to change in population?

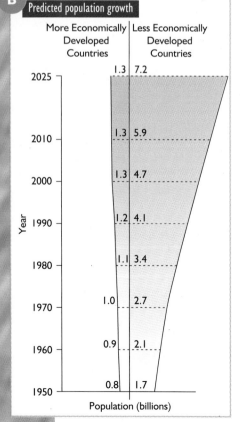

A

World population	
Year	**(billions)**
1830	1
1927	2
1960	3
1974	4
1987	5
1998	5.8
2000	Best estimate: 6
1 billion = one thousand million	

Birth rates

Increasing birth rates and falling infant mortality have been important contributors to population growth in many countries.

Many countries have made efforts to decrease birth rates through the introduction of family planning. However, there is a debate about the effectiveness of family planning programmes. Some believe they are only effective if combined with greater wealth and progress in women's education. However, Bangladesh has used family planning successfully without economic change or increased education. Despite this, education does appear to play a key role in most places. Increasing education for women provides them with information on ways to control fertility, lengthens the time girls spend in school, raises the age of marriage and delays the child-bearing years.

Death rates and

B

Predicted population growth

	More Economically Developed Countries	Less Economically Developed Countries
2025	1.3	7.2
2010	1.3	5.9
2000	1.3	4.7
1990	1.2	4.1
1980	1.1	3.4
1970	1.0	2.7
1960	0.9	2.1
1950	0.8	1.7

Year / Population (billions)

life expectancy

World-wide death rates are falling rapidly. In 1993 about 51 million people died, of whom 39 million lived in LEDCs. About one third died from disease. The causes of death by disease vary between MEDCs and LEDCs. In MEDCs there is adequate health care, yet heart disease and strokes account for nearly half the deaths. Cancer kills 1 in 5 people in MEDCs. Infectious diseases kill 1 person in 100 in MEDCs, but 1 in every 2 people in LEDCs. They include diarrhoea, tuberculosis, malaria, cholera, dengue and yellow fever. Yet rapid progress with immunisation programmes by WHO (World Health Organisation) has helped considerably and LEDC death rates are now relatively low.

Life expectancy and the **infant mortality rate** are part of the study of death rates. They are important signs of human well being in an area. Increasing life expectancy indicates progress socially and in health care. Between 1980 and 1993 world-wide life expectancy increased from 61 to 65 years.

There is a gap of 35 years between life expectancy in the least developed country (43 years) and the most developed (78 years) (**C**). This gap is expected to widen in certain LEDC countries due to AIDS. In the 45 least developed countries, 850 million people, 15 per cent of the global population, life expectancy is below 60 years.

C

Life expectancy	Male	Female
MEDCs	71.2	78.6
LEDCs	62.4	65.3
Least Developed Countries	51.5	53.6

CASE STUDY *Russia and Central Africa*

D

Life expectancy in Russia		
	Male	Female
1992	62	75
1993	59	73
1994	57	71

For many years life expectancy has steadily increased. Some recent examples, however, suggest that this is no longer happening everywhere.

Decreased life expectancy in Russia

In Russia average life expectancy has been falling for both men and women (**D**). Suggested reasons for the falls include increased heart disease, alcoholism, suicide, crime, poor job prospects, heavy smoking, inflation cutting, the falling value of wages and pensions, poor health services and environmental pollution.

Decreased life expectancy in Central Africa

Life expectancy is falling in the 15 nations of Central Africa including Kenya, Uganda, Malawi, and Tanzania. It is expected to fall to 49.6 years because of the AIDS **pandemic**. Without AIDS it is estimated that life expectancy would have been between 60 and 65 years.

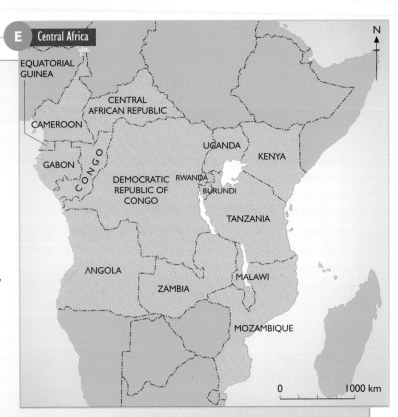

Infant mortality rates

A particular aspect of death rates is **infant mortality** (**F**). This is one of the most important indicators of health improvements in a country as healthy babies are dependent on healthy parents. Between 1980 and 1993 world infant mortality fell by 25 per cent. Despite this success, three million babies born in the developing world during the same period did not survive one week. The main causes of high rates of infant mortality are:

- low income
- limited access to safe drinking water
- disease
- poor health care
- lack of sanitation.

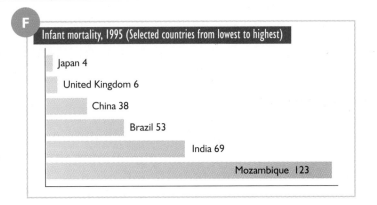

DEFINITION

The **infant mortality rate** is the number of children who die before their first birthday (expressed per 1,000 live births).

Questions

1 Why do you think life expectancy at birth is less than life expectancy at age one? (2)

2 Using the figures in **G**, write a statement for the relationship between
   a) birth rates and infant mortality, and
   b) birth rates and female literacy. (2)

3 Suggest reasons for women's education being the key to reducing birth rates. (6)

4 Explain why life expectancy has increased in the UK since 1945. (6)

5 For an LEDC in table **G**, or another of your choice, explain the main factors, other than women's education, affecting its birth rate. (9)

G

1998	Nigeria	Bangladesh	Cuba	Thailand
Birth rate	45	27	15	17
Infant mortality	84	77	10	30
Female literacy (%)	47	26	96	92

Total: 25 marks

DEMOGRAPHIC TRANSITION

Demography is the study of population. Researchers in demography have suggested that many countries are following a similar path in the way their population is changing. This pathway can be described using the Demographic Transition Model.

The Demographic Transition Model

This model describes the way the total population of an area changes through time because of variations in birth and death rates. The model was drawn after studying changes in total population of industrialized countries in Western Europe and North America. Some of these countries had records of birth and death rates for up to 200 years.

The Demographic Transition Model is like any other model – it is useful but only gives part of the answer.

Uses

- Helps study changing population sizes.
- Brings together changing birth and death rates which influence population change.
- Used to predict changes in population and future needs for education and health services.

Limitations

- The falling death rates of MEDCs were dependent on medical discoveries. If LEDCs could afford these medicines they could move to Stage 3.
- The falling birth rates in Stage 3 have been less rapid than expected in some LEDCs because of social beliefs linked to large numbers of children and religious beliefs.
- The 'One Child Policy' in China decreased birth rates more quickly than expected by the model.
- Some of the newly industrialized countries of the Pacific Rim (Malaysia and Hong Kong) have moved more quickly through the stages than countries in Western Europe.

A

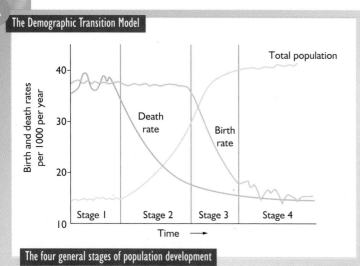

The Demographic Transition Model

The four general stages of population development

Stage	One	Two	Three	Four
Birth rate	High	High	Falls	Low and fluctuates
Death rate	High and fluctuates	Falls	Low	Low
Population change	Small growth	Rapid growth	Slower growth	Stable
Places	Amazon rainforest	Kenya	China	Japan
UK	Before 1750	1750–1880	1880–1950	1950–2000
Quality of life	Survival, subsistence agriculture, high infant mortality	Improved food supply, disease control, no birth control, high infant mortality	Better living conditions, health care, birth control, factory jobs, urbanization	Industrial employment, high standards of living, affluence, delayed marriage, free secondary education

B

Population in England and Wales (1800–1990)

Year	Birth rate (per 1000)	Death rate (per 1000)	Total population (millions)
1800	38.5	22.0	9.0
1820	36.0	20.5	12.0
1840	31.0	20.0	15.5
1860	34.0	22.5	20.0
1880	34.0	20.0	25.9
1900	28.0	17.0	32.5
1920	20.0	12.5	37.0
1940	14.5	13.0	41.5
1960	17.5	11.5	46.0
1980	14.0	12.0	49.5
1990	14.0	11.0	50.5

Q

1 Use **B** to draw a graph for birth rates, death rates and total population for England and Wales, 1800–1990. Use the left-hand 'y' axis for birth and death rates and the right-hand 'y' axis for total population. Label the three lines clearly.

2 Use the data for the UK from **A** and divide your graph into the four stages of the Demographic Transition.

3 Does your graph support the expert's view that England and Wales entered stage 3 of the model around 1880?

CASE STUDY *LEDC: Mauritius*

D Port Louis, Mauritius

The Republic of Mauritius is an island with an area of 1,865 sq km, situated in the south west of the Indian Ocean (**C**). It is 2,400km from the southern tip of Africa. The island had a population of 1,145,000 in 1997. The capital is Port Louis and the official language English. The island has a regular water supply and nearly all the population has access to clean water and sanitation. The whole island has electricity which is mainly thermal. The airport is at Plaisance in the south of the island. Since Mauritius became independent in 1968 its basic problem has been to provide for its ever-growing population.

Mauritius was in Stage 1 of the Model between 1900 and 1945 (**F**). Total population was steady or rising slightly. Over the 45 years various disasters and epidemics increased the death rate. In 1945, after the anti-malaria campaign, death rates fell, birth rates remained high and total population began to increase (**E**). The changing population of Mauritius matches the Demographic Transition Model.

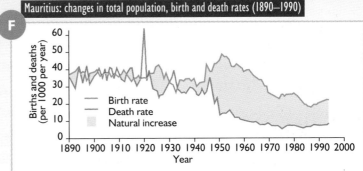

F Mauritius: changes in total population, birth and death rates (1890–1990)

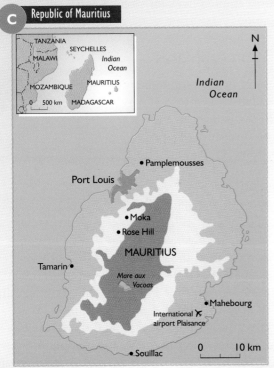

C Republic of Mauritius

Questions

1 Use **G**.

  a) Describe the main trend in the birth rate in Japan. *(2)*

  b) How would the changes in birth and death rates have affected the total population in Japan between 1900 and 1996? *(3)*

  c) Suggest a reason for the unusual figures between 1940 and 1950. *(4)*

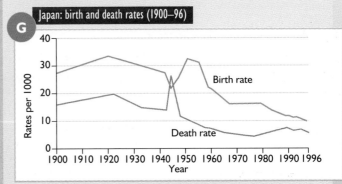

G Japan: birth and death rates (1900–96)

2 a) Write a brief paragraph describing the location of Mauritius. Include references to latitude, longitude, hemisphere and nearby seas or oceans in your answer. *(4)*

  b) In what stage of the Demographic Transition Model is Mauritius in at the moment? Justify your decision. *(6)*

  c) Explain the factors causing specific changes in the death rate of Mauritius. *(6)*

Total: 25 marks

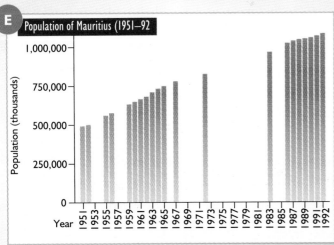

E Population of Mauritius (1951–92)

How is global population changing?

A study of the way total population is changing can help in planning for the supply of water, energy and food. Some experts have produced very alarming forecasts for the future.

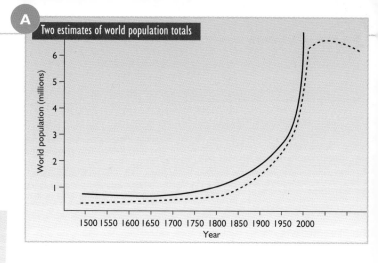

Two estimates of world population totals

Fast train to overpopulation

Every second, three more people are born into the world. The human race is expanding by the equivalent of the population of Liverpool and Birmingham every week. This growth in world population is happening faster than ever before. It has doubled since 1950 and now stands at 5.4 billion in what has been called a 'population explosion'.

The Guardian, 1991

However, there are two very different views of what might happen.

The number of humans will outstrip food supply. Population will be 'checked' by famine, war and disease. Overpopulation is inevitable and population will be checked.	Population growth will stimulate increased food production. Farming techniques will improve as 'necessity becomes the mother of invention'. New crop strains will be found and new methods of cultivation discovered to feed the growing population.
View 1 Thomas Malthus (1766–1834)	View 2 Esther Boserup (1965)

In 1998 United Nations' reports suggested that world population growth was slowing down. These estimates and forecasts give rise to concern as well as optimism.

Causes for optimism

- In many MEDCs the total population is growing slowly and in some even falling.
- Some LEDCs are moving rapidly to stable population totals.

Causes for concern

- High growth rates are still found in several LEDCs.
- High population growth rates are usually linked to poverty, limited lives for women and high migration.

Population estimates

Estimates of future population size are highly uncertain. It may level off to a plateau in the twenty-first century (**A**). Some experts think the population will stay below 10 billion (compared to 5.8 billion in 1998). The United Nations' estimates for 2050 range from 7.7 billion to 11.2 billion. Their average estimate is 9.37 billion which is lower than their estimate of 9.83 billion people made in 1994. Predictions of population totals are difficult because they have to be based on **fertility rates** and **mortality rates**, family planning programmes, wealth and poverty and the status of women. The key factor in forecasting population growth in the next few years is fertility. A fertility rate of 2 would mean each couple is replacing itself with 2 children.

Fertility rates (number of children per woman aged between 15–49)		
	1950	1995
World	6.0	3.0
MEDCs	2.8	1.7
LEDCs	6.2	3.4

Differences between LEDCs and MEDCs

The main pattern of population change is of declining totals in many developed countries including Japan, Germany, Denmark, Greece, Italy, Spain, Portugal, Belarus, Bulgaria, Hungary, Romania, Russia and the Ukraine. The USA is an exception where population increase is projected. On the other hand the population of Africa is projected to double by 2025 and Asia to grow by 40 per cent.

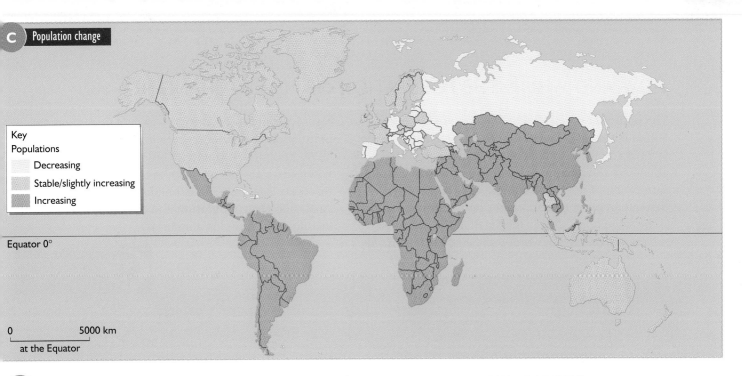

Key
Populations

Decreasing

Stable/slightly increasing

Increasing

Equator 0°

0   5000 km

at the Equator

D

Progress in reducing population growth	
China	The world's most populous nation. Fertility now 2.0 but growth will continue because of large numbers of women in child-bearing years.
Thailand	Fertility rate of 2.1 has nearly reached population stability.
Indonesia	Great progress has been made to reach fertility rate of 2.8.
Cuba	Fertility rates below 2.0.
Argentina / Brazil / Chile / Colombia / Jamaica / Uruguay	Fertility rate well below 3.0.
India	After stalling at 4.0 in the 1980s, the UN estimates a fertility rate of 3.8. India government figures suggest 3.4.
Sub-Saharan Africa	Fertility rate of 6.5 has fallen only slightly from 6.6 in 1960.

Q

You are a reporter working for one of the television news channels. You are attending a press conference given by a Swedish organization to explain how Sweden is encouraging people to have more children. You know world population is growing and that people are hungry in some LEDCs. However, the Swedish expert explains that in Sweden they:

- pay family allowances as long as a child is in education
- pay extra non-taxable allowances for a third child
- enforce payment of maintenance by absent parents
- pay pregnant women four months paid leave before the baby is born
- give one-year paid leave after the baby is born
- provide nursery facilities for all children over 18 months.

Write a one-minute talk that you can read to the cameras. You want to report the actions taken but also to suggest alternatives to help Sweden sustain its population and maintain a workforce and home market for goods. One possibility would be to encourage migrations from more crowded, poorer countries.

Questions

1 Table **E** shows world population for the years 1950–98.

   a) Draw a line graph to show global population totals between 1950 and 1998. (3)

   b) Write a paragraph describing the trend shown by your graph of total population growth. Add a second paragraph describing the changing rate of growth since 1950. (6)

2 a) Why do you think China has laws to reduce the rate of its population growth? (5)

   b) Why do countries such as Sweden and Singapore reward people who help increase their population? (5)

3 The United Nations makes frequent projections of world population change. Suggest reasons why it is important for them to do this. (6)

Total: 25 marks

E

Year	Total (billion)
1950	2.5
1955	2.8
1960	3.0
1965	3.3
1970	3.7
1975	4.1
1980	4.5
1985	4.9
1990	5.3
1995	5.7
1998	5.8

HOW AND WHY IS THE POPULATION OF PLACES CHANGING?

The **optimum population** is the size of population which is the most favourable to the people for the level of resources and technology in an area. It allows for the maximum income per person. If you can use more resources and improve technology, then an area can carry a higher optimum population. If the population total is higher than the optimum, the area is said to be overpopulated. This means the resources and technology are unable to support the population at their current living standard. China is an overpopulated country. **Underpopulation** happens when there are too few people to exploit the resources available, for example Canada and Australia. **Overpopulation** and underpopulation can lead to a fall in living standards.

CASE STUDY *Underpopulation: Singapore*

Singapore is a small island (only 623 sq km) in South-East Asia between Malaysia and Indonesia. Its climate is tropical, with no pronounced seasons. Thunderstorms occur on 40 per cent of all days. The island is low and gently undulating to a maximum height of 166m. The key resources of this island are its people and its position as a deep water port. Singapore has a population of 3.4 million. It has a relatively low population growth rate of 1.9 per cent. The fertility rate is 1.65 children born per woman.

Singapore has had problems with its population total for many years. After the Second World War in 1945, birth rates increased dramatically. During the second half of the 1960s the Singapore government set up a Family Planning and Population Board. This gave family planning advice and 62 per cent of women used the service. By the end of the 1960s the birth rate had fallen. Between 1971 and 1975 education and publicity promoted the two children per family policy – 'Two is enough'. The programme was very successful and by 1975 the fertility rate fell to the replacement level of 2.1. Between 1975-80 fertility fell to 1.7 children per woman, then in the 1980s to 1.4 children. In 1986 the Family Planning and Population Board closed and a new policy was adopted to encourage population growth. A package of incentives (**B**) was introduced under the slogan 'Have three or more (children) if you can afford it'. The number of births has increased.

A

What are the reasons for Singaporeans marrying late?

"I think the reason people are getting married late [ages 27/28] is that they are concentrating on their careers, and they have to save a lot of money for house, car, wedding, honeymoon, children's education, daily living expenses. The 'official' view is that people are marrying late due to better qualified females having higher expectations. I think it's because it is too expensive to get married."
Tan Wah Tze

"People marry when the economy is doing well and they have enough money to buy houses and afford kids' education. In the context of Singapore you can't have rising costs of living and expect people to have more kids."
Skyjuice

"I would add two more reasons: one, they prefer single life styles and two, they just patiently wait for the right one. The Singapore government expect women with higher education to find highly educated Mr Right. I have educated friends who date people who don't even have high school diplomas."
Wu Huei-Fen

"You get $90,000 for a woman under 29 having her third child. Who says it is too expensive?"
Toh Yung Cheong

B

Actions by the Singapore government to encourage births include:

- a Social Development Unit to help single people to meet
- child care centres so that working mothers can continue careers
- flexible working hours and part-time employment
- extended maternity leave
- tax rebates for the third child born
- subsidies for children attending care centres
- priority for housing
- a publicity campaign on the benefits and joys of marriage
- portrayal of happy family life on television, radio and newspapers.

CASE STUDY *LEDC: overpopulation: China*

China has a land area of 9.3 million sq km (**C**). It is slightly larger than the USA. In 1998 its population was estimated at 1,300 million (about one-quarter of all the people in the world). The population growth rate is 1.2 per cent as births exceed deaths in the ratio 8:3. Males outnumber females in all age groups up to 64 years. The fertility rate, at 1.8, is below the replacement level.

Some of China's problems include low economic growth, air pollution, future water shortages, a lack of clean water (less than 10 per cent of sewage is treated), deforestation and soil erosion.

China has a population crisis. It has 21.4 per cent of the world's population but only 7.1 per cent of its arable land. China faces the difficult choice of rigid population control or more poverty and suffering.

In 1980 the government launched the 'One-Child Policy' which allows every married couple only one child. It was promoted by a series of measures (**D**). The aim is now to reduce the fertility rate from 1.84 to 1.0 children per woman (it had been 6.0 in 1970).

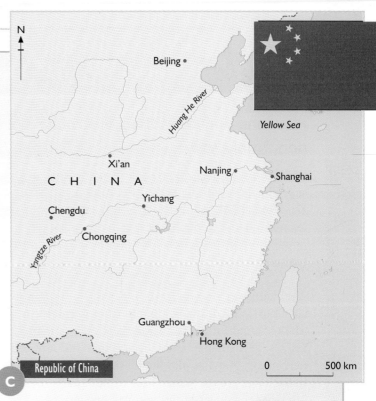

C Republic of China

0   500 km

D   Actions by the government as part of the 'One-Child Policy'

- permission and a certificate needed for all pregnancies
- birth quotas per area are published as targets for each provincial governor
- pregnancies without a certificate may be ended by abortion
- compulsory birth control for all women with one child
- compulsory sterilization of all couples with two children
- fines, night raids on houses where there is a second child
- no grain rations; no schooling; disadvantages at work where there is a second child
- no permission certificates if someone else in village has unauthorized birth
- free contraceptives and birth control education
- a couple with a second child pay a fine and a tax each year
- couples with one child get a 10 per cent wage bonus
- one-child families get priority in education, health and housing.

The birth rate in China has fallen from 33 per 1000 in 1970 to 17 in 1996. The policy has been criticized. In the cities it has been possible to supervise, but in rural areas, where 80 per cent of the population lives, the policy has been less successful. Also modern ultra-sound machines allow prediction of the sex of babies. The prestige of a boy baby means girls are aborted or abandoned. The natural ratio of boy babies to girls is 1:1, but in China the figure is 3:1.

One severe critic of the policy, Peter Zang, a Chinese geographer, points out that the birth rate began falling in 1970 well before the policy began. The fertility rate of 1.8 hides a rural figure of 2.5. He feels China should have followed Japan and Singapore through the Demographic Transition Model where population growth naturally slows without the cruel One-Child Policy.

Questions

1. Use the diagram to explain the terms 'optimum population', 'overpopulation' and 'underpopulation'. *(4)*

2. Countries such as Mexico and India have rapidly growing populations. What alternatives might they develop to reduce the rate of population growth? *(5)*

3. a) Compare the population policies of Singapore and China. *(5)*
   b) Suggest one criticism of each policy. *(2)*

4. Governments adopt plans to influence birth rates. For a country of your choice, describe how they have done this, and explain why they have done it. *(9)*

Total: 25 marks

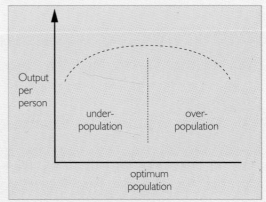

Population structure

How and why does the age structure of populations vary?

Population can be broken up into age groups and by sex. This is called the structure of the population. Knowing about the structure of population helps us, for example, predict changes in the working population or the demand for houses. It also allows for comparisons between LEDCs and MEDCs.

The main way in which we find out about population structure is by drawing a **population pyramid** (A). The pyramid for Brazil, which is typical of many LEDCs, gets smaller as the age group rises, and the percentage of males and females is much less equal in each age group. Notice how in this LEDC the higher percentages are in younger age groups.

It has the following characteristics:

• the higher percentages are in the younger age groups

• the pyramid gets smaller in the higher age groups

• the percentages of male and female are more or less equal.

If a country has this type of pyramid, it suggests high birth rates, fairly high death rates and little migration out of the country. Of course, the population pyramids of LEDCs can be affected by disasters such as floods, wars and the migration of young men to work in another country nearby.

The population pyramid for the MEDC France is quite different (B).

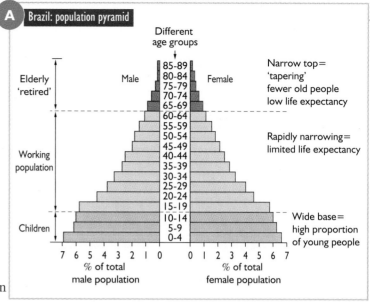

A Brazil: population pyramid

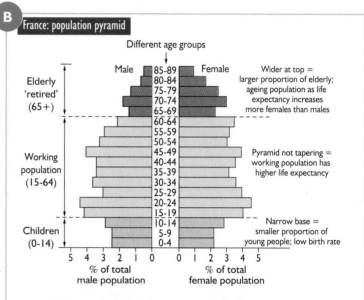

B France: population pyramid

C Young people in Brazil

Steps in reading a population pyramid

1 Read the title to note which country, city or group is shown. Groups could be different racial groups, urban/rural, or for two dates, town centre/suburbs, immigrants.

2 Look at the general shape. It could be broad based, rectangular or narrow based.

3 Note the proportions in the 0–16, 17–60 and above 60 age groups.

4 Look at the height of the pyramid to form an idea of life expectancy.

5 Examine the proportion of males to females – the sex ratio. There are usually more females in the older age groups. A sudden large working age group, usually male, suggests immigration.

Q

Look at **A** and **B**.

a) In Brazil over half of the total population is in the 0-19 age group. What percentage of the total population of France is in this age group?

b) Describe how sex ratios and life expectancy differ between the two countries.

c) In each pyramid, which age band contains the largest percentage of the population?

D | Examples of population pyramids

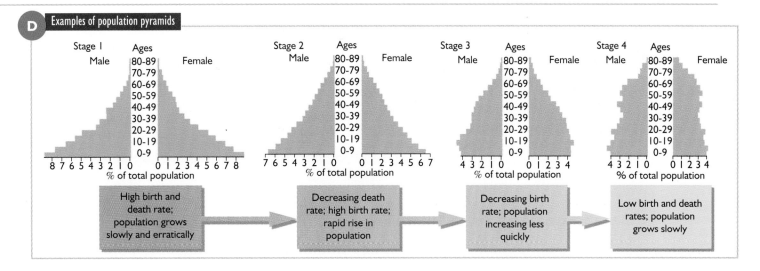

Population pyramids and the Demographic Transition Model

The four stages of population change in the Demographic Transition Model can be seen in the population pyramids (**D**). Notice the following general characteristics:

- as birth rates fall the pyramid base narrows
- as death rates fall and life expectancy increases, the pyramids grow taller
- as the country moves towards Stage 4, the pyramid becomes more barrel shaped.

Dependency ratio

This is the ratio of the number of dependents to the number of working population in a country:

$$\text{Dependency ratio} = \frac{\text{Number of dependents}}{\text{Number of working population}}$$

In the UK, people in the 0–16 age group are known as young dependents and those females over 60 and males over 65 as elderly. In some LEDCs the young dependents are 0–14, though in many areas children under the age of 14 work.

A dependency ratio of 1 means a dependent is supported by a member of the working population. Higher figures show more people dependent on fewer workers. LEDCs tend to have higher dependency ratios because of so many children.

Population pyramids and urbanization

A key feature of the structural change of population is that the world is becoming more urban. People move to cities for jobs, higher incomes and better health and education services. In cities their fertility tends to decline.

The population pyramids for cities show a greater proportion of people aged 15–65. In LEDCs men aged

15–65 outnumber women because of inward migration of people looking for work. Children under 15 and the elderly form a smaller proportion of the population than those of working age.

There are differences between urban areas in LEDCs and MEDCs. In LEDCs

- unemployment rates are higher
- social and health services do not meet demand
- levels of health care, e.g. immunization, are low.

Questions

1998	Brazil (% population)		Japan (% population)	
Age	Male	Female	Male	Female
0-14	18	17	8	7
15-29	14	14	11	10
30-44	9	10	10	10
45-59	5	5	11	11
60-74	3	3	7	9
75+	1	1	2	4
	50%	50%	49%	51%

1 Use the data above to draw two population pyramids. Annotate each pyramid with its main population features.

(6,6)

2 Suggest reasons for the differences and similarities between the two pyramids. (9)

3 A growing population can be looked on as an asset to a country, region or tribe. Suggest two reasons for this. (4)

Total: 25 marks

AGEING POPULATIONS

The population of the world is growing older. Life expectancy is increasing. While the total population is increasing by 1.5 per cent, the over-65 population is increasing by 2.7 per cent. The growth in the numbers over 65 is most rapid (over 400 per cent) in some LEDCs. In the next 30 years there will be a dramatic increase in the numbers over 80.

In 1900 one in twenty people was aged 60 or over (the 'Third Age'). Today it is one in seven. This is placing an increased tax burden on those in work. Table **A** shows this pattern for selected European Union countries.

A

	Population over 60 (%)							
	Netherlands	France	Germany	UK	Spain	Portugal	Italy	Denmark
1950	11	16	14	15	11	10	12	13
2025 est.	30	26	31	26	22	22	27	30

CASE STUDY *Life expectancy in England*

B

'Men living in Cambridge, Guildford and Woking can expect to live nearly seven years longer than those in Manchester and Liverpool. Life expectancy has risen much faster in wealthy parts of the country, while in Inner London it has increased at a rate well below the national average. Men in Cambridge can expect to live 76 years, in Manchester 69, compared to a national average of 74. In Cambridge life expectancy for women is 81 years, 76 in Manchester, with a national average of 79.5. The areas with the lower life expectancy show higher levels of social deprivation. The life expectancy variances are widening. The most deprived areas have life expectancies below the most affluent areas ten years ago.'

The Times, December 1997

Q Read extract **B**. Draw a table to compare male and female life expectancy for Cambridge and Manchester. Include a row or column showing national averages.

This increase in the number of elderly people is a worry for health providers. An elderly person uses three times the health services of a person between 15 and 60 years. More elderly people will be dependent on fewer working people.

C

Life expectancy in England				
	1974	1984	1994	1997
Male	69.2	71.5	73.8	74.0
Female	75.5	77.4	79.1	79.7

D

The effects of global population growing older

MEDCs	LEDCs
Some of the 'oldest' countries are Sweden, Germany, Japan and Italy with over 20% of the population over 59.	Some LEDCs have rapidly increasing life expectancy, e.g. China.
Shortage of hospitals and homes to care for the elderly.	Few health programmes for the elderly.
Pension schemes under pressure as number of retired increases and younger workers declines. Longer life expectancy after retirement. In the USA life expectancy has risen from 62 (three years less than retirement) in 1970 to 76 (11 years more) in 1997.	Often no social security or pension schemes. Older generation depends on younger family. Urbanization, loss of traditional values and greater movement make this dependency difficult.
Women outnumber men and on average live eight years longer – in some places twice as many women over 59 as men.	Older women, widows, face extreme poverty in old age.
Money has to be diverted from programmes for young.	Nation has more pressing priorities than the elderly.
Elderly play important role in community: use university of the Third Age; heavy use of leisure facilities.	In Chile, over half the elderly people help in the schools with basic and vocational skills.

E

Elderly people in China

CASE STUDY *Population changes in the EU*

In 1994 the population of the EU was 370 million (6.5 per cent of the total world population). Twenty four years previously, in 1960, the figure for the same European countries was 10.4 per cent of the total world population. In other words, although the population of Europe has continued to grow, its share of the world's population has fallen. This is because the populations of the LEDCs have been growing more rapidly to take a larger share of the world's population.

F

Population under 20 years of age (%)	
EU	24.4
Republic of Ireland	34.9
Germany	21.5
USA	28.8
Japan	25.5

The rate of natural increase for the EU was one of the lowest in the world at 0.1 per cent in 1990. In **F** all have ageing populations but the percentage of young people was lower in the EU and Germany the lowest of all. The consequences of these population changes will cause major problems for the EU in the twenty-first century.

A summary of the main characteristics of the European population includes:
- a population where the average age is increasing
- a decreasing number of births
- increased life expectancy, especially for women
- one of the lowest infant mortality rates in the world
- an increasing age for couples marrying for the first time
- smaller households with a larger number of single parent families
- a smaller economically active population.

Belgium, Italy and the UK are the worst affected. The problems they face include:
- funding state pension schemes
- funding health and social services
- building enough special housing.

Ageing Asian population

This table shows that many Asian countries have a significant increase in the number of elderly people in their populations. This has come about through decreasing birth rates and extended life expectancy, and is known as **demographic ageing**.

	Demographic profile	% of population aged 65+			Decade when dependency rates will show marked increase
		1990	2010	2025	
Hong Kong	Mature	7.5		18	2010
South Korea	Mature	4.8	9.0	12	2010
Singapore	Mature	5.8	10.4	21	2010
China	Rapidly ageing	5.8	8.3	13	2020
Indonesia	Ageing	3.0	5.9	10.5	2025
Malaysia	Ageing	3.7	5.0	8	2025
Thailand	Ageing	4.0	7.2	13	2025

Demographic indicators

Global gender issues

Is the quality of life the same for both sexes?

Since 1990 the United Nations has used the Human Development Index (HDI) to study human well being globally. This has included equity, poverty and **gender** issues. The most recent reports on the HDI have focused on gender issues. They have noted some global progress:

- female life expectancy has increased 20 per cent faster than male since 1975
- fertility rates have fallen by a third since 1975
- female **literacy** has increased from 54 per cent of the male rate in 1970 to 74 per cent in 1990
- female primary and secondary school enrollments have increased from 67 per cent of the male rate in 1970 to 86 per cent by 1990.

However they note progress still has to be made in:
- reducing female poverty, where 70 per cent of the people living in poverty are female
- increasing the number of females in paid employment – only 40 per cent achieving equal pay – female wages are 75 per cent of those of men
- increasing the number of female white collar workers
- gaining political influence (in the UK only 10 per cent of parliamentary seats are held by women and only 6 per cent of cabinet seats).

Countries with a good record on women's rights include Norway, Sweden, Finland and Hong Kong.

Q

1 With a partner, discuss ways of resolving the remaining issues on gender shown by the United Nations HDI study. Prepare a 200-word report.

2 Is increased life expectancy a major cause for celebration? Justify your views.

Migration

Population **migration** is a small part of the many movements made by people every day. When people move 'permanently' (defined as for more than one year) from one place to another they are described as migrating and they are part of population migration.

A

Types of migration

There are four types of migration according to the origin and destination of the migrant:

Type 1 Rural to rural In the UK this could be a farmer's son or daughter moving to a nearby farm, or an elderly couple moving nearer to their children.

Type 2 Rural to urban – urbanization This type of movement was very common in the nineteenth and early twentieth century in the UK as rural people moved into the growing industrial cities. Young people are still moving to urban areas as they seek greater opportunities and better paid jobs. Some very poor people also move to cheap, low quality rooms found in urban areas. However, some richer people are also moving back into very expensive new or refurbished accommodation – **reurbanization**.

Type 3 Urban to rural – deurbanization This is a strong movement at the end of the twentieth century. People, especially those with families, money and a car, are moving to rural areas around cities where they can live in villages and commute daily into the nearby city. Retired people also often leave the urban area. Families with cars find the congestion of city centres inconvenient and prefer the out-of-city shopping and entertainment complexes.

Type 4 Urban to urban There are two main groups who move from one urban area to another. The first group are like Type 2 movers. They move their home to an urban area near to the city in which they are living. Each day they travel back to the city to work. For example, around London, towns such as Bedford, Orpington, Sevenoaks, Maidenhead and High Wycombe have rapid rail services to the centre. The second group migrate from urban area to urban area because their company is moving, or they may have lost or changed their job. Governments have encouraged some companies to move their head offices out of the centres of big cities. After 1945 people were also encouraged to migrate to new towns.

What causes people to move?

There are many reasons for people to migrate. A useful way of looking at them is to divide them into push and pull factors (**B**).

How far do people move?

Many factors influence the distance that people migrate. These include:

1 **The attractiveness of the destination** Migrants tend to move in a series of steps. From home into the local town, then a larger city, a regional centre and finally the capital or primate city. Not every migrant completes all of these steps. Destinations become more attractive as jobs in industry and commerce grow. In large cities a reverse series of steps can be seen as families move out.

B

Push factors	Pull factors
Conditions in the home area (origin) that make people feel they should move to improve their quality of life	Opportunities in another area (destination) which attract people to move there for a better life
Lack of job opportunities, e.g. • in remote rural areas • in former coal mining areas • in textile and pottery areas • in shipbuilding, iron and steel	Job opportunities, e.g. in tourist honeypots in IT industries in service industries in new car assembly plants
Poor housing, e.g. in inner city areas	Housing, e.g. houses with gardens
Poor environment, e.g. crime, noise, pollution, traffic	Safety, privacy, green areas
War and civil strife	Political stability
Poor schools	Quality schools and educational opportunity
Lack of health care	Provision of health care for young and elderly
Increased wealth and car purchase	Opportunities to use wealth to improve quality of life, e.g. home with garage, golf club
Age, e.g. new workers and recently retired	Age, e.g. people with similar social habits
Family breakdown, e.g. divorce	Presence of family and friends
Personal restlessness	Desire for new experiences
Loss of sense of community	Recognition of sense of community

2 **The origin of the migrants** People in rural areas, especially in less developed or remote areas, tend to migrate more than those in larger towns. As the negative features of urban areas have increased – crime, traffic congestion, noise and pollution – people leave for rural areas nearby.

3 **Obstacles between the origin and the intended destination**, e.g. the distance between the two places. The greater the distance the fewer people are likely to migrate between them. Distance may be measured in kilometres, time or cost. This is the **Distance-Decay effect**. Migration increases as transport improves and travel costs fall. Another obstacle to movement is the existence of other opportunities. These are called 'intervening opportunities'. These include jobs found along the way, frontier controls, lack of money, language changes and homesickness.

4 **Personal factors** People are different. Some are more restless and see opportunities in new places and migrate. Others prefer the familiar places they know. These 'behavioural' characteristics have to be taken into account. People willing to take risks to get what they see as the most from life are called 'optimizers'. Those satisfied with their way of life are called 'satisficers'.

The new border wall on the USA and Mexican border (**C**) has been built to stop the flow of illegal immigrants and drugs. It replaces 100km of rusting steel, chain-link fences. When the government of the USA ordered the wall they said they wanted it to be:

- resistant to repeated physical assaults by means of welding torches, chisels, hammers, firearms, climbing over or penetration by vehicles
- friendly looking to evoke friendship between the two countries; to allow light and have a feeling of openness
- 4.3m high and called a fence, not a wall.

The USA officials living on the north side, in Nogales, Arizona feel the fence works well with its salmon colour, blue trimmed openings and inlaid stone chips. In Nogales City, Mexico to the south, there is less enthusiasm. Some would prefer no fence and free movement to be allowed between the two countries. They believe the fence will become an eyesore. Graffiti has already started to appear on the Mexican side.

C The border between USA and Mexico

The Schengen Agreement is named after a small town in Luxembourg. At Schengen, Austria, Belgium, France, Italy, Germany, Luxembourg, Netherlands, Portugal, Spain, Greece, Denmark, Sweden and Finland agreed that by 1999 they would have got rid of all internal borders. In addition their police forces would work together to control illegal immigration, crime and the drugs traffic. The map (**D**) shows the position in 1998 when some of the countries had begun to operate the Schengen Agreement. Six major weak points are shown as well as the reactions of French and German governments. They have reacted angrily to inefficient controls by Mediterranean countries. Illegal immigrants included those from India, Pakistan, Sri Lanka, Turkey, Algeria, Egypt and Iraq (**E**).

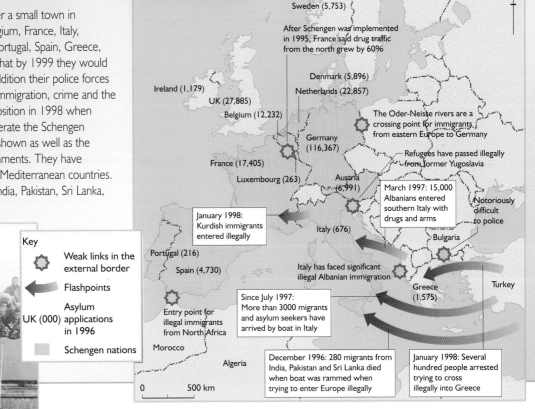

D Europe without frontiers

Finland (771)

Sweden (5,753)

After Schengen was implemented in 1995, France said drug traffic from the north grew by 60%

Denmark (5,896)

Ireland (1,179)

Netherlands (22,857)

UK (27,885)

Belgium (12,232)

The Oder-Neisse rivers are a crossing point for immigrants from eastern Europe to Germany

Germany (116,367)

Refugees have passed illegally from former Yugoslavia

France (17,405)

Luxembourg (263)

Austria (6,991)

March 1997: 15,000 Albanians entered southern Italy with drugs and arms

Notoriously difficult to police

January 1998: Kurdish immigrants entered illegally

Italy (676)

Bulgaria

Portugal (216)

Italy has faced significant illegal Albanian immigration

Greece (1,575)

Turkey

Spain (4,730)

Since July 1997: More than 3000 migrants and asylum seekers have arrived by boat in Italy

Entry point for illegal immigrants from North Africa

Morocco

Algeria

December 1996: 280 migrants from India, Pakistan and Sri Lanka died when boat was rammed when trying to enter Europe illegally

January 1998: Several hundred people arrested trying to cross illegally into Greece

0   500 km

Key

⬡ Weak links in the external border

◀ Flashpoints

UK (000) Asylum applications in 1996

Schengen nations

The Kurds from Iraq are a large group. They are **refugees** from an unsympathetic regime in Iraq

E

Questions

For the EU or an MEDC you have studied:

1 Describe how the population is changing through migration. (4)

2 Explain the push and pull factors that have led to this migration. (9)

3 How has the migration affected the structure of population at the destination and origin? (6)

4 What other effects have the migrants had on the destination area? (6)

Total: 25 marks

The location of settlement

The word location is used here to include the site and situation of a settlement. Writing about location includes a description of the position of the settlement within its region and in relation to other settlements. The search for reasons to explain a location includes detail of the features of its site and the social, historical, economic and political factors which have had an influence (table **A**).

CASE STUDY EU: Littleton – a growing village

Littleton is really three rural settlements in Gloucestershire that have merged. Together they show many of the features of modern villages. It lies at the foot of the Cotswold scarp. A series of streams provide a water supply even in the driest weather. Most of the land around the village is too steep or too wet for crops so pasture land dominates. The village is 16km from the nearest large town, Cheltenham.

Villages are always changing. Those located within range of large cities have become attractive places in which to live. People who can afford to commute to the city often choose to live in a village in the surrounding countryside. In addition some people who retire from a job in the city buy a house in a village nearby. Note how the village has changed (**B**). It covers more land as new housing estates have been built; the church, post office/shop and village hall remain. However the school and bus stop have gone. In 1955 the village had football, darts and cribbage teams, and an amateur dramatics group. All of these had ceased until an enterprising landlord revived interest. Now a retired actress has re-formed the amateur dramatics group and an industrialist has organized an art group. The crib team is doing well but is composed entirely of newcomers – teachers, bank managers, ICT specialists, a cabinet maker and an administrator. The village has celebrations together at Christmas and New Year, a May Day maypole

and a summer fete. The newcomers from the city, together with the retired people in the village, have brought new life to the community.

This process is called **deurbanization**. People move from urban areas to live in the country around the city. This is the reverse of the movement of people into the city in the previous 100 years called urbanization.

A

Factors influencing the location of settlements

Main factor	Explanation	Example
Water supply	Water is needed every day. Originally streams and rivers provided a clean and safe supply. Spring-line settlements can be found at the foot of chalk and limestone scarps. Wet-point settlements can be found in dry areas, e.g. oases.	Gretton, Gloucs. Longnor, Staffordshire
Defence	This was needed in earlier less peaceful times. Inside of a meander	Durham
	Commanding view across countryside	Edinburgh
	Near boundary of kingdom	Conwy
Routeways	Where several valleys meet	Carlisle
	Where two rivers meet (confluence)	Tewkesbury
	Routeway gap in line of hills	Dorking
	Bridging point over river	Oxford
	Lowest bridging point	Newcastle upon Tyne
Relief	Risk of flooding	
	Dry sites in marshy area	Ely
	Shelter and aspect, south-facing	Torquay
Distance	From other settlement, commuter town	Bedford
Resources	Mining coal	Wigan, Rhondda
	Salt extraction	Nantwich
Ports	Sheltered sea inlets	Dartmouth
	Fishing grounds	Grimsby
	Deep water harbour	Southampton
Market centres	Services for surrounding area, county town	Norwich
Manufacturing centres	Car assembly	Coventry
	Light industry	Slough
Resorts and spas	Holiday places	Blackpool
	Spa towns	Cheltenham, Buxton
	Retirement towns	Eastbourne
Educational centres	University towns	Cambridge
Religious centres	Cathedral towns	York, Canterbury
Railway towns	Major junctions	Crewe
Planned towns	New towns	Harlow, Stevenage
	Expanded towns	Peterborough

B Littleton, 1955 and 1998

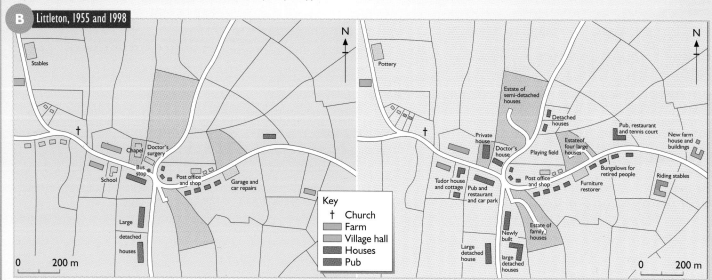

Key
† Church
Farm
Village hall
Houses
Pub

CASE STUDY *EU: Durham City – a regional defensive site*

The city of Durham, with 30,000 inhabitants, is in the north of England. Its twelfth century cathedral and castle stand on a hill in the centre of a meander loop of the River Wear (**C**). The cathedral and castle are designated as a World Heritage site. Durham also has the third oldest university in England; it is a market centre, has good road links, the A1(M), and has the east coast inter-city rail line nearby.

Durham was built on a defensive site. The River Wear acts as a moat or defensive barrier on three sides of the town. In the past this made the site easier to defend. Gates could be closed so that the only way into the town was through the heavily defended wall in the Market Place.

Q Produce a tourist brochure advertising the interesting site of Durham City. You can include its new shopping centre, good restaurants, range of hotels and caravan park nearby. The brochure must emphasize the uniqueness of the site.

CASE STUDY *EU: Harlow – a planned town*

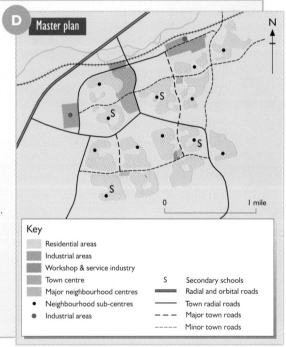
D Master plan

Key

Residential areas	
Industrial areas	
Workshop & service industry	
Town centre	S Secondary schools
Major neighbourhood centres	Radial and orbital roads
• Neighbourhood sub-centres	Town radial roads
● Industrial areas	– – – Major town roads
	- - - - Minor town roads

Fifty years ago many cities in the UK were prevented from sprawling over the countryside by a Green Belt. These were fields around the urban areas where it was made very difficult to get permission to build. These Green Belts still exist and have preserved areas of countryside. New developments have had to be located inside the urban area or outside the Green Belt in smaller urban areas.

Since 1946 the government of the UK has planned and built a large number of New Towns. They are one of the success stories of British town planning. Harlow, Essex is one of these towns. The town is now over 50 years old. It was based upon a series of neighbourhoods surrounding a planned pedestrianized town centre. Two industrial areas were also built on the edge of the town. The Master Plan was the responsibility of a single architect/town planner (**D**). Over the 50 years changes have been made to the original plan mainly because of mass car ownership.

The key point in understanding the location of Harlow is that it was selected by planners. They needed a site near to, but separate from, London to take its overspill population. The planners were told to avoid good agricultural land and to take account of existing railway lines. The site had to be big enough to take a town of 50,000 people.

Q Study **B**.

1 Make a table of the advantages and disadvantages, to the people living there, of the growth of a village near a large city.

2 Make a list of the changes you can see in the village between 1955 and 1998.

Questions

1 How have the following affected the popularity of living in a village:
   a) Increased car ownership
   b) Public transport
   c) New locations of industry
   d) Views on rural life. (8)

2 Why might estate agents, people living in suburbs and farmers have different ideas of what a village should be like? (9)

3 Study a copy of your local Ordnance Survey map. Using map evidence, suggest reasons for the location of a named settlement on the map. (8)

Total: 25 marks

The functions of settlement

Are settlement size, location and function linked?

A family is going on holiday and driving towards a settlement in East Anglia. It is 12.30 pm and everyone is hungry. One thought fills everyone's mind – is there a McDonald's in this settlement? The eldest child, a geography student, looks ahead and says there will be at least a chip shop and probably a McDonald's, which proves to be right. How did he come to his correct decision?

Central Place Theory

The other members of the family may have seen the settlements they had passed through as a mixture – some large, some small, some close together, others far apart. The student had been seeing the settlements as part of **Central Place Theory**. He had been seeing the settlements as places to which people travel to purchase something. They travel to a central place from a **market area** or **sphere of influence**.

Some people will travel only a short distance for goods that they need regularly, such as bread and milk. So the sphere of influence for shops selling bread and milk is small. For furniture, shoes and other high **order** comparison goods they will travel further from a larger sphere of influence. The distance people are willing to travel is called the **range of the good**.

In some villages there are only one or two different shops (functions) but in market towns there will be more. Cities will have all the functions of towns and villages plus higher order ones of their own – this is known as the **settlement hierarchy** (**C**). In an area you will find many villages, a smaller number of towns and one or two cities.

Key
- • Village
- • Low-order central place
- ⬤ High-order central place
- — Low-order market area boundary
- — High-order market area boundary

A

Pattern of settlement predicted by Central Place Theory

A shows how Central Place Theory works out for a very flat area with an even population distribution. The real world does not fit this theory exactly. The theory helps understanding of the real world.

Q

1 Name a village and a town you know and describe the services in each.

2 How do you think you could test the idea that village shops have small spheres of influence?

CASE STUDY EU: Cambridgeshire

In East Anglia, the population of the area around the City of Cambridge has grown rapidly, by 35 per cent, in the last ten years. Cambridge and the six towns which surround it (**B**) lie on the relatively flat floodplains of the rivers Ouse and Cam.

Cambridge with a population of about 100,000, has four major functions:
- a university town since the thirteenth century
- a tourist centre for visitors to the colleges, river and surrounding area
- a growing industrial centre of employment in high-tech, agricultural-related employment and resources linked to the university
- a shopping and regional centre.

Villages around Cambridge

In the villages, for example Linton, 14 km south-east of Cambridge, there is usually a primary school, a small supermarket, pub and post office. Pensioners and people looking after young children are in the village street each weekday morning to use the services. There is less choice than in Cambridge and prices are a little higher, but it is friendly and

convenient. In most villages parking is not a problem. These are low order settlements with a small range of goods.

The six towns around Cambridge (B)

These are busy places, especially on market day and each day that the secondary school is open. They attract people from the town and surrounding villages for shopping and other services. They have more to offer than a village but less than Cambridge. These are middle order settlements with a higher range of goods. They have a bigger sphere of influence than villages and are found further apart.

B

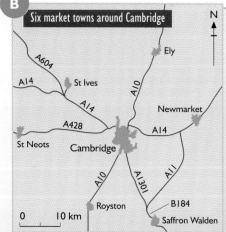

Six market towns around Cambridge

N

Cambridge as a shopping and regional centre

The number of people using the services in Cambridge is far greater than its population of 100,000. People come from the surrounding villages and towns to Cambridge each day to work and to use its services. They come for the wide range of employment available and the choice of shops and other services (specialist hospital, legal and other professional services). In Cambridge you can use the large superstores on the ring roads to do your weekly shopping or use the Park and Ride to travel to the high quality shops and supermarkets in the centre. They offer a wide choice including internationally famous clothes, shoe shops, large bookshops and varied places to eat. There is choice, variety and size to attract the users of the centre.

The services in Cambridge and its towns and villages show an interesting pattern (D). The key points to note are:
- cities have the wider range of services
- villages have a small range of services.

However, not all villages have so many functions. Why might this be so?

Study of these three types of settlement (D) shows that:

- people shop locally for low order goods such as bread (especially pensioners who do not tend to drive to busy towns and cities)
- service centres, such as villages, towns and cities, attract people from outside to use their services – the sphere of influence of the settlement
- people travel further for more specialist goods, e.g. CDs, electrical goods, clothes
- there are fewer large service centres (such as Cambridge) than there are small market towns (C).

D

Summary chart of settlement services

	Village	Town	City
Primary school	✔	✔	✔
Chemist	✔	✔	✔
Small supermarket	✔	✔	✔
Bus service	✔	✔	✔
Pub	✔	✔	✔
Post office	✔	✔	✔
Baker	✔	✔	✔
Grocer	✔	✔	✔
Bank		✔	✔
Florist		✔	✔
Furniture		✔	✔
Newsagent		✔	✔
Take-away		✔	✔
Secondary school		✔	✔
Market		✔	✔
Butcher		✔	✔
Clothes		✔	✔
Building society			✔
Designer clothes			✔
Hospital			✔
Out of town superstore			✔
Dry cleaner			✔
Auctioneers			✔
Jeweller			✔
Railway			✔
College			✔

Examples		Use
Department stores, hospitals, cinemas and leisure centres	High order	Least frequent
Supermarkets, restaurants	Middle order	More frequent
Newspaper shops, post offices, off licences	Low order	Most frequent

Hierarchy of shops and services **C**

Q

1. Select a location in your local area where you might open a video shop. Explain the choice of location you make.

2. Define the terms 'range', 'threshold' and 'hierarchy' when used to explain the link between the size of a settlement and its functions.

3. Why might you find McDonald's restaurants in the town centre and on the ring roads of many towns?

E Shopping trips to shoe shops in North Humberside

Key
- Selected households
- Towns

Scale
0 — 8km

Questions

1. Study C:
   a) Which order of goods will be more common in a large city? *(1)*
   b) What do you understand by the term 'market area'? *(2)*
   c) Describe and explain the difference in market area of a greengrocer and a leisure centre. *(3)*
   d) Suggest ways in which shop owners could extend their market area. *(4)*

2. Study E:
   a) Describe the pattern of trips shown on the map. *(3)*
   b) How might the pattern change if a retail park, with two shoe shops, was opened 8km to the south east of Driffield? *(3)*

3. For a region you have studied, what links are there between size and location of settlement and its functions? *(9)*

Total: 25 marks

Land use patterns

Where are the different activities located within settlements?

Most of the land in a modern residential area is used for housing. Some land is used by local shops, for example a newsagent and general store, and there is open space. This pattern of land use is very different from the centre of a city where larger shops and offices are the main land users. Urban land use appears to be arranged into zones (**A**).

In the 1920s an American, Burgess, studied land use in Chicago. He found a roughly circular pattern (**B**). In 1939 another American, Hoyt, improved on the model. He studied 142 cities in the USA and produced model **C**. In 1965 a geographer named Mann matched the Burgess and Hoyt models to three English cities – Huddersfield, Nottingham and Sheffield. Ten years later a British geographer, Robson, matched them to Sunderland and Belfast. Their British version is shown in **D**.

None of these models will fit your town perfectly nor in LEDCs where the cities have grown rapidly. LEDCs show some of the zones of these models but they have their own characteristics as well.

The Central Business District This is the core of the city. It is the city centre and contains the chief shops, offices and places for entertainment It will also include banks and local authority offices. Sites are very expensive in the **CBD** because of its accessibility and shortage of space. Only the bigger shop chains can afford the high rents. Buildings often have several storeys to increase the floor area. Indoor shopping

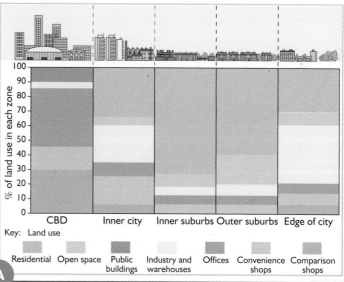

A A generalized view of the land use zones that may be found along a transect from the centre of the urban area to its edge.

malls are popular where temperatures are controlled, and security and cleanliness are high. The area has a low residential population, but high pedestrian numbers during the day. Traffic is restricted in the CBD and parking difficult and expensive. There is always rebuilding taking place in or on the edge of the CBD.

The inner city This area of mixed land use is on the edge of the CBD. It may have small industries, such as printing, car repair, garages and larger houses converted to flats and offices. Often the area feels as if it is decaying while waiting for renewal. Housing is often in small rented rooms. Crime rates are relatively high and governments have given special attention to these areas. Problems include poverty, poor housing, health (lower life expectancy and higher infant mortality), educational attainment, noise and air pollution. A series of planning programmes have taken place in partnership with local people to improve these areas.

Q

Explain why tall buildings are found close to the centre of many cities.

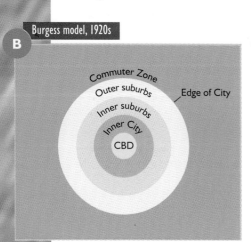

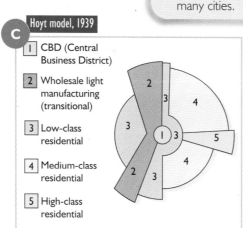

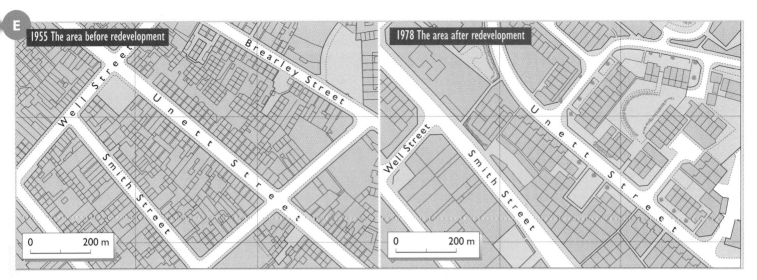

E

1955 The area before redevelopment

1978 The area after redevelopment

0   200 m

0   200 m

Inner suburbs Much of this area of housing was built 80–100 years ago. The terraced houses were for workers who walked to factories near the city centre. Streets are lined with cars, especially at night. Sometimes three or four houses have been demolished for off-street parking. Houses have backyards rather than gardens. Many have been redeveloped (**E**).

Outer suburbs Areas of semi-detached houses were often built between 1930 and 1940 as suburban trains and buses allowed people to travel further to work. Since 1945 large areas of local authority housing (council estates) and private housing have been built. Today many families on these estates have a car. They can shop at the local small parade (take away food, video library, newsagent, baker and small supermarket, DIY shop). The houses have space for a car and front and back gardens. On the outer edges of these suburbs, large shopping areas have sometimes been built. These sites have car parking and are close to ring roads. They cause extra traffic and damage the shops in the CBD. In

the future it will be more difficult to get permission to build these out-of-town centres.

Industrial areas The older industrial areas are on the edge of the city centre, next to the railway which was the main way goods were transported. Today they are in difficulties because of traffic congestion and cramped sites. Where industry has closed, the government is trying to re-use the site. These are called brownfield sites. New users include small factories, leisure sites, shops and housing. Government aims to build half the new houses on brownfield sites. The new industrial areas are in the outer suburbs on estates close to ring roads. Many working in these factories live on outer suburban estates.

Commuter zone Green belts around urban areas stop sprawl. In this area and beyond it the small towns and villages become desirable places to live for people able to afford the high house prices and cost of travelling daily to the city.

Q

1 In groups of three of four, make a **transect** map of land use in your town.

  a) Select four sites in your town. They should be in the CBD, near the CBD, in the suburbs, and near the edge.

  b) Visit each site and record the land use of about 20 properties on a grid like the one below.

  c) Write a brief description of each of the areas you visited. Mention the main users of land, traffic conditions, people in the area and any changes you noticed taking place. Explain how you got an idea of the age of the buildings.

  d) Mark the areas on a map of the town. Annotate your map with any pattern you

see as you move from the CBD to the edge of the town.

  e) Draw a diagram similar to **A** to show your findings.

  f) What differences do you notice in the main users of each area?

2 On an A3 sized piece of paper, arrange four to six photographs or sketches to show different areas of land use within a town you have chosen. Annotate each photo.

Bungalow Residential 1960s	Church Leisure 1870	Vicarage Residential 1870	Fire Station Services 1940	Shop Antiques 1900	Shop Grocer 1900	Public House Leisure 1900	Shop Fast food 1900	Shop Newsagent 1900	Shop Post Office 1900
Name of road or street									
House Residential	House Residential	House Residential	House Residential	Shop Cards	Shop Optician	Shop Antiques	Shop Building Society	Shop Bank	Shop Grocer

Changing land use within settlements

The effect of changes in transport

Cities in the UK have become increasingly congested. This affects everyone every day. Journeys take longer; roads and pedestrian areas become more dangerous; air quality becomes poor; noise pollution invades homes and workplaces and cars become a huge visual intrusion. More people own a car because of the door-to-door convenience in travel but increased car ownership threatens the access it brings. The Confederation of British Industry has estimated that congestion and accidents cost £25 billion per year. In the UK the government is aiming to reduce traffic by 5 per cent below 1990 levels by 2005 and 10 per cent by 2010.

A, **B**, **C** and **D** give information on the increase in traffic. They show that the number of cars has increased while the number of public transport vehicles, such as buses, has fallen (**A**). The number of kilometres travelled by buses has increased but they are carrying fewer passengers (**C**).

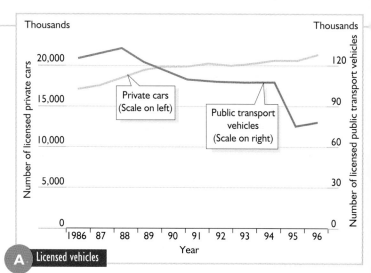

A Licensed vehicles

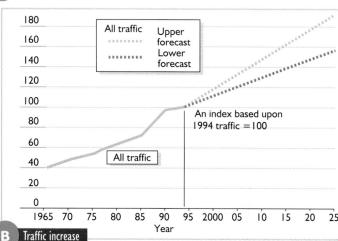

B Traffic increase

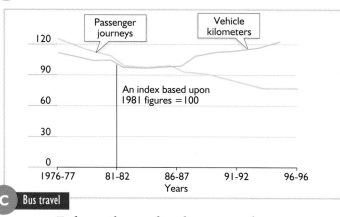

C Bus travel

E shows the results of a survey of car users. **F** is a list of problems caused by traffic.

D

Average annual miles travelled per person			
	1975/76	1985/6	1995/96
Car	3,199	3,796	5,082
Foot	255	244	200
Bicycle	51	44	38
Local bus	129	297	258
Train	289	292	302
Motorbike	47	51	29
Taxi	13	27	40
Van/lorry	187	228	296
London Underground	36	44	54
Other public	222	262	244
Other private	16	33	29
Total	4,740	5,317	6,570

E

Public opinion poll

A recent survey found the following:

- congestion adds 2.5 hours per week to commuter journeys
- only 7% of commuters using cars said they would switch to public transport if congestion doubled
- 25% of commuters said they would continue to drive into traffic-related pollution even if it was a health hazard
- doubling the price of petrol is opposed by 95% of road users
- charging £5 to travel into a local city is opposed by 72% of road users
- people are willing to suffer upheaval if the revenue raised goes into improved public transport
- toll roads are opposed by 68% of road users.

F

Traffic problems listed in a national newspaper

- Air and noise pollution result from traffic
- 3.5 million people suffer from asthma in the UK
- Millions of children are unable to play in the streets
- Older people are trapped at home due to lack of public transport
- New roads create more demand for more roads – there are 600 areas waiting for a by-pass.

Options for reducing traffic

In order to reduce traffic, the government has to be clear what options are available. Some towns have introduced trams (J), others have 'park and ride' schemes, but how successful are they? What other options are there? The information on this page should be used in the Decision Making Exercise on page 195.

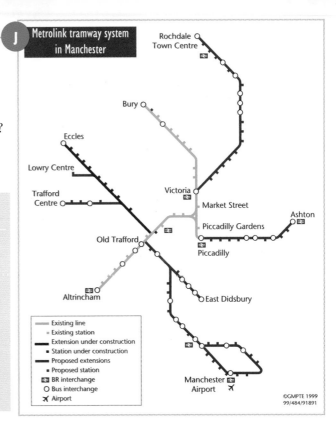

J Metrolink tramway system in Manchester

G Transport 2000 agenda

Ways to reduce the problem of traffic:

- Introduce traffic calming, low speed zones and bus lanes
- Introduce pedestrian zones, car free areas and cycleways
- Increase car parking charges and the price of fuel
- Encourage commuters to share cars
- Create safe routes to school
- Encourage supermarkets to introduce home delivery services
- Refuse planning applications for out-of-town shopping and entertainment centres
- Build car parks next to bus and rail stations
- Introduce Park and Ride schemes
- Introduce cheap, easy to pay flat rate fares on public transport.

Manchester Metrolink (J)

- The city links are running well through the streets of Manchester
- Bus services do compete with the tram
- Impact on getting cars off the road is modest
- Main users have come from buses.

H A green budget

Ideas to reduce pollution:

- Raise the tax on fuel to encourage people to move to energy-saving cars
- End tax concessions on company cars
- Tax private parking at the workplace
- Raise the road fund tax on larger vehicles
- Cut back on the new roads programme and improve public transport

K Some of the planners' conclusions

- Attractive low floor buses needed in urban areas
- Buses, trams, light rail and heavy rail need to be integrated
- Cars do have advantages for their users
- The problem is most urgent in urban areas
- Car users will only use public transport if it is good
- Land use has to be planned
- Car users should pay the real cost of using their car
- 'Quick fix' solutions will not get people out of their cars.

I Research by Lancaster University

Commuting journeys are getting longer, the average is now ten miles per day. People put up with long journeys because:

- they do not want to uproot home and family
- jobs are insecure
- people having a company car are more likely to commute.

Research from London University

Reducing road space causes traffic to evaporate. Delays cause motorists to:

- try alternative routes or change their destination e.g. for shopping
- share cars.

Persuading parents not to use their cars to get children to school may quicken other people's rush hour journeys by eleven minutes.

Government research reports

Effectiveness of Park and Ride

- No evidence that it reduces congestion on its own
- Takes traffic from other public services

Road pricing

- One of the most promising ways to reduce congestion
- Consumers change behaviour rather than pay.

L Survey of people's attitudes, UK, 1995 (%)

	Strongly agree/ agree	Neither agree or disagree	Disagree strongly/ disagree	Cannot choose/not answered
Many more streets in towns should be reserved for pedestrians only	68	16	11	5
Cyclists and pedestrians should be given more priority in towns even if this makes things more difficult for car drivers	64	16	15	5
Buses should be given more priority in towns even if this makes things more difficult for car drivers	61	16	18	5
The UK should do more to improve its public transport system even if the road system suffers	58	19	16	7
Car drivers are still given too easy a time in UK towns	29	26	37	8
Local rail services that do not pay for themselves should be closed down.	13	17	62	8
Local bus services that do not pay for themselves should be closed down.	12	16	66	6

Cambridge

Cambridge became a boom area in the 1980s (**M**) and 1990s. The boom brought with it disadvantages as well as advantages including:

- housing became very expensive
- traffic congestion grew
- wages became high because of skills shortages
- higher costs started to make 'hotspots', such as Cambridge, uncompetitive compared to European rivals
- public transport was unable to cope with demand.

M Congestion in Cambridge City

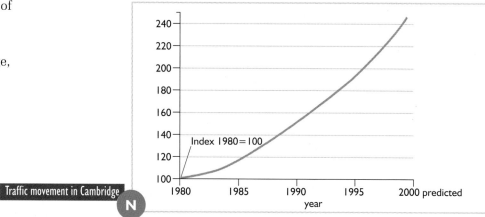

Traffic movement in Cambridge **N**

Index 1980=100

O Sketch diagram of Cambridge

Reasons for growth

Sketch diagram of Cambridge based on the map on page 188

A10

A14

A428

A14

M11

Effects of growth on local population

Problems of growth

Decision making exercise

This section has focused on problems caused by traffic in towns. It has looked at ways to reduce traffic and encourage people to use public transport. Cambridge is an example of a town with serious traffic problems. Using your own knowledge, opinions and the resources on pages 192–194, complete the following tasks based on Cambridge. You may find pages 188–189 useful.

The background

1 a) Describe the main trends shown in the graphs **A**, **B** and **C**.

  b) Some experts say that time is running out for cities and their traffic. Use the information provided and your own knowledge to explain this view. (6)

2 O is a simple map of the Cambridge area. Using a copy of the map, fill in the boxes with notes. Select only the important points and be careful not to repeat. Make sure you include the following points:

  • important road links include the M11 and A14
  • London is 50 minutes away by rail
  • London is about 70 km away by motorway
  • the population of the built-up area has increased by 100,000
  • house prices have risen dramatically
  • there are 4,000 people on the waiting list for council houses
  • only 20 per cent of first-time buyers can buy in the city
  • traffic congestion in the rush hour is severe on all approach roads
  • several farmers on the edge of the city are willing to sell their land to developers
  • the university provides a highly skilled workforce
  • the colleges are a tourist attraction all year. (8)

3 Study **N**. The 'Index of Traffic Movement' is a measurement of traffic relative to every 100 vehicles in 1980.

  a) Describe what the graph shows about traffic movement in the city of Cambridge between 1980 and 2000.

  b) Give three reasons for the changing amount of traffic in urban areas.

  c) What problems are likely to have been caused in Cambridge by these changes? (8)

The options

How can the quality of life of people living and working in cities be sustained as car ownership and traffic increases? Here are three options for Cambridge:

A • Restrict parking in the historic city centre and provide park and ride spaces on the edge of the city. This would mean closing some public car parks with a loss of income. Much of the town centre would only have access for buses and emergency vehicles.
  • Build one multi-storey car park for shoppers needing to drive to the centre. Parking fees would be high: £1 per hour with a maximum of 2 hours.
  • Employ traffic wardens.
  • On the north, west and southern edges of the city provide large spaces for park and ride. Charges of 50p per return journey would not cover the full use of the service.

B • Allocate land at two or three places on the edge of the city for employment, e.g. Cambridge Science Park and large out-of-town shopping centres. Ensure they have plenty of car parking. These could be placed near the ring road and motorway (M11) for the large middle order shops used once per week.
  • Introduce toll gates on the main entrances to the city.

C • Build a by-pass around the city to allow traffic travelling from east to west (the coast to the Midlands) and north to south (Northern England to Stanstead Airport and London) to miss the city.
  • To ease housing problems develop some of the smaller towns as growth poles some ten to twenty miles from Cambridge.
  • Provide employment in these towns.

How do these plans affect the quality of life for people living in the area?

4 For each of the options **A**, **B** and **C**:

  a) explain its advantages and disadvantages

  b) state, with reasons, the likely views of one of the groups listed (i-vi):

    i) A two car family, with no children. The husband has retired and the wife is working near to the centre of Cambridge. They live in one of the growth pole towns to the north of Cambridge.

    ii) A family with one car living in a small terraced house 1km to the north of the city centre.

    iii) An elderly couple with a car who find city centre traffic difficult. They live in a village 12km to the north of Cambridge. They need to visit the hospital which is in the southern suburbs.

    iv) A young couple, both working in the city centre, who have a car but would like to walk to work and entertainment.

    v) A family of four with two children at secondary school on the other side of town.

    vi) Ambulance and fire services. (18)

The decision

5 Imagine you are on work experience with the Cambridge City Traffic Planning Team. Concentrate on the morning rush hour during term time and on the northern part of the city.

Using all the information on these pages, suggest how you think the planners can reduce the traffic demand. You could suggest one approach or a combination of several. Give reasons for your decision. Cambridge City Council, as part of their planning for traffic in the town, have to consider:

  • the future of town centre shops
  • the large number of tourists coming to the town centre
  • the needs of those attending schools, offices, shops and places of entertainment in the town centre
  • the need to preserve the historic buildings in the narrow streets of the town centre. (20)

Total: 60 marks

The effect of changes in economic activity

How and why is settlement land use changing?

Economic activity is changing in the CBD and on industrial estates. This is largely due to changing ways of life.

Industrial change

In the nineteenth century many urban areas grew up as the new factories offered employment to the rural poor (**A**). They were pulled to the city by the prospects of a better life and well-paid employment. A very similar pattern of migration is happening in the cities of many LEDCs today.

In the nineteenth-century city in the UK, most working people lived in terraced housing within walking distance of the factory, which was usually near the city centre. As steam trains and buses were introduced people moved to the new suburbs. Between 1920 and 1939 cities sprawled rapidly into the countryside. Factories needed to grow and moved outwards as well to suburban industrial estates. In the 1970s and 1980s many moved again to be near to motorways. This gave space for modern production techniques and motorway access to bring in supplies and distribute goods. In the past they had been pulled to the city centre by the need to be close to sources of power, to link to supplies and have contact with bankers and other services. Electricity, motorways and telecommunications have removed

B

Wembley Park Industrial Estate – these sites are known as 'brownfield' sites a government policy is to attract people, housing, shopping and employment b to them. This will help to save the CBD and reduce demand for 'greenfield' si

this need and factory owners have greater freedom of choice. They are more influenced by the sites available, road communications, availability of skilled labour and the type of environment (**C**).

Central Business District Change

The centre of a town or city is known as the Central Business District (CBD). During the day it is very busy – people shop, meet, visit the bank, the building society, or the pub. Even in small towns quite a number of people work in this central area as bankers, solicitors, estate agents and accountants, and those working in shops and services. In a small town the edge of the CBD is where the businesses end and other land uses such as housing, fire stations, schools and car parks appear. Sometimes the bus or railway station is on the edge of the CBD. In larger cities the CBD has high rise offices and the headquarters of large companies. Specialist shops and services, department stores, national chain stores, major banks, theatres, cinemas and concert halls are all found here.

Many of the original nineteenth-century factory sites close to the urban centre, with often the river, canal, railway and main road nearby, have become derelict. They are part of the problem area called the inner city.

A

Cambridge Business Park – open plan factories and offices with many parking spaces are convenient for modern production techniques

C

The CBD developed because of its accessibility. The roads and railways of the area focused upon the centre. Competition for the land meant that prices rose and few land users could afford to pay. More recently many high streets have been pedestrianized.

Many CBDs are changing and many are under threat. Large shopping areas and offices in edge-of-town business parks and multi-plex entertainment centres for cinemas, theatres and sports stadiums are being built. Mass car ownership means people can drive there and avoid the traffic congestion and lack of parking space in the CBD. In some urban areas the CBD is struggling because of the competition from these new centres.

Inner-city change

Many inner-city areas (**A**) are vibrant communities benefiting from mixtures of culture, nationalities and lifestyle. However, problems can occur and these include: poorly paid jobs, poor housing, traffic congestion, noise and air pollution and low-quality open spaces.

The factors contributing to the unattractiveness and decline of inner-city areas include:

- decline of older traditional manufacturing industries such as steel making, shipbuilding, clothing manufacturing, e.g. Sheffield, Newcastle, Manchester
- loss of trade from port cities, e.g. Liverpool
- lack of attraction for new growth industries because of cramped sites and the low skill level of the work force (skilled workers have moved to the suburbs)
- inadequate and complex road systems
- old worn-out housing in poor state of repair which cannot attract new buyers
- noise and air pollution
- derelict factories and disused railway and dockyards
- higher levels of vandalism, graffiti, crime, prostitution and drugs

The Government and local authorities have, especially since 1980, launched a series of plans to make inner cities better places to live. These include:

1 the Urban Programme of small project grants to tackle economic, social and environmental problems

2 derelict land grants to fund reclamation for specific schemes, e.g. old factories, steelworks

D New urban development: Canary Wharf, London

3 Enterprise Zones: some of which are special areas in inner cities where local rates and taxes are reduced

4 Urban Development Corporations: to encourage companies to invest in the inner city, e.g. London Docklands (**D**), Trafford Park (Manchester)

5 City Challenge: a competition for local authorities to revamp inner-city areas, e.g. Dearne Valley, Hulme (Manchester), Brick Lane (Tower Hamlets).

It is difficult to know if these schemes have been a success. Much has been achieved and many inner-city areas are showing a new vitality. However, much of the improvement has benefitted newcomers to the area rather than the original local people.

Questions

1 The people arriving to live in a recently converted inner-city house (originally the large house of a factory owner) include:

- a retired couple on a low pension without children
- a young couple who live together – he is a computer technician in the city-centre and she is a beauty therapist
- an employed single parent with one young daughter
- a taxi driver and his wife who have always lived in the area
- three students attending the university nearby

Choose **two** tenants. For each list the advantages and disadvantages of their choosing to live in the inner city. (12)

2 None of the following live in the inner city. They live in a village ten miles from the city centre:

- a college lecturer and her partner, who works from home
- a retired managing director of a computer firm and his wife, who runs a healing clinic
- a finance manager of a growing agricultural chemicals company and his wife and young family

Suggest reasons for their decision not to live in the inner city. How could they be persuaded to live near the city centre? (9)

3 The inner parts of some cities in the UK have been called the 'winter cities'. Why do you think this is so? (4)

Total: 25 marks

The effect of changes in ways of life

The nineteenth century

By 1900 the population of England and Wales had quadrupled in the 100 years since 1801. The populations of rural areas and small market towns decreased as people moved to the factory employment available in the urban areas.

People living in urban areas in the UK a hundred years ago did not have cars and buses, telephones, televisions and microwave ovens. Few remained at school after the age of eleven. Most men, women and children walked to work. Few couples were used birth control and families were large.

Today

In England and Wales today 70 per cent of the population have cars, 99 per cent have TVs and fridges, 92 per cent have telephones and 55 per cent have central heating.

A Regions of England

B Percentage change in average dwelling price, (1991–97)

Key	
Region	**Counties**
North	Cleveland, Durham, Northumberland, Tyne and Wear, Cumbria
North West	Cheshire, Greater Manchester, Lancashire, Merseyside
Yorkshire and Humberside	North, South and West Yorkshire and Humberside
East Midlands	Derbyshire, Leicestershire, Lincolnshire, Northamptonshire, Nottinghamshire
West Midlands	Hereford, Worcester, Shropshire, Staffordshire, Warwickshire, West Midlands
South West	Cornwall, Devon, Dorset, Gloucestershire, Somerset, Wiltshire
East Anglia	Cambridgeshire, Norfolk, Suffolk, Bedfordshire, Essex, Hertfordshire
South East	Berkshire, Buckinghamshire, East Sussex, Hampshire, Isle of Wight, Kent, Oxfordshire, Surrey, West Sussex
London	Greater London

C

	England /Wales '91	England /Wales '97	North '91	North '97	North West '91	North West '97	Yorks./Humbs '91	Yorks./Humbs '97	E Midlands '91	E Midlands '97	W Midlands '91	W Midlands '97	South West '91	South West '97	E Anglia '91	E Anglia '97	South East '91	South East '97	London '91	London '97
Average gross weekly earnings (full time)																				
Male (£)	332	372	314	332	320	354	308	350	306	352	312	360	315	364	321	341	355	387	434	514
Female (£)	232	266	221	241	224	254	218	252	215	248	216	257	225	261	221	245	247	275	308	364
Population (000s)	49,500	51,800	3,117	3,099	6,396	6,412	4,918	5,029	3,852	4,123	5,186	5,306	4,381	4,826	1,893	2,104	10,205	10,902	6805	7007
Economic activity rate (%) (dependency ratio '97)		63		58		59		62		64		63		62		65		66		64
Population over pensionable age (%)	7	18	7	19	7	18	7	18	7	18	6	18	8	18	7	20	6	18	7	16
GDP (100 = average per head)	100	100	90	89	94	90	95	90	98	98	91	95	94	95	102	102	110	111	123	123
Unemployment rate (%)	7	8	12	11	9	8	7	8	5	7	8	7	5	6	4	6	6	6	8	9
Average dwelling price (£000)	60	65	44	46	53	56	47	57	53	60	55	65	65	68	61	59	79	78	86	95
Deaths of infants under 1 per 1,000 live births	7	6	7	6	7	6	8	6	8	6	9	7	6	5	6	5	6	5	7	6
Crime offenses (000s per 100,000 population)	9	10	2	8	11	11	12	13	10	11	9	10	9	8	8	8	8	8	13	11

Investigating data

The next page explores the information on ways of life that emerge from the data in **C**. In the numbered points Gloucestershire is used as an example in an investigation of house prices. The tinted boxes show you how to complete a similar investigation on a different set of data, for example earnings, unemployment, infant mortality, etc.

1 How your region compares: summary

Example: Gloucestershire, the West Midlands region.

- The West Midlands have male and female gross weekly earnings below the national average in 1991 and 1997.
- The economic activity rate is on the national average with the three northern regions and the south west below it.
- The percentage of the population over pensionable age is close to the national average.
- The North and East Anglia are the two regions with a higher percentage of elderly people.
- GDP in pounds per head is below the national average because of the high value produced by people in East Anglia, the South East and London.
- Unemployment rates, infant mortality, house prices and crime rates are also close to the national average.

In summary the West Midlands tends to be close to the national average.

Your own survey

- In which county and region do you live? (If you live in the same area as the example, choose another area.)
- Write a commentary on your pilot survey to compare your region with the national average.
- Complete your commentary with a summary statement about how your region compares to the national average.

2 Testing an hypothesis or idea

The hypothesis: house prices in the West Midlands have increased more rapidly than in some regions but still lag behind London.

Your own survey

- Write a sentence about one of the lines of data on ways of life. Be sure to include your region in your sentence. Here are a few examples:
- Total male and female weekly earnings decrease with distance from London.
- Unemployment rates are higher in the north and decrease to the south and east.
- Crime is higher in eastern England with Yorkshire and Humberside the highest.

3 The data

- House prices in the West Midlands have certainly increased. In 1991 they were below the national average (£5000 less), but by 1997 were on the average.

Your own survey

- Select the row or rows of data you need to explore your hypothesis. Copy out the data in a space below your hypothesis.
- Describe the general impression of the message in your data. Mention any regions which do not appear to be fitting with the hypothesis.

4 Developing the messages in the data – taking percentages

- The percentage figures show the increase in the West Midlands is second only to Yorkshire and Humberside and well above the national average. Note the negative figures for the East Anglia and South East regions.

Percentage change in average dwelling price (1991–1997)

England/Wales	North	NW	Yorks/Humbs	E Mids	W Mids	S W	E Anglia	S E	London
8%	5%	0	21%	13%	18%	5%	–3%	–1%	10%

data which compares each region with the national average.
- If your hypothesis is about change, then taking percentages is always a good idea. It brings the data to a common scale from 1 to 100. Note also any growing and declining regions.
- Another possibility is to make a table of the
- You need to study the data you have calculated against your hypothesis. Write another paragraph describing the new set of data.

5 Is there a special message in the data? Drawing a map

- On an outline map of the standard regions, bars have been drawn to show the percentage increase in house price (**B**). This is better than the usual bar graph because it shows, on the map, where the increases took place. If you draw a map based upon data, be sure to add a title and key. Be careful with the wording of the title and be accurate with your key.
- The map shows a core area of increased house prices in the East and West Midlands, Yorkshire and Humberside. In the more peripheral areas house prices have risen less quickly and in the case of the North have been static. East Anglia and the South East show falling house prices. London does not fit the pattern for this part of the country.

Your own survey

One of the key tasks in geography is to search for patterns on maps. Use an outline map of the regions of England and Wales to draw a map. You can draw symbols on the map.

Ideas for symbols include:
- Stick people to show population, e.g. 1 per 100,000
- Bar columns on each region
- Proportional circles on each region
- a £ sign whose height shows amount of money.

After your map is drawn give it a title and key. These are essential for other readers of your map. Now write a few sentences to describe what the map shows. Link your sentences to the hypothesis you have in mind.

6 Drawing a conclusion

The West Midlands does not have the highest rate of house price increase. It is second to Yorkshire and Humberside. House prices fell in some parts of the country.

Your own survey

Review your findings at each stage. Do not worry if your original idea has to be changed now that your work is nearly complete. Write a clear paragraph to state your findings.

7 What I could do next

- Clearly there is a pattern of house price increase. The next task is to explore possible reasons. One idea would be to calculate the percentage increase in total income for each region. This could be graphed against house price change.

Your own survey

- When you start an enquiry you know it will take you to a first conclusion. But you can carry on understanding the pattern you have discovered.
- Make a note of possible future work.

The growth and decline of settlements

Bournemouth

Urban population growth		
	Bournemouth	Middlesbrough
1821	7,585	–
1831	7,908	–
1841	8,246	–
1851	8,904	2,485
1861	9,366	25,790
1871	25,137	58,320
1881	40,277	87,947
1891	75,444	107,076
1901	95,220	137,625
1911	126,374	165,705
1921	146,393	181,531
1931	174,998	195,245
1951	252,850	212,420
1961	291,875	227,120
1971	321,819	256,283

Middlesbrough

Why are some settlements growing while others are declining?

In 1800 only three per cent of the world's population lived in urban areas. In Europe, in the nineteenth century, factory-based industry grew rapidly. This increased the demand for labour and urban areas began to grow. This increase in the percentage of the population living in urban areas is called urbanization. Today about 70 per cent of the people in the world live in urban areas. In MEDCs 80 per cent live in urban areas compared to 37 per cent in LEDCs. However, the rate of urban population growth in LEDCs is three times that of MEDCs.

Settlement is divided into rural settlement (villages, hamlets and farms) and urban settlement (towns, cities and metropolitan areas). It is difficult to define when a large village becomes a town.

Defining the boundary of an urban area is also difficult. The figures given for the population of an urban area are usually based upon a count (census) of people living within the administrative boundary of the local authority. Every city authority has an area for which it is responsible. If you live outside that area, yet go to school in it, you are not counted in its population. Every day the urban area is filled by people who commute to work there but do not live there. Other people use the urban area for shopping and leisure. If they live beyond the edge of the administrative area, which will probably not coincide with the built-up area, they are not included in its population total. So, usually, the total number of people using an urban area is much larger than the figure given in the census.

Urbanization is the word used to describe the way places and people become urban. It includes rapid growth of population, expansion of the built-up area, a growth of secondary and tertiary employment and a change to an urban way of life.

Settlement changes in MEDCs

There are four changes associated with urbanization in MEDCs, particularly in the EU and USA.

1 Population growth

Urban areas grew rapidly as people migrated from rural areas. This combined with rapid natural increase to produce high rates of population growth. Table **B** shows the rapid growth of two towns, Bournemouth and Middlesbrough. Both towns were developed from near vacant sites during the nineteenth century.

Bournemouth (**A**) is an example of a special group: the seaside resorts. The town did not record an urban population until 1821. Local landowners developed estates by the sea. The country estates gradually merged and sea front hotels were built as roads and railways made the town more accessible. Today the town remains a popular holiday town, and has extended its 'season' by becoming a centre for conferences.

Middlesbrough is an example of a newly created Victorian town. No other English town grew faster in the nineteenth century. In 1801 there were four houses on the site of Middlesbrough. The development of coal, iron and steel and shipbuilding industries led to the creation of the town on the banks of the River Tees. As these industries have declined, the town's function has changed to one of a regional centre.

2 Built environment

Urban areas are covered in bricks, mortar and concrete, although of course these urban areas include some green spaces. The availability of transport (trains and buses) allowed the cities to sprawl and produce suburbs.

Between 1930 and 1939 more efficient trains and buses allowed people to travel from their suburban homes to work. In London the suburbs grew around newly built tube stations. City authorities and planners became so concerned about this spread of building into the countryside that they established Green Belts where building is prohibited around the urban areas.

3 Economic activity

Jobs change. People moving to urban areas change from working in primary industry, such as agriculture, to secondary manufacturing and tertiary services. Secondary and tertiary activities merge for greater efficiency. Secondary industry has declined in the UK and service employment now dominates.

4 Way of life

People in urban areas live close to neighbours; they know more people but have fewer close friends. They have access nearby to education, health services and entertainment. They tend to see the countryside as of value for leisure. They live away from their place of work. Residential areas tend to contain people with similar income.

DEFINITION

The word **conurbation** or **megalopolis** is used to describe an urban area where a large city has grown and absorbed several large towns. For example in the UK London is a core city; the cities and towns that have been absorbed into its conurbation include Kingston upon Thames, Croydon and Dartford.

The decline of cities in MEDCs

Since the 1970s many people have left large urban areas to live in small towns and villages. Frequently their small business moves with them as they work from home using telecommunications. This process is called deurbanization.

Reviving cities in MEDCs

However, in the 1990s there are signs of people and jobs moving back into cities. This is called reurbanization. These people tend to be the young, affluent professionals attracted to life in the city. They often have highly paid jobs in financial services, marketing or telecommunications. They live in small high-rise apartments, built on former industrial sites close to the city centre. They can walk to work and have high quality leisure activities nearby, for example London Docklands.

Population in large cities: the millionaire cities

In 1900 only London and Paris had populations greater than one million ('Millionaire Cities'). By 1990 it was estimated that there were 295 of these very large cities (remember that counting the population of large cities is difficult because of boundary problems).

The majority of the millionaire cities were, at first, in the developed countries of the northern hemisphere. Today the number has grown by the addition of cities from between the tropics, especially in LEDCs. However there are signs that the rapid growth of these large cities in LEDCs is slowing down. Some of the population totals of older millionaire cities in Europe and North America are falling. By 2005 it is estimated that 20 of the 25 largest cities in the world will be in LEDCs. Mexico City is expected to be the second largest at 20 million. In 1998 its population was 16.9 million.

Q

1 Imagine you win a prize of a ten-mile hot air balloon ride. Locate your starting point and wind direction. Select a settlement over which you will pass. State the day of the week and time, describe the view of the settlement, its layout and the activity you see.

2 Why do you think it is difficult to give a precise figure for the population of a large city? Give at least three reasons.

SETTLEMENT CHANGES IN LEDCS

CASE STUDY *Urbanization in Africa*

Towns and cities have existed in LEDCs for a long time. Since 1950 LEDC towns and cities have grown rapidly as people have moved from the countryside. Their populations have also increased, until recently, because of high birth rates.

Urbanization in LEDCs is different from that found in MEDCs in the speed and scale of change. The three main differences are that population growth rates are higher, income levels are lower and the urban areas have weaker planning and administration to cope with the extra population.

The average percentage of the population in urban areas is 37 per cent but it does vary. In Latin America the figure is 66 per cent, whereas in China and SE Asia it is only 25 per cent. In Africa the figure increased from 25 per cent to 33.4 per cent between 1990 and 1995. Africa has the most rapid rate of urban growth of population (**C**).

LEDC governments often encourage urbanization, despite the problems caused, because, per person, they are three to four times more productive than rural areas. However, dealing with the problems of urban areas often causes governments to neglect their rural people.

Experts think that the urban population of Africa will have huge increases in the next few years. High fertility, fewer infant deaths and increasing life expectancy suggest the urban population could double by 2010. Cairo has already emerged as a mega-city with more than 12 million people in 1995, and Lagos is expected to soon.

Cairo

A

B

Problems in the large cities of Africa:

- high unemployment and large informal sector
- poverty
- poor quality and overcrowded housing
- failing transport, water supply and sewerage systems, e.g. in Accra only about half the houses are connected to a sewerage system and only about 66 per cent of the solid waste produced by houses is collected. In Dar-es-Salaam 65 per cent is collected, in Kampala only 10 per cent
- water is often contaminated and there is too little of it, e.g. in Accra only 35 per cent of houses have indoor piping of water, 24 per cent use a stand pipe and 28 per cent buy from water vending carts. The remaining houses collect rainwater and use open waterways.
- overcrowded education and health facilities
- rapid growth of a young population through migration from nearby smaller towns and increasing life expectancy
- destruction of any free land in the urban area, especially along water courses, and the felling of trees for firewood
- inadequate enforcement of the law especially on the environment and health.

C

African cities with populations over 1 million

	1970	1990	Examples
North Africa	4	8	Cairo (12m) — largest in Africa. Algiers, Alexandria, Casablanca, Khartoum, Rabat, Tripoli, Tunis
West Africa	1	2	Ibadan, Jos, Kedina, Lagos, Abidjan, Accra, Conakry, Dakar
East Africa	0	6	Addis Ababa, Nairobi, Dar-es-Salaam, Harare, Lusaka, Kampala
Central Africa	1	6	Kinshasa, Kananga, Luanda, Maputo, Yaoundé, Douala
Southern Africa	2	5	Johannesburg, Cape Town, Durban, Pretoria, Port Elizabeth. (None in Botswana, Lesotho, Swaziland and Namibia.)

Q

1 There are at least 20 cities in the world with populations greater than five million. Use your atlas to name one in North America, South America, Europe, Africa and SE Asia (there are none in Australia).

2 a) Make a table of the large cities in Africa. Using **C**, for each city name the country in which it is located. Indicate which is the capital of the country.

b) On a map of Africa, mark and label the large cities.

CASE STUDY *LEDC: The growth of Mexico City*

It is estimated that Mexico City (**A**) will have a population of nearly 20 million by the year 2002. Its population density is well over 10 000 people per sq km. Its population has been growing rapidly because of the arrival of large numbers of migrants from the countryside, high birth rates and falling death rates. It is estimated that 40 per cent of its population live in 'informal settlements' or '**shanty towns**'.

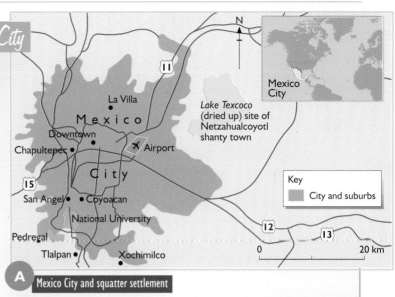

A Mexico City and squatter settlement

C		
Year	Population (millions)	Rate of growth per year
1970	9	4.5%
1980	14	2.7%
1990	15	0.7%
1995	15.5	0.7%

However, Mexico City is not all poor houses (**B**). The city has a long history with many magnificent buildings as well as broad highways flanked by multi-storey corporate headquarters. There is a an extensive metro system within the built-up area, an international airport and university. One Internet site describes the city as 'crowded, polluted, and chaotic but also passionate, exotic and beautiful'.

Why has Mexico City grown?

1 Rural to urban migration

Factors that push people from the rural areas and factors that pull them to urban areas are listed in (**D**). About 1,000 new migrants arrive in Mexico City every day. Of course there are positive things about living in the countryside and negative ones in the urban areas. The 'bright lights' of the urban areas make them more attractive than they really are.

D	Push factors	Pull factors
	Poverty	Richer people
	Low pay	Better pay
	Unemployment	More jobs
	Few schools	Primary and secondary schools
	Few doctors	Health care and hospitals
	Poor roads	Cars
	Poor electricity and water supply	Electricity and water
		Entertainment

In LEDCs migrants often move first to a local town and then to Mexico City. This is called 'step-wise' migration. However, as birth rates remain high in rural areas and health care is improving, the population total in rural areas is not falling.

There are jobs in the cities – 65 per cent of Mexico's economic activity is in Mexico City. There are oil, chemical and food processing industries. In addition cement, glass, paper, clothing, electronics, household appliances and cars are made in the city. Most of the main banks have their head offices here. The people of the city have very varied ways of life. There are houses for the rich in elegant suburbs such as Pedregal (**A**) as well as crowded squatter settlements, such as Netzahualcoyotl, which is located on the dry bed of Lake Texcoco (**A**).

2 High birth rates

When the migrants arrive in Mexico City, they find life hard with little or no employment available. All the family works to get money for food and to pay the rent for their tiny room in a shanty town. Many children miss school, have a low level of education and many girls are

B Mexico City

pregnant by their sixteenth birthday. Only 55 out of every 100 children attend primary school despite free education. Few parents are educated to use contraception. Many of the people moving to the city are from younger age groups. As a result birth rates are high (24.6 per 1,000 in 1998).

3 Death rates are falling

In the past, poor water supplies, little sanitation, rubbish in the streets and sewage in open drains meant that death rates were high. Old cars and buses have made the air so polluted that to breathe in Mexico is like smoking 25 cigarettes per day. The city planning authorities however, with the help of overseas aid, are improving health. There are more doctors and hospitals; there are restrictions on car use; new buses that use lead-free petrol have been purchased; a metro train service has been introduced, and self-help housing schemes have been started. All these actions improve the quality of life for people and reduce the death rate (5 per 1,000 in 1998). This means more people in Mexico City.

There are signs that the growth rate of cities in LEDCs is falling. This is mainly because, as women become more educated and job seeking, they start to use contraceptive methods such as the birth control pill. In addition, other cities in Mexico have started to grow rapidly (3.7 per cent in 1995 which is higher than the national growth rate of 2 per cent) as industry leaves the expense and congestion of Mexico City.

Problems

Housing

In Mexico City, as in other LEDCs, housing is seen as the highest priority. Unlike most cities in MEDCs the houses of the poor are mostly found on the edges of the city. These are often found in unplanned, illegal settlements called 'shanty towns'. Mexico city has become ringed by a series of shanty towns – 'villages' – often built illegally but on public open space or even on farmer's land. They are built from scrap materials and are usually one-roomed shacks. They lack the basic amenities of housing such as running water and sanitation. Some houses have electricity by connecting illegally to the main supply, which runs outside the town. No one knows how many people live in the shanty towns.

Water, land and air pollution

Water pollution is a problem because rainwater is not kept separate from industrial and domestic users. This leads to the pollution of drainage channels. The high temperatures and heavy rainfall make this worse. In some cities sewage is still drained directly into rivers. Most shanty towns have no sewerage system and use pits dug in open spaces. On hillsides, such as those around Rio de Janeiro, the sewage may seep down into other people's drinking water supply. In Mexico City only about 75 per cent of the rubbish is collected by the refuse collection service. In some areas women collect human excrement to dump in refuse pits nearby. Illegal dumping of industrial waste and refuse from the 'informal sector' creates land pollution. Because Mexico City is sited in a basin surrounded by hills the air pollution from four million cars and industry is not blown away. Car and bus fumes are a problem because of old inefficient engines and low quality petrol.

Subsidence

Parts of 'downtown' Mexico City are built on the soft deposits of an old lake. Some areas have fallen by 6m damaging buildings and breaking water and sewerage pipes. New buildings have to be erected using steel piles and concrete drums.

Q There have been suggestions that the conditions in some areas of Britain are nearly as poor as those found in LEDC cities. In areas such as South Yorkshire the unemployment level is over 15 per cent since the closure of steel works and coal mines. Earnings are low and the amount of derelict land is five times the national average. This is the area where the film 'The Full Monty' was made. What similarities can you recall between this area and conditions in LEDC cities.

The way forward?

Discourage rural to urban migration The key thing to do is to improve conditions in other areas so that people do not wish to migrate for the apparent advantages of the city. This can be done by providing employment in other areas as well as by improving their educational and social services. Better transport allows people to live out of the city even if they commute in each day. In Indonesia the authorities tried to ban migration by issuing people with identity cards and requiring permits to change residence.

Build satellite New Towns to disperse population
Hong Kong and Singapore have built high-density housing to reduce their problems of housing shortage. They could afford to build high-rise blocks of flats in new settlements outside the city. Kuala Lumpur used the same solution but built low-rise four storey blocks. In all three cases the new residents were able to pay rents for their flats.

Increase employment Tourism is a key area for the growth of jobs. Tourists provide foreign currency that is vital to countries' development. They demand many services and this creates jobs. Many cities in LEDCs have features that attract tourists. City growth, increased traffic and neglect can threaten these attractions, for example the historic colonial core of Kuala Lumpur, the mangrove areas near Santos in Brazil, the beaches of Rio de Janeiro and the Taj Mahal in India. City authorities need to publicize the importance of conserving these important sites. A key feature of this strategy is to involve local business people, schools and residents.

The 'informal sector' is being recognized as one way to encourage employment. There are two main types of informal employment:

1 Services such as shoeshine boys, street vendors, repairers, newspaper sellers, unofficial guides, and food and drink sellers.
2 Small-scale manufacturers of pottery, crafts, soaps, traditional ornaments, etc.

The informal sector supplies everyday goods at cheap prices as well as meeting the needs of some tourists. The traders are usually operating outside the law and without a license. In parts of India and Kenya the government has appreciated the role this group places in growing trade and has given some protection to the people. The governments recognize that the informal sector employs large numbers of people though conditions and wages may be poor. Unfortunately the informal sector has a reputation for employing children and illegal immigrants. The sector is very adaptable and ready to try to supply to most demands. Encouragement of this sector may lead to the growth of more stable industries and the money that changes hands fuels the economy of the city.

Provide self-help housing These are schemes where the local authority provides a concrete base and water supply to a small plot of land. The owner, often helped by neighbours, builds a house for the family. A second floor may be added as the town gets older. Gradually the self-built estates are upgraded as electricity is added.

Elect stable government In many cities in LEDCs, bureaucracy, corruption and unrest, including terrorism, have not helped to sustain the quality of life in the area. Foreign investors have to consider these problems when they consider where to locate their production plants. The low wages they would have to pay and the lack of trade union activity attract them but they fear disruptions to production and the safety of key workers.

Improve transport The governments would like to encourage people to use public transport, but they have to have the finance to fund new buses and rail routes. Some successes have been achieved in Hong Kong, Singapore and Malaysia where wealthier governments had the funding.

Obtain international aid to repair infrastructure, e.g. sewers and education system Education, especially for women and children including the street children and homeless adults as well as the mentally ill, would reduce population growth and provide better skills to help with employment.

Introduce legal restrictions and fines to reduce pollution The Mexico City authorities have joined with the national government and PEMEX (the national petroleum manufacturer) to agree an eight-point strategy costing £8 billion. The eight points are as follows:

- checking car and bus exhaust fumes with restrictions on use until unleaded petrol used
- all new vehicles to be fitted with catalytic converters

- fines for companies found disposing of waste by illegal means
- monitoring of human solid and liquid disposal especially on beaches and public open spaces
- new cleaner technologies to be used in factories
- introduction of cleaner fuels
- education about environmental issues
- improved public transport.

Involve citizens Local authorities have formed Citizens Councils to involve local people. Similar movements exist in the UK as well. Local people are able to suggest the best ways forward to meet their needs. Local authorities formed Environmental Councils to:

- propose methods of preserving the local environment
- receive complaints about threats to open spaces and vegetation
- be a public voice influencing the City Council.

Questions

Table (**B**) shows conditions in rural and urban areas in Mexico.

B	Rural (%)	Urban (%)
Lack of health care	60	80
Access to safe drinking water	49	82
Inadequate food	50	15
Below poverty line	43	23

1 Compare conditions in rural and urban areas of Mexico. (4)

2 Explain how the figures in **B** help to explain rural–urban migration to Mexico City. (4)

3 Describe the main problems associated with the growth in Mexico City. (8)

4 How has the growth in Mexico City affected the quality of life for the population? (5)

5 What benefits are associated with the growth of Mexico City? (4)

Total: 25 marks

SETTLEMENT GROWTH IN THE UK

Much new housing has been built on greenfield sites. The Government is worried about this loss of rural land. They have asked local authorities to plan for 50 per cent of housing to be on brownfield sites. Behind this change of policy is the bigger question of where and how people want to live. Here are some trends:

- builders find expensive housing easier to sell on exclusive estates. Prices can be well above the local average
- people are mobile and willing to commute long distances
- families are ready to travel longer distances to take their children to school
- loss of farmland is not an issue in terms of food supply
- single as well as married owners of homes want 2 or 3-bedroom houses with a garage and garden
- people in jobs have plenty of choice of houses
- the low paid and those on benefits can rarely afford to buy a house and have little choice
- cheaper housing for rent is often in a poor state of repair.

The danger is that these trends tend to separate rich and poor. So where should the homes for rich and poor be provided to produce a sustainable environment and society?

Before houses can be built in an area, the developer has to get planning permission. Permission is granted by the local authorities after they have looked at their plans and those provided by the developers such as architects, engineers and builders.

CASE STUDY *EU: Winchcombe, Gloucestershire*

The background

In this area of Gloucestershire the 1997 housing survey showed that nearly half the people had moved into the area in the last five years. The average house price is over £90,000, well beyond what many locally employed people can afford. Two hundred and forty affordable houses are needed in the Winchcombe area in the next five years. A decision has to be made about where these houses are to be built. The following groups play important roles in the decision.

The role of National Government

The Government forecasts population total and housing needs based upon the census and other information, e.g. the reduced size of households. For Gloucestershire they predict the need for 53,000 more houses by 2011. The Government expects county councils to have plans to supply land to meet this target. Through the Department for the Environment the Government has stated the following guidelines for building land:

- where possible the main urban areas should take new development
- any further growth should be in settlements near the main urban areas if they have good transport connections
- development should be in settlements where employment, shopping and leisure can be found
- in rural areas housing should be within or close to settlements
- the focus should be on sustainable and affordable housing
- developers should use brownfield sites when available.

The role of the County Council

Every County Council has to have a plan for the future of its area. This is called a Structure Plan. This plan has to show how Gloucestershire will meet the target set by government and take account of local circumstances. **C** shows how Gloucestershire is split into Districts. The Gloucestershire Structure Plan will try to:

- reduce the use of the private car, especially for getting to work
- ensure convenience for employment, services and community facilities
- use brownfield sites or greenfield sites close to urban areas
- provide affordable housing
- avoid turning settlements into dormitory areas.

The role of the District Council

The Tewkesbury District Council has to prepare plans for its local area to meet the targets and guidelines set by the County Council. Their plans aim to:

- meet local needs
- provide different types of housing
- provide more locally based work
- encourage people to use public transport
- encourage a sense of community.

B shows three possible sites for building 200 houses including affordable housing:

Site 1: Opposite Winchcombe School: by creating new village streets of high townscape value

Site 2: Becketts Lane: on former railway land including the station yard.

Site 3: Filling in spaces in small villages around Winchcombe.

A

Gloucestershire

N

0   200 km

The role of local people

Into every house in the area a group of local people placed a pamphlet (**D**). They have some idea of the Structure Plan and Local Plan. They mention Bishops Cleeve which is a former village about 6km from Cheltenham, which has been expanded to double its size. These people are defending the area where they have chosen to live. Their response takes only one point of view and they do not mention affordable housing for local people.

Q

1 Some people have been described as NIMBY (Not In My Back Yard) when reacting to new planning proposals.

   a) Explain why the local people of Winchcombe could be described as NIMBY.

   b) Describe a project that could happen in your local area where you might become a NIMBY.

2 Each of the plans mentions building 'affordable' housing.

   a) Describe what you think this term means. People in regular employment can usually buy a house for about 2.5 times their income.

   b) Some couples are called DINKY (Double Income No Kids Yet). How does this fit in with house purchase?

D

DO YOU WANT 240 NEW HOUSES IN WINCHCOMBE AND GREET?

Tewkesbury District Council is proposing to allow 240 new houses to be built in and around Winchcombe and Greet. If this is allowed to go ahead, think what this means for your town. Consider the following:-

- The lack of any employment in Winchcombe to sustain 240 new families.

- 240 new families will mean 300 or more additional cars, thus increasing the amount of congestion in the town centre and along Back Lane and Gloucester Street.

- Children going to or coming from Winchcombe School and the Junior School will be at increased risk from traffic on Greet Road and Back Lane.

- The lack of public transport available to reduce dependence on the car.

- The intrusion into an area of High Landscape Value/Area of Outstanding Natural Beauty of such a major development.

- The inevitable decline in the magic of what is Winchcombe, as it becomes another Bishops Cleeve.

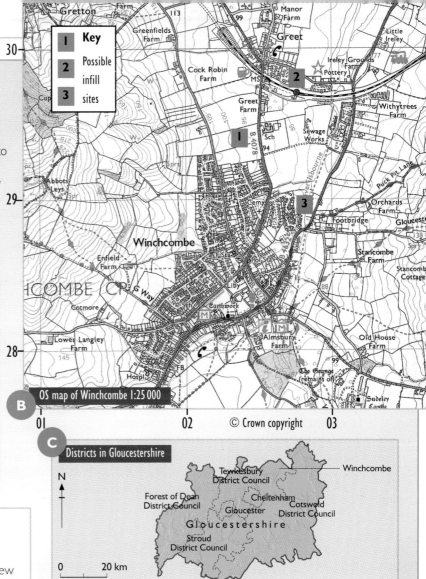

B OS map of Winchcombe 1:25 000

© Crown copyright

C Districts in Gloucestershire

Decision making exercise

The options

Tewkesbury District Council needs to decide how best to manage their area bearing in mind the views of the three other groups. Possible approaches include:

- Development of greenfield sites where a comprehensive plan can provide a range of housing to a well designed layout.

- Development of brownfield sites where well designed housing can fit the site once it has been cleared.

- Infill of small sites in five or six villages around Winchcombe .

The decision

a) Suggest with reasons which one of these three approaches would be most appropriate for Winchcombe.   (8)

b) What reservations do you have about the plan you have chosen?   (4)

c) What advantages do the two rejected plans have?   (4)

d) Give your reasons for rejecting them.   (4)

Total 20 marks

Settlement change in Europe

In the EU there is a core of areas with a high population density stretching, nearly continuously, from central and south-east England through to southern Italy (**A**). This contains most of the largest urban areas in Europe (**B**).

Europe was the birthplace of manufacturing industry. The manufacturing areas of Europe developed with the help of their own cheap coal. As late as 1962 only Italy and the Netherlands in Europe used more oil than coal. By 1972 oil had become the main energy source. Founded on the coal-producing areas of the UK, France, Belgium, Luxembourg and Western Germany, a broad zone of industry developed. London's population reached 1 million by 1810 and 2 million by 1850. Paris reached 1 million by 1850 and Berlin, Vienna and Moscow by 1900. By 1994 some 68 metropolitan areas had developed in Europe. The large urban areas of Europe are London, Paris, Randstad (Holland), Rhine-Ruhr and Moscow.

A Core and periphery of Europe

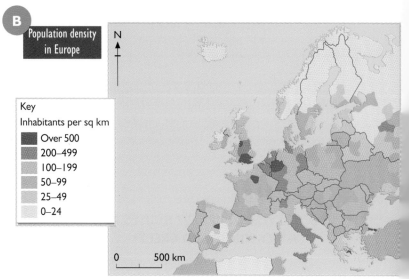

B Population density in Europe

Key
Inhabitants per sq km

- Over 500
- 200–499
- 100–199
- 50–99
- 25–49
- 0–24

0   500 km

European urban problems

The successful growth of large urban areas also brings problems including:

- shortage of good quality housing, overcrowding and the creation of slums
- congested living in inner-city areas
- dangers of urban sprawl using up the countryside
- restless migrant populations
- long journey to work
- city transport system under strain
- widespread car ownership and traffic congestion
- need to renew central areas
- migration of people out of the tax area of the city they use.

Deurbanization

Since 1965 people have been leaving the urban areas of Europe to live in the semi-rural areas on the urban fringes. As a result the total populations of the large built-up areas have been falling. This has been made possible by improved transport which has made long distance commuting, by better paid people, a possibility.

There are many causes of deurbanization, including:

- increased life expectancy and longer retirements
- increased earned wealth of people retiring from urban employment
- decline of traditional heavy industry and textiles
- anti-urban feelings – viewed as crowded, congested, polluted, stressful as opposed to rural peace.

Reurbanization

In the 1990s a number of governments have become concerned about the decline of their urban areas and plan to make them more attractive.

CASE STUDY *EU: Urban Europe: Randstad, Holland*

Randstad is the name given to a ring of cities in the Netherlands (**D**). By 1995 these urban areas contained over 6 million people (40 per cent of the Dutch population). The map shows how the cities, towns and villages have nearly merged and yet they have kept their individuality. Randstad differs from London in that the big city functions are distributed around the urban areas. The specialist functions are located as follows:

- commerce and industry – Amsterdam and Rotterdam
- finance and culture – Amsterdam
- government – The Hague
- road and rail communications – Utrecht
- exhibitions, conferences – Utrecht.

Issues and conflicts for Randstad

In a very large urban area such as Randstad, where change is always taking place, it is very difficult to maintain or improve the quality of the lives of the people living there. The issues and conflicts the planners face include:

- the quality of housing in the cities, especially good housing
- shortage of land on which to build if the green areas are to be protected
- traffic congestion due to large numbers of people commuting, especially in the rush hours
- lack of green space for recreation – most green areas are used for agriculture
- environmental pollution – water, air, soil and noise pollution
- new housing and 'out-of-town' offices and service sector facilities are threatening the green areas
- falling populations in the four major cities threaten their economic future.

Planned solutions for Randstad

The planners in Randstad have abandoned their policy of putting growth poles in other parts of the country to draw people away from Randstad. They found this movement weakened the big cities and increased traffic. Instead their plans are to:

- locate new housing inside the major cities on brownfield sites and by infill
- preserve the green areas as much as possible
- allow development around Zoetermeer to the east of The Hague, around the railway line from The Hague to Rotterdam, near Schipol Airport and to the west of Utrecht
- protect green buffer zones between the urban areas
- preserve historic town centres, especially in Amsterdam

- renovate and replace worn-out housing in the inner suburbs of the big cities
- build attractive waterside housing around abandoned dock areas and waterways
- replace high rise blocks of flats with family homes, many of them with gardens
- encourage the use of public transport by developing a metro system. (Underground railways are very difficult to build in the marsh and peat soils of the area.)

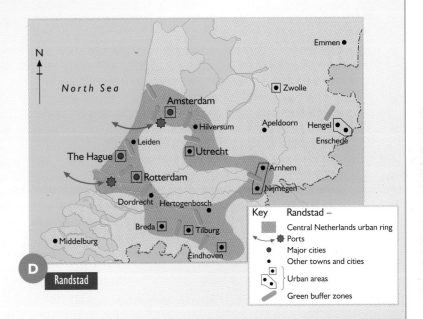

D Randstad

Questions

1 Describe the main problems arising from urban growth in the Randstad. (5)
2 Write five newspaper headlines you might expect to find in the Utrecht daily newspaper about these problems. Justify your choice. (8)
3 Make a list of the planned solutions to the problems found in the Randstad. (6)
4 Show how **two** of these planned solutions will affect the quality of life for local people. (6)

Total: 25 marks

GLOSSARY

Birth rate   The average number of births per 1000 of the population.

Census   The collection of demographic, economic, and social information about a sample of people in a defined area at a particular time. The information collected usually includes: total population, age, sex and marital status, place of birth and nationality, literacy and educational attainment, family and household structure, fertility and rural or urban residence.

Central Business District   Commercial centre of a town or city in which businesses are concentrated.

Central place   A village, town or city that provides goods and services to people living in and around it.

Central Place Theory   Central Place Theory describes the sizing and spacing of settlements according to the services they offer.

Death rate   The average number of deaths per 1,000 of the population.

Demographic ageing   An increasing number of older people in a country's population.

Deurbanization   The movement of people, services and industry out of towns and cities.

Distance-decay effect   The level of interaction between two places decreases as the distance between them increases.

Emigration   When people move from one area and settle in another, usually moving from one country to another.

Fertility rate   The number of live births per 1,000 women aged 15-49 years.

Gender   Male or female.

Immigration   People arriving in a country with the intention of settling there.

Infant mortality rate   The average number of deaths of infants under 1 year of age per 1000 live births. High infant mortality is often a sign of limited medical services and malnutrition.

Life expectancy   The average number of years a person may be expected to live.

Literacy   Being able to read and write.

Market area   The area in which residents favour a particular central place over its competitors.

Migration   The movement of people. Can be internal, within a country, or external, to and from different countries.

Mortality rate   The number of deaths per year per 1,000 population.

Optimum population   The number of people that can live most effectively in any area in relation to the resources available.

Order   The ranking of a central place. High order places, such as cities, provide many services.

Overpopulation   When the population of an area reaches a level at which it cannot be supported by the available resources in that area.

Pandemic   Something that affects a whole country or the whole world, e.g. a disease.

Population density   The number of people per unit area, usually per square kilometre.

Population distribution   The way in which people are spread over an area.

Population pyramid   A device to show the population of a specific area, with males on one side and females on the other.

Range of the good   The maximum distance people are willing to travel to obtain goods from a central place.

Refugee   A person who flees to a place of refuge, especially during times of war or political persecution.

Reurbanization   The movement of people, services and industry back to a previously urbanised area.

Settlement hierarchy   A series of settlements of different order, with a few cities spaced far apart, and increasingly more settlements of lower order placed closer together.

Shanty town   A poor part of a town, consisting of hastily-built housing, found mainly in cities in LEDCs.

Shopping hierarchy   The way shops and services are ranked according to their useage.

Sphere of influence   The area in which a central place distributes services, recruits labour and takes in school children.

Suburb   An area of town, away from the centre, which has some of its own shops, schools, housing and industry.

Threshold population   The minimum number of customers needed to support a service from a central place.

Transect   A line drawn across an area which allows a sample to be made. The observations made along the lines are taken to be representative of the whole area.

Underpopulation   When the population of an area is too few to exploit the available resources there.

Urbanization   A growing concentration of people and activities in towns and cities, increasing the scale of settlement, changing the economy and changing the population structure.

Using practical skills

Practical skills are a very important part of a geographer's 'tool kit'. Up to 35 per cent of the total assessment in the GCSE exam course is awarded for the use of skills. These skills are described as:

🌐 using appropriate geographical terms

🌐 using and interpreting different types of maps at a variety of scales

🌐 selecting and extracting information from primary and secondary sources of information, including photographs, satellite images, graphs, statistics, journals and ICT

🌐 using a range of practical and fieldwork techniques and procedures

🌐 using instruments for collecting and recording geographical information

🌐 applying suitable methods and ideas to investigate and explain geographical situations and issues

🌐 presenting your information by drawing maps, sketches, graphs and writing reports

🌐 planning and carrying out a geographical investigation, supported by fieldwork

🌐 using evidence to analyse and collect data to reach a conclusion and critically evaluate findings.

Many of the skills are used in exercises throughout this book. This section will focus particularly on the type of skills that may be used when carrying out a coursework investigation, i.e.:

• collecting and selecting data or information
• analysing and presenting data or information.

A Pupils collecting information

B Land use within settlements

D Planning a by-pass: resolving environmental issues

C Coastal landscape : geomorphic processes and landforms

COLLECTING AND SELECTING DATA

Up to 25 per cent of the total GCSE assessment is based on coursework. Some of the work will require collecting information from both primary and secondary sources. Both types of data are important, but most examination syllabuses require at least one piece of coursework to be based on the collection of primary data.

Preparing for data collection

Before collecting data it is important to be specific about exactly what is required and where to get the information. Careful planning is needed.

Primary data

- Think about the best sites to visit for fieldwork. How accessible are they? How effectively can data be collected?
- Make sure that all data is *relevant*. Regular checking back to the title and the aims of the work is a good idea. It is easy to collect irrelevant information when out on fieldwork – a lot of glossy brochures are *not* a good idea! Yet, well used, relevant extracts and quotes show efficient data selection.
- Collected data must be recorded

on some type of data collection sheets in the form of surveys, questionnaires, or sketches (see the following pages for guidance).
- Photographs are always a good addition to any coursework, but only if they are relevant and well labelled and annotated.
- Personal safety is of prime importance. Safety instructions must always be

Pupils collecting secondary data **B**

followed carefully. Pupils should aim to collect data in groups rather than alone, particularly in isolated or potentially dangerous places.

Secondary data

- Plan well in advance and be very specific about what

you want, particularly if writing letters to request information. People are often busy and need time to deal with requests. It is likely that you will need to look carefully through a lot of irrelevant data to extract exactly what is needed. This is an important skill.
- Check to see if someone else in the class needs the same information and write the letter together, instead of sending duplicate letters to the same place.
- Think about where to find other resources, e.g. a good library may be a source for census data (**B**).
- CD ROMs and the Internet offer a huge amount of information, but again these need careful selection and sometimes give rather biased information.

A Pupils collecting primary data

What sampling methods?

Sampling is an important skill to understand when collecting data. Taking a sample using a recognized sampling method avoids bias and will give a more representative range of results.

Decisions have to be made about *where* to go to collect the data, *which* people need to be asked as well as *when* and *what* you are going to ask.

A *target* sample will focus on a particular group of people or trees or shops, etc.

Samples can be taken in different ways:

- A *systematic* sample (**C**) takes only a selected sample at set intervals or numbers, for example every fifth or sixth person, house or item. Stones might be measured every five metres.

- A *stratified* sample (**D**) takes a proportional sample from each group. For example, when conducting a questionnaire in a village which has 20 new private houses, 40 old private houses and 40 local authority houses, a representative opinion from each housing type is needed. By selecting 25 per cent of each group (5, 10 and 10) a proportional sample is collected. This could also be done with tree types, rock types, age groups, etc.

- A *random* sample (**E**) selects a sample by chance. You may select people in a street at random or drop a quadrat frame down at random to count plant species. A 'random number table' helps to select a sample by using a set pattern of numbers. These tables are published in textbooks or found on computers.

In addition, a decision must be made whether your sampling will be of points, areas or lines. *Transects* (or *line sampling*) are a method which involves collecting data along a straight line. Changes in temperature, vegetation type or size of beach material could be sampled by using a transect line from one point to another.

Whatever method of sampling is used sufficient numbers must always be taken to ensure an accurate representation of features or opinions. The more opinions you collect, the more reliable or *significant* your conclusions will be. A sample of at least 20 people answering questionnaires is needed to achieve a significant result. In a shopping survey in a town centre, for example, if only three or four opinions are collected the result is going to be rather limited and unreliable. Also, if the information is then graphed or mapped, only one or two responses will not be enough to draw a meaningful diagram.

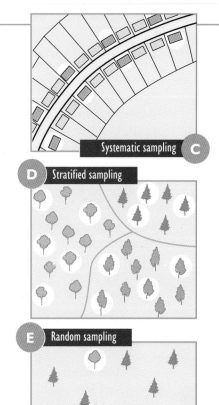

Systematic sampling **C**

D Stratified sampling

E Random sampling

How can primary data be collected?

The following few pages describe a limited number of techniques that can be used when collecting primary data on fieldwork trips. There are many other techniques that are suitable for a range of different environments.

1 Field sketching

Field sketching does not require outstanding artistic ability. The important skill in making a field sketch is to focus clearly on the relevant features and emphasize the important detail by adding labels and annotations. The end product should be a clear pencil sketch which shows understanding of the relevant features, rather than something to hang in a gallery (**F** and **G**)!

F

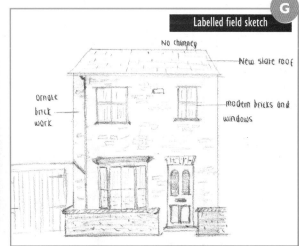

G

Labelled field sketch

No chimney

New slate roof

ornate brick work

modern bricks and windows

2 Measuring physical features

Measuring is a very important fieldwork skill and is used to collect lots of different types of data. Measuring landforms and then analysing the results can help identify and understand many of the natural processes that shape the landscape.

Physical sites such as rivers, beaches or woodlands provide good locations at which to measure and identify processes at work. The width, depth and velocity of a stream or small river could be measured (**A**) and the figures used back at school to draw up a river cross-section (**B**). If this takes place at several sites along the river, it is possible to identify where processes of erosion or deposition are taking place along the course of the river.

Useful measurements to take when studying river processes are:
- channel width (from bank to bank)
- stream/river width
- bed profile by measuring the depth of the river at regular intervals in a straight line from bank to bank
- height of the bank above the river level
- the velocity or speed of flow in different sections of the river using a flowmeter or a cork and stopwatch over a set distance.

A Measuring a stream cross-section

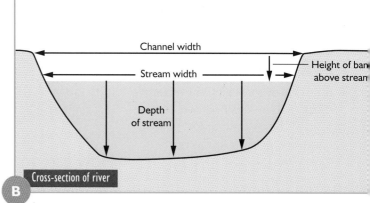
B Cross-section of river

Channel width · Stream width · Depth of stream · Height of bank above stream

3 Measuring human flows

Measuring pedestrian and traffic flows can give a clear picture of patterns of movement in a town or along a route (**C**). This helps to identify areas of congestion or times of peak and low flow. Traffic and pedestrian flows vary depending on the time of day and which day they are counted on. Counts must be taken at regular intervals on different days to get an overall pattern and overcome sampling variations. This is what road builders do before they make a decision about altering a road junction or building a by-pass. Counts for ten minutes can be multiplied by six to give an hourly flow. The table in which you record your traffic or pedestrian count data needs

C Traffic movements

to be set out clearly (**D**). A tally system is useful when you need to make a note of things quickly. Back at school, traffic flows can be converted into pcus or passenger car units. These give a better idea of the volume of flow.

D

Location	Day	Date	Time
Type of vehicle	**Number**		
Motorbikes (1/2 pcu each)			
Cars (1 pcu each)			
Vans (2 pcus each)			
Lorries/buses (3 pcus each)			
(pcu = passenger car unit)			

4 Questionnaires

Questionnaires are used to collect both quantitative (numerical) and qualitative (written opinions) data. The results could be graphed and used in written analyses. This is a good way to discover the opinions of local people in the area you are investigating. Remember to think about the sample group and size (see p 213 on sampling). It is essential to ask the right questions to receive reliable information. The following examples give some guidance on how to write a questionnaire.

E Good questionnaire

Date_____ Time _____

Location _____

Excuse me, I am a pupil from the _____ School and I am conducting a questionnaire about shopping patterns in the town centre. Would you please help by answering some short questions?

I Are you here to shop today?   Yes / No

2 How often do you shop here?
- ❏ More than twice a week   ❏ Once a week
- ❏ 2-3 times a month   ❏ Once a month
- ❏ Less than once a month

3 Where do you live? _____

4 How did you travel here today?
- ❏ Walked   ❏ By bicycle
- ❏ By car   ❏ By bus
- ❏ Other

5 Which of the following types of shops and services do you use in this town centre?
- ❏ Food   ❏ Clothes
- ❏ Furniture   ❏ Banking facilities
- ❏ Electrical goods ❏ Other

6 Please select three factors from the following list which best describe why you use this shopping centre:
- ❏ It is close to home
- ❏ There are good parking facilities
- ❏ There is good public transport
- ❏ There are a good range of shops and amenities
- ❏ The shops are close together and under cover
- ❏ Prices are cheaper
- ❏ Other

7 How do you think this shopping centre could be improved?

_____

Thank you for your help

> This questionnaire is good because it has a mixture of open and closed questions. There are not too many questions, but people have the opportunity to give more information if they want to.

F Bad questionnaire

Date_____ Time _____

Location _____

Excuse me, I am a pupil from the _____ School and I am conducting a questionnaire about shopping patterns in the town centre. Would you please help by answering some short questions?

I Why have you come here today?

_____
_____

2 How often do you shop here?

_____

3 Where do you live?

_____

4 How did you travel here today?

_____

5 How far have you travelled?

_____

6 Which shops and services do you use?

_____
_____

7 Why do you like shopping here?

_____
_____

8 How could this shopping centre be improved?

_____
_____

Thank you

> This questionnaire asks the same questions as the first example, but all the questions are open ended. This causes problems because it will take longer to answer and write down. There will be more variety in the answers and the data will be difficult to group together. Question 5 is pointless because the distance can be worked out from question 3.

Constructing a questionnaire

- Think carefully about the questions you want to ask. Make sure there are enough questions to find out the information needed but not too many to frighten people off! Give them an approximate idea how many there are before you start.
- Include a brief, polite introduction telling people why you are doing the questionnaire and requesting their help.
- Quantified questions make data analysis easier (i.e. numbers instead of written responses). For example when asking for opinions about the appearance of a new building use numbers: 1 – it is unsightly; 2 – it is acceptable; 3 – it is attractive. These types of responses are easier to graph.

- A range of 'open' and 'closed' questions should be asked. Open questions give scope for individual opinions and begin with how, what, where, why, etc. Closed questions are answered with 'yes' or 'no' or a set response as in question 2 in the 'good' questionnaire on page 215.
- Some questions do not need to be asked, such as the sex of the person you are interviewing. You can fill that in yourself. If you need to ask people their age, it is better to put a range of ages into groups, for example, 16-25, 26-35, 36-45, 46-55, over 55. Leave this question until the end of your questionnaire.
- Consider whether you or the person you are questioning will fill in the questionnaire. You could use a table to collect a large number of responses. If

you need the individual to fill in their own responses at home, you will need to collect them at a later date.
- The results could then be put onto a spreadsheet. There are many computer programmes such as 'Pinpoint' which will give a framework for a questionnaire and then collate the information and turn it into graphs.

5 Bipolar surveys

This method of data collection involves giving a numerical value to peoples' personal opinions to compare the qualities of different areas or environments. Draw up a list of features which are important qualities or indicators of an area or a

particular environment, then decide on a scoring system using a '**best**' to '**worse**' scale (**A**). You must then ask people to circle a number which best describes their opinion. This is a good method of collecting numerical or quantitative data which could be shown by using a graphical technique in a final report.

6 Land use mapping

Land use mapping techniques are useful in both urban (**B**) and rural environments. Skills in map orientation as well as classifying and plotting data accurately are important in this exercise. Land use may be plotted along a transect line (see p 213). You should include a suitable key for land use (**C**).

A

When comparing two or more residential areas the following descriptions may be used:				
Best				**Worse**
Friendly	3	2	1	Unfriendly/threatening
Well maintained	3	2	1	Shabby and in need of repair
Well landscaped	3	2	1	Few green areas
Quiet, with little traffic	3	2	1	Busy traffic flows
Lots of local amenities	3	2	1	Few amenities
Clean environment	3	2	1	Evidence of pollution

B

Two land use maps of street

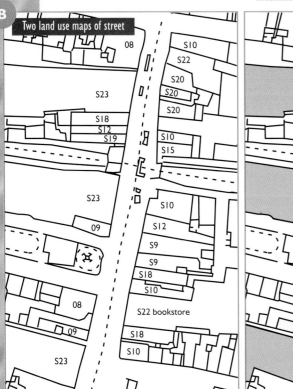

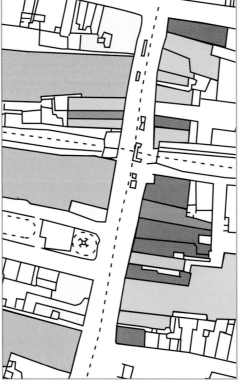

C

Classification of land uses

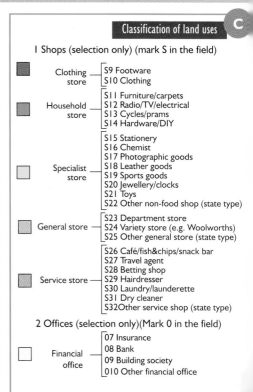

1 Shops (selection only) (mark S in the field)

Clothing store
- S9 Footware
- S10 Clothing

Household store
- S11 Furniture/carpets
- S12 Radio/TV/electrical
- S13 Cycles/prams
- S14 Hardware/DIY

Specialist store
- S15 Stationery
- S16 Chemist
- S17 Photographic goods
- S18 Leather goods
- S19 Sports goods
- S20 Jewellery/clocks
- S21 Toys
- S22 Other non-food shop (state type)

General store
- S23 Department store
- S24 Variety store (e.g. Woolworths)
- S25 Other general store (state type)

Service store
- S26 Café/fish&chips/snack bar
- S27 Travel agent
- S28 Betting shop
- S29 Hairdresser
- S30 Laundry/launderette
- S31 Dry cleaner
- S32 Other service shop (state type)

2 Offices (selection only)(Mark 0 in the field)

Financial office
- 07 Insurance
- 08 Bank
- 09 Building society
- 010 Other financial office

HOW CAN DATA BE PRESENTED AND ANALYSED?

The skills described in this section can be used in coursework and any other part of your GCSE course where you need to analyse data or draw maps and graphs.

After collecting data (this is called raw data), it needs to be analysed to identify patterns and draw conclusions. This raw data can be used to draw up maps, graphs and diagrams or used in statistical techniques to show patterns and trends. These will help describe the data collected. To analyse the data you should give full explanations and reasons for the patterns shown. Remember that the data collected on one particular day will only give you a 'snapshot' in time. The situation may be different on another day or at a different time of day – the weather may change, the number of shoppers may increase or decrease. To get a really reliable picture of human activities data needs to be collected over a period of time. Remember, the larger the sample, the more accurate the findings. Landform and land use patterns are more permanent, so the need to collect data over a period of time is not as important.

Maps

Drawing maps is an essential skill for all geographers both in coursework and in the exam. Examiners really appreciate well-drawn sketch maps (**D**). There are some basic rules to follow when drawing maps:

- put the map in a frame
- use appropriate colours for different features
- add a scale and don't forget the North sign
- write the heading neatly
- label in neat print and include a key if necessary.

1   Land use maps (**B** and **E**)

2   Isoline maps join up features of the same value on a map. They are used in weather forecasts in the newspapers or on television. All maps with contour lines are isoline maps. The values may measure the same air pressure, the same temperature or the same height above sea level. The isolines can show temperature variations around the school grounds (**F**) or pedestrian movements in a town.

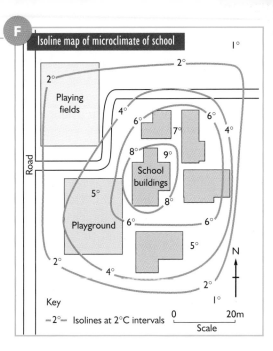

Playing fields

Road

School buildings

Playground

Key

—2°—   Isolines at 2°C intervals

Scale   0   20m

N

The success and accuracy of isoline maps depend on the data collection process and the drawing up of the map. A large number of evenly spread out values should be collected. Decide on an interval when drawing the lines. Ideally a regular interval such as the contour interval on OS maps (10m), should be chosen.

Drawing the isolines is more than just joining up the points with the same values. Sometimes the line has to pass between two points where one is higher and the other lower than the value of the isoline. In this case the position of the lines is estimated. This skill is called interpolation.

Advantage:
- a good way of showing a pattern or distribution of a particular feature over an area.

Disadvantages:
- sometimes they tend to be too generalized and miss out small variations. They are not always completely accurate and depend on estimated values between measurement points.
- they can be difficult to draw
- they need a lot of sampling points to be meaningful.

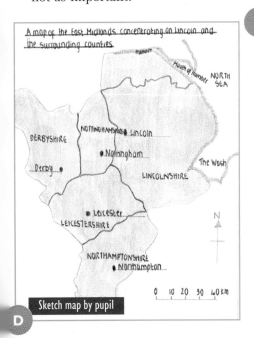

A map of the East Midlands concentrating on Lincoln and the surrounding counties

Humber

Mouth of Humber   NORTH SEA

DERBYSHIRE

NOTTINGHAMSHIRE   Lincoln

Nottingham

Derby

The Wash

LINCOLNSHIRE

Leicester

LEICESTERSHIRE

NORTHAMPTONSHIRE   Northampton

N

0   10   20   30   40 km

Sketch map by pupil

D

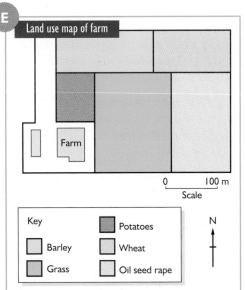

E   Land use map of farm

Farm

Scale   0   100 m

Key

Barley

Grass

Potatoes

Wheat

Oil seed rape

N

3 Choropleth maps are often known as density shaded maps (**A**). The density of shading reflects the intensity of whatever data is being shown. They are used to compare areas on a map in terms of their grouped values. For example, percentage changes in population between two census years in different regions of Britain could be shown using a choropleth map. Sort the data into groups first then decide on a style of shading to show the values of the groups. The map used should show clearly defined boundaries such as regional or county boundaries. The style or density of shading should represent the value being shown, with the higher values having the stronger or darker shading. If colours are used then they should be selected from the same spectrum. The darkest colour would show the highest value as shown in **A**.

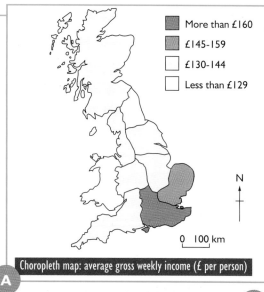

Choropleth map: average gross weekly income (£ per person)

A

Advantages:
- they give a good visual impact   • they help compare values
- they identify patterns easily.

Disadvantages:
- the shading gives a very generalized picture
- local values are unclear within large areas.

4 Dot maps are another way of plotting information and one which gives a more precise picture of distribution than choropleth maps. Dots can show a more localized pattern. Again a scale must be worked out, for example one dot can represent so many people. Once the scale has been decided the information can be plotted on the map (**B**).

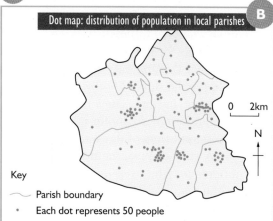

B

Dot map: distribution of population in local parishes

Key
~ Parish boundary
• Each dot represents 50 people

Advantage:
- this gives a more localized pattern.

Disadvantage:
- a decision about the scale can be difficult sometimes. Figures must be rounded up or down which means a lot of fine detail can be lost. For example if one dot represents a million people then the same dot would be used for 800,000 as for 1,480,000.

5 Flow line and **desire line** maps are used to plot volumes or numbers of movements in set directions or along particular routes on a map. Flow lines may be used to show the number of pedestrians or traffic moving along a particular road (**C**). Desire lines may be used to show where people travel to or from for a particular service (**D**).

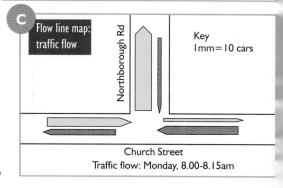

C

Flow line map: traffic flow

Northborough Rd

Key
1mm=10 cars

Church Street
Traffic flow: Monday, 8.00-8.15am

Care must be taken when selecting a scale – the highest and lowest values need to be considered so that a scale will enable both values to be shown clearly. The thickness of the line then represents the volume of flow on the flow map. Desire lines are all the same width and the length is drawn to scale to show a distance or journey. Also, care is needed when showing the direction of flow – this is sometimes difficult if it is not in a straight line, for example along a road.

Advantage:
- they give a good visual image of direction and volume or distance.

Disadvantage:
- it is sometimes difficult to devise a scale for the flow lines when there is a wide range of values.

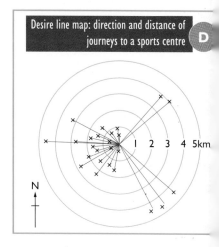

Desire line map: direction and distance of journeys to a sports centre

D

Different types of graphs and diagrams

Graphs and diagrams are probably the most common method of showing numerical or quantitative data. They always give a good visual impression and are relatively easy to construct. The different types of graphs and diagrams can be drawn separately to show results or they may also be plotted onto maps to locate the data.

The choice of diagram is very important and by selecting the appropriate method and using a variety of them you will show an understanding of the techniques you are using. Just choosing bar or pie graphs gives the examiner a very clear message about your lack of ability to select appropriate techniques!

1 Line graphs

Line graphs are used to map continuous data, such as traffic counts over a day collected every hour, monthly temperature changes or population changes between census years. The amount or value should be plotted on the vertical axis and the time interval on the horizontal (**E**). By using a different style or colour of line you can plot more than one set of information on the one graph (**F**).

Advantages:
- you can pick out trends, that is changes from year to year, and predict future patterns
- you can see a clear pattern of peaks and troughs and possibly explain reasons for these changes.

Disadvantage:
- it is easy to make assumptions about the interval between the recording points which are not always reliable.

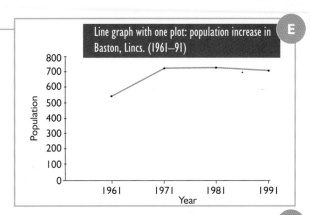

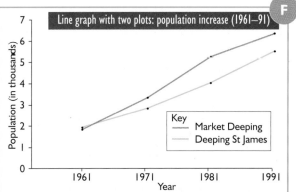

2 Bar charts and histograms

Bar (or block) charts or graphs are easy to plot and commonly used to illustrate a range of data. The vertical axis is used as a numerical or quantitative scale. The horizontal axis is then used for groups or categories of data (**G**). Histograms are slightly different – they have numerical data on both axes. The frequency is on the vertical axis, the same as with a bar graph. The horizontal axis is used to plot sizes, classes or values such as pebble or field sizes (**H**).

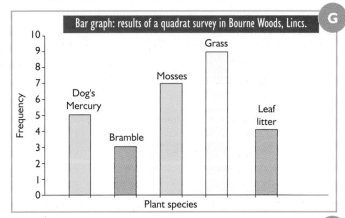

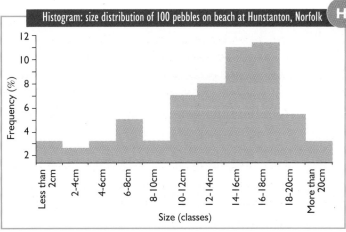

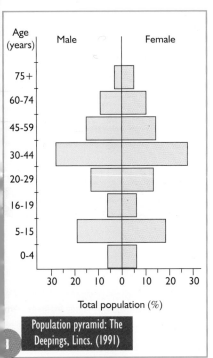

Population pyramid: The Deepings, Lincs. (1991)

There are many different variations on the theme of the bar graph or histogram (**A**, **B** and **C**, page 220).

Mirror graph: survey of shops in two high streets

(one high street with out-of-town shopping centre close by and other without)

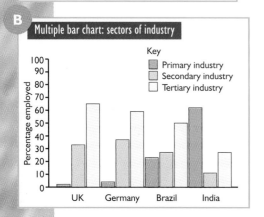

Without   With

- Take away foods
- Furniture
- Electrical retail
- Book shops
- Super-markets
- DIY
- Charity shops
- Clothes
- Banks

5 4 3 2 1   1 2 3 4 5

Number of shops

B

Multiple bar chart: sectors of industry

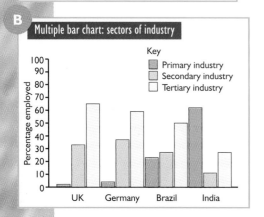

Key
- ▨ Primary industry
- ▦ Secondary industry
- ☐ Tertiary industry

Percentage employed

UK   Germany   Brazil   India

C

Cumulative/composite chart: sectors of industry

Key
- ▨ Primary industry
- ▦ Secondary industry
- ☐ Tertiary industry

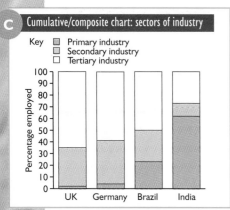

Percentage employed

UK   Germany   Brazil   India

3 Pie charts

This type of graph is a favourite for many students but it is often overused and incorrectly used. A pie chart is a circle which is divided up in proportion to show group values (**D**). As it is a circle the values are first converted into percentages (relative values) then into degrees (absolute values). A common error in

choosing to use a divided pie chart is not having enough groups or categories to plot. It is not a good idea to plot the results of a questionnaire where the answer is **yes** or **no** onto a pie graph. A circle showing just two responses, or even worse just one response, is of limited use. You should have a minimum of three groups or categories of information to plot, and no more than eight. Pie charts can be effectively plotted onto maps to locate data.

When drawing the pie charts there are certain rules to follow:
- when dividing the pie chart up, start at the 12 o'clock position
- draw the segments in order of size, unless several pies are drawn to compare the same data (e.g. primary, secondary and tertiary employment in different regions) then the same sequence must be used in all pies
- avoid ending with a very small segment if possible
- when plotting pie charts on a map they should not overlap.

4 Proportional circles

Proportional circles can be used effectively on maps to show different relative values in data, such as population figures (**G**). The *area* of each circle is in direct proportion to the *quantity* of data represented. Follow these steps to draw proportional circles.

1. The areas of the circles are being compared so you need to use the

square root of each value to calculate the radius of each circle. For example, if your circle needs to represent 10,000 people, first find the square root of 10,000, which is 100 (**E**).
2. Then decide on the size of the largest circle to fit comfortably on your map, for example a circle with a radius of 2 cm. Remember that the smallest circle also needs to be large enough to be seen.
3. Draw the largest circle's radius onto the scale (see **F** below). Then draw a line to the far left corner of the scale. Move along the scale line to find the radius needed for each value.

Example of use of square roots

E

Population of settlements in South Lincolnshire (1991)

		Square root
Baston	705	27
Langtoft	1,079	33
The Deepings	11,312	106
Thurlby	1,386	37
Bourne	9,327	95

F **Example of scale**

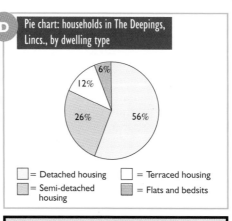

Largest radius

0   20   40   60   80   100

27 33 37   95 106

G

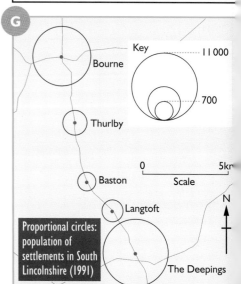

Key
- 11 000
- 700

Bourne

Thurlby

Baston

Langtoft

The Deepings

0   5km

Scale

N

Proportional circles: population of settlements in South Lincolnshire (1991)

D **Pie chart: households in The Deepings, Lincs., by dwelling type**

6%
12%
26%
56%

☐ = Detached housing   ☐ = Terraced housing
▤ = Semi-detached housing   ▨ = Flats and bedsits

Conversion: percentages to degrees

$1\% = 3.6°$ $10\% = 36°$ $100\% = 360°$

5 Scattergraphs

Scattergraphs do a bit more than just give a visual display of data. They attempt to show if there is a link between different sets of information. If you were investigating the shopping and movement patterns of people in a Central Business District of a large town or city, you might ask how far the shoppers travel to get to the shopping centre and how long they spend there. You could then plot the information on a scattergraph to see if there is a link between the two variables (**H**, **I** and **J**).

A *line of best fit* or *trend line* may be drawn on scattergraphs. This is a line drawn by eye through as many of the plotted points as possible. The line may be straight or curved and be roughly central to the group of points. If there is a pattern or trend to the values, this line will make the direction clearer. Sometimes there are odd values which do not fit the general pattern. These are called *residuals*. An example of a residual is clear in **H**. In this case the residual may be explained by somebody who came in shopping to meet some friends and have lunch then go to the hairdresser and shop later. This means the length of time they have stayed is not linked to the distance travelled. The average trend shows a positive correlation.

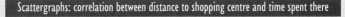
Scattergraphs: correlation between distance to shopping centre and time spent there

H

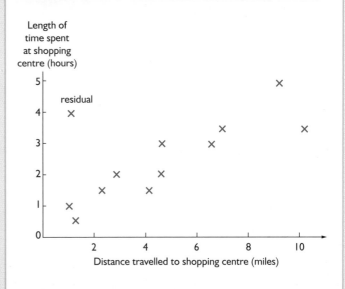

The pattern shown on this graph runs from the bottom left-hand corner where the values are lower up to the top right-hand corner where the values are higher. This suggests that as the value gets higher on one axis it does so on the other as well. In this case the further people travel then the longer they stay in the centre. This is a *positive correlation*.

I

If the pattern was running in the opposite direction – bottom right to top left – it would give a *negative correlation*. This means the shorter the distance they travel, the longer they stay.

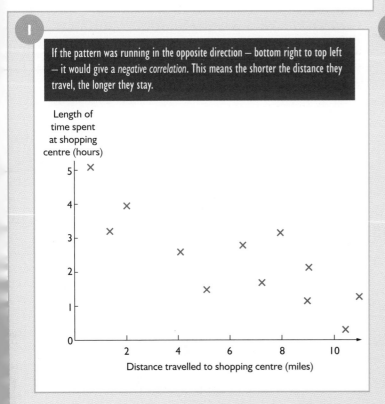

J

Sometimes there is no pattern on the graph, so there is no correlation.

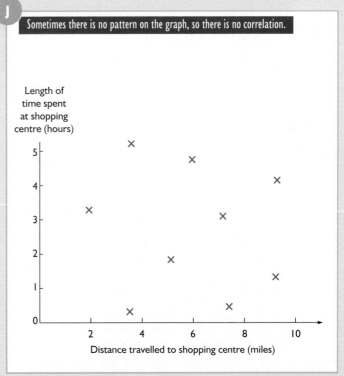

6 Triangular graphs

These are graphs where three variables are plotted on the same graph (**A**). Examples of their use include showing proportions of sand, silt and clay in soil samples, or the proportions employed in primary, secondary and tertiary employment in the UK (**A**).

Only relative values or percentages that add up to 100 can be plotted, for example 2 per cent primary, 33 per cent secondary and 65 per cent tertiary. Each side of the triangle or axis must be divided up into 100 representing the percentages. The axis lines are drawn at an angle of 60 degrees to each other and form a triangle.

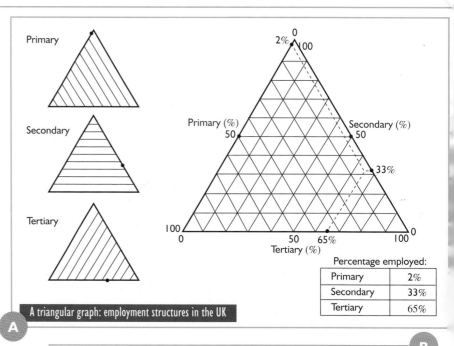

Percentage employed:	
Primary	2%
Secondary	33%
Tertiary	65%

A triangular graph: employment structures in the UK

A

7 Rose diagrams

These are best used when you need to show values for different directions. The classic example of this is for wind strength. A wind rose shows where the winds are blowing from (**B**). It can also show their strength (**C**). This method can also be used in urban geography, for example to show the number of people travelling from different directions to a city centre.

D Measuring wind strength

B Rose diagrams: wind direction and strength

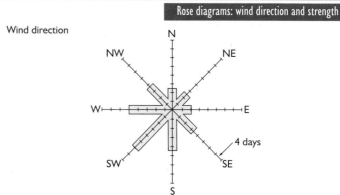

Wind direction

Wind direction is recorded over a period of time. The bars on each compass line indicate the number of days the wind has blown in that direction.

Wind direction and strength

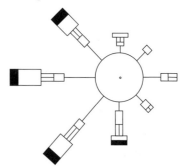

C

Key
Wind strength
(width and style of line shows strength of winds according to Beaufort scale)

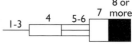

Wind direction
(length of line shows how often wind blows in that direction)

0   10   20   Frequency (%)

Statistical techniques

These techniques allow data to be quantified as opposed to the visual way of graphs and maps. They can also use mathematical formulae to test how significant or meaningful the data is.

Mean, median, mode

The mean, median and mode are terms used in statistics. These represent different ways of finding the average or most frequently occurring values in a set of data. When measuring the speed of a cork floating in a stream, several readings could be made and graphed. The mean, median and mode values can then be calculated.

- The mean is the average of all values – calculated by adding all values and dividing by the number of readings.
- The median is the middle value of all the readings taken.
- The mode is the value which occurs most often.

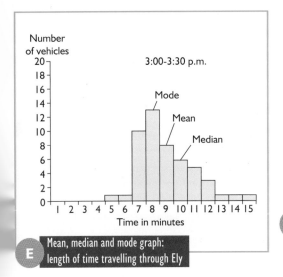

Mean, median and mode graph: length of time travelling through Ely

E

Spearman Rank Correlation

This statistical technique tests how strong the link is between two sets of data. The example shown tests the relationship between the life expectancy of people in selected countries and the number of people per doctor. This may show that there is a link between the level of health care and the length of time people live on average.

To work through this test follow this procedure using the example:

a) Rank the values depending on what is to be tested. In **F** the highest life expectancy would be given rank 1 and the lowest number of people per doctor (which in this case is better) would also be given rank 1. If there are two or more places with the same rank in the same set of data then find the average. In **F** Saudi Arabia and Brazil have the same life expectancy, so they should rank 5 and 6. Instead they both become rank 5.5, the average between 5 and 6.

b) Calculate the difference between the ranks of each set of data – life expectancy and number of people per doctor (in **F**, Japan = 3)

c) Square the differences and record them in column 7 (Japan = 9).

d) Add up the squared differences (in **F**, 12.25). This is $\sum d^2$.

e) Put your results in the following equation:

$$R = 1 - \frac{6\sum d^2}{n^3 - n} \quad \text{where}$$

R = the significant value

d = the difference in ranks (in **F**, Japan 1 and 4 = 3)

n = the number of items (in **F**, 7 countries)

$\sum d^2$ = sum of the differences (in **F**, 12.25)

f) The closer the figure is to plus or minus 1 then the stronger the relationship or correlation.

Example

$$R = 1 - \frac{6(12.25)}{343 - 7}$$

$$= 1 - \frac{73.5}{336}$$

$$= 1 - 0.2188$$

$$= 0.78$$

Country	Life expectancy	Rank	Number of people per doctor	Rank	Difference (d)	Difference squared (d²)
Japan	79	1	780	4	3.0	9.0
USA	76	2.5	520	2	– 0.5	0.25
Italy	76	2.5	340	1	–1.5	2.25
UK	76	2.5	650	3	0.5	0.25
Saudi Arabia	66	5.5	1,670	6	0.5	0.25
Brazil	66	5.5	1,660	5	–0.5	0.25
Bangladesh	53	7	7,810	7	0	0
					$\sum d^2 = 12.25$	

F

This result gives a good positive correlation, which means that there is quite a strong link between the life expectancy of these countries and the number of people per doctor.

If the answer had been 1, then it would mean that there was a perfect positive correlation.

If the answer had come up as high but with a minus sign before it then it would mean that there was a negative correlation, i.e. the longer the life expectancy then the higher the number of people to each doctor.

If the answer had been below 0.5 then it would mean there was no real correlation between the two values.

Index